City Money

Political Processes, Fiscal Strain, and Retrenchment

CITY MONEY

Political Processes, Fiscal Strain, and Retrenchment

Terry Nichols Clark
and
Lorna Crowley Ferguson

New York Columbia University Press *1983*

Library of Congress Cataloging in Publication Data

Clark, Terry N.
City money.

Bibliography: p.
Includes index.
1. Municipal finance—United States. I. Ferguson, Lorna C. (Lorna Crowley) II. Title.
HJ9145.C5 1983 336'.014'73 83-7375
ISBN 0-231-05688-5
ISBN 0-231-05689-3 (pbk.)

Columbia University Press
New York Guildford, Surrey

Clothbound editions of Columbia University Press books are Smyth-sewn and printed on permanent and durable acid-free paper.

Contents

Preface

The New York City fiscal crisis of 1975 was the impetus for this volume. New York officials made many trips to Washington that summer seeking federal aid. One argument was that other large, old, northeastern cities were suffering strains similar to New York's, and the federal government should help all such cities. A counter-argument held that New York was unique since its leaders chose to spend at high levels, for which city-specific solutions were more appropriate. How many other cities were close to similar crises was thus a critical question. At the time no federal agency had the immediate capacity to answer it; most policy discussions thus used anecdotes about what seemed to be happening outside New York. T. N. Clark spent that summer at the Brookings Institution and Department of Housing and Urban Development where people asked if the Permanent Community Sample (PCS) could speak to these issues. The PCS is a national sample of 62 cities which range from New York down to cities of 50,000 population. The same cities have been studied repeatedly for fifteen years, which has made the PCS into the most extensive political and fiscal data bank available for American cities. We used PCS fiscal data to create 29 indicators of fiscal strain, and presented initial results in *How Many New Yorks?* (Clark et al. 1976).

Fiscal strain was a brand new issue in the mid-1970s, but its importance has increased as cities have suffered local taxpayer revolts, state spending limitations, and cutbacks in federal and state aid. Most fiscal studies consider expenditures on individual functions, or common functions which most cities provide, like police and fire. But fiscal strain often involves debt and functions not common to all cities, like education, welfare, housing, and hospitals. We thus had to develop new procedures to capture fiscal strain involving all municipal functions.

While measuring fiscal strain is an essential beginning, to explain its sources and consider solutions, one must deal with political decision making. Past work on fiscal policy has often dismissed politics as idiosyncratic and hence amenable to anecdotal treatment. Yet the PCS has perhaps become best known for its success in measuring urban political decision making. Over a hundred books and articles have used PCS data on preferences and power of mayors, business leaders, municipal employees, ethnic groups, and how they variously affect urban public (especially fiscal) policies. Building on this foundation, the current volume pursues specific linkages between the economic base, political decision making, and urban fiscal policies. Many surprises emerged in the process. Virtually every chapter reports how widely accepted views (which we often held too) were incomplete or wrong.

Just one example: urban fiscal retrenchment did not begin with federal cutbacks by the Reagan administration in the early 1980s. Nor were state tax and spending limits like Proposition 13 the proximate cause. In fully half our PCS cities, retrenchment began in 1974, due mainly to local processes. We concentrate on detailed analysis of fiscal decision making in individual cities from 1960 to 1977, which makes possible isolating and documenting such counter-intuitive results. This necessitates combining data from numerous sources, many of which appear only with some delay. We present some data for the 1980s, but the importance of policies reached in the 1960s and 1970s, and widespread misunderstandings about them, led us to concentrate on these critical years.

We build on several specialized fields, but matters not essential for the general reader are in footnotes and appendixes. The issues are sufficiently pressing that we have written not just for researchers, but also for mayors, civic leaders, and others who deal directly with urban fiscal policy.

The Twentieth Century Fund and U.S. Public Health Service, NICHD, HD-08916-03 and HD-13121-01 aided in financing research for this work. Smaller grants came from University of Chicago sources: The Albion Small Fund, Social Science Divisional Research Fund, and Biomedical Research Support Grant.

Many ideas developed from working with mayors and other officials in our PCS cities, sometimes via the U.S. Conference of Mayors, with encouragement from Melvin Mister.

Research assistants who helped with early conceptualization were Ester Fuchs, Thomas Panelas, and Erwin Zimmermann. Data analysis was supervised successively by Robert Shapiro, Thomas Panelas, Margaret Troha, Mark Eckel, and Barbara Bieniewski. Tom Bonczar worked on migration; Ken Hoffman, Hai Hoang, John Raz, James Lucas, N. M. Triet, and Thomas Lamberty on fiscal indicators; Robert Rosenberg, Terry Alf, Bryn Walstrom, and Paul Gronke on political leaders; Paula Kline on the poor; Barbara Smith on intergovernmental relations; Stuart Michaels and Caroline Jumper on statistical modeling; Bruce Conforto, Robert Sullivan, John Aquino, and Dale Miller on data analysis; and Teresa Friend, Peter Cha, Inchul Choi, Daniel Emberly, Ken McBride, Andrea Woyt, Tod Heath, James Leong, Connie Gaglio, Sara Rubin, Tom Semereau, Charlene Seifert, and Laura Wohlford on everything else. Some are coauthors of sections below. All worked hard and long.

Drafts of the book were used in seminars we taught with George Tolley, Doris Holleb, Paul Peterson, and James Coleman. So many persons commented on drafts that we acknowledge them by citing their work below. We must still separately thank Amy Bridges, Ron Burt, Reid Charles, Robert Lineberry, Susan MacManus, Gerald Suttles, James Sheffield, Frank Thompson, Herman Turk, Norman Walzer, Sally Ward, and Lynne Zucker.

Clearly this book could not have been written without the help of many associates and friends. We hope they find the results useful or at least provocative.

T. N. CLARK
L. C. FERGUSON

Chicago
December 1982

City Money

Political Processes, Fiscal Strain, and Retrenchment

Introduction

New York's quasi default publicized fiscal strain in 1975. Subsequent difficulties in Buffalo, Yonkers, and Cleveland led many to ask if the same might occur elsewhere. Many city leaders were alarmed when California voters passed Proposition 13 in 1978. Tax and expenditure limitations elsewhere gave them little peace of mind. The future role of government is clearly at stake. The 1960s prosperity and optimism seem distant; what to preserve under austerity is the more common concern.

American cities provide an opportunity to consider general ideas about growth of government and support for the welfare state. Many factors have been identified as affecting the direction and rate of government growth: the expansion of citizenship rights (Bell 1976), heightened citizen participation (Verba, Nie, and Kim 1978; Stigler 1972), collective social movements (Genevie 1978), special interest group pressures (Lowi 1969), network ties among groups (Wilensky 1975; Turk 1977; Marsden and Laumann 1977), class conflict (Dahrendorf 1959), government bureaucrats (Wildavsky 1964; Niskanan 1971; Borcherding 1977), the New Class of professionals (Bruce-Briggs 1979), capitalism (O'Connor 1971), business pressures (Schattschneider 1960; Friedland and Bielby 1981), regional decline (Sternlieb and Hughes 1975), dissolution of the family and civil morality (Janowitz 1978), Protestant individualism (Lipset 1979), a conservative New Right (Howe 1978). The basic theories apply to cities as well as national societies. Contemporary national analyses are constrained to one case, while cross-national and historical studies are plagued by limited data. American cities permit systematic comparisons and provide striking contrasts not found inside many countries of the world. Quantitative data for them are richer and more comparable than for national societies. This combination of circumstances provides an opportunity to formulate more rigorous propositions about the sources of government growth and retrenchment, and to test them more systematically, than in studies of entire societies. Nevertheless, values, politics, and competing theories are so interrelated that consensus among experts has not emerged. This makes the area challenging. The sums are huge: in 1982, American local governments spent some $200 billion, about 8 percent of the gross national product (GNP) or roughly the total GNP of Italy or the United Kingdom.

The range of views on fiscal strain and its remedies is suggested in statements about New York:

> John Kenneth Galbraith—"No problem associated with New York City could not be solved by providing more money. . . . It's outrageous that a person can avoid income tax by moving to New Jersey or Connecticut. Fiscal funkholes are what the suburbs are."
>
> Milton Friedman—"Go bankrupt. The only other alternative is . . . [to] live within its means and become an honest city again."
>
> Edward Banfield—"I'm afraid that real trouble is that it's [New York] run by the upper and middle classes and they're too moral and too righteous to do the painful and sometimes wrong things that have to be done to run a big city."
>
> Michael Harrington—"By passage of three laws in Washington you could end the crisis immediately—the federalization of welfare, the Kennedy-Corman health-security bill, and the Hawkins-Humphrey full-employment bill."
>
> Jane Jacobs—"I don't know that New York can recover now. A city can't let its skills, manufacturing plants and suppliers' plants wither away and then not suffer the consequences" (*New York Times*, July 30, 1975).

An enormous literature bears on urban fiscal strain, but little serious work directly focuses on it. Most writers, like those quoted, posit different causes and hence different solutions. This study differs by formulating a systems analysis of urban fiscal strain and by assessing it using both a national city sample and individual cities.

Overview of Discussion by Chapter

Chapter 1 outlines our distinctive approach: a systems analysis of urban fiscal strain. The main elements are summarized in figure A. *Citizen preferences* are analyzed using sectors—portions of a city's population holding common fiscal policy preferences. Major sectors are the middle class, blacks, and municipal employees. *Equilibrium* is defined as fiscal policy consistent with citizen preferences. When such equilibrium is not present (the usual case), citizens may migrate out of the city, thus changing sector sizes. Or they may become more politically active via *organized groups* which can press for favorable policies. *Political leaders*, primarily mayors and council members, respond to citizens or organized groups with fiscal policies. Leaders may be *invisible* in implementing only preferences of others, or *dynamic* in imparting their own preferences to the policy. Preferences of citizens, organized groups, and leaders are analyzed concerning fiscal liberalism

Figure A. A Systems Analysis Framework for Urbal Fiscal Strain

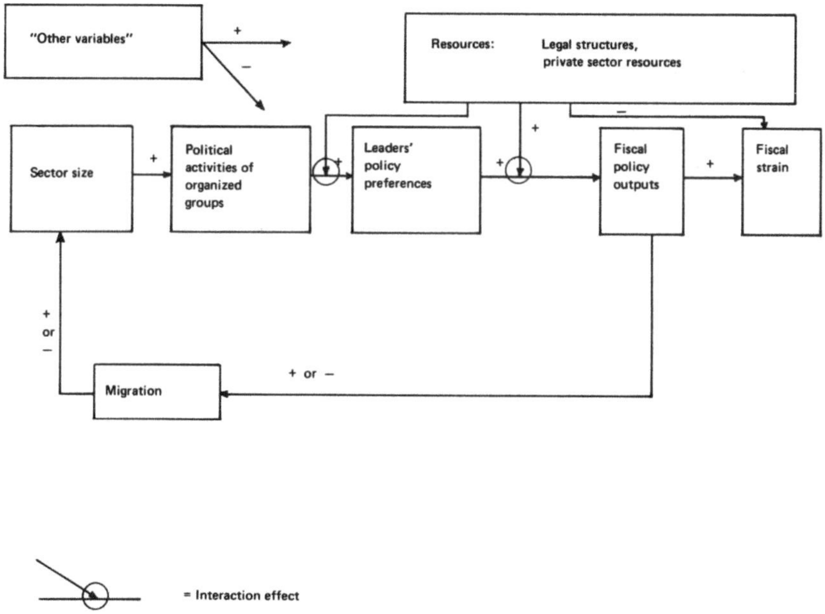

(more government spending) and social liberalism (especially concern for minorities and disadvantaged). Citizens, organized groups, and leaders can implement their preferences more fully if they have more *resources*. Resources themselves are inert, only means to ends defined by the participants, thus interacting with other variables in our model rather than exerting direct effects.

The components of our systems model have been analyzed separately in most earlier work. Our distinctive concern is specifying the dynamics by which separate general processes—involving citizens, groups, leaders, and migration—combine with systemic consequences. These are stated in a system of propositions and equations, analyzed using data from our 62 cities. The processes shift in importance according to transformation rules defined by four *political cultures* which state how the general processes operate in specific cities and time periods. The four political cultures used throughout the book are those of New Deal Democrats, Ethnic Politicians, New Deal Republicans, and New Fiscal Populists. The political cultures direct the processes which generate specific fiscal policies.

In the late 1960s, the dominant style in Washington and many cities was set by *New Deal Democrats* like Lyndon Johnson. They were fiscally liberal in their ambitious government programs and socially liberal in concern for blacks and the disadvantaged. This political culture built on organized groups—unions, civil rights organizations, and especially the Democratic party—but overlooked the "silent majority" of individual citizens. Many leaders were dynamic, like Mayor Ivan Allen, who implemented racial integration after the "sit-in" was first used in his Atlanta. Such leaders persuaded their councils to enact more ambitious programs than ever before. Government expanded accordingly, with federal grants, local taxes, and borrowing. New Deal Democratic leaders emphasize both public goods, shared by all citizens, and separable goods like patronage jobs or contracts, which can reward supporters. Broad support for this political culture helped government grow for decades, but over the 1970s citizens increasingly questioned the legitimate role of government. The bright ideas that fueled the New Deal began to fade—for some because of government failures, for others because the New Deal program had been achieved.

Ethnic politicians resemble Democrats but stress ethnicity more in formulating policies. White ethnic groups did this for years, while more recently blacks have been important in increasing social service programs and expanding municipal work forces to create jobs for underemployed blacks.

New Deal Republicans see the individual citizen and taxpayer as a more legitimate force than unions or other organized groups, and the private market as more efficient than government. Taxes are thus kept low. Republicans are also conservative on social issues, or at least less willing than Democrats to use government to address social problems like racial prejudice. Republican cities are more affluent, white, suburban, and western than those with Democratic leaders. However, in most Republican cities, council members are elected through nonpartisan voting, so that issues are discussed in less partisan terms.

The newest type is *New Fiscal Populism*, illustrated by Jimmy Carter or Mayor Peter Flaherty in Pittsburgh. Often liberal Democrats in background, they became fiscal conservatives through personal conviction or fiscal constraint. They seek to ease the burden on the average taxpayer while still responding to the disadvantaged. They are fiscally conservative, but liberal on social issues like race. They differ from New Deal Democrats in their appeal to individual citizen-voters and are less attentive to "special interest groups," especially municipal employees, hence our populist designation. Many observers label this combination of policies confused or impossible, but this is only in terms of New Deal ideology. The New Deal coalitions have broken down, and New Fiscal Populist leaders have devised new modes of governance and specific policies consistent with more limited resources and current citizen preferences. Subsequent chapters show how citizens, groups, and political leaders each affect urban fiscal policy differentially according to the type of political culture.

Chapter 2 introduces our approach to urban fiscal strain, contrasting it with two others. One sees the municipal bond market as recording cities' fiscal conditions. If reasonable for the investor, this does not indicate which specific factors cause market reactions. The second approach views a declining economic or population base as generating fiscal strain. We differ in treating jobs and population as only environmental resources. *Private sector resources*, like employment and population, are generated primarily by local private sector dynamics. While outside the city government, they may be potentially tapped via taxes or charges. We view government as a system which must adapt to its environment; our conception of *fiscal strain* is the degree to which government expenditures and debt are adapted to the city's private sector resources. A city losing jobs and population can be fiscally sound if its public leaders trim expenditures in proportion to declining resources. Pittsburgh did this in the early 1970s; New York did not. *Fiscal policy outputs* are four—general expenditures, long-term debt, a city's own revenues, and common functions—analyzed throughout the book as per capita levels in 1977 and changes for several periods from 1960 to 1977. *Fiscal strain indicators* are primarily ratios of such fiscal policy outputs to private sector resources, of the following sort:

$$\text{Urban fiscal strain} = \frac{\text{City government spending and debt}}{\text{Private sector resources}}$$

The ratio reflects adaptation by local public leaders if city spending declines when the tax base declines (as in Pittsburgh). But if the numerator increases while the denominator does not, this indicates that the city is not adapting, and the ratio increases (as in New York). High spending alone, however, does not cause fiscal strain if the tax base is sufficiently strong (as in Palo Alto). Fiscal strain scores are presented for our 62 sample cities to illustrate the ratio approach. Causes of fiscal strain may act on either the numerator or denominator. That is, strain can increase from either a growing government or a declining tax base, but the reasons governments grow may be quite different from the reasons the tax base declines. Governments grow through essentially political decisions. But people and firms move in and out of cities for reasons often minimally political. Public and private sector dynamics are distinct. This is a central argument which the book develops in separate chapters on public and private sector sources of fiscal strain.

One popular view holds that fiscal strain is part of the "urban distress" of large, old cities in the Northeast, declining in jobs and population. In the 1970s, "targeting" criteria for federal grants and the Carter National Urban Policy assumed this view. How adequate was it? We consider it in chapter 3 first by examining the strength of intercorrelations among several private sector measures (population size and change, median family income, etc.) for our 62 sample cities. Because the correlations are only modest, we question the "Northeast syndrome" characterization. Next we correlated the same private sector measures with fiscal policy outputs of city governments. Relations were very weak, indicating that some local officials adapt their fiscal policies to private sector resources, but others do not. These weak relations illustrate the distinctiveness of public and private sector dynamics. Chapter 3 also considers inflation and recession. While important for local firms and individuals, these trends affect city governments less. City revenues rise almost as fast as expenditures with inflation and do not fall much in recession. Private sector perturbations thus demand adaptation, but do not determine city government responses.

Chapter 4 analyzes political processes using our systems analysis framework. Results differ for three periods in conjunction with the political cultures. Dynamics of the first period, the early 1960s, were marked by New Deal Republicans and Democrats. Citizen preferences explained most spending increases, although organized groups were important in Democratic cities like New York, San Francisco, and Boston. In the second period, the late 1960s and early 1970s, Democrats and ethnic politicians set the main dynamics. Racial disturbances and strikes by employees encouraged leaders to respond to organized groups and party ideologies more than to citizens. The third period, 1974–77, saw the resurgence of citizen preferences, championed by Republicans and New Fiscal Populists who implemented more fiscally conservative policies. Yet they were analytically invisible leaders; the only measure significantly driving fiscal policy was the size of the middle class. Results for fiscal strain indicators and fiscal policy outputs were almost identical, indicating the importance of political processes compared to private sector resources. Our core statistical model, like all scientific analyses, involves simplification; many further variables are analyzed in subsequent chapters and appendix 5.

Chapter 5 considers the style of ethnic politics which European immigrants developed, built on friendship, trust, and personal loyalty. Patronage jobs enlisted campaign workers but also increased expenditures. Blacks reacted against exclusion from white ethnic politics by organizing, first with civil rights in the rural South, followed by the black power movement in cities in the late 1960s. Black political activities encouraged fiscally liberal mayors who in turn implemented expansive fiscal policies—primarily in cities with large black populations, but interestingly black population size had no direct effect on fiscal policy. Only if blacks were politically active, and the mayor sympathetic, did fiscal policy respond. Both white and black ethnic politics were thus (1) fiscally liberal due in part to (2) responsiveness to organized groups and (3) corresponding de-emphasis of individual citizens, (4) use of ethnicity as a political criterion, and (5) preference for separable goods like jobs over abstract issues like low taxes. However, by the late 1970s the black power movement weakened, due in part to its success. Black leaders entered mainstream politics, pursuing policies with broader appeals—and spending less.

Chapter 6 examines organized groups active in Democratic and Republican cities. The "liberal-labor" Democratic coalition was never so important locally as nationally, and has generally broken down. We thus analyze municipal employees as a separate, organized group, but surprisingly find that where they are better organized, cities do *not* spend more. While about half of municipal expenditures go to personal services, these have two distinct components: the number of employees and compensation per employee. The product of the two is the personal services item in a city budget. Municipal employees are not powerless, but affect most those policies critical to current members, as emerges clearly when these two components are separately analyzed. City characteristics and general political processes largely explain *numbers* of municipal employees: cities have more employees if they perform more functions, have a smaller middle class, politically active blacks, and political leaders who favored more services in the late 1960s. But municipal employee's organization and political activities do not affect their numbers, despite stereotypes about "featherbedding." By contrast, employees' activities do increase their *compensation*.

Cities thus differ substantially according to union power. Those with strong unions, like New York and Detroit, paid fewer workers more. In time of retrenchment, they cut employees (and probably services), but kept increasing salaries, such that in 1977 average compensation exceeded $17,000 per employee. By contrast, cities with powerful blacks and political leaders, and weak unions, hired more workers but paid them less. Gary is a good example, paying only about one-third that of New York or Detroit: $6,208 per employee.

Chapter 7 probes the taxpayers' revolt. Retrenchment in our sample cities began in 1974, four years before Proposition 13. It was a middle class populist reaction against taxes and spending raised by liberal organized groups. Did conservative groups lead the way? Business is often cited, but had no consistent impact on fiscal policy. The New Deal tradition of most Democratic political leaders led them to ignore the taxpayers' revolt. Citizen surveys had shown support for low taxes over many years, accentuated in the 70s by inflation, recession, and government growth. But on social issues like racial tolerance and civil liberties, citizens remained liberal. These preferences led many citizens to support new leaders—like Mayor Peter Flaherty in Pittsburgh. We label them New Fiscal Populists (NFPs) due to their political culture of (1) fiscal conservatism, (2) social liberalism, (3) populist concern for citizen preferences, (4) disregard for traditional party organization, and (5) new policies following from such preferences. We include a case study of Mayor Flaherty to show how one NFP implemented dramatic changes: he reduced taxes several times, cut the work force, yet maintained services. NFPs have been important carriers of a distinctive political culture in transforming rules of the game in Pittsburgh, as well as other cities like New York or San Francisco, helping them adapt to declining private sector resources and reduce their fiscal strain.

Chapter 8 shows citizen support for fiscal conservatism in *migration* analyses. Net (in minus out) migration was higher to places with lower taxes. People, especially whites, left places with high tax burdens for those with lower burdens. However, net migration by nonwhites was to places with higher welfare benefits. Many variables affect migration besides tax burdens and welfare. Yet over time these fiscal policies change cities' population sectors, as shown by the figure A feedback loop. Volatile migration and job patterns both reflect and support individualistic life styles and New Fiscal Populist politics.

Chapter 9 reviews strategies that have often failed. Intergovernmental aid is frequently suggested to ease fiscal strain. But cities like New York which receive most aid still have fiscal problems. Our analyses suggest that local processes generate most expenditures and are surprisingly unchanged by intergovernmental revenues. Cities with more functions (welfare, hospitals, etc.) have more Democrats, organized employees, and leaders who prefer more spending. Transferring functions from such cities to state or federal governments would very likely *increase* service costs, even to less affluent residents, for reasons ignored in most public discussions. Many legal reforms have been passed, like debt and expenditure limits, but they are best seen as (only) resources. They have little impact if local participants support other policies.

Chapter 10 lists twelve options for local officials: policies already in use in some cities. To help assess policies, we classify them by their responsiveness to the four political cultures. Policies include user charges, making visible efforts to improve productivity, privatization, use of volunteers, capital versus labor trade offs, and contracting out for services. Federal and state officials can strengthen local general government by providing funds through general rather than categorical grants. Allocation formulas can be made fairer, and grant administration streamlined. States can facilitate municipal borrowing via bond banks or earmarking state aid for bond payments.

Conceptual Contributions for Social Scientists

Our main conceptual innovation is a complex systems model of urban fiscal policy making, incorporating citizen preferences, organized groups, political leaders, and migration, as summarized in figure A. Key decisions pass through political institutions, but the system includes characteristics like sector size which some political analysts consider "environmental."

We build on Anthony Downs, Robert Dahl, Floyd Hunter, and Charles Tiebout, but stress interdependence among processes which these theorists usually treat separately. Earlier theories defined partial equilibrium conditions for citizen preferences, organized groups, competing leaders, and migrants. But a general equilibrium including all these processes depends on variables omitted from some of the separate traditions. By considering the processes together in a single system, we pose questions—and answers—they did not. We identify city characteristics which shift the processes generating fiscal policy. Contradictions among earlier theories are resolved by shifts in rules of the political game in different cities and time periods. The systemic approach avoids positing any single type of characteristic as consistently determining others; change in one affects others throughout the system. We show how policy preferences and rules of the game variously combine in the four political cultures of New Deal Democrats and Republicans, Ethnic Politicians, and New Fiscal Populists. The political culture thus defines transformation rules for the deep structures of the system (involving citizens, groups, and leaders) which are included in a system of structural equations and estimated with data for the 62 PCS cities.

Our systems approach reinterprets several past studies. We transcend or recast debates about the relative importance of economic versus political variables (Hofferbert 1972), demand versus supply determinants of public expenditure (e.g., Bahl, Johnson, and Wasylenko 1980; Inman 1979), and citizen versus organized group versus elite importance (e.g., Dahl 1961; Turk 1977; Caro 1974) by including each set of variables and showing how each is important under certain circumstances. Our concepts of resources and political culture partially resolve the stratification versus pluralist view (e.g., Polsby 1980; Stone 1980), suggest which nondecisions become decisions (Bachrach and Baratz 1970; Crenson 1971), which structural characteristics (Castells 1972) shift actual behavior, and how patterns differ across issues (Lowi 1964; Peterson 1981) and over time (Gilbert 1968). Our analysis points to the incompleteness of economic determinisms which explain urban fiscal strain by shifts in jobs and population (e.g., Muller 1975), movement of capital (e.g., O'Connor 1973; Friedland, Piven, and Alford 1977), or financial and business elites (e.g., Alcaly and Mermelstein 1977; Newfield and DuBrul 1977). Similarly, the political determinism implicit in many "city biographies" (e.g., Dahl 1961; Caro 1974; Allen 1971) is relativized by placing leaders in their social and economic contexts.

Methodological Contributions for Social Scientists and Municipal Fiscal Analysts

We retained elements in the systems model of fiscal strain only if they found empirical support; data and analysis strategies are thus integral to the enterprise. The foundation is the Permanent Community Sample (PCS), the most extensive political and fiscal data file available for American cities. Acquired through some fifteen years of surveys, it includes social and political indicators seldom systematically analyzed, like leaders' influence and spending preferences, and political activities of organized groups. The several processes which combine in our systems analysis involve multiple linkages which no one type of data can adequately capture. Hence the importance of analyzing several data sources in distinctive ways. Economic, social, and political data for the 62 PCS cities are included in a core regression model for most fiscal analyses; PCS county areas are used to measure the total tax burden and welfare benefits for migration analyses of individuals and jobs; survey data for individuals help define fiscal preferences of middle class citizens, blacks, and other potential sectors. We pool data for all mayors and council members to document operation of their political cultures.

Fiscal policy levels in the PCS cities are analyzed cross-sectionally, and their changes studied over several periods from 1960 to 1977. This isolates statistical interaction effects involving different causal patterns in three time periods. We transcend the split between quantitative work and case studies by presenting case study materials for cities chosen from scatterplots of critical relationships including all PCS cities. Our functional performance (FP) approach is a new method to analyze determinants of municipal revenue, debt, and noncommon function expenditures, making unnecessary analysis of only common functions or data for overlapping governments. The method permits assessing the overall fiscal condition of city governments and isolating city-specific decision-making processes.

Implications for Municipal Fiscal Analysis

The study suggests several lessons for municipal credit analysts, federal and state agencies, municipal financial officials, and citizen groups monitoring local finances. It casts doubt on funds flow-type measures such as "deficits" or "surpluses" in a city's general fund, or short term debt outstanding at the end of a fiscal year. For a city in such straits as New York about 1975, these may be meaningful. And if a city holds to consistent fiscal and accounting procedures, such indicators may be useful for a single city over time. However, comparing one city with another on funds flow measures is seldom meaningful, largely because of differences in state and local laws and the ease with which monies may be shifted across funds. An aggregate "surplus" or "deficit" for all state and local governments combined, common in macroeconomic analyses (e.g., ACIR 1979a), is particularly misleading because cities differ so from states and from one another.

By contrast, ratios similar to those currently employed by municipal analysts are useful indicators, especially ratios of expenditures or debt divided by population, income, and taxable property value. We refine such indicators beyond earlier work, for example, with a City Wealth Index that combines median family income and equalized taxable property value using weights reflecting the revenue structure of the individual city. Our interpretation of these ratios, however, departs substantially from traditional approaches. Fiscal analysts often stress private sector resources; cities losing population and jobs are widely considered "distressed." Investors in the 1970s who downgraded or refused to buy most or all bonds in the Northeast illustrate the fallacy of this approach.

Fiscal strain determinants are twofold, including both city fiscal policies and private sector resources. Informed analysts should consider each. Our twofold approach shows that population and job loss can bring fiscal strain, but only if local leaders do not adapt. To write off most older northeastern cities as "poor risks" is an enormous simplification, denigrating local leaders by assuming that they cannot adapt to private sector changes.

Chapter 3 shows that relations are weak between municipal fiscal and private sector indicators; that is, many cities which lose jobs and population do *not* become fiscally strained. Brief case studies of Pittsburgh and Chicago document how local leaders adapted policies to changing circumstances. Similarly, the sister cities of Albany and Schenectady have both lost jobs and population, but Schenectady moderated its fiscal commitments more and is less fiscally strained.

Variables are considered in a reasoned and coherent manner to assess their meaning. To identify patterns it is not enough to "look at" many variables and read a brief city description. Some leading municipal analysts may succeed at this, but have not conveyed their secrets to most others. No one knows precisely what is in the mind of credit analysts or investors. Sharper analysis could change this.

We stress both fiscal strain levels and changes as indicators, a point simply stated but often ignored. To consider tax burdens, we include all overlapping local governments and the state government, especially important for migration of individuals or location of firms.

Our principal contribution, however, is to analyze these indicators with a formal model incorporating social, economic, and political characteristics. Equations are specified modeling the basic processes generating urban fiscal decisions. Detailing their logic to permit quantitative analysis forces the analyst to transcend the anecdotal, state assumptions, and document hypothesized causal linkages so that they are explicit, amenable to criticism and future refinement. Whether one is monitoring city finances generally (by a federal or state agency) or specific policies (by a city agency or citizens' group) or investing in a portfolio of bonds, one implicitly posits processes generating fiscal strain or health. Our approach makes these more explicit. Similar approaches have been used in the private sector. Only by refining this approach can "early warning signals" be demonstrated as valid. The major bond rating agencies—Moody's and Standard and Poor's—have been properly criticized for continuing casual procedures in a multibillion dollar industry. Since the 1975 New York fiscal crisis, many financial institutions and public agencies have begun more serious analyses. They could elaborate this approach.

Using sound judgment to evaluate individual municipalities will remain critical. Our approach is not an alternative, but a complement, a sharper tool for analysts. Judgment was essential in the past as critical variables had not been measured, but we have shown how to quantify many processes. The interested analyst need not replicate our complete systems analysis, but could adapt individual measures for different years or cities. Examples: the Index of Staffing, middle class sector size, the Index of Functional Performance, fiscal strain indicators, and mayors' and council members' preferences and political resources (see appendix 1).

PART I
A Framework

CHAPTER ONE

A Systems Analysis of Urban Fiscal Strain

The public finances are one of the best starting points for an investigation of society, especially though not exclusively of its political life. The full fruitfulness of this approach is seen particularly at those turning points . . . during which existing forms begin to die off and to change into something new, and which always involve a crisis of the old fiscal methods. . . .

We may surely speak of a special set of facts, a special set of problems, and of a special approach—in short, of a special field: fiscal sociology, of which much may be expected.

Joseph Schumpeter "The Crisis of the Tax State" (1918)

Schumpeter's expectations were premature; social and political dynamics of public finance were long neglected. But in the last decade, fiscal crises in several cities and public debates over the legitimate role of government have underscored the importance of clearer theory. The 1970s were a "turning point" of the sort Schumpeter identified. Underlying assumptions about government were questioned and new developments emerged. Past theories were inadequate to explain the new developments. A good theory indicates important causal relationships and thereby helps clarify meaningful policy options.

This chapter formulates a systems analysis of urban fiscal strain. It concentrates on general fiscal policy, rather than specific policy areas (like police or fire). National trends like growth of the economy are considered insofar as they shift local resources. Local citizens, organized groups, and political leaders are the major participants. When fiscal policy is consistent with citizen preferences, the local system is in equilibrium. But this seldom occurs. As fiscal policies increasingly conflict with citizen preferences, some citizens become politically active or move elsewhere. Political leaders may then modify policies to reduce such dissatisfaction. Preference patterns and activities by citizens, groups, and leaders shift according to the city's political culture. These ideas are sharpened below.[1]

Previous Approaches

We build on four types of literature, dealing with: citizen preferences; organized interest groups; leaders' preferences; and residential choice. Each stresses a different cause of political decisions, contributing a necessary but not sufficient element. Each defines an equilibrium which assumes constant variables in the other traditions. These four processes constitute the "deep structures" of our systems analysis of urban fiscal strain. We briefly discuss past theories concerning each process before stating our own propositions about the processes and how the processes combine and complement each other.

Citizen Preferences

Following Anthony Downs, the citizen preference approach sees policies as a direct expression of voter demands. The rational voter supports officials whose policies are closest to his interests. The elected official pursues policies that secure enough votes for reelection. For expenditure decisions, "governments continue spending until the marginal vote gain from additional expenditures equals the marginal vote loss from financing" (Downs 1957:73). In a strict version of the model, policies flow entirely from citizen preferences and assumptions are those of a perfect market, including competition among political leaders and complete information.[2] Given these, Downs suggests that the system will reach equilibrium when the political leader provides policies consistent with preferences of the median voter.

We too use citizen preferences to define system equilibrium, and use uncertainty partially building on Downs. But we differ from him on the structure of citizen preferences. Preference aggregation problems, as in Arrow (1963), have many solutions (see Sen 1970), and are handled by Downs largely by assuming a two-party system and single-peaked, unidimensional citizen preferences. We find the sector concept more convenient. Sectors, as discussed below, are citizens sharing policy preferences.

Interest Groups

The interest group tradition sees policy shaped by groups. Citizens have vague policy preferences and seldom participate politically. Politicians thus respond to those with well-articulated demands. Limited interests and resources lead individuals to concentrate on selected policies. Moreover, resource and communication advantages of organized pressure imply that organized groups are effective (only) on those issues which concern them. Important works in this tradition include Truman (1951), Key (1958), and Dahl (1961). Authors vary, but some hold that groups from block clubs to taxpayers' associations emerge to represent all major interests (see Truman 1951:5ff.), and conclude in Darwinian manner that policy outputs reflect the balance of interests among major groups. But note that if groups mirror individual interests (preferences), and policies in turn reflect group activities, then group theory reduces to citizen preference theory. Group theory is often consistent with this argument, but seldom takes it so far. Certainly, most empirical work in this tradition focuses on groups themselves. Our model includes groups as potentially independent sources of fiscal policy. But instead of assuming that existing groups represent major citizen interests, we analyze how much this is so with separate citizen and group measures.

Leaders' Preferences

However strong are interest group pressures or voter preferences, elected officials still make most fiscal decisions. Leaders themselves are critical in a long tradition emphasizing their personal characteristics and preferences. Elite theories from Mosca, Pareto, Schumpeter, and Michels have influenced case studies of individual cities (e.g., Hunter 1953; Dahl 1961), and biographies of leaders (e.g., Caro 1974; Allen 1971). Mayors John Lindsay, Richard Daley, and Richard Hatcher showed leadership affecting fiscal policies of their cities. More abstract work on "political entrepreneurs" (e.g., Frohlich, Oppenheimer, and Young 1971) focuses on leaders' strategies yet specifies major constraints on leadership. Most theory in this tradition considers sources of leaders' political activation more than why leaders have a distinct policy impact. Empirical work has developed measures of leaders' preferences permitting comparison with citizens (e.g., McClosky 1964). We draw on this tradition for procedures to measure leaders' preferences. Acknowledging that leaders, like groups, can independently affect fiscal policy, we differ from theorists who omit leaders with the argument that they reflect citizen preferences. If their position is reasonable for a stable system in the long term, it is unreasonable to assume a priori. While leaders generally seek policies responsive to their citizens, leaders play independent roles under conditions specified below.

Residential Choice

Residential choice theories, often building on the Tiebout (1956) hypothesis, stress individual choices in the aggregate. When local policies diverge from the individual's preferences, he moves, rather than attempting to change policies. Since citizens' tastes differ, leaders in different cities should maintain distinctive policies to retain residents. Equilibrium is encouraged if cities provide differentiated market baskets; residents can then locate in the city with their preferred mix of taxes, services, and amenities.

Like this tradition, we stress that citizens are not immovable, as some citizen preference theories imply. Rather than considering just isolated individuals and long-term equilibrium, however, we use our sector concept to clarify residential choices, suggesting that if policies diverge from sector ideals, dissatisfied sector members will move, decreasing the sector's size.

In the 1970s, advocates of these approaches often grew deterministic, especially when influenced by economic-inspired theorists writing in *Public Choice*. Models are more tractable when only one type of actor can maximize. For example, the median voter approach was seen as extending consumer behavior theory, and groups or leaders dismissed as largely superfluous "transactions costs." Healthy competition among leaders assured that "the party machinery is essentially neutral, and its personnel wish merely to win elections" (Stigler 1972:96). The consumer-citizen was sovereign. Emphasis on citizens was perhaps heightened by the mathematical elegance of some formulations (in *Public Choice*); populist appeals to decentralization, community control and the ethnic distinctiveness they afforded (e.g., Altschuler 1970); plus an interest in tracing implementation of policies from who governs? to who benefits? by studying who consumes which services? (see Lineberry 1977). Yet over the 1970s, as "special interest groups" grew more salient, some theorists like Buchanan and Tullock, Niskanan (Borcherding 1977), Stigler (1975: chs. 8–11), and Becker abandoned citizen preferences. Rather than suggest that citizens might still play an occasional role, however, they were largely dismissed: "voters receive little attention because they are assumed mainly to transmit the pressure of active groups" (Becker 1982:1). These last theorists often concluded that government growth was inexorable.

Just as active special interest groups left earlier median voter theories in disarray, so is the recent slowdown in government growth inconsistent with most group theories. In each case the problem lies in positing a single factor as driving government growth. While cast as comprehensive, these are only partial equilibrium theories propped on fragile ceteris paribus assumptions. We suggest that a more adequate approach includes citizens, groups, and leaders as plausible sources of government policies. Rather than dismissing one altogether when times change, analytical conditions generating such changes should be specified, as outlined below.

A Systems Analysis of Urban Fiscal Strain

We begin with definitions of central concepts. *Fiscal policy outputs* are expenditures, debt, or revenues of the local political system. *Fiscal strain* arises when fiscal policy outputs grow more than private sector resources of the city. Fiscal policy outputs and strain (discussed in chapter 2) are types of *fiscal policies*. Fiscal and nonfiscal public policies may be classified on a continuum from public to separable goods. *Public goods* like clean air are indivisible—it is hard to exclude persons from their use. *Separable goods*, like patronage jobs, may be allocated to specific neighborhoods or individuals (Samuelson 1969; Clark 1974a). Public and separable goods may have equal costs, but emerge from different dynamics, elaborated below. The main empirical system to which our theory applies is the American city government, although much seems applicable to democratic political systems which include citizens, organized groups, elected political leaders, and citizen migration. More specificity is added as we proceed, especially in positing particular combinations of general processes in the political cultures.

Sectors and Organized Groups

Individuals striving to achieve their interests are the building blocks of social systems. The major interests we address involve urban fiscal policy, yet fiscal decisions are made not by individuals, but governments. How are individual interests linked to such collective decisions? The task is simplified by considering not particular programs, but overall spending. If some supporters vary by program, social bases of general fiscal policy are more stable. This does not imply that decisions need be made on overall spending, but that preferences can be analyzed in these terms.[3] Rather than dealing with individuals, we use the concept of a *sector* to refer to citizens with common interests concerning urban fiscal policy. This simplifies aggregation by reducing the number of participants and conversion of their preferences into policy—whether through organized groups or other means of articulating and aggregating citizen preferences. Sectors are particularly appropriate for comparing cities, as sectors differ so in size across cities. Some cities have large homogeneous middle classes, others small ones, in combinations that vary more dramatically than for larger systems like national societies.

Our sector resembles Marx's class or group theorists' concept of group.[4] Sector interests derive from sectors' differing relations to the means of production of public services. In elementary, deductive manner, we thus initially distinguished three sectors—the poor, nonpoor, and municipal employees. The poor pay few taxes and depend on government for much of their income or income substitutes in the form of public services. The nonpoor pay more taxes than the poor and may receive fewer services.[5] Municipal employees are the most dependent on government. The poor and municipal employees share an interest in expanding government and taxes. The nonpoor should oppose taxes for services not in their interests. These sector interests are qualified below. Our concern here is to elaborate the general logic as stated in two basic propositions:

1. *The larger a sector in a city, the more fiscal policy is responsive to the sector.*
2. *The more organized and politically active an organized group, the more fiscal policy is responsive to the group.*[6]

What are the major sectors and groups? An infinite number are conceivable, but only a few meaningful for general fiscal policy. The threefold typology above was modified by surveys of individuals and city-level analyses considered in subsequent chapters. The major change was adding blacks as a sector. The poor were too few and weak to affect fiscal policy, but blacks often did. Black individuals at all income levels reported decidedly higher spending preferences than whites.

Municipal employees have the clearest interests and best organization of any sector. They favor more compensation for themselves, although not necessarily other government expenditures. Municipal employees, of course, are not quite like the two other sectors, but we use the same term to simplify exposition. Their numbers are small, but intensity of interest is great—channeled by unions and professional associations which mobilize employees, families, and friends.

The third sector is hardest to distinguish. We use the term middle class, but in contemporary America this often means simply nonpoor. Our city-level analyses use literally the percentage of middle income families. Middle class subsectors—homeowners, the aged, environmentalists, and the like—often press for spending on their special interests. But the middle class as a whole prefers lower spending and taxes. This is clear in many surveys, but not always in public discussions, in part because organized groups almost never represent the general middle class. Vigorous low spending advocates often seemed to be business groups, which led us to include several measures of their political activity; but these are inconsistently important. The middle class is the preeminent sector in that its size alone is important for fiscal policy. Our focus on general fiscal policy is especially important for the middle class, which holds down the size of the government pie, even if it is too diffuse in its interests to slice the pie.

Sector members share policy preferences, but not unanimously. Leaders and groups seek to capture general sector preferences in their policies; in similar spirit we identify interests of (most) sector members, but not of each individual as our concern is city-level decisions. Intensity of interest and a sector's ability to mobilize vary with overlapping memberships. For example, municipal employees have strong and clear preferences because of the centrality of their occupational status. But middle class taxpayers have weaker preferences due to competing statuses.[7] While we thus identify certain sources of sector preference, the empirical analysis focuses more on their consequences.

Political Leaders

Political leaders are primarily mayors and council members. While representing citizens and groups, they can still create distinct "political bases" with fiscal consequences. For example, John Lindsay appealed to the affluent and minorities, while Abraham Beame relied more on municipal employees. Political leaders also vary in personal preferences and activities concerning spending, the main leadership dimension we consider. John Lindsay actively pressed taxpayers, the governor, and lenders for more funds. Simultaneously, Richard Daley was cautious about expanding programs, even though Chicago and New York had similar social problems.

Leaders act in two analytically distinct ways. They may be *invisible* in only implementing others' preferences, or *dynamic* in imparting their own preferences to fiscal policy. Invisible leaders might be termed "democratic" or "responsive," for the invisible label by no means implies that they moderate their demands or are unnoticed by constituents. On the contrary, leaders are often most outspoken when a large and unified constituency stands behind them. But they remain analytically invisible if their own preferences are not distinctively important: they act like Adam Smith's invisible hand in the private market, supplying products the consumer demands. By contrast, dynamic leaders impose their own preferences, which may reflect distant experience or immediate interest. A dynamic leader exerts a distinct impact beyond propositions 1 and 2 (concerning citizens and groups), necessitating a third independent variable:

3. *The more city leaders favor a policy, the more likely the policy is to be adopted.*

Leaders' actions "aggregate" citizen and group preferences. Leaders' own preferences may be clear, but most policies emerge from bargaining and compromise which no leader dominates, and for which it is difficult to derive logical "decision rules" (e.g., Sen 1970; Luce and Raiffa 1957). Budget votes evolve from interactions among mayors and council members whose individual positions come from assessments of sectors, organized group activities, and leaders' personal preferences in mixtures shifting across issues and time. Our concern is not each decision, but processes characterizing cities over several years, especially the degree to which propositions 1, 2, and 3 apply.

Migration

Propositions 1, 2, and 3 suggest causes of fiscal policies; these in turn feed back to citizens. If voting and political activity prove ineffective, citizens move to locations with more acceptable policies. Residential choice can thus reflect political protest, but as a normal act of unpoliticized citizens, it seldom is noticed by leaders and organized groups, at least in the short term. Fiscal policy is obviously just one of many, many factors affecting migration, but insofar as it does, it may be analyzed as follows:

4. *The more urban policy outputs are consistent with sector members' preferences, the greater the expansion of that sector through migration.*

This incorporates residential choice into our systems analysis, but uses the sector concept to facilitate empirical work. Chapter 8 tests this idea by analyzing net migration as a function of tax burdens and welfare benefits.

Resources: Facilitators of Influence

Some Neo-Marxists (e.g., O'Connor 1973) and urban economists (e.g., Muller 1979) see resources as largely determining government policies. But if the posited relationships are deterministic, they are often empirically weak, which suggests a misspecified partial equilibrium model. We suggest instead that resources are properties of individuals or collectivities that can facilitate attainment of their interests. They shift effects of the four above propositions. Resources themselves are inert; they have no direct effects, but strengthen or weaken other relations.

5. *The larger the quantity of resources at the disposal of a participant (sector, organized group, or political leader), the greater the participant's potential effects on other participants and on fiscal policy outputs.*

This idea appears simple, but is difficult to analyze empirically due to the complexity of specific mechanisms by which resources and leadership interact. For example, elected officials in a wealthy city may prefer excellent services because "the city can afford them." Middle-class voters may mildly disagree, but are seldom well-informed so they acquiesce. Capturing such interactions demands detailed data for each type of participant. It is simpler to estimate the "direct" effect of wealth, which may appear significant not because the actual process is direct, but because interactions are so hard to measure. We thus show two types of paths for resources in figure A.[8] One direct path is to policy outputs and fiscal strain; other paths interact with sectors, groups, and political leaders. Figure A is a "complex systems model" suggesting the main lines of causal influence, and feedback via migration.[9] Basic relations are estimated with a system of multiple regression equations which comprise our "core model." A sector's preeminent resource is its size; we thus identify sectors largely as percentages of the city population.[10] Of course, not all sector members are eligible or vote. But as they can be mobilized if dissatisfied, elected officials usually stay attuned to their interests. How much so depends on other resources of which we consider four. Most previous writing considers them not (only) as resources, but as direct causes of fiscal policy.

Legal structures, like the mayor's appointment powers, can enhance his ability to achieve his preferred policies. Conversely, state limits on city debt or revenue can constrain local leaders.

Wealth permits wealthy cities to provide policies which others do not, despite similar citizen preferences.

Intergovernmental revenues, like local wealth, are means to respond to local policy preferences. General Revenue Sharing is an almost pure resource, but most others include "strings" which discourage some cities from pursuing them.

National social movements assisted blacks and municipal employees, sometimes directly—as when AFL-CIO organizers helped local employees. More diffuse were black urban disturbances. Their new and radical character was such that the media and experiences elsewhere suggested tactics to local participants and elected leaders. The national "taxpayers' revolt" similarly reinforced local activities. While we strive for theoretical parsimony, local developments are hard to interpret without these social movement elements. But we analyze them using indicators of their local importance—like the magnitude of black urban disturbances.

Resource Activation and System Responsiveness

Consider a hypothetical city with near total citizen participation. Votes would overshadow other resources, and proposition 1 about sector size would explain fiscal policy. Yet in representative democracies, voters seldom influence decisions directly; organized groups and leaders are the main participants, especially between elections. Resources besides votes then become important. The critical theoretical point about resources is that they often are not used. When they are, influence is exercised.[11] Nevertheless, people seldom use many of their resources to affect urban policy. Even in the activist late 1960s, only 47 percent of Americans reported that they always voted in local elections, 13 percent ever contributed money to a party or candidate, and 8 percent were members of a political club or organization (Verba and Nie 1972:31). Such unused resources provide "slack" in the system which permits independent effects by organized groups or political leaders intensely concerned about specific issues. Participants need not even conflict. That is, policies vary from "zero sum" to "positive sum" games. In zero sum games, one player's gain is equalled by another's loss; not so in positive sum games. Few political issues are pure zero sum games.

If low participation and slack are business as usual, what affects participation and resource activation levels? One answer is the disparity between policies desired and obtained.

6. *The greater the disparity between existing policies and the preferences of a sector, organized group, or political leader, the greater its tendency to mobilize resources at its disposal in an effort to achieve its preferences.*[12]

Even large disparities lead few sector members to participate. Still an increased rate of participation may shift policies toward citizen preferences, again with systemic consequences:

7. *The closer public policies of a political system are to citizen preferences, the more stable the system.*

Leaders are endorsed or replaced through elections, such that votes and citizen preferences periodically have the final word. We thus define equilibrium as the situation where citizens are satisfied with public policy. Services are then provided in a manner consistent with citizen preferences, as is the budget constraint which citizens choose for themselves and their elected officials. At equilibrium, organized groups and political leaders are invisible in basically representing citizen preferences, out-migration is low (proposition 4), and citizens mobilize few resources (proposition 6). A dynamic equilibrium would experience external shocks, but political leaders could soon adapt such that the system would be self-correcting by operating in the cybernetic manner of general systems theory (e.g., Wiener 1948; Parsons 1951; Miller 1978). Political systems often move toward such equilibrium, but it usually remains a desired end state, a goal, rather than an achieved condition. If equilibrium is difficult for a national government, it is more feasible for certain local governments. The degree to which the system deviates from equilibrium varies with the specific policy. Equilibrium may be achieved in semi-trivial policies like having police arrest criminals, or dispatching firefighters to fires. Indeed the routine character of basic city services was the origin of the famous reform slogan: "There is neither a Republican nor a Democratic way to pave a street." These examples indicate that partial equilibria may obtain on certain issues, even if general equilibrium on all issues does not.

System stability concerns the types of demands transmitted into specific policy outputs. An unstable system is one where the flow of policy demands results in a shifting pattern of policy outputs, such as recorded by volatile spending patterns. A city near equilibrium should generate a relatively stable pattern of fiscal policy outputs.

Our sector concept was introduced to simplify analysis of preference aggregation. Equilibrium is facilitated where all citizens have identical policy preferences, i.e., belong to a single sector. But this tractable model grows more complicated if we consider that cities generally have more than one sector. Adding a sector ipso facto implies conflict and less than perfect equilibrium, since sectors differ in fiscal policy preferences.[13] One may so dominate, however, that its members are in near-perfect equilibrium, while other sectors have little impact. Examples have been described in the South before black voter registration, or in towns where older residents dominate newcomers (Present 1971; Laumann and Pappi 1976). Such sector-specific equilibrium is unlikely to endure. Why? If dissatisfied sector members grow more numerous (proposition 1), they would mobilize resources (proposition 6), and when these are sufficient (proposition 5), policy outputs move toward their preferences. Such political mobilization permits the new sector to implement its preferred policies. For example, in some newly developed towns, older residents left rapidly after newcomers raised tax and service levels. More commonly, however, two or more sectors coexist.

Searching for equilibrium is complex with two or more sectors, for practical politicians or social scientists. Policy outputs shift with relative sector size, intensity of preference, consideration of more than one preference dimension, and decision rules for preference aggregation. Consideration of these many issues would take us far afield,[14] but one central variable is homogeneity of citizens.

7a. *The more homogeneous are citizens in terms of characteristics linked to policy preferences, the more easily leaders can provide policies consistent with citizen preferences, and the more stable the system.*

Even if leaders have preferences distinct from citizens, the clearer citizen preferences are to them and to others, the more citizens become a constraining force. Competing candidates can advocate citizen-supported policies if incumbents do not. Similarly, mass media and citizen groups can more easily point out deviations.

If some changes in urban systems can be described as "equilibrating," to many participants "nonequilibrium" is more obvious. Equilibrium is theoretically attractive for sharp analytical models, but specifying conditions necessary for their operation clarifies how often these conditions are absent from American cities. Three conditions are especially important, but sufficiently complex that a path diagram is useful (figure 1.1). The basic ideas may also be stated in propositional form:

Figure 1.1. Sources of Alternative Decision-Making Processes

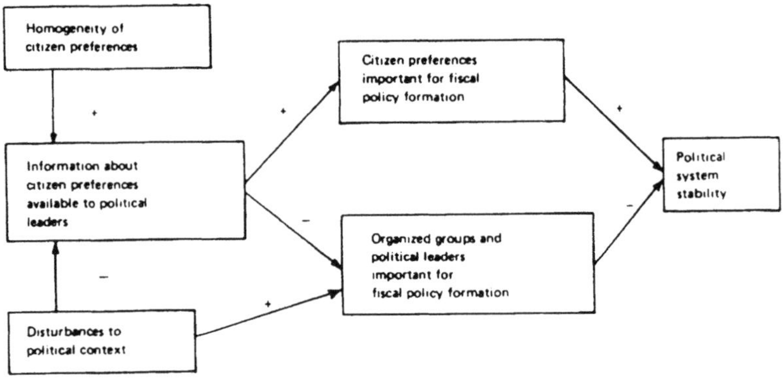

8. *Citizen preferences are more important, and organized groups and political leaders less important, for fiscal policy when: (a) citizen preferences are more homogeneous, (b) political leaders have more information about them, and (c) there are fewer disturbances to the political system. Further, the more important citizen preferences are for fiscal policy, the more stable the political system.*

Consider these ideas separately. Homogeneity facilitates leaders' responsiveness (proposition 7a), which follows from information about citizen preferences. Where citizen preferences are more homogeneous, leaders can learn of and act on them more easily. Indeed lack of information is a major reason that leaders stray from citizen preferences. Citizen preferences are less clear in systems with diverse residents. Disturbances to the political system also increase uncertainty about preferences and resources for leaders. Disturbances arise from myriad sources; some recently important for cities include:

Changes in resources. Especially changes in intergovernmental revenues. Both increases and decreases can generate disturbances. The Great Society programs helped mobilize blacks and poor to upset existing arrangements; fiscal cutbacks can generate counterreactions.

Social and political disruptions. Examples since 1960: civil rights demonstrations, race-related riots, strikes by municipal employees. Still, disturbances can simultaneously generate more information for elected officials about policy preferences of underrepresented groups.

Population changes. Major sector changes disturb the political system by undermining old political bases and creating new ones. Immigrations from Europe near the turn of the century, and later of blacks from the South, were accompanied by out-migration of middle class whites and major political changes.

In systems with new and fluid sectors, preferences and realistic policies are hard to define sharply for citizens or leaders. Such uncertainty encourages pressure by organized groups to increase their share of the pie. Even if leaders seek to respond to citizens, their uncertainty about citizen preferences leads them to request advice about sectors from organized groups qua informants. Disturbances (sometimes intentionally) precipitate crises that leaders must resolve with groups; time prohibits broad citizen input. Competing leaders are also more likely to assemble different winning coalitions than in more stable circumstances. Resources change as coalitions of parties, organized groups, and council members join and divide on different issues. Failure by leaders is then more likely, with turnover rates higher, generating shifting policies. Political leaders become more "dynamic" than in stable systems.

Consider, by contrast, a stable political system typified by a small middle class town where leaders are in close contact with citizens. They "keep in touch" because the town is small enough to encourage direct contacts and homogeneous enough that polls are unnecessary. Few changes disrupt the political climate, and informants soon report minor developments. Population shifts and federal programs are small, voting turnout low, and organized groups few and low-keyed.[15] Many places approximate this type. Consider a Chicago suburb which saw few changes in years. A new city manager had city staff mow the grass next to street curbs. A trivial issue elsewhere, it provoked citizen opposition because it was new and might eventually bring tax increases. The program was discontinued. In such cities, candidates for public office still actively compete for the best means to their constituents' preferred ends, but seldom disagree over ends. Hence, leaders, and organized groups, generally remain invisible.

A corollary of proposition 8 is that organized groups and political leaders are more important for governments serving larger and more heterogeneous populations. Citizens should similarly feel less satisfied with leaders and policies of larger political systems, and given a choice, seek to decentralize policies; organized groups and dynamic leaders should prefer the opposite. This applies to federal vs. state vs. local government, and to cities differing in size.

To summarize, in an unstable system, leaders have more options and their uncertainty about citizen preferences is greater. To overcome uncertainty, they rely more on their personal views or those of organized groups, and thus become more dynamic. By contrast, a more stable political system, with more homogeneous citizen preferences, has fewer points of conflict and more stable rules of the game. Citizen preferences become clearer to political leaders, who are then more likely to remain invisible and implement citizen preferences, which increases stability of the political system.

Four Types of Political Culture

A fourfold typology of political cultures extends earlier propositions by indicating how policy preferences, citizens, and organized groups variously combine. The four types can guide an empirical, positive analysis. They also serve as widely shared normative models defining standards against which alternative policies may be assessed.

The analytical role of the political cultures is clarified by some basic concepts from linguistic theory (e.g., Chomsky 1968). Citizen policy preferences, legitimacy of citizens versus organized groups, and reliance on public or separable goods are "deep structures" common to many political systems. The political cultures define "transformation rules," summarized in figure 1.2, indicating how the deep structures shift their operation in different political systems. The transformation rules encourage interpretation of the "surface structures" of each political culture in more general terms. Examples of surface structures are specific sentences such as Democrats are big spenders, Republicans believe in the market, ethnic politicians use patronage, etc. The political cultures show how such surface structures link together and may be analyzed as a system including preferences, organized groups, and political leaders. The political culture is analogous to cybernetic control in mechanical systems or the genetic code in biological systems.

General characteristics defining the four political cultures are in figure 1.2. The four types are outlined here briefly, stressing their distinctive combinations of the general characteristics. Subsequent chapters elaborate each type. New Deal Democrats and Republicans are

Figure 1.2. General Characteristics Generating Four Types of Political Culture

	Policy preferences		Legitimate sources of input to the political system:		Public goods emphasized as resources
	Fiscal liberalism	Social liberalism	Individual citizens	Organized groups	
New Deal Democrats	+	+	–	+	+ and –
New Deal Republicans	–	–	+	–	+
Ethnic Politicians	+	–	–	+	–
New Fiscal Populists	–	+	+	–	+

well known. The two other types have had less attention, especially New Fiscal Populists (NFPs). Each type evolved in reaction to the others, seeking to capture political territory and elective office. Emergence of the NFPs marks the most profound shift in political alignments since the 1930s, suggesting the end of New Deal coalitions.

With the New Deal, *Democrats* mobilized on fiscal and social liberalism. Fiscal liberalism meant an active role for government; creating jobs through government spending was a central New Deal innovation. Related fiscal policies were unemployment insurance, social security, and welfare, plus a general posture that business should be regulated and monitored. The Democratic Party emerged as a coalition of organized groups, especially labor unions, many Catholics, and ethnic minorities who sought tolerance and respect. More generally, Democratic theorists, like John Kenneth Galbraith, hold that "countervailing groups" to business—like unions and the Democratic Party—are necessary and legitimate political forces affecting public policies. New Deal Democrats are thus defined by (1) fiscal liberalism, (2) social liberalism, and (3) mobilization by organized groups and the party. More educated reform Democrats stress the "public interest" and socially liberal causes, while union and minority groups emphasize more fiscal issues and favors for their supporters. While most American citizens were Democrats in the early 1970s, by the late 1970s, these and other strains split the party apart; the three other types then gained ground.

Republicans opposed Democrats on these issues as the New Deal was debated in the 1930s. Republicans thus lost many black voters who had stayed with the party of Abraham Lincoln after the Civil War, and other poorer ethnic groups (e.g., many Italians). A laissez faire approach sees the market as the least bad mechanism for economic and social decisions. When Democrats call for "countervailing groups" like unions, Republicans counter that the market makes better decisions to increase growth for everyone, and with the exception of monopolies, generally "that government is best which governs least." On social issues Republicans may personally oppose ethnic prejudice, but are cautious about government intervention in matters better handled privately. As Republicans are more often white, Protestant, and affluent citizens, they are less sensitive than Democrats to symbolic "social issues" concerning the disadvantaged. Achievement is emphasized over equality, and individualism over collectivism (Lipset 1963). Disadvantaged persons should work their way up through individual initiative rather than seek special favors from government as a group. Correspondingly, individual citizens are more legitimate than organized groups in providing inputs to public policies. If some Republican leaders do occasional favors for constituents and use patronage, Republican political culture still treats such separable or private goods as less legitimate than public goods (those indivisible and shared by all).

Ethnic politicians are fiscally liberal but socially conservative, at least in using ethnic criteria for political decisions. Ethnic city politics in the mid-nineteenth century saw native-born Americans side against recent immigrants. "Machines" in cities like Boston, New York, and Chicago were built on ethnic loyalties. Blacks in the South had grown up with ethnic politics of white Southern Democrats who rejected the social liberalism of the national party on racial issues. In the 1960s, "red neck" leaders like "Bull" Connor of Birmingham became symbols attacked by the civil rights movement, with considerable success. Black leaders applied direct action tactics from the civil rights movement to city politics, but abandoned integration for the racial distinctiveness of "black power." New black leaders shared with past ethnic politicians a responsiveness to ethnic organizations, churches, neighborhood associations, and other groups that mobilize voters and provide legitimate input to the political process. Like Democrats, they see the normal workings of society as deserving change, which demands special organization. If this disrupts a citizen-defined equilibrium, so much the worse for equilibrium. As lower status individuals join few organizations, leaders feel compelled to speak for the unorganized. Proponents point to the low mobilization of lower-status Americans compared to other countries (Verba, Nie, and Kim 1978) due to weak party structures in the United States. Critics suggest that a group-minded approach blinds one to individual responses, and encourages policies like forced busing, designed to integrate schools but inadvertently causing white flight (Coleman, Kelly, and Moore 1975). Ethnic leaders have usually joined New Deal Democrats on national fiscal issues, favoring an expanding government, albeit stressing "states rights" or "local autonomy" in intergovernmental programs. From

David L. Lawrence to Richard Hatcher, ethnic politicians have openly used federal funds to bolster their political organizations. Patronage along ethnic lines has long been a legitimate way of doing politics for such leaders and their supporters.

New Fiscal Populists (NFPs) emerged last. With continual growth of government through the 1970s, many Democratic voters grew conservative on fiscal issues. They did not abandon social liberalism in the form of civil liberties for persons of disparate ethnic, religious, and racial backgrounds. But like Republicans they prefer eliminating barriers to achievement instead of organizing by groups. Indeed, cooptation of established groups into the two major parties led NFPs to appeal to individual citizen-voters in populist manner. Jimmy Carter, John Anderson, Jerry Brown, Edward Koch, and many newer leaders variously illustrate New Fiscal Populism. Besides (1) fiscal conservatism, (2) social liberalism, and (3) a populist appeal to individual citizens, NFPs often (4) come from Democratic backgrounds, in part because most voters declared themselves Democrats in the 1970s. They represent (5) a *new* configuration of policies and style from past political leaders due to their combination of traits. These lead them to search for (6) new policies, often public goods like increased productivity via contracting out, or user charges, sometimes avoided by New Deal Democrats due to their dependence on unions for political support. Such policies ideally maintain services while reducing taxes. NFP leaders can thus play a critical role in helping traditional Democratic and ethnic political systems adapt to their declining private sector resources. Cities like New York, Philadelphia, or San Francisco are unlikely to elect Republicans but they elected NFP mayors in the late 1970s who helped transform the rules of the game generating fiscal policies in these cities, and reduced their fiscal strain.

The Dynamics of Political Culture

The political cultures include both policy preferences and rules of the political game, as in past usage (see Knoke 1981). But we do not posit cultural characteristics as consistently driving others. Different components respond to different factors. Fiscal conservatism follows from higher income, heightened by government growth and a stagnant private sector. Higher income leads to less dependence on government services and favors (separable goods), and thus to preferences for less government in general and for public over separable goods. Social liberalism increases with education, which also encourages public goods. Catholics have supported organized groups as political participants, whereas Protestants have more often acted as individuals. More ethnic group members in a city encourage ethnic politics. Heterogeneity in socioeconomic characteristics leads to organized group activities, which in turn generate separable goods as policy outputs. Active organized groups could in principle generate legitimate and stable leadership in Democratic or ethnic cities, but citizens often support organized groups while opposing consequences like high taxes. Poor white and black citizens favor more services but not more taxes.

These conflicting pressures generate conflict and instability in Democratic and ethnic cities. NFPs may define policies responsive to broad citizen preferences, but their conflicts with municipal employees and other groups often generate political difficulties, and unstable leadership. Patronage and specific, short-term favors to supporters are used in Democratic and ethnic political cultures due to their appeals to poorer, less educated, and (at least in the past) Catholic citizens. By contrast, the "public interest" is stressed by more affluent, highly educated Protestant and Jewish citizens (see Wilson and Banfield 1964; Elazar and Zikmund 1975; Clark 1975c; Knoke 1981). Of course, an individual leader or city need not conform to the ideal type, and to state a norm does not imply it is never violated. But leaders often redefine policies to make them consistent with local norms rather than violating norms. When Mayor Daley was asked why he gave city contracts to his sons' insurance firm, he replied, "It's a father's duty to help his sons," illustrating the legitimacy of open patronage in Chicago. A Republican or NFP leader helping his sons would more likely defend the action as consistent with competitive bidding procedures.

Democrats and ethnics see groups and leaders as legitimate policy making vehicles, such that uncertainty about citizen preferences troubles them less than NFPs or Republicans. In New York, Chicago, or Boston, for example, Democratic and ethnic leaders conduct few citizen preference surveys, or such surveys remain unpublicized. In Chicago's Democratic political culture, legitimate information about citizens, often as requests for favors, is passed up from Democratic precinct captains and ward committeemen to city government staff. When decentralization and citizen participation were mandated in certain federal programs, these were largely organized by Party staff to retain control. In Boston Mayor Kevin White used Little City Halls in a manner similar to the Party in Chicago. These organizations thus feed in citizen requests and deliver back favors. The press, radio, and television are competitors in defining citizen preferences (via spot interviews, or "in depth" reports). In cities with Democratic and ethnic leaders, the media often publicize views of NFP and Republican council members and civic leaders who appeal to "overtaxed and underrepresented" citizens. Media persons may or may not hold these views themselves; in any case such dissent makes good "news." "Good government reformers" from the turn of the century to present have attacked Democratic and ethnic rules of the game. Reformers have proposed rules more responsive to individual citizens and public goods—like nonpartisan, at-large elections and the city manager. Day-to-day decisions can be delegated to professional staff (only) if allocating favors is not a leader's duty in the political culture. City managers, finance directors, and their professional norms thus influence fiscal policy more in NFP and Republican dominated cities. Information about citizen preferences and legal rules of the game are resources which proponents of each political culture use in ways that advance their respective positions. Everyone may be equally "nasty, brutish, and short" or "utility maximizing," but NFP or Republican leaders are constrained by their political cultures to appeal to "the public good" while ethnic and Democratic leaders seek to debunk such appeals and follow their own rules.

As these examples suggest, we introduce political culture not as consensually shared values, or as an abstraction opposed to material conditions, but as a tool to codify the patterned conflicts, constraints, and rewards to which participants must adapt. Still, because of the generality of the components in figure 1.2, much specific behavior remains unregulated or "noninstitutionalized" (Parsons 1969) by any political culture. This leaves room for creative leaders to mobilize new resources, and create new coalitions and policies, which over time can institutionalize new components of political culture (Clark 1972b, 1975c).

Distinguishing these four ideal types does not imply that they fully define any given city. Most cities are hybrids and include proponents of all four types. We still introduce examples of more pure types to illustrate their dynamics. Over time, policy outputs shift sector size; higher spending and tax burdens depress the middle class sector. Social, economic, political, and cultural characteristics thus affect one another as elements of a complex system.

NFPs have not been identified or explicitly considered in past research. Yet citizen surveys in chapter 7 suggest that many Americans are NFPs. Americans have grown more concerned with fiscal issues, and more fiscally conservative since the 1970s, especially on redistributive issues like welfare. Higher income trends generate more fiscal conservatism, and higher education trends more social liberalism. Both increase numbers of NFPs, who deserve more serious attention.

Are the four types analytically necessary? The normal answer is yes if the dimensions comprising them cluster and interact to create more than additive linear effects. Answers may thus vary with the specific analysis. Some cities are also hard to score clearly on some dimensions, especially cities with nonpartisan elections. They vote predominantly Republican in national elections, but it is mistaken to introduce unrealistic partisanship. Our empirical analyses thus often use separate dimensions of the four types. The next chapter introduces important fiscal measures, which chapter 4 then joins with measures of citizens, groups, and leaders to test the ideas from this chapter.

PART II

Fiscal, Economic, and Population Characteristics

CHAPTER TWO

Fiscal Strain and Its Measurement

Fiscal strain reflects lack of adaptation by a city government to its private sector environment. How measure it? Economic and population base measures, used to index "distress" in federal formulas, capture half the story, that of the private sector. Bond prices and ratings concern municipal bond performance, but what else they show is unclear. Defaults are too few to study. Short term measures, like fund balances and deficits, vary with specific accounting practices and are hard to interpret across cities. Our preferred fiscal strain indicators are thus ratios using as numerators fiscal policy outputs of city government: general (total) expenditures, own revenues, common function expenditures, and long-term debt. Denominators are private sector resources like income and taxable property value. This chapter introduces indicators analyzed throughout the book.

The strain scores are strictly fiscal and limited to the period measured. They do not reflect inadequate capital maintenance or dissatisfaction by citizens whose services are trimmed. A "city social welfare" index including such nonfiscal indicators might be desirable, but as cities vary across indicators, and indicators vary for different reasons, we avoid global indexes.

Three Concepts of Fiscal Strain

From the frequent discussions of fiscal crises, strain, and distress, three conceptions may be distinguished. One is that a city suffers fiscal strain if it has a weak or declining economic base, especially characterized by population loss. This conception often leads to classifying cities as declining northeastern central cities or growing suburbs and Sunbelt cities. It informed many federal policies in the 1970s, such as the Carter National Urban Policy of seeking to encourage jobs and population in cities losing them. Often implicit here is the notion that a city's economic base either defines or so fully determines the city government's fiscal strain that little further analysis is necessary. Developing the economic base follows logically as the primary solution to urban distress. This view is elaborated in chapter 3.

A second conception stresses the municipal bond market which summarizes the judgment of informed investors (see Petersen 1974). Fiscal strain is registered by (1) the offering price of a new issue, or (2) the issue's price in the secondary bond market, both of which are considered related to (3) the probability of regular principal and interest payments and perhaps (4) bond ratings by Moody's and Standard and Poor's. Bond prices (1 and 2) reflect many types of information significant for investors, but few analysts would hold prices as synomous with fiscal strain since the bond price leaves undefined what *determines* the probability of regular payments (3). Bond ratings (4) might provide the answer, but in practice they have performed dismally, as we discuss below.

The economic base of a city and probability of paying debt service are two extreme conceptions of fiscal strain. We consider neither adequate, but propose a third incorporating them as components. It moves back an analytical step from the municipal investor's perspective to include explanations of debt policy. But not so far back as to define fiscal strain by the economic base. Our conception of the city government as a complex system leads us to focus on how it obtains resources from its "environment." The main flows of service demands and resources are in figure A (see Introduction). Like all systems, cities must adapt as their environments change. Municipal leaders play a key role in keeping city government policies in balance with their private sector environment. As the socioeconomic base changes, municipal officials must formulate new policies to maintain balance between resources and expenditures. Cities that do not adapt rapidly enough suffer fiscal strain. A simple example of adaptation involves population growth or decline. A growing city must construct new roads, sewers, sidewalks, and schools. Local officials must assess the rate and duration of population growth, and manage capital expenditures and debt accordingly. The few defaults since the 1930s have often involved small but rapidly growing towns that became overextended. Cities with declining populations face the opposite problem: reducing expenditures, which employees may particularly resist. Again, local leaders may or may not adapt to changed circumstances. Fiscal strain increases if they do not.

Our conception stresses that the political system must adapt to its environmental resources if it is to survive. Political leaders are central in maintaining balance between fiscal policy and the social and economic base. In the short term, local leaders only modestly affect changes in population movement and private sector economic activities; these social and economic base characteristics are more influenced by national trends. By contrast, the city government has considerable control over its expenditures, debt, and many revenues. Changes in such fiscal policies immediately affect fiscal strain, and over a decade or more, they may exert considerable impact on population and job growth.

How measure fiscal strain? If strain is poor adaptation of (1) fiscal policy outputs of the city government to (2) private sector activities, both components must be measured and combined. The clearest combination is a ratio dividing fiscal policy outputs by private sector activities. We present such ratios below, but because fiscal policy outputs are not always simple to measure, we initially consider them separately.

Fiscal Policy Outputs

Analyzing Changes. Consider first a type of measure often used in Washington: aggregate expenditure or revenue change for all U.S. cities. The measure indicates smooth and continuous growth, free of peaks and troughs, from World War II to the late 1970s (see figure 3.1). Yet it is also misleading: the growth and continuity both change in more sensitive measures. Consider instead percentage changes for individual cities in per capita general expenditures, which are total expenditures from all sources including debt and intergovernment revenue. These vary from Bloomington's average annual decrease of 4 percent in 1960–70 to San Francisco's and New York's growth of 19 percent (table 2.1). Change rates also vary for an individual city over time, like Pittsburgh's annual increase of 13 percent in the 1960s, which dropped by almost half in the early 1970s. Such discontinuities conflict with "incrementalist" theories which hypothesize (1) constant changes over time, and (2) "small" changes.[1]

If we consider separate components of general expenditure by city, a different, more striking pattern emerges: after 1974 about half our cities began retrenchment. Debt and capital outlays are often easiest to trim, and 31 of the 62 cities cut back one or both. Similarly, 23 reduced their work forces (table 2.2).[2] Note that these cutbacks began four full years before Proposition 13. But apart from New York City, retrenchment was barely mentioned in national urban discussions until after the California referendum. The downturn was ignored in part because it did not appear in the widely used aggregate measures for all U.S. cities.

Levels of Fiscal Policy. Changes, however, are distinct from levels. A city like New York may spend at a high level but change slowly. Both types of measures are thus important to consider. Percentage changes can be readily compared across cities, but per capita levels cannot, primarily because cities differ in functions they perform.

The Functional Performance (FP) Approach. American cities traditionally performed most local functions, including education and welfare. But influenced by the reform movement in the late nineteenth century, most founded after that time were assigned fewer functions. Special districts were created separate from city governments for certain functions. By the mid-twentieth century, cities thus differed considerably in service responsibilities. New York City provides welfare, public eduction, public health and hospitals, but the City of Los Angeles almost none of these. Los Angeles residents receive most of the same services as New Yorkers, but often from special districts, school districts, county, and state governments. Such differences have long troubled fiscal comparisons of cities. One solution compares only "common functions," like fire and police, common to most cities.[3] This is one approach we use here. But common functions are less than half the total expenditures of cities which perform many noncommon functions, and the approach does not work for revenues or debt which

Table 2.1. Cities Differ from One Another and over Time in Their Rates of Change

Cities	Average Annual Rate of Growth in General Expenditures per Capita		
	1960-70	1970-74	1974-77
1. Akron, OH	11.64	8.39	17.86
2. Albany, NY*	--	--	--
3. Amarillo, TX	7.68	8.46	57.39
4. Atlanta, GA	13.56	15.21	9.20
5. Baltimore, MD	17.91	10.09	14.73
6. Berkeley, CA	12.16	12.84	18.41
7. Birmingham, AL	13.16	30.47	3.81
8. Bloomington, MN	-4.31	8.39	3.92
9. Boston, MA	9.11	13.72	14.22
10. Buffalo, NY	12.61	19.19	13.21
11. Cambridge, MA	12.31	13.34	16.48
12. Charlotte, NC	3.19	16.87	9.34
13. Chicago, IL	7.99	11.45	8.78
14. Cleveland, OH	11.54	17.05	16.72
15. Clifton, NJ*	--	--	--
16. Dallas, TX	10.48	16.96	4.95
17. Detroit, MI	7.96	17.26	10.27
18. Duluth, MN	11.58	21.47	23.55
19. Euclid, OH	7.24	22.41	3.60
20. Fort Worth, TX	8.77	10.19	27.66
21. Fullerton, CA	4.01	10.59	19.65
22. Gary, IN	4.86	27.90	-9.43
23. Hamilton, OH	7.33	10.46	12.21
24. Hammond, IN	7.13	13.60	-1.06
25. Houston, TX	4.87	12.58	24.93
26. Indianapolis, IN*	--	--	--
27. Irvington, NJ*	--	--	--
28. Jacksonville, FL*	--	--	--
29. Long Beach, CA	5.52	4.98	24.14
30. Los Angeles, CA	7.19	12.75	10.34
31. Malden, MA	6.09	17.55	15.28
32. Manchester, NH	11.55	15.89	20.92
33. Memphis, TN*	--	--	--
34. Milwaukee, WI	8.80	7.89	7.06
35. Minneapolis, MN	8.23	22.53	15.51
36. New York, NY	19.33	16.20	5.96
37. Newark, NJ	11.76	17.85	8.99
38. Palo Alto, CA	11.24	8.03	10.34
39. Pasadena, CA	8.50	22.91	9.96
40. Philadelphia, PA	11.48	13.00	10.98
41. Phoenix, AZ	10.46	24.08	13.74
42. Pittsburgh, PA	13.09	6.93	12.50
43. St. Louis, MO	9.82	16.22	12.62
44. St. Paul, MN*	--	--	--

Table 2.1. (Continued)

Cities	Average Annual Rate of Growth in General Expenditures per Capita		
	1960-70	1970-74	1974-77
45. St. Petersburg, FL*	--	--	--
46. Salt Lake City, UT	3.93	25.07	9.03
47. San Antonio, TX	8.87	14.26	25.28
48. San Diego, CA	9.09	11.69	8.43
49. San Francisco, CA	19.59	6.62	12.36
50. Santa Ana, CA	4.73	10.86	27.45
51. San Jose, CA	6.87	5.08	24.78
52. Santa Monica, CA	4.94	2.08	15.09
53. Schnectady, NY*	--	--	--
54. Seattle, WA	14.46	18.39	10.54
55. South Bend, IN	9.51	24.35	.56
56. Tampa, FL	4.16	18.11	47.57
57. Tyler, TX	7.52	9.10	18.88
58. Utica, NY	8.37	3.89	-.03
59. Waco, TX	19.05	6.03	.44
60. Warren, MI	2.72	29.74	7.61
61. Waterbury, CT	13.71	10.84	4.99
62. Waukegan, IL	20.30	10.16	12.85
MEAN	9.50	14.37	13.67

Note: An asterisk after the city name indicates a significant change in functional responsibility over the period, such as transferring hospitals to the county government.

-- indicates omitted.

are not readily matched to expenditure categories. New York City resembles many other cities in its common function expenditures, but differs in debt and noncommon functions. Another approach is thus called for.

We developed Functional Performance (FP) analysis to overcome shortcomings of past approaches. It permits comparing debt and noncommon function expenditures of cities differing in functional responsibilities. It uses an Index of Functional Performance measuring the range of municipal responsibilities as a control in statistical analyses. City finances have two dimensions: the *range* of functions performed and the *level* of expenditure. The FP Index measures just the range. Some functions are small while others are large, so to weight all equally is misleading. The FP Index thus uses as weights the average per capita expenditure on 67 subfunctions by all U.S. cities over 50,000 in population which perform the subfunction. For example, New York City provides public hospitals; but so do many others. The weight for "public hospitals-current operating expenditures" is the average per capita expenditure on this subfunction by all U.S. cities performing it. New York's expenditure *level* may be above or below the U.S. average. But for its FP score, New York is assigned the U.S. average as a weight. We thus estimate the *range* for the FP Index by using the *average level* for U.S. cities.

The FP Index is a weighted measure of the range of functions per-

Table 2.2. When Individual Cities Are Classified as Increasing or Decreasing Their Expenditure Levels over Several Periods, Retrenchment Is Clear for Many Cities after 1974

	1960-70	1970-74	1974-76	1974-77
Long Term Debt				
Number of cities increasing	50	42	34	36
Number of cities decreasing	4	12	20	17
Missing or Zero	8	8	8	9
General Expenditures				
Number of cities increasing	53	54	50	50
Number of cities decreasing	1	0	4	3
Missing or Zero	8	8	8	9
Capital Outlays				
Number of cities increasing	49	37	37	35
Number of cities decreasing	5	17	17	18
Missing or Zero	8	8	8	9
City's Own Revenues				
Number of cities increasing	54	54	50	51
Number of cities decreasing	0	0	4	2
Missing or Zero	8	8	8	9
Intergovernmental Revenues				
Number of cities increasing	52	52	50	49
Number of cities decreasing	1	1	3	4
Missing or Zero	9	9	9	9
Number of Municipal Employees				
Number of cities increasing	52	41	39	39
Number of cities decreasing	1	12	23	14
Missing or Zero	9	9	0	9

Note: We show 1974-76 as the downturn after 1974 is clearer on some indicators than for 1974-77.

formed by an individual city government. To compute it the city is assigned 1 for each of 67 subfunctions it performs, and 0 for those it does not. These 67 1's or 0's are then multiplied by the 67 respective weights, and products summed to generate the FP Index for the city.[4] FP Index scores for PCS cities are in table 2.4. Insights from the approach are exemplified by comparing New York City with Baltimore. These two topped the list in per capita general expenditures (in table 2.3, column one). Both perform many functions and have high FP scores, $583 and $567 respectively (table 2.4). But how do their expenditures look when we control (as explained in the table 2.3 note) for differences due simply to functional responsibilities? New York still ranks above most other cities, but Baltimore falls near the bottom (columns three and four of table 2.3). Baltimore's high (unadjusted) general expenditures are thus largely explained by its broad functional responsibilities, but not New York's. These results sharply undercut the common argument that New York suffers fiscal strain because it is responsible for so many functions.

The FP approach is our preferred adjustment for "nondiscretionary" expenditures. Nondiscretion, like truth or justice, clearly exists, but only where a political culture is clearly institutionalized, well indexed by leaders who themselves feel bound to it. If one asks different informants to list nondiscretionary items, it soon grows clear that nondiscretionary often means "politically unfeasible," or "nonnegotiable" to the informant. This can mean until the contract expires, the council acts differently, the staff changes its operating procedures, the city takes the case to court or lobbies in Washington or the state capitol for new laws or administrative procures. This is least true of state-mandated functions like welfare or public eduction, but the FP approach is a reasonable solution to these. "Nondiscretion" is a more appropriate concept at lower administrative levels (Padgett 1981) than for top leaders. We were most convinced on this point by participating in (private) workshops with mayors where those who declared items "non-discretionary" were counseled by others concerning solutions. Chapter 9 pursues these issues.

The FP Index is strongly related to certain fiscal level measures, explaining over 80 percent of the variance (the r^2) in general expenditures, general revenues, and personal services. Similarly, other var-

Table 2.3. Illustration of FP Approach

Cities	(1) General Expenditures per Capita 1974	(2) Long Term Debt per Capita 1974	(3) Residual of (1) FP Adjusted	(4) Residual of (2) FP Adjusted
	GENEXP77	FS01Y77	GEXPFA77	FS01FA77
1. Akron, OH	411	334	.55	-.27
2. Albany, NY	439	499	.83	.26
3. Amarillo, TX	355	225	.53	-.53
4. Atlanta, GA	484	1348	1.12	2.96
5. Baltimore, MD	1293	585	-.53	-1.30
6. Berkeley, CA	384	45	.58	-1.14
7. Birmingham, AL	336	1083	-.12	2.09
8. Bloomington, MN	200	592	-.51	.67
9. Boston, MA	1224	772	1.32	-.14
10. Buffalo, NY	905	543	.50	-.49
11. Cambridge, MA	1034	407	.09	-1.25
12. Charlotte, NC	335	562	-.03	.45
13. Chicago, IL	377	365	-.47	-.35
14. Cleveland, OH	500	543	.97	.33
15. Clifton, NJ	377	111	-2.68	-1.67
16. Dallas, TX	305	572	.12	.57
17. Detroit, MI	517	453	-.31	-.28
18. Duluth, MN	482	787	1.16	1.18
19. Euclid, OH	267	351	-.17	-.13
20. Fort Worth, TX	318	513	.07	.35
21. Fullerton, CA	247	37	-.18	-1.10
22. Gary, IN	174	157	-1.32	-.85
23. Hamilton, OH	222	228	-.27	-.47
24. Hammond, IN	183	261	-.69	-.39
25. Houston, TX	294	594	-.21	.58
26. Indianapolis, IN	418	396	-1.87	-.65
27. Irvington, NJ	367	128	-.50	-1.10
28. Jacksonville, FL	411	966	-1.49	1.27
29. Long Beach, CA	537	382	1.05	-.23
30. Los Angeles, CA	334	952	-.50	1.59
31. Malden, MN	818	502	.66	-.43
32. Manchester, NH	752	566	-.16	-.30
33. Memphis, TN	540	1127	-2.19	1.39
34. Milwaukee, WI	348	357	-.20	-.26
35. Minneapolis, MN	494	542	.89	.32
36. New York, NY	1628	1806	1.81	2.55
37. Newark, NJ	981	460	1.08	-.76
38. Palo Alto, CA	459	173	1.43	-.67
39. Pasadena, CA	511	478	1.44	.21
40. Philadelphia, PA	603	800	-.17	.70
41. Phoenix, AZ	360	592	-.22	.45
42. Pittsburgh, PA	336	266	.00	-.48
43. St. Louis, MO	511	310	-.10	-.68
44. St. Paul, MN	488	1131	1.13	2.26

Table 2.3. (Continued)

Cities	(1) General Expenditures per Capita 1974	(2) Long Term Debt per Capita 1974	(3) Residual of (1) FP Adjusted	(4) Residual of (2) FP Adjusted
	GENEXP77	FS01Y77	GEXPFA77	FS01FA77
45. St. Petersburg, FL	304	443	.10	.15
46. Salt Lake City, UT	282	190	-.08	-.65
47. San Antonio, TX	241	716	-1.11	.86
48. San Diego, CA	252	168	-.48	-.76
49. San Francisco, CA	1045	849	2.35	.65
50. Santa Ana, CA	239	31	-.27	-1.13
51. San Jose, CA	328	227	-.04	-.61
52. Santa Monica, CA	278	83	-.17	-1.01
53. Schenectady, NY	275	165	-.38	-.79
54. Seattle, WA	476	963	.94	1.70
55. South Bend, IN	223	258	-.69	-.47
56. Tampa, FL	583	540	2.14	.44
57. Tyler, TX	188	346	-.74	-.14
58. Utica, NY	281	469	-.44	.15
59. Waco, TX	250	317	-.80	-.36
60. Warren, MI	268	194	-.42	-.69
61. Waterbury, CT	589	497	-1.94	-.65
62. Waukegan, IL	223	107	-.35	-.87
MEAN	466	491	0	0

Note: The data in columns (1) and (2) were regressed on the Index of Functional Performance. Residuals of these regressions appear in columns (3) and (4). The procedure is elaborated in the text and appendix 4.

iables are intertwined with FP, like Democratic voting and unionized employees (table 9.4). Careful analysis is thus essential to isolate effects of each. But this is unnecessary for percentage changes—as long as cities do not change functional responsibilities over the period analyzed. For this reason we usually delete cities that change functional responsibilities.

Fiscal Strain Indicators

If fiscal strain indicators are ratios of fiscal policy outputs of city government over private sector resources, which resources are appropriate? Several socioeconomic characteristics are considered in chap-

Table 2.4. Functional Performance Scores for the 63 Cities in the Permanent Community Sample

Cities	FP Score	Cities	FP Score
1. Akron, OH	47	34. Milwaukee, WI	65
2. Albany, NY	43	35. Minneapolis, MN	66
3. Amarillo, TX	20	36. New York, NY	583
4. Atlanta, GA	46	37. Newark, NJ	301
5. Baltimore, MD	567	38. Palo Alto, CA	14
6. Berkeley, CA	31	39. Pasadena, CA	39
7. Birmingham, AL	53	40. Philadelphia, PA	193
8. Bloomington, MN	10	41. Phoenix, AZ	73
9. Boston, MA	409	42. Pittsburgh, PA	45
10. Buffalo, NY	301	43. St. Louis, MO	142
11. Cambridge, MA	394	44. St. Paul, MN	48
12. Charlotte, NC	47	45. St. Petersburg, FL	23
13. Chicago, IL	98	46. Salt Lake City, UT	24
14. Cleveland, OH	64	47. San Antonio, TX	71
15. Clifton, NJ	243	48. San Diego, CA	35
16. Dallas, TX	22	49. San Francisco, CA	250
17. Detroit, MI	158	50. Santa Ana, CA	14
18. Duluth, MN	43	51. San Jose, CA	44
19. Euclid, OH	22	52. Santa Monica, CA	27
20. Fort Worth, TX	31	53. Schenectady, NY	39
21. Fullerton, CA	12	54. Seattle, WA	54
22. Gary, IN	51	55. South Bend, IN	34
23. Hamilton, OH	6	56. Tampa, FL	20
24. Hammond, IN	13	57. Tyler, TX	19
25. Houston, TX	38	58. Utica, NY	47
26. Indianapolis, IN	211	59. Waco, TX	55
27. Irvington, NJ	95	60. Warren, MI	39
28. Jacksonville, FL	182	61. Washington, DC#	554
29. Long Beach, CA	78	62. Waterbury, CT	302
30. Los Angeles, CA	78	63. Waukegan, IL	12
31. Malden, MA	246		
32. Manchester, NH	268		
33. Memphis, TN	294	MEAN	118

#There are further complications for the District of Columbia that have led us to omit it from some analyses (such as the correlations in this chapter). The FP score is still presented here, calculated as if it were a city like any other, for purposes of comparison.

ter 3, but our concern here is to select resources convertible into revenues for city governments. City revenues are themselves resources, but balanced budget requirements normally force city revenues to equal expenditures in the same fiscal year.

We thus use three private sector measures: population size and change, change in median family income, and a City Wealth Index. The Index includes two leading wealth measures in research to date:

taxable property value and income. Taxable property value is used since the property tax is the largest city revenue source. Still it generates over 80 percent of own source revenues in Gary and Boston, but under 15 percent in others like Birmingham. Such revenue structure differences are incorporated in the City Wealth Index. Its two components, taxable property value and median family income, are weighted by the city's revenue structure to capture differences across cities. The weight for property tax revenues is the proportion they represent of the city's own revenues, while the weight for median family income is the proportion of revenues from all other sources (including charges and fees, sales, income, and wage taxes):

$$\text{City Wealth Index} = \text{CWI} = W_i I + W_t T$$

where I is median family income, T is equalized taxable property value, W_t is the percentage of own revenues from property taxes, and $W_i = (1 - W_t)$.

Conversion of private resources into revenues is of course not automatic. Assessment levels and tax rates come from political decisions. Wealthy cities suffer fiscal strain if citizens oppose high "tax effort."[5] Private resources are still potential revenues, while a declining tax base exacerbates other problems.

A past barrier to urban fiscal strain indicators was non-comparability in functions across cities. We handle this in different indicators by (1) using common function expenditures, or (2) comparing changes (not levels) in general expenditures and own revenues, or (3) adjusting levels of noncommon functions with our FP Index. Our ratio indicators use four different numerators: *general expenditures* capture total city spending; *own revenues* show local contributions by removing intergovernmental transfers;[6] *common functions* are core municipal services; *debt* indicates future obligations. Denominators are *median family income*, *population change*, or the *City Wealth Index*. Changes and levels of fiscal strain were computed for the same years as the fiscal policy outputs. Five indicators used general expenditures:[7]

Acronym	*Numerator*	*Denominator*	*Year*
NGXMI607	General expenditures	Median family income	1960–70

NGXPO607	General expenditures	Population change	1960–70
NGXPO704	General expenditures	Population change	1970–74
NGXP0747	General expenditures	Population change	1974–77
GENNET77	General expenditures	City wealth index	1977

Five similar measures were constructed for own revenues, five for common functions, and five for debt (appendix 1 lists details.)

Table 2.5 illustrates the indicator construction procedure. It uses a ratio of two periods' expenditures over a ratio of two periods' resources.[8] Column (1) shows general expenditures per capita in 1960, and column (2) the same for 1970. Column (3) is simply the ratio of (2) to (1); it reflects the rate of expenditure increase from 1960 to 1970. A similar measure (6) captures population change by dividing 1970 population (5) by 1960 population (4). Finally, expenditure change (3) is divided by population change (6) to generate (7) the fiscal strain ratio of general expenditure/population 1960–70. Consider some results. General expenditures doubled 1960–70 (column (3) scores are near 2). By contrast, population was about the same in 1970 as 1960 (column (6) scores are about 1). In 1960–70 general expenditures per capita thus grew about twice as fast as the population of most cities (column (7) is about 2). But cities differ substantially. New York and San Francisco raised general expenditures almost three times as much as their populations, scoring near 3 on the column (7) indicator, while fiscal strain increased by less than half as much in other cities.

Ratios for 1977 levels are in table 2.6. Column (1) shows common function expenditures. While Amarillo rose substantially in 1974–77, in 1977 it still spent less than half as much as Newark and Palo Alto, two of the highest cities. Still, these two substantially differ on the City Wealth Index in column (2), so Newark remains at the top of the fiscal strain ratio in column (3), while Palo Alto falls below average. Wealthy Palo Alto still scores about twice as high as Gary whose large black population often leads it to be discussed with Newark. Yet Gary and Newark are far apart in terms of fiscal strain, due both to spending and wealth differences.

Table 2.5. Fiscal Strain Indicators Using General Expenditures and Population

Cities	(1) General Expenditures per Capita in 1960	(2) General Expenditures per Capita in 1970	(3) Ratio of 1970/1960 General Expenditures per Capita	(4) Population in 1960	(5) Population in 1970	(6)=(5)/(4) Ratio of Population in 1970/ Population in 1960	(7)=(3)/(6) Ratio of General Expenditures/ Ratio of Population
	GENEXP60	GENEXP70	NGXP6070	POP60	POP73T	NPOP6070	NGXPO607
1. Akron, OH	92	200	2.16	290221	275	.94	2.28
2. Albany, NY	154	316	--	129760	116	.89	--
3. Amarillo, TX	55	97	1.76	137947	127	.92	1.92
4. Atlanta, GA	100	236	2.35	487279	497	1.02	2.30
5. Baltimore, MD	229	639	2.79	938610	906	.96	2.89
6. Berkeley, CA	73	163	2.21	111238	117	1.04	2.11
7. Birmingham, AL	58	135	2.31	340529	301	.88	2.62
8. Bloomington, MN	236	134	.56	50492	82	1.62	.35
9. Boston, MA	289	553	1.91	697555	641	.91	2.08
10. Buffalo, NY	162	366	2.26	532547	463	.86	2.60
11. Cambridge, MA	202	451	2.23	107718	100	.93	2.39
12. Charlotte, NC	118	156	1.32	201516	241	1.19	1.10
13. Chicago, IL	113	205	1.80	3543545	3369	.95	1.89
14. Cleveland, OH	91	198	2.15	876366	751	.85	2.51
15. Clifton, NJ	138	220	--	82109	82	1.00	--
16. Dallas, TX	77	158	2.04	679701	844	1.24	1.64
17. Detroit, MI	130	233	1.79	1668141	1514	.90	1.98
18. Duluth, MN	70	152	2.15	106884	101	.94	2.29
19. Euclid, OH	73	127	1.72	62986	72	1.13	1.51
20. Fort Worth, TX	65	123	1.87	356398	393	1.10	1.70
21. Fullerton, CA	78	109	1.40	56120	86	1.53	.91
22. Gary, IN	77	115	1.48	178099	175	.98	1.50
23. Hamilton, OH	66	114	1.73	72086	68	.94	1.84
24. Hammond, IN	71	122	1.71	111530	108	.96	1.77
25. Houston, TX	75	111	1.48	937905	1233	1.31	1.13
26. Indianapolis, IN	77	90	--	475147	745	1.56	--
27. Irvington, NJ	145	287	--	59390	60	1.00	--
28. Jacksonville, FL	164	131	--	201013	504	2.50	--
29. Long Beach, CA	167	260	1.55	343886	359	1.04	1.48
30. Los Angeles, CA	98	169	1.71	2485536	2810	1.13	1.52
31. Malden, MA	204	329	1.60	57684	56	.97	1.65
32. Manchester, NH	131	282	2.15	88284	88	.99	2.16
33 Memphis ,TN	147	294	--	497810	624	1.25	--

Cities	(1) General Expenditures per Capita	(2) General Expenditures per Capita	(3) Ratio of 1970/1960 General Expenditures per Capita	(4) Population in 1960	(5) Population in 1970	(6)=(5)/(4) Ratio of Population in 1970/ Population in 1960	(7)=(3)/(6) Ratio of General Expenditures/ Ratio of Population
	GENEXP60	GENEXP70	NGXP6070	POP60	POP73T	NPOP6070	NGXPO607
34. Milwaukee, WI	116	218	1.88	740831	717	.96	1.94
35. Minneapolis, MN	97	177	1.82	482646	434	.90	2.02
36. New York, NY	285	838	2.93	7778183	7896	1.01	2.89
37. Newark, NJ	207	450	2.17	405490	382	.94	2.31
38. Palo Alto, CA	124	265	2.12	52460	56	1.06	1.99
39. Pasadena, CA	111	205	1.85	116757	113	.96	1.91
40. Philadelphia, PA	139	298	2.14	2000625	1950	.97	2.20
41. Phoenix, AZ	63	129	2.04	439275	582	1.32	1.54
42. Pittsburgh, PA	82	191	2.31	604143	520	.86	2.68
43. St. Louis, MO	113	225	1.98	749682	622	.83	2.38
44. St. Paul, MN	148	213	--	313704	310	.98	--
45. St. Petersburg, FL	120	121	--	181264	216	1.19	--
46. Salt Lake City, UT	79	110	1.39	189454	176	.92	1.50
47. San Antonio, TX	46	87	1.88	587861	654	1.11	1.69
48. San Diego, CA	71	137	1.90	572834	697	1.21	1.56
49. San Francisco, CA	203	602	2.95	740097	716	.96	3.06
50. Santa Ana, CA	69	102	1.47	100851	156	1.54	.95
51. San Jose, CA	92	156	1.68	204163	446	2.18	.77
52. Santa Monica, CA	118	176	1.49	83213	88	1.06	1.40
53. Schenectady, NY	110	148	--	81613	78	.95	--
54. Seattle, WA	85	208	2.44	557072	531	.95	2.56
55. South Bend, IN	57	111	1.95	132703	126	.94	2.06
56. Tampa, FL	98	139	1.41	274986	278	1.01	1.40
57. Tyler, TX	50	88	1.75	51215	58	1.12	1.55
58. Utica, NY	132	243	1.83	100719	91	.90	2.02
59. Waco, TX	68	199	2.90	97770	95	.97	2.98
60. Warren, MI	78	99	1.27	89216	179	2.00	.63
61. Waterbury, CT	150	357	2.37	107176	108	1.00	2.35
62. Waukegan, IL	37	114	3.03	55681	65	1.17	2.58
MEAN	116	221	1.95	562221	584	1.10	1.91

-- indicates omitted.

Table 2.6. Fiscal Strain Indicators for 1977 Levels of Common Function Expenditures and General Expenditures

Cities	(1) Common Function Expenditures Per Capita in 1977	(2) City Wealth Index	(3)=(1)/(2) Common Functions/ City Wealth Index	(4) General Expenditures per Capita in 1977	(5) Residual of (4) on Functional Performance Index	(6)=(5)/(2) Residual of General Expenditures per Capita in 1977 on Functional Performance Index/City Wealth Index
	FS08Y77	NTWRTH70	CFNETW77	GENEXP77	GNXP77FP	GXPFNT77
1. Akron, OH	197	9526	.021	411	72	.008
2. Albany, NY	212	12148	.017	439	108	.009
3. Amarillo, TX	107	10463	.010	355	69	.007
4. Atlanta, GA	201	10453	.019	484	146	.014
5. Baltimore, MD	257	6084	.042	1293	-69	-.011
6. Berkeley, CA	171	10822	.016	384	76	.007
7. Birmingham, AL	183	7853	.023	336	-15	-.002
8. Bloomington, MN	133	13334	.010	200	-66	-.005
9. Boston, MA	280	9222	.030	1224	171	.019
10. Buffalo, NY	195	7897	.025	905	65	.008
11. Cambridge, MA	228	12319	.019	1034	12	.001
12. Charlotte, NC	152	11555	.013	335	-4	.000
13. Chicago, IL	188	11004	.017	377	-62	-.006
14. Cleveland, OH	240	8020	.030	500	126	.016
15. Clifton, NJ	108	11875	.009	377	-348	-.029
16. Dallas, TX	155	15298	.010	305	15	.001
17. Detroit, MI	223	9270	.024	517	-41	-.004
18. Duluth, MN	197	8406	.023	482	151	.018
19. Euclid, OH	167	11771	.014	267	-23	-.002
20. Fort Worth, TX	122	8625	.014	318	9	.001
21. Fullerton, CA	134	13750	.010	247	-23	-.002
22. Gary, IN	91	11262	.008	174	-172	-.015
23. Hamilton, OH	113	9251	.012	222	-36	-.004
24. Hammond, IN	108	9658	.011	183	-89	-.009
25. Houston, TX	142	13320	.011	294	-27	-.002
26. Indianapolis, IN	159	9356	.017	418	-244	-.026
27. Irvington, NJ	133	8774	.015	367	-65	-.007
28. Jacksonville, FL	140	7525	.019	411	-193	-.026
29. Long Beach, CA	289	11017	.026	537	136	.012
30. Los Angeles, CA	190	11411	.017	334	-65	-.006
31. Malden, MA	247	7863	.031	818	86	.011
32. Manchester,	175	8004	.022	752	-21	-.003

Table 2.6. (Continued)

Cities	(1) Common Function Expenditures per Capita in 1977	(2) City Wealth Index	(3)=(1)/(2) Common Functions/ City Wealth Index	(4) General Expenditures per Capita in 1977	(5) Residual of (4) on Functional Performance Index	(6)=(5)/(2) Residual of General Expenditures per Capita in 1977 on Functional Performance Index/City Wealth Index
	FS08Y77	NTWRTH70	CFNETW77	GENEXP77	GNXP77FP	GXPFNT77
33. Memphis, TN	161	8350	.019	540	-284	-.034
34. Milwaukee, WI	177	10194	.017	348	-26	-.003
35. Minneapolis, MN	239	10949	.022	494	116	.011
36. New York, NY	252	11725	.046	1628	235	.020
37. Newark, NJ	223	5505	.019	981	141	.026
38. Palo Alto, CA	294	18212	.016	459	185	.010
39. Pasadena, CA	236	11807	.020	511	187	.016
40. Philadelphia, PA	244	8410	.029	603	-22	-.003
41. Phoenix, AZ	164	10131	.016	360	-29	-.003
42. Pittsburgh, PA	144	7703	.019	336	0	.000
43. St. Louis, MO	201	8172	.025	511	-13	-.002
44. St. Paul, MN	206	10681	.019	488	146	.014
45. St. Petersburg, FL	165	7532	.022	304	13	.002
46. Salt Lake City, UT	151	9637	.016	282	-11	-.001
47. San Antonio, TX	261	7638	.020	241	-144	-.019
48. San Diego, CA	115	10602	.015	252	-62	-.006
49. San Francisco, CA	146	13241	.014	1045	306	.023
50. Santa Ana, CA	147	10973	.012	239	-35	-.003
51. San Jose, CA	148	12108	.014	328	-5	.000
52. Santa Monica, CA	149	12480	.012	278	-22	-.002
53. Schenectady, NY	134	10110	.013	275	-49	-.005
54. Seattle, WA	269	12092	.022	476	123	.010
55. South Bend, IN	153	7485	.021	223	-90	-.012
56. Tampa, FL	197	6931	.029	583	278	.040
57. Tyler, TX	93	5402	.017	188	-96	-.018
58. Utica, NY	144	5503	.026	281	-58	-.011
59. Waco, TX	131	7977	.016	250	-104	-.013
60. Warren, MI	167	15569	.011	268	-54	-.004
61. Waterbury, CT	151	9064	.017	589	-253	-.028
62. Waukegan, IL	133	11591	.012	223	-46	-.004
MEAN	178	10079	.020	466	0	0

Fiscal strain indicators for the other three level measures (general expenditures, own revenues, and debt) were more complex. Per capita general expenditures were regressed on the FP Index to generate a residual, which was divided by the City Wealth Index (table 2.6).[9] New York, Chicago, and Los Angeles all scored about $11,000 per capita on the City Wealth Index, but New York spent about five times as much as the two others (column 4). Differences remain large, even adjusting for New York's functional responsibilities (5). Finally, (6) shows that New York's fiscal strain level is surpassed only by Newark and San Francisco.

The fiscal strain ratios for long-term debt show increases for most cities in all periods, like the expenditure ratios, but fluctuate more as cities issued and retired debt.[10] Capital construction can be financed from current revenues or debt. If debt is issued, current revenues can be spent elsewhere; this postpones repayment of the principal, but generates immediate interest costs. If the tax base grows, it helps pay off these deferred obligations. But if the tax base is declining, and the city experiences short term problems, it could fail to meet debt payments.

There are no absolute criteria to distinguish fiscal strain from fiscal health. Individual cities change as do national standards. Rather than labeling cities using somewhat arbitrary categories like "sound" or "BBb," we find it more useful to list scores which permit comparisons with other specific cities at the same time. These can also be statistically analyzed.

Fiscal Management Problems

Ratios of the above sort seldom make headlines, but defaults and bond ratings do. Why not analyze them? Defaults are useful historical indicators as dozens of cities defaulted in each major recession in American history (see Hemple 1971). New York City and Yonkers experienced "quasi-defaults" in 1975 and Cleveland defaulted in 1978, but since the 1930s defaults have been too few to study systematically.[11] Bond ratings by Moody's and Standard and Poor's use admittedly "judgmental" procedures and may include the population and economic base as well as fiscal measures. Ratings should predict bond payments, but have performed poorly. In 1921, 48 percent of defaulting issues held Moody's top rating of Aaa; in 1975, New York City was rated A by Moody's and Standard and Poor's a few months before it essentially defaulted. Still the ratings are widely used and may influence borrowing costs. This view was vividly expressed by a New York City official who asserted that downgrading the city's bonds from A to BBB in 1968 cost $20 million in additional interest costs, or equivalently hospital space for 500 patients, seven elementary schools, or 2,000 more policemen (*The Bond Buyer* 1968, p. 17). The displeasure of New York City officials with their lowered ratings led to a Congressional inquiry and subsequent upgrading. These events not only illustrated the susceptibility of the agencies to political influence, but also forced them to begin to disclose their procedures and defend them publicly. Many observers were distressed at the low quality of analysis and called for improvements. The Twentieth Century Fund's Task Force on Municipal Bond Credit Ratings (Petersen 1974), among others, challenged the rating agencies to disclose fully and explicitly what the ratings measure and the specific factors entering the rating judgment. The rating agencies responded in general terms (W. Smith 1979; Standard and Poor's 1979) but held that quantitative weights could not be assigned to ratings, since their procedures were inherently "judgmental."

If one considers not determinants of ratings but their effects on bond prices, results are again unclear. The most dramatic testimonies to the importance of the ratings come from impressionistic accounts of individual cities (like the quoted cost estimates for New York City) or from simple statistical studies which tabulate ratings against bond prices yet include few or no controls (reviewed in Petersen 1974, 1981). The "effects" of the ratings are thus upwardly biased by omission of other important variables, such as disclosure of political scandals, poor financial practices, or a bad cash flow situation. In bonds actively traded in the secondary market, such events can be rapidly incorporated in bond prices. When bonds are next sold, and the issue requests a rating to accompany the sale, the rating agency can then incorporate the market information and downgrade the issue. Of course, the rating then does not cause the bond price, but vice versa. Virtually no study to date has adequately captured such dynamics. With only about a dozen analysts in each agency, covering some 12,000 municipalities, it is no wonder that ratings are "judgmental." Still, rating agency spokesmen have declared for years that they are improving their procedures. Over time, studies simply replicating certain standard analyses could help monitor any progress. The lack of clear criteria and heavy workload of small staffs currently make the agencies' ratings too unsystematic for careful analysis.[12]

Much attention focused on finding cash and short term obligations in the New York, Cleveland, Chicago school board fiscal crises. Are deficits, short-term debt, and cash flows useful strain indicators? Sometimes.

Deficits indicate an imbalance between a city's revenues and expenditures. But deficits can reflect temporary problems, like a snowstorm, causing one-time expenditures or revenue decline. However, persisting deficits indicate disparity between revenues and expenditures, signaling problems. Ideally, a funds flows measure for a consolidated financial statement or by specific city funds would reflect meaningful surpluses or deficits. But the requirement that cities balance their budget means that deficits seldom appear in financial statements. Legal constraints against deficits vary by state and city. Some regulate fund balances, other revenue or expenditure changes. These lead cities to vary in handling and disclosing fiscal policies, but all lead revenues to equal expenditures in the public record. Surpluses or deficits for cities are less visible than for private corporations, which since the 1930s have been compelled to accept standardized accounting, financial disclosure, and investigation by the Securities and Exchange Commission to assure compliance. Municipal governments have few such constraints. Some maintain careful records and disclose financial practices thoroughly. But in others, accounting practices vary by department and from year to year, some figures are estimates, and sometimes no independent auditor reviews the statements. Further problems complicate comparison of deficits and surpluses across cities:

—Most cities use fund accounting, with separate funds for items like capital construction, intergovernmental revenues, bond repayment, and general operation. Financial statements report receipts and disbursements for separate funds, not the whole city government. The number and type of funds vary across cities (see appendix 6), making even "general funds" noncomparable.

—Surpluses in one fund can cover deficits in another. Especially where funds differ in timing of receipts and disbursements, and restrictions on use, interfund transfers can hide potential deficits.

—Budgets are issued at the outset of the fiscal year and are only planning documents. Official statements of actual receipts and disbursements are issued after the fiscal year and reflect only the year-end position. Despite problems during the year, adjustments may be timed so the year-end statement is more favorable (and in compliance with appropriate laws and ordinances).

—The accounting base differs across cities, and sometimes departments and funds within the same city: cash, accrual, and various degrees of modified accrual are all in use.

—Interfund transfers are difficult to net out. Some cities do, but few disclose adequate data for a reliable "consolidated" statement, i.e., reporting total net receipts and disbursements for all funds, like consolidated statements of private corporations.

—An apparent deficit in one year may come from spending a surplus from a previous year.

—For expenditures including capital outlays, apparent deficits can be covered by issuing long-term debt.[13]

There is such variation across cities in these problems that cross-city comparisons of surpluses or deficits are likely to be substantially biased.[14] Within a single city, an historical time series might still be useful, but financial staff even in one city have trouble ascertaining if these issues have been handled in a comparable manner over time. For most outsiders it is extraordinarily difficult. If local officials do not wish to disclose a deficit, innumerable options are available to facilitate their efforts. To track precise surpluses or deficits for numerous cities probably must await adoption of more standardized accounting and reporting practices. Cities without deficits are thus not necessarily fiscally sound. Still, despite such problems, some cities do generate unambiguous deficits. When these can be detected, they are good indicators of short-term management problems.

Short-Term debt, issued for less than one year, is often used to cover immediate financial difficulties. Alternatively, it may simply reflect operating procedures to overcome a lack of synchronization of cash flows. A common example is using short-term debt annually when dates of tax collection and expenditure do not fall close together (as in Chicago and many other cities). State law often sets tax collection dates, and cities unable to change them may use revenue anticipation notes. Similarly, cities may float several bond anticipation notes, subsequently consolidating them in a long-term debt issue when market timing is fortuitous. Many cities have also issued housing and urban renewal notes guaranteed by the Department of Housing and Urban Development. These were carried over several years until completion of the project, and then converted into long-term debt or paid off by HUD.

The Census unfortunately does not distinguish types of short-term debt, but reports just one total. Of the 30 largest PCS cities, 21 had some short-term debt. To refine this indicator, we reviewed city financial statements and Census worksheets, and deleted short-term debt guaranteed by HUD. Only nine cities remained, shown in table 2.7.[15] Thus adjusted, short-term debt signals fiscal difficulty if it persists over several years, as for Buffalo, Detroit, New York, and Cleveland. But due to the accounting problems listed, we do not systematically analyze short-term debt below.

Overall liquidity is the third fiscal management indicator. It sums all cash, restricted and unrestricted, and all nonpension fund investments. Much of a city's cash, particularly in bond funds, is legally restricted to specific purposes. Such reserves have still been used in past crises to relieve cash flow problems (see Hemple 1971), so they are included in our measure.[16] Overall cash is divided by general expenditures to generate the overall liquidity ratio. PCS cities range from having enough cash to cover almost two years of general expenditures at current spending rates, to having only enough for about one month (table 2.8). While one month coverage may be too little, two years is high. Large cash reserves increase tax burdens. The 62 city mean is .704, or enough reserves for over eight months of current operations. Albany, Cambridge, Newark, and Schenectady fall notably lower. Moreover, all cities with recurrent short-term debt also had low overall liquidity, except Seattle and Cleveland, and only bond fund deposits improved Cleveland's score.[17] We were dissatisfied with overall liquidity for the reasons above, but unlike short-term debt it was available for all 62 cities, so we included it in selected regressions.

Table 2.7. Among the 30 Largest Cities, Few Have Short-Term Debt Outstanding at the End of the Fiscal Year after HUD-Guaranteed Debt Is Deleted

Cities	Short-term debt per capita, excluding HUD notes, for the fiscal years: (in millions) 1970	1973	1974
Atlanta, GA	0	0	0
Baltimore, MD	0	0	0
Birmingham, AL	0	0	0
Boston, MA[a]	0	0	16
Buffalo, NY	119	72	25
Chicago, IL[b]			
Cleveland, OH	10	97	120
Dallas, TX	0	0	0
Detroit, MI	13	7	0
Fort Worth, TX	0	0	0
Houston, TX	0	0	0
Indianapolis, IN	0	1	0
Jacksonville, FL[c]	0	0	71
Long Beach, CA	0	0	0
Los Angeles, CA	0	0	0
Milwaukee, WI	0	0	0
Minneapolis, MN	0	0	0
New York, NY	163	97	120
Newark, NJ	55	28	9
Philadelphia, PA	0	0	0
Phoenix, AZ	0	0	0
Pittsburgh, PA	112	0	0
St. Louis, MO	0	0	0
St. Paul, MN	2	0	1
San Antonio, TX	0	0	0
San Diego, CA	0	0	0
San Francisco, CA	0	0	0
San Jose, CA	0	0	0
Seattle, WA	0	4	7

[a]Boston: Includes only short-term notes issued for the General Fund.
[b]Chicago: Data were temporarily unavailable from the Census.
[c]Jacksonville: These short-term notes are Bond Anticipation Notes issued for sewer system development.
Comparable data were unavailable for our smaller cities.

Pensions: The Problem of a Deferred Obligation

Alarming facts about pensions were reported in the mid-1970s by Congressional committees, state pension commissions, and the mass media. Example: "Los Angeles spent more on pensions than on anything except schooling and policing" (Fogelson 1979). Do pensions exacerbate fiscal strain?

Table 2.8. Most Cities Have Enough Cash and Securities to Cover More Than Six Months of Current Operations

Cities	Overall Liquidity 1974	Cities	Overall Liquidity 1974
1. Akron, OH	.66	33. Memphis, TN	.53
2. Albany, NY	.15	34. Milwaukee, WI	.58
3. Amarillo, TX	.89	35. Minneapolis, MN	.46
4. Atlanta, GA	1.17	36. New York, NY	.29
5. Baltimore, MD	.37	37. Newark, NJ	.18
6. Berkeley, CA	.23	38. Palo Alto, CA	1.16
7. Birmingham, AL	1.53	39. Pasadena, CA	.78
8. Bloomington, MN	.94	40. Philadelphia, PA	.31
9. Boston, MA	.28	41. Phoenix, AZ	.70
10. Buffalo, NY	.38	42. Pittsburgh, PA	.84
11. Cambridge, MA	.09	43. St. Louis, MO	.44
12. Charlotte, NC	.92	44. St. Paul, MN	.38
13. Chicago, IL	.44	45. St. Petersburg, FL	1.82
14. Cleveland, OH	.77	46. Salt Lake City, UT	.82
15. Clifton, NJ	.22	47. San Antonio, TX	1.31
16. Dallas, TX	1.08	48. San Diego, CA	.82
17. Detroit, MI	.54	49. San Francisco, CA	.62
18. Duluth, MN	.42	50. Santa Ana, CA	.52
19. Euclid, OH	.47	51. San Jose, CA	.89
20. Fort Worth, TX	.75	52. Santa Monica, CA	1.14
21. Fullerton, CA	.62	53. Schenectady, NY	.14
22. Gary, IN	.29	54. Seattle, WA	1.44
23. Hamilton, OH	1.29	55. South Bend, IN	.45
24. Hammond, IN	.27	56. Tampa, FL	.73
25. Houston, TX	1.31	57. Tyler, TX	1.93
26. Indianapolis, IN	.47	58. Utica, NY	.25
27. Irvington, NJ	.39	59. Waco, TX	.32
28. Jacksonville, FL	1.95	60. Warren, MI	.86
29. Long Beach, CA	1.38	61. Waterbury, CT	.49
30. Los Angeles, CA	1.20	62. Waukegan, IL	.75
31. Malden, MA	.27		
32. Manchester, NH	.35	MEAN	.70

Note: Overall Liquidity 1974 = Cash and Securities/General Expenditures

Many Cities Do Not Administer Their Own Pension Funds. Pension arrangements vary considerably. The 1977 Census of Governments counted 3,075 state and local government public employee retirement systems, of which 78 percent are administered by municipalities. Most are small; 80 percent of the municipal systems have under 100 members. Our concern with cities leads us to consider only city-administered systems. Some cities include only police and fire, with other employees usually in state-operated systems (table 2.9). Only 38 of the 63 PCS cities administer some part of their own pension system. Membership is concentrated in large, state-administered systems. If a city

Table 2.9. Only 38 of the 63 PCS Cities Administer Their Own Employee-Retirement System

	Type of Employee Covered by City Administered Pension System				
Cities	General[a]	Police and Fire (one system)	Police (separate systems)	Fire (separate systems)	Other
Atlanta, GA	X		X	X	
Baltimore, MD	X	X			
Birmingham, AL	X	X			
Boston, MA[b]	X				Teachers
Cambridge, MA	X				
Charlotte, NC				X	
Chicago, IL	X		X	X	Laborers Retirement Board
Dallas, TX	X	X			
Detroit, MI	X	X			
Fort Worth, TX	X				
Gary, IN				X	
Houston, TX	X		X	X	
Indianapolis, IN			X	X	
Jacksonville, FL	X	X			
Los Angeles, CA	X	X			Water and Power Syst.
Malden, MA	X				
Memphis, TN	X				Utility Systems Employees
Milwaukee, WI	X				
Minneapolis, MN	X		X	X	
New York, NY	X		X	X	School Employees, Teachers
Newark, NJ	X				
Pasadena, CA		X			
Philadelphia, PA	X				
Phoenix, AZ	X				
Pittsburgh, PA	X		X	X	
St. Louis, MO	X		X	X	
St. Paul, MN			X	X	
St. Petersburg, FL	X		X	X	
San Antonio, TX		X			
San Diego, CA	X				Transit
San Francisco, CA	X				
San Jose, CA	X	X			
Seattle, WA	X		X	X	
South Bend, IN			X	X	
Tampa, FL	X	X			
Warren, MI	X	X			
Washington, DC					Teachers
Waterbury, CT	X				

Source: 1977 Census of Governments. Vol. 6. Topical Studies. No. 1. "Employee-Retirement Systems of State and Local Governments." Table 8.

[a]Which employees are included in General varies by city. In some instances Police and Fire are part of General. Police and Fire have only been listed separately where they are separate pension systems.

[b]The Boston system is operated jointly with the Commonwealth of Massachusetts.

system failed on its obligations, it would reflect on the city's financial status. By contrast, if a state pension system defaulted, its members would blame the state system more than the city government contributing to it.

Pension Payments As a Future Fiscal Obligation. The basis for funding ranges from fully funded to "pay-as-you-go." A pay-as-you-go system has no accrued assets; benefits are paid from current pension receipts or city revenues when the employee retires. By contrast, in a fully funded system, contributions are paid into the fund when the employee earns them so that assets cover all future benefits accrued to date. Few systems are fully funded, just as few have no assets. There is no consensus on an ideal level or system of funding (Tilove 1976: ch. 8; Bacon 1980). With clear criteria unavailable for funding levels, we compared systems using two relatively undemanding measures: the level of assets, and flows of funds in and out of the system.

$$(1) \qquad A = \frac{\text{Assets (Cash and Security Holdings)}}{\text{Annual Payments}}$$

$$(2) \qquad R = \frac{\text{Annual Receipts}}{\text{Annual Payments}}$$

A (for assets) indicates how many years of payments existing assets cover (at current rates). *R* (for receipts) indicates whether annual receipts exceed annual payments; if so, assets can be accrued for the future.[18] Table 2.10 presents scores for the PCS cities administering their own systems. For cities with more than one system, we include the one largest in membership. Funding levels vary considerably. Pittsburgh marks the low ebb, with no accumulated assets ($A = 0$) and current receipts below current payments ($R < 1$). Indianapolis, South Bend, and Washington, D.C. cluster at the lower end with assets for under three years at current payout rates ($A < 3$) and current receipts less than payments ($R < 1$). A and R covary; a city low on one is usually low on the other. Clearly, just a few systems have assets for over 20 years of current payments ($A > 20$), yet more than half have assets for over 10. These results suggest that pension problems are limited to selected cities.

It Can Get Worse. The *A* and *R* ratios still capture only some of the problems. They do not forecast the future if benefits increased in

Table 2.10. Indianapolis, South Bend, Newark, Pittsburgh, and Washington, DC Have the Lowest Levels of Pension Funding

Cities	System Coverage	(1) Assets / Annual Payments	(2) Annual Receipts / Annual Payments
Atlanta, GA	General	16.9	5.37
Baltimore, MD	General	14.1	1.92
Birmingham, AL	General	29.3	4.7
Boston, MA	General	4.0	1.06
Cambridge, MA	General	4.0	1.99
Charlotte, NC	Fire	18.8	3.2
Chicago, IL	General	9.4	1.83
Dallas, TX	General	20.0	3.65
Detroit, MI	General	12.4	2.02
Fort Worth, TX	General	18.0	3.7
Gary, IN	Fire	.21	1.18
Houston, TX	General	13.1	3.56
Indianapolis, IN	Police	.03	.97
Jacksonville, FL	General	1.97	1.29
Los Angeles, CA	General	15.7	2.86
Malden, MA	General	4.18	1.35
Memphis, TN	General	17.2	2.9
Milwaukee, WI	General	21.0	3.2
Minneapolis, MN	General	11.9	2.26
New York, NY	General	11.7	2.32
Newark, NJ	General	.16	1.02
Pasadena, CA	Police & Fire	8.45	1.5
Philadelphia, PA	General	5.79	2.37
Phoenix, AZ	General	25.0	5.0
Pittsburgh, PA	General	0.0	.99
St. Louis, MO	General	15.6	3.09
St. Paul, MN	Police	5.3	1.89
St. Petersburg, FL	General	5.8	.89
San Antonio, TX	Police & Fire	7.43	2.3
San Diego, CA	General	12.8	2.6
San Francisco, CA	General	9.15	1.8
San Jose, CA	General	29.3	6.6
Seattle, WA	General	12.1	1.78
South Bend, IN	Fire	.20	.92
Tampa, FL	General	10.75	2.46
Warren, MI	General	44.5	7.69
Washington, DC	Teachers	2.42	.89
Waterbury, CT	General	9.53	1.57
MEAN		11.79	2.5

Source: Computed from 1977 Census of Governments. Vol. 6. Topical Studies. No. 1. "Employee-Retirement Systems of State and Local Governments." Table 8.

the last 20 years or so, unless assets are increasing commensurate with benefits. Early retirement also imposes future burdens. Police and firefighters have lowered the retirement age, following the military model of a young and active force. Criteria for disability retirement also grew more liberal in the last few decades, with minor physical ailments often sufficient cause.[19] As the average retirement age falls, burdens on the system may increase (not necessarily, as some have actuarial equivalent benefits differentiated for younger and older employees).

Increased benefits and younger retirement imply more fiscal commitments. For a system with few assets and which does not change its revenue flows, such commitments could lead to bankruptcy. Many pension funds have also grown less than inflation—not a good fiscal practice. But nothing is inevitable; cities can change pension policies. It is not clear that pay-as-you-go funding is bad. High funding levels demand higher taxes and employee contributions, and tie up cash over many years. But by not funding a pension system, more responsibility falls upon local officials, some of whom have been pressured to extend benefits unwisely.

Whether to finance retirement benefits from tax increases or larger employee contributions,[20] to restrict benefits for all current or just newly hired employees, or to adjust in some other way—these are policy questions that more careful accounting cannot answer. Yet current data are so inadequate in many cities, and so little used in working out revenue, tax, and expenditure policies, that improving them could help city officials do more responsible jobs.

Fiscal Strain and Fiscal Management

Fiscal management problems reflected in deficits, short-term debt, or low cash reserves need not imply fiscal strain. This point is clarified by cross-classifying the two (figure 2.1). The obvious situations are illustrated by San Diego and New York City. But the two other cells show how fiscal strain is distinct from fiscal management. Cities like Chicago can borrow short-term and thus have apparent fiscal management problems without being fiscally strained. Conversely, others like Tampa can be fiscally strained on our ratio measures, but show no visible fiscal management problems. A city with both fiscal strain and management problems may have trouble resolving the management problems, but this is because they are the top of an iceberg of strain. A fiscally unstrained city can usually solve financial management problems with short-term solutions like borrowing or fund transfers. But if problems recur and grow more acute, and such management solutions prove inadequate, this probably reflects more profound problems of the sort captured by our above indicators of fiscal strain.

A general monitoring system should include fiscal strain, financial management, pensions, and other indicators. Fiscal strain indicators normally lead, providing "early warning signals" before fiscal management indicators record problems. Given the distinct causes and solution of each, they need not covary closely.

Is Fiscal Strain a General Phenomenon?

A general fiscal strain index is of great practical value to help decide whether or not to buy or sell a bond, to award state or federal grants, to raise taxes, etc. We are concerned to address these issues, but for several reasons—including the analytical focus of the book, and rapid changes in specific indicators—do not present a single index.

Close to the policy question of should one use a single index is the analytical question of how distinct are separate indicators. This is addressed in table 2.11 which shows intercorrelations among our principal

Figure 2.1. Cities Can Have Fiscal Strain and Fiscal Management Problems Separately or Combined

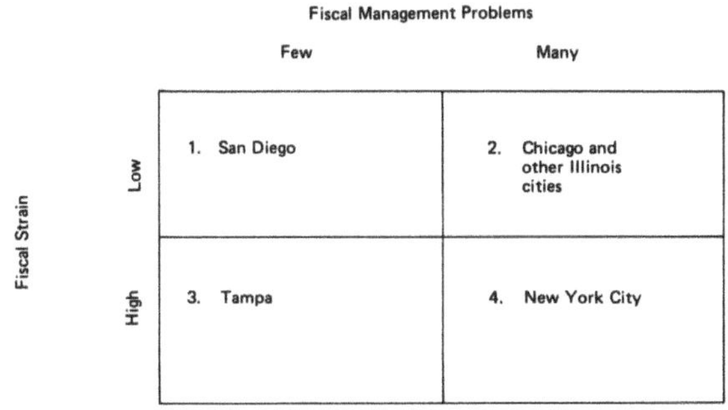

Table 2.11. Correlation Matrix of Fiscal Strain Indicators

	LOL74	LNCFP607	LNCFM607	LNGXP607	LNGXM607	LNDPO607	LNDMI607	
LOL74								
LNCFP607	-0.35							
LNCFM607	-0.27	0.90						
LNGXP607	-0.27	0.75	0.48					
LNGXM607	-0.23	0.56	0.45	0.92				1960-1970
LNDPO607	-0.39	0.55	0.32	0.56	0.42			
LNDMI607	-0.36	0.29	0.22	0.32	0.29	0.93		
LNCFP704	0.06	-0.10	-0.19	0.10	0.05	0.02	-0.04	
LNGXP704	-0.21	0.24	0.11	0.17	0.05	0.15	0.04	1970-1974
LNDPO704	0.05	0.25	0.18	0.15	0.07	-0.06	-0.18	
LNCFP747	0.27	0.02	0.06	-0.14	-0.16	-0.20	-0.22	
LNGXP747	0.26	-0.05	-0.05	-0.00	0.00	0.01	0.02	1974-1977
LNDPO747	-0.11	0.25	0.11	0.16	0.05	0.14	0.02	
LCFNTW77	-0.11	0.30	0.29	0.57	0.47	0.34	0.16	
LFS177FP	0.32	0.01	0.03	0.01	-0.01	-0.06	-0.10	
LLTDFT77	-0.26	-0.03	-0.02	0.06	0.11	0.10	0.14	1977 level
LGXP77FP	-0.06	0.38	0.32	0.33	0.27	0.08	-0.05	
LGXPFT77	-0.01	-0.36	-0.28	-0.34	-0.27	-0.17	-0.04	

Right half of table continued on next page.

Table 2.11. (Continued)

	LNCFP704	LNGXP704	LNDPO704	LNCFP747	LNGXP747	LNDPO747	LCFNTW77	LFS177FP	LLTDFT77	LGXP77FP
	1970-1974			1974-1977			1977 level			
LOL74										
LNCFP607										
LNCFM607										
LNGXP607										
LNGXM607										
LNDPO607										
LNDMI607										
LNCFP704										
LNGXP704	0.41									
LNDPO704	0.32	0.47								
LNCFP747	-0.13	0.17	0.26							
LNGXP747	-0.08	-0.22	-0.10	0.42						
LNDPO747	-0.03	0.26	0.17	0.35	0.26					
LCFNTW77	0.10	0.21	0.24	0.26	0.23	0.40				
LFS177FP	0.29	0.20	0.25	0.17	0.07	0.39	0.15			
LLTDFT77	-0.27	-0.15	-0.17	-0.12	-0.08	-0.37	-0.13	-0.88		
LGXP77FP	0.17	0.20	0.25	0.12	0.37	0.42	0.39	0.28	-0.25	
LGXPFT77	-0.10	-0.11	-0.29	-0.00	-0.33	-0.28	-0.23	-0.18	0.24	-0.76

Note: These are logged versions of indicators presented in earlier tables. The first letters or LN are for log to the base N. The middle letters are OL for overall liquidity, CF for common functions, GX for general expenditures, LTD, LT, D, or FS1 for long term debt. Next are the denominators in ratio indicators, P or PO for population, M or MI for median family income, NTW for net worth. Two 1977 level indicators also include FP at the end for FP residuals. The years are 607 for 1960-70, 704, for 1970-74, 747 for 1974-77, and 74 or 77 for 1974 or 1977.

fiscal strain indicators. Change indicators cluster by period. That is, cities show roughly similar patterns on several indicators for the same period (in table 2.11), with r's often .4 or higher. But change patterns differ considerably across periods. This is because some cities that increased fiscal strain dramatically in the 1960s made substantial adjustments in 1970–74; Baltimore and Pittsburgh are two conspicuous examples. Others which increased less in 1960–70, rose rapidly in 1970–74, like Gary and Birmingham. The 1977 level indicators were strongly correlated with each other and moderately related to changes in each period (but not to liquidity). Levels are thus the type of indicator most strongly correlated to others, but correlations still remain generally low, implying that each indicator is sufficiently distinct that it is best to analyze them separately in considering their causes and formulating solutions.[21] This we undertake in subsequent chapters.

CHAPTER THREE

Private Sector Resources and Urban Fiscal Strain: How Tight Are the Linkages?

This chapter addresses private sector processes widely held to influence urban fiscal strain. Large, old, declining cities of the Northeast are often seen as particularly prone to fiscal strain, and distinct from those of the "Sunbelt." This view informed the Carter National Urban Policy, "targeting" federal funds to "distressed" cities, and programs like the Urban Development Action Grants and "enterprise zones". This implies that public sector leaders are incapable of adapting to a changing private sector. Our results question the adequacy of this view. Regional differences are less than often implied. Low relations between many widely discussed (private sector) measures of "urban distress" and urban fiscal policies suggest that causal linkages between the two are only weak to moderate. Many cities do adapt. Inflation and recession are two further processes often considered to generate fiscal strain. Yet their importance is unclear in studies to date. We address private sector processes here so as to control for them properly in subsequent chapters on mainly public sector processes.

When Are the "Northeast" and "Sunbelt" Useful Concepts?

The mid-1970s saw population growth in the South and West and decline in the Northeast. Although underway for decades, these trends received special attention in debates on federal aid to New York City, devising federal grant formulas, and the Carter administration's National Urban Policy. Regional voting blocks occasionally emerged in Congress. Felix Rohatyn, chairman of New York's Municipal Assistance Corporation, articulated a widespread view: "It is no coincidence that our cities under the greatest strain are tied to our industries in most severe difficulty. An arc of industrial and social crisis extends today from Baltimore to St. Louis" (*Chicago Tribune*, February 1981). How useful are such regional classifications of cities? Despite the many debates, there has been limited serious research. Are northeastern cities actually more fiscally strained?

To compare cities, Thomas Muller and George Peterson at the Urban Institute have used population change over a decade or two as a measure of a declining city syndrome (e.g., Muller 1975; Peterson 1976). Richard Nathan, Paul Dommel, and their Brookings Institution associates developed indexes usually including population change, poverty or income, and old housing (see Nathan and Dommel 1981). We have used a "Northeast syndrome" measure combining northeastern region, city age, and population change (Clark 1977a). Is such a composite measure reasonable to capture the private resource base of cities? It might be if most northeastern cities were large, losing population, densely populated, and included many poor and black residents—and "Sunbelt" cities the opposite. Casual accounts often imply as much, but few such discussions have been informed by a systematic conception; rather a diffuse idea of "distress" often leads to interchangeable use of "Northeast syndrome" indicators. This may follow logically if one posits an economic base definition of fiscal strain, but neither the more casual discussions nor the research (by Peterson, Nathan, etc.) have addressed the question of how closely such measures are interrelated and thus how well they reflect different aspects of fiscal strain.

We consider this issue in several ways. One instructive analysis consists of simply intercorrelating those variables often discussed as defining distressed or growing cities, such as northeast and northcentral region, population change, and similar measures (table 3.1). Most striking is the low level of most correlations. The characteristics do not "go together" as neatly as popular accounts suggest. There is some, but limited, clustering. No correlations with the northeastern region measure exceed .5 except for an overlapping regional measure, north central region. While several correlations are statistically significant, no single dimension emerges. We experimented with several procedures to construct a composite measure including many of these variables, but decided against using one because of difficulties of interpretation.[1]

How Closely Linked Are Private Sector Resources and Fiscal Policy Outputs?

If private sector characteristics like those just analyzed were major sources of fiscal difficulties, we would expect large, older cities in the Northeast to spend more than others. But they do not. Few of the 13 private sector resource measures correlate significantly with 17 measures of fiscal policy; this is true of both level and change measures (table 3.2).[2] This suggests that private sector processes do not determine fiscal policies, rather the two are only weakly related. Some cities that are large, old, northeastern, etc. spend at high levels, but not others. Some city officials adapt to private sector changes; others do not.

This same point is illustrated by expenditure levels for basic services in 13 cities, all of which are in the Northeast, large in population, old, and densely populated—see table 3.3. Yet their expenditures differ markedly; Boston spends almost twice as much as Pittsburgh. Similarly, outside the Northeast are cities like Atlanta and San Francisco which share many socioeconomic characteristics and fiscal problems with cities like New York and Philadelphia. The presence of so many "exceptions" to the stereotype generates the low correlations in the tables. Social and economic characteristics of cities provide resources which their city governments may or may not draw upon; one cannot explain fiscal policy outputs by private resources alone.[3]

How About Population Change?

Population decline is a widely used measure of urban "hardship" or "distress" (e.g., Nathan and Dommel 1977). Others have seen population loss as a direct cause of fiscal strain.[4] The idea that population loss either defines or causes fiscal strain was sufficiently accepted to

Table 3.1. There Is Moderate but Limited Clustering among Variables Commonly Used to Distinguish Northeastern and Other Cities

		North-East 1=In Region 0=Not	East-Central 1=In Region 0=Not	Population Size	Population Change 1960-75	Population Density	Age of City
		LNEAST	LEASTCEN	LPOP75T	LPOP6075	LCITDE70	LCITYAGE
Northeast (1=in region, 0=not)	LNEAST						
East-Central (1=in region, 0=not)	LEASTCEN	.50					
Population Size	LPOP75T	.04	-.06				
Population Change, 1960-75	LPOP6075	-.28	-.39	-.06			
Population Density	LCITDE70	.45	.40	.41	-.39		
Age of City	LCITYAGE	.46	.23	.57	-.58	.48	
Percentage of Old Housing	LPC70OLH	.43	.40	.15	-.86	.53	.78
Percentage Black	LPC70NW	-.03	-.15	.53	-.39	.33	.54
Pct. Families Below Fed. Poverty Level	LPC70PIN	.13	-.18	.47	-.40	.21	.70
Median Family Income	LMED70IN	-.21	.05	-.24	.46	-.08	-.63
Market Value of Taxable Property	PRSV70LA	-.31	-.28	.05	.34	-.07	-.37
City Wealth Index	LNTWRT70	-.34	-.20	.03	.43	-.08	-.46
Change in Median Family Income, 1960-70	LMDF1607	-.09	-.07	-.07	.59	-.30	-.42

Table 3.1. (Continued)

		Percent-Age of Old Housing	Percent-age Black	Percentage Families Below Fed. Poverty Level	Median Family Income	Market Value of Taxable Property	City Wealth Index
		LPC70OLH	LPC70NW	LPC70PIN	LMED70IN	PRSV70LA	LNTWRT70
Northeast (1=in region, 0=not)	LNEAST						
East-Central (1=in region, 0=not)	LEASTCEN						
Population Size	LPOP75T						
Population Change, 1960-75	LPOP6075						
Population Density	LCITDE70						
Age of City	LCITYAGE						
Percentage of Old Housing	LPC70OLH						
Percentage Black	LPC70NW	.41					
Pct. Families Below Fed. Poverty Level	LPC70PIN	.50	.75				
Median Family Income	LMED70IN	-.51	-.49	-.89			
Market Value of Taxable Property	PRSV70LA	-.41	-.19	-.41	.61		
City Wealth Index	LNTWRT70	-.49	-.24	-.54	.74	.95	
Change in Median Family Income, 1960-70	LMDF1607	-.60	-.28	-.37	.39	.27	.39

Note: These are simple r's (Pearson correlation coefficients) for the 62 PCS cities. If $r \geq .21$, $p \leq .10$; if $r \geq .32$, $p \leq .01$.

Table 3.2. Thirteen "Northeast Syndrome" Characteristics Are Often Unrelated to 17 Fiscal Policy Output Measures

		Total Tax Burden	Change in Long Term Debt			Change in Common Functions			Change in Own Revenues 1960-70
			1960-70	1970-74	1974-77	1960-70	1970-74	1974-77	
		LFS27072	LFS01607	LFS01704	LFS01747	LFS08607	LFS08704	LFS08747	LONRV607
Northeast (1=in region, 0=not)	LNEAST	.07	.23	.13	.22	.19	-.35	-.20	.02
East-Central (1=in region, 0=not)	LEASTCEN	.07	-.08	.22	.05	.09	-.02	-.21	.06
Population Size	LPOP75T	.04	.05	.18	.22	.02	.24	.00	.06
Population Change, 1960-75	LPOP6075	-.09	-.19	-.20	-.24	-.42	.16	.16	-.42
Population Density	LCITDE70	.43	.00	.09	.12	.30	-.28	-.20	.06
Age of City	LCITYAGE	-.03	.44	.23	.48	.16	.03	-.13	.32
Percentage of Old Housing	LPC700LH	.05	.28	.19	.38	.17	-.15	-.22	.39
Percentage Black	LPC70NW	.09	.21	.00	.04	.06	.17	-.24	.24
% Families Below Federal Poverty Level	LPC70PIN	-.10	.42	.05	.30	.00	.05	-.09	.26
Median Family Income	LMED70IN	.20	-.43	-.18	-.38	.00	.06	-.05	-.23
Market Value of Taxable Property	PRSV70LA	.11	-.16	-.14	-.17	.10	.10	-.07	-.04
City Wealth Index	LNTWRT70	.13	-.25	-.14	-.25	.11	.11	-.07	-.07
Change in Median Family Income, 1960-70	LMDFI607	-.13	-.28	-.01	-.04	.05	.10	.06	-.13

	Change in Own Revenues		Change in General Expenditures			General Expenditures in 1977	Long Term Debt in 1977	Own Revenues in 1977	Common Functions in 1977
	1970-74	1974-77	1960-70	1970-74	1974-77	(FP Adjusted)	(FP Adjusted)	(FP Adjusted)	
	LONRV704	LONRV747	LGXP6070	LGXP7074	LGXP7477	LGXP77FP	LFS177FP	LORV77FP	LF SO8Y77
LNEAST	-.09	.00	.28	-.02	-.01	-.16	-.26	.09	.09
LEASTCEN	.04	-.37	.05	.19	-.30	-.11	-.16	.11	.01
LPOP75T	.10	.04	.21	.10	.08	.12	.32	-.12	.39
LPOP6075	-.14	.25	-.47	-.14	.14	-.13	.00	-.04	-.36
LCITDE70	.00	-.16	.29	-.02	-.02	.11	-.16	.00	.44
LCITYAGE	.07	-.07	.58	.06	.03	.09	.18	-.14	.38
LPC700LH	.09	-.24	.62	.11	-.09	.03	-.05	-.02	.33
LPC70NW	.16	-.27	.43	.03	-.16	.21	.30	-.19	.29
LPC70PIN	.00	-.08	.44	.07	.02	.23	.34	-.18	.18
LMED70IN	.06	.00	-.34	-.14	-.09	-.14	-.25	.15	-.03
PRSV70LA	.17	.12	-.18	-.02	-.05	.04	-.04	.38	-.09
LNTWRT70	.19	.09	-.24	-.02	-.05	.00	-.09	.34	.06
LMDFI607	.12	.03	-.39	.01	-.01	-.13	.14	.05	-.18

Note: These are simple r's (Pearson correlation coefficients) for the 62 PCS cities. If $r \geq .21$, $p \leq .10$; if $r \geq .32$, $p \leq .01$. The fiscal policy output (rev., expend., or debt) measures presented here are deflated by resource measures in ch. 2 to generate fiscal strain indicators. Undeflated here to assess the degree of interrelation between private sector resources and FPO's.

Table 3.3. Differences in Cities' Expenditures on Basic Municipal Services

A. Several Large, Old, Densely Populated Northern Cities Differ Substantially in Their Expenditures on Basic Municipal Services

	Common Function Expenditures per Capita, 1977
Boston, MA	$280
Baltimore, MD	258
Newark, NJ	252
Philadelphia, PA	244
Cleveland, OH	240
Minneapolis, MN	239
New York, NY	224
Detroit, MI	223
St. Paul, MN	207
St. Louis, MO	201
Chicago, IL	188
Milwaukee, WI	178
Pittsburgh, PA	144

B. But There Are Also High Spending Cities in the South and West

	Common Function Expenditures per Capita, 1977
Palo Alto, CA	$294
Long Beach, CA	289
Seattle, WA	270
San Francisco, CA	262
Pasadena, CA	236
Atlanta, GA	201

Note: These are subsets of the 62 PCS cities. Common functions include basic services common to most American cities: police, fire, highways, sewerage, sanitation, general buildings, parks and recreation, general control, and financial administration.

be emphasized in the background report for President Carter's National Urban Policy (Urban and Regional Policy Group 1978), to help justify the Urban Development Action Grants and aim them toward the "neediest cities" (Nathan et al. 1977:506), and to incorporate population change in the 1978 dual formula for Community Development Block Grants (Bunce 1979).[5]

What is the evidence that population loss is actually related to fiscal policy outputs of city governments? If population declines, and spending does too, the city will not suffer fiscal strain. Per capita changes in spending then should not correlate with changes in population. But inertia of policy makers and expectations of citizens and organized groups, especially city employees, can make it hard to adjust fiscal policy directly to population changes. New York City is a common example of the long lag between population decline and fiscal policy adjustment.

Closer analysis of our PCS cities indicates that relations between population change and expenditure vary over time. From 1960 to 1965, changes in general expenditure per capita and in population were unrelated. But from 1965 to 1972 and 1970 to 1974, the relationship was negative; that is, cities losing population increased expenditures faster than cities gaining population. But in 1974 to 1977 this relationship reversed itself: cities decreasing in population also decreased in expenditures. The same patterns hold for own revenues, indicating that intergovernmental revenues did not change these relationships (table 3.4).[6] If these were the only available data, we might posit a process of lagged adjustment to population decline.

But this interpretation should not be applied mechanically. For population loss to generate fiscal problems (1) city government revenues must decrease with population declines, and (2) decrease more than expenditures necessary to service a smaller population. Consider these two linkages, expenditures first. Expenditures could increase if the remaining population were older, poorer, and more costly to local government. Cities losing population do have slightly more poor and black residents (table 3.1). Still, these relationships are not overwhelming and population composition is analytically distinct from population decline (see Frey 1979). If economies of scale were significant, population loss could increase per capita costs. Research to date, however, suggests *dis*economies of scale for services like police and fire (e.g., Ostrom 1972; Ostrom et al. 1973).[7] Trimming expenditures when population falls may be constrained by constituents' demands, and especially by an inflexible labor force. The evidence is weak that population loss inherently increases service costs; many other variables complicate the relationship.

Consider then the other linkage: does population loss decrease revenue? Not per se. The link must go through specific revenue sources, of which the property tax is the most important. Does population loss

Table 3.4. Only from 1965 to 1974 Did Municipal Expenditures and Revenues Increase in Cities Losing Population

Percent Change in General Expenditures	Percent Change in Population 1960-70	1970-75
	LPOP6070	LPOP7075
1960-65 (LGEXP605)	.038	
1965-72 (LGEXP6572)	-.396	
1970-74 (LGEXP7074)		-.207
1974-77 (LGEXP747)		.195

Percent Change in Own Revenue	Percent Change in Population 1960-70	1970-75
	LPOP6070	LPOP7075
1960-70 (LONRV607)	-.441	
1970-74 (LONRV704)		-.241
1974-77 (LONRV747)		.315

Note: These are simple r's (Pearson correlation coefficients) for the 62 PCS cities. If $r \geq .21$, $p \leq .10$; if $r \geq .32$, $p \leq .01$.

The dates on the two axes of the table do not exactly match. We could have added additional shorter periods for population change, but decided not to for several reasons. The population figures between the decennial censuses (unlike the fiscal data) are only estimates, so it is better not to overinterpret them. Rankings across cities would also differ little if we used population change for 1960-65 instead of 1960-70, and would complicate presentation.

decrease property values and in turn property tax revenues? No doubt it can eventually, but have recent population losses generated such effects? Not clearly. Effects are weakened by other factors. One is the increase in illegal aliens.[8] Another is the size of urban households, which has declined for several decades via longer life spans, later marriages, fewer children, and more singles (e.g., Alonso 1978). These factors all generate more demand for housing and increase property values. Property values are still high and increasing in many "declining" cities.[9]

Concern about population decline often reflects a projection of what might occur if it continues. Decline was a new public issue in the mid-1970s, and initial reactions were often exaggerated. Yet local officials in Pittsburgh, for example, point out that population declines helped eliminate slums and crowding, permiting construction of more spacious parks and more desirable land use. Public debates emerged in the mid-1970s on such themes as "urban conservation," "small is beautiful," and "gentrification." The popular criticism of gentrification—more rich residents are bad—reversed the criticism of population decline. But the extent of gentrification has been exaggerated in many discussions (see Laska and Spain 1980). The idea that any population decline is undesirable seems less widespread than just a few years ago. Such a shift in attitude is consistent with our results. Still, for city staff, adapting to declining resources is usually more difficult than adapting to growth. When decline is rapid, and unions and civil service boards are strong, it is especially hard for leaders to adapt. But many cities still do.

Empirical analyses in this section are deliberately simple: like most earlier studies they involve bivariate (two-by-two) relationships, but instead of contingency tables we use correlations which make the low relationships clearer. The weak results surprised us too. Our concern here is not to refute any single theory, only to show that relations are weak enough that further variables are important, as considered in subsequent chapters.

In brief, population changes, and other demographic and social characteristics can indicate problems to which local officials must adapt. But whether and how they adapt is not determined by the problems, as is clear from large differences in fiscal policies across cities confronting similar social and demographic circumstances. Social and economic characteristics are important resources; they are not fiscal policies.

Inflation and Recession: How Large Are Their Effects?

Like regional demographic movements, inflation and recession are major national trends. Many discussions imply that city governments participate in them like the rest of the economy, and anecdotal accounts cite their deleterious effects.[10] But what systematic evidence is there to indicate the magnitude of their effects? Unfortunately little. This section reviews the few available studies, paying special attention to actions of local officials.

A. National Business Cycles and City Government. Two obvious bases of comparison for cyclical effects on cities are the private sector and federal and state governments. City governments clearly fluctuate less than the private sector. Growth curves of city revenues are smooth over several decades, varying little with business cycles (figure 3.1). By contrast, several private sector indicators show sharp cyclical patterns.[11]

How do cities compare to federal and state governments in these same respects? Revenues of higher-level governments fluctuate more

Figure 3.1. Trends in City General Revenue from Selected Major Sources, 1959–80 (Billions of Dollars)

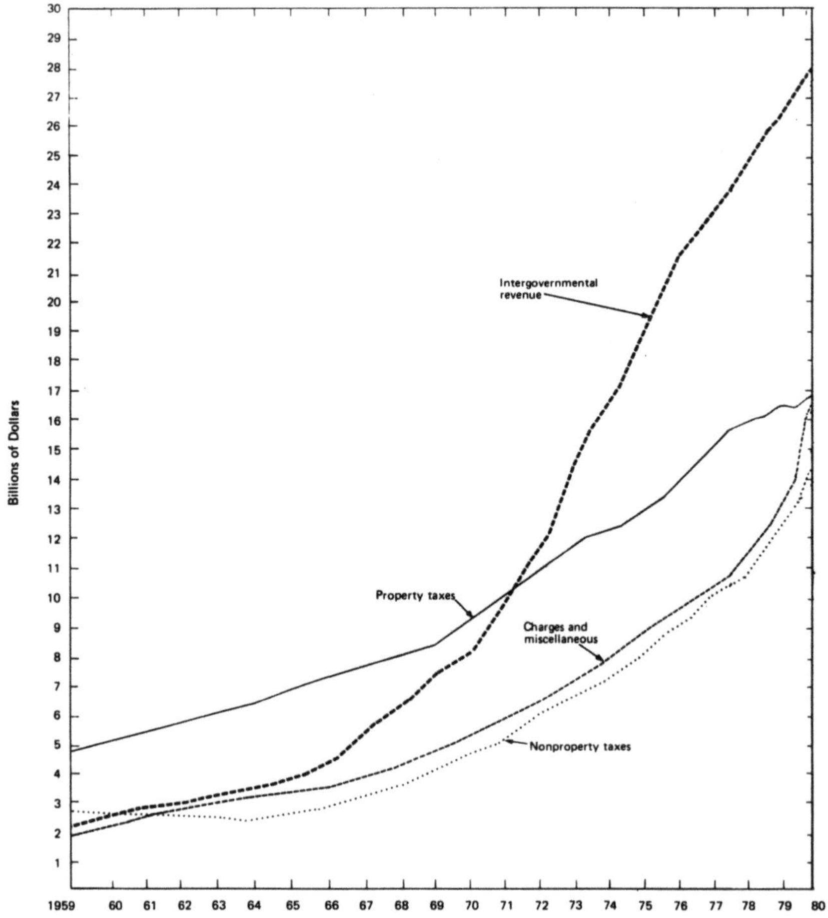

Source: U. S. Bureau of the Census, City Government Finances (annual). Data are for all U. S. cities.

due to their more elastic sources, especially income, corporate, and sales taxes.[12] Expenditures also vary with differences in functional responsibility. The federal government's management of the national economy, following Keynesian policies, has often increased deficit spending in recession. Similar patterns hold for state governments responsible for unemployment compensation and related benefits. More elastic revenue sources, combined with anticyclical program responsibilities, create cyclical deficits and surpluses for state and especially federal governments unparalleled locally.[13] But how large are these differences?

Funds flow indicators, such as total revenues minus total expenditures, are often used to gauge cyclical fluctuations of the federal government. Similar indicators for the "state and local sector" from the National Income Accounts are widely discussed as "surpluses" or "deficits" in Washington and national news media. They indicate far more cyclical fluctuation by the federal government than by state and local governments.[14] Their major advantage is that they are more current than city-specific indicators. But they are current because they are only estimates from a sample of states and localities. And they ignore differences among states, other local governments, cities, and variations among cities. They may help macroeconomic analyses, but are poor indicators of urban fiscal strain.

If aggregate indicators are misleading, how assess effects of recession and inflation? This is best posed as two separate questions:

1. Do city expenditures increase faster than revenues with inflation?
2. Do revenues decrease faster than expenditures with recession?

Both questions stress comparing marginal revenue and expenditure changes. One should determine for both how much such changes are "automatic" or amenable to local intervention.

B. Inflation and Cities. Inflation experts suggest addressing the first question by comparing cities on city-specific price indexes to capture inflation responses. Only one study has done this carefully for local governments (Greytak and Jump 1975). On the expenditure side, the authors estimated the inflation-induced increment to 1974 expenditures that would have resulted had each of the sample jurisdictions purchased the same market basket of input in 1974 as in 1971. A similar approach was taken on the revenue side. By assuming a circumstance in which jurisdictions had the same revenue structures in 1974 as in 1971, the authors estimated the potential increment to revenue that would have been produced had the communities simply captured the inflation in their revenue bases.[15] Practically no area gained as much in inflation-induced potential revenue as it lost in inflation-induced expenditures (table 3.5). However, the extent to which potential expenditure increases surpassed potential revenue increases varied considerably, from a potential net loss of over 13 percent in Atlanta to a small potential gain in Orange County.

Still, local governments choose whether or not to increase revenues and expenditures at the same rates as such indexes. These six governments varied considerably, both from one another and by revenue type. Consider two major local revenues, property and sales taxes. Property taxes are often criticized as increasing less than the inflation rate for expenditures. This was true in four of the six Greytak and Jump cases; in two others the inflation index for property taxes (column 4 of table 3.6) increased as much or more than the expenditure inflation index (column 1 of table 3.5).[16] A city can increase property tax revenues four ways: growth in the value of existing property, addition of new taxable property, increase in assessments, and increase in property tax rate.[17] Much of the first is due to inflation. The other three

Table 3.5. Comparison of Local Revenue and Expenditure Inflation Indices for Six Locations

Location	(1) Total Current Expenditure Inflation Index	(2) Total Local Revenue Inflation Index	(3) Difference Between (1) and (2)
Atlanta, GA	127.9	114.1	-13.8
Lexington, VA	121.0	120.4	-.6
New York, NY	121.4	115.8	-5.6
Erie County, NY	124.1	116.7	-7.4
Orange County, CA	117.3	117.6	.3
Snohomish County, WA	123.9	119.5	-4.4

Source: Adapted from Greytak and Jump (1975). Tables II-B and III-B.

Table 3.6. Comparison of Total Local Revenue Growth with Local Revenue Growth due to Inflation, 1971-74

Location	Revenue Growth Index[a] (1971=100)			Inflation Index for Local Revenue[b] (1971=100)		
	Property Taxes	Sales Taxes	Total[c]	Property Taxes	Sales Taxes	Total[c]
Atlanta, GA	103.9	---	121.8	121.9	---	114.1
Lexington, VA	99.0	128.6	123.5	116.5	123.4	115.8
New York, NY	124.2	116.6	133.1	120.6	114.4	116.7
Erie County, NY	101.2	267.9	121.1	123.6	118.6	120.4
Orange County, CA	126.0	165.6	133.9	121.0	115.9	117.0
Snohomish County, WA	115.7	161.7	160.0	124.7	121.6	119.5

Source: Adapted from Greytak and Jump (1975). Tables III-A and III-B.
[a]Revenue Growth = Percentage increase in actual amounts of revenue
[b]Inflation Index = Potential increase in revenue for property taxes due to increase in value of existing property in 1971. Assumes amount of taxable property and tax rate remains constant. Inflation indices calculated separately for different types of sales taxes in each city and county. Total calculated by summing each type of tax and weighting by proportion contributed to total local revenue.
[c]The Total Indices include all types of revenues. Only property and sales taxes are listed separately here.

are predominantly local public decisions (such as annexation, taxing previously tax-exempt property, reassessing property, increasing the assessment ratio, or increasing the actual tax rate). Yet the property tax, as a visible, lump sum payment, is much disliked.[18] City officials are thus understandably reluctant to raise property tax revenues. New York City still increased revenues from property taxes (column 1 of table 3.6) more than its inflation indexes (column 4 of table 3.6); Atlanta and Lexington followed the opposite policy.

What of sales taxes? For four of the six governments, sales tax inflation indexes (column 5 of table 3.6) increased less than the property tax indexes (column 4 of table 3.6). This contradicts earlier discussions which suggested that property tax revenues were less responsive to inflation than sales taxes (see Netzer 1966:3–8). The early 1970s apparently marked a change from earlier periods in this regard. A related argument for sales over property taxes is that sales taxes increase automatically with inflation, so the government need not increase the tax rate to capture increased revenues; but for all six governments, actual collections (column 3 of table 3.6) equaled or exceeded inflation index increases (column 6 of table 3.6).

These results conflict with much common wisdom in that while all six governments experienced inflation, magnitudes varied considerably. Further, the six governments seldom let revenues or expenditures increase or decrease simply with inflationary forces; they substantially intervened through local decisions.

C. Recession and Cities. How about recession? The property tax then is a blessing; it seldom declines even if property values do, since assessments and tax rates are usually unchanged in recession.[19] By contrast, sales tax revenues drop with local sales receipts. No study like that of Greytak and Jump is available for recession. Still, for the 1974–75 recession, Dickson (1978:35) finds that of 31 cities only four showed declines in tax receipts (from property, sales, and income). But she did not determine the degree to which revenue flows were maintained by changes in tax rates.[20]

What policy implications emerge in this area? A decade ago two recommendations were common: avoid the property tax and diversify revenue sources. Many cities followed these policies, primarily by expanding nonproperty tax revenues. The major arguments against the property tax were that it was regressive and inelastic. Both arguments have been undermined by more recent work.[21] The argument for diversifying revenues was based on these two criticisms plus the view that downturn in one source could be offset by strength in others. This argument in turn depended on timing differences in cycles by industry. These do exist, but more important than diversification per se seems to be the type of industry, since some industries are far more cyclically sensitive than others. (See Vernez et al. 1977.)

Summary of Inflation and Recession Effects

Inflation and recession are fiscally troublesome, but cities generally suffer less than private firms and the federal government. While these national trends are often blamed, their effects are difficult to separate from local processes involving municipal employees, taxpayers, and others. Some cities suffer from inflation in that their revenues increase less rapidly than expenditures. But others benefit from inflation, and the single largest expenditure item—personnel—is locally determined.

Property values in the early 1970s generally increased as fast as most expenditure indices, contradicting the traditional view that property tax revenues are inelastic. In recession, property taxes have the advantage of seldom decreasing, while sales and other revenues do. Yet the extent of such decreases is unclear in research to date.

Conclusion: The Role of Private Sector Resources

Public and private sector processes are distinct. It is naive for local officials to expect to have major impacts on basic private sector trends—movements of jobs and population, recession, inflation, and the like. These trends can be buffered by some federal policies and astute local officials; but such effects are limited. Conceptions like "declining Northeast cities" and "Sunbelt cities" should be used cautiously in research. Such characteristics as region, population size, population change, and city age are only loosely correlated. And such private sector measures only weakly predict fiscal policies of city governments. Population change in particular has been overused as an indicator of "urban distress"; it is better treated as one more private sector resource. Inflation and recession affect city governments, but far less than casual examples imply.

Subsequent chapters analyze private sector resources in several ways. We use the City Wealth Index to assess the impact of wealth on fiscal policies. Our analyses are structured to minimize inflation and recession effects, since we compare the 62 PCS cities by period to explain changes or levels of fiscal policies. There is clearly room for other variables besides private sector resources to explain fiscal policy outputs. These are introduced in the next chapter.

PART III

Four Political Cultures and Their Fiscal Policies

CHAPTER FOUR

Political Processes: How Citizens, Organized Groups, and Political Leaders Affect Fiscal Policy

This chapter presents results addressing the propositions of chapter 1, which pointed to three processes driving fiscal policy. At their respective sources lie citizen preferences, organized groups, and political leaders. The processes differ by time period and political culture. (1) In the early 1960s, fiscal policy was influenced mainly by citizen preferences, with dynamics set by New Deal Democratic and Republican Parties. (2) But in the late 1960s and early 1970s, Democrats and black power leaders were more important for spending increases. (3) Then in the mid to late 1970s, New Fiscal Populists and Republicans won ground as champions of the taxpayers' revolt.

We begin with an overview of the operational model and political process measures. Next we summarize results from the 62 PCS cities. We then turn to dynamics of each period, considering individual cities illustrating major processes. The last section compares results for fiscal policy outputs and fiscal strain indicators.

The Core Model

We developed a model for statistical analysis whose basic components are: (1) citizen sector size, (2) political activity of organized groups, and (3) political leaders' policy preferences—corresponding to propositions 1, 2, and 3 in chapter 1. The three major participants

Figure 4.1. Path Diagram of Variables Used to Specify Core Model

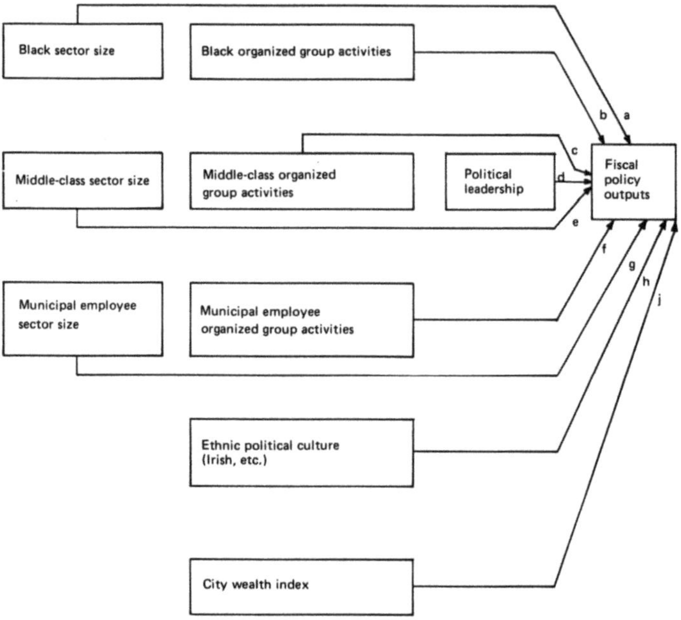

considered were the middle class, blacks, and municipal employees. Figure 4.1 shows their direct effects on fiscal policy outputs. Variations of the figure 4.1 model were analyzed since 62 cities permit only about 10 independent variables. Our "core" model simplified figure 4.1 as follows. Sector and organized group measures for blacks were strongly correlated, so just one or the other was included (only path a or b). Several middle class organized group measures were insignificant, and thus omitted. All other relationships were important for some time periods; the core thus includes paths d through j. The ethnic political culture measure is elaborated in chapter 5. The City Wealth Index assessed the impact of wealth and removed wealth effects operating through other core variables.[1]

Measures of Core Variables

This section briefly explains the core model measures for our 62 Permanent Community Sample cities. Appendix 1 adds details and sources.

Sector Size. We started with four sectors—poor, blacks, middle class, and municipal employees—since their members reported distinctive fiscal policy preferences, as subsequent chapters detail. Surveys of middle class citizens showed that they generally preferred less government spending, while the poor and blacks preferred more. Size measures were thus constructed for these sectors using data from the best city-level source, the 1970 Census of Population.[2] The poor were the percentage of families below the federal government definition of "low" income. Thus defined, they averaged only 9 percent of the population in our 62 cities, and never more than 18 percent (in Newark and San Antonio). In analyses with both poor and blacks, the poor sector was largely insignificant and thus deleted. Blacks are more than twice as numerous as the poor, averaging 18 percent of the population in our PCS cities in 1970, and an absolute majority in a few (53 percent in Gary, 55 percent in Newark, and 51 percent in Atlanta). The middle class was measured in several ways described in appendix 2.E. The core model used the percentage of families with annual incomes between $10,000 and $15,000 (in 1969), which ranged from 18 to 41 percent of the families in our 62 cities, the unambiguous core of the middle class. The Index of Functional Performance measured the municipal employee sector; it was used instead of the actual number since the two were similar and some analyses were to explain the number of employees.

Political Activities of Organized Groups. These were measured in two PCS surveys. In 1976 the mayor and council members listed the five most active groups affecting city government, and how often they contacted or were contacted by each. Our political activity measures sum such contacts for each group. In 1967 local leaders were asked about the importance of different groups in mayoral elections, air pollution control, urban renewal, municipal bond referenda, and antipoverty programs. These led to power measures, which tap potential but not necessarily actual influence. Influence was measured by participation of groups in decisions.[3] Political activity measures for several groups were constructed from these two surveys. Most were insignificant and thus omitted from the core, including power and influence measures of the poor, business groups, civic groups, neighborhood groups, all nonpoor groups combined, and an index of agreement between the mayor and business groups. The core retained black political activities and the percentage of municipal employees who were members of a union or professional association (the latter is discussed in chapter 6).

Leaders' Policy Preferences. These were measured in 1967 using issues stressed by the mayor in his campaign, as reported by the mayor and party chairmen to a National Opinion Research Center (NORC) interviewer. Issues were coded as favoring or opposing city government spending. In 1976 the mayor and council were asked if they favored more, same, or less spending in 11 policy areas. These preference measures, following proposition 5 on resources, were weighted by the power of the mayor (in 1967) or mayor and council (in 1976).

The City Wealth Index. This included the equalized taxable property value and median family income, weighted by the dependence of local revenues on these respective sources. (see chapter 2.)

Fiscal Indicators. The fiscal policy outputs and fiscal strain indicators, introduced in chapter 2, were for 1977 levels per capita, and percentage changes in 1960–70, 1970–74, and 1974–77.

General Results

Results of multiple regression analyses for the core model appear in table 4.1. They differ by period. For 1960–70, expenditures increased if cities had larger black sectors. But the larger the middle-class sector, the less the increase. These two results support proposition 1 concerning citizen preferences. Political activity and leadership measures were insignificant. In the second period, 1970–74, sector size declined and political leadership rose in importance. Cities with powerful leaders who favored higher spending increased expenditures, although leaders' preferences were linked in turn to organized groups as discussed below.

Table 4.1. Regression Results of Sources of Fiscal Policy Outputs and Fiscal Strain Using Core Model

Independent Variables	Dependent Variables			
	Fiscal Policy or Strain Measure			
	Changes			Level per Capita
	1. 1960-70	2. 1970-74	3. 1974-77	4. 1977
Middle class sector size (LPC70UMC)	-	0	-	-
Black sector size (LPCBLK70)	+	0	0	0
Index of Functional Performance (LFPDEC4)	0	0	0	+
Organized activity of municipal employees (LPEMPO72)	0	0	0	0
Ethnic political culture (IRISHL70)	0	0	0	+
Political leaders' spending preferences X resources (LRPNTALK or LLEAD3W2)	0	+	0	+
Index of City Wealth (LNTWRT70)	0	0	0	+

Note: This table summarizes the general results from separate regressions for our four principal fiscal measures involving general expenditures, own revenues, long-term debt, and common functions.

See note 1 and appendix 2.

The third period, 1974–77, resembled the first: no longer was political leadership important, sector size was. The larger the middle class sector, the less expenditures increased. Finally, the 1977 expenditure level captures major processes from earlier years: spending is higher in cities with smaller middle-class sectors, which perform more functions, have more Irish residents, leaders who preferred more spending, and greater city wealth.

The importance of political leaders in the politically unstable middle period, and insignificance in the first and third periods, fits proposition 8: "Citizen preferences are more important, and organized groups and political leaders less important for fiscal policy, when: (c) there are fewer disturbances to the political context." Propositions 6 and 7 concerning sector activation help explain why one sector process followed the other, but are discussed below in chapters on the major participants. This chapter concentrates on distinguishing the three periods. The next sections consider each period.

Growth in the 1960s: The Importance of Sector Size

The 1960s were a decade of general growth in city expenditures. Growth was faster in cities with larger black sectors, and slower in cities with large middle classes. Both findings illustrate proposition 1: The larger the sector in a city, the more fiscal policies are responsive to it. This assumes that middle class citizens prefer less spending, and black citizens more, but citizen surveys in chapters 5 and 7 are clear on these points. Organized groups and political leaders had few effects.

These findings are for the 62 cities combined. Scatterplots in figures 4.2 and 4.3 indicate how individual cities fit the general pattern. Figure 4.2 shows the percentage of middle-class residents on the horizontal axis, and the 1960–70 percentage change in general expenditures on the vertical axis. For example, New York City had about 24 percent middle class residents, and increased expenditures about 190 percent. Individual cities consistent with the national trend in a scatterplot are those near the regression line—the line best summarizing the pattern for all cities. One can also observe consistency from how close all cities are to the line. "Deviant cases" are those well above or below it. Cities below the figure 4.2 regression line increased expenditures less than one would expect from the size of their middle class—especially Bloomington, Minnesota, Tampa, and Charlotte. Additional data are necessary to explain deviations from the national trend. For example, they may have had a particularly conservative newspaper or conservative business leaders.

Consider Waukegan, Illinois, well above the regression line. Waukegan thus increased expenditures more than predicted by its middle-class sector. Why? Perhaps Waukegan had a large black sector? Figure 4.3 shows this is not the case. The increase seems largely due to Mayor Sabonjian, a dynamic and influential leader, proud of his extensive contacts with citizens. For personal reasons he split with the party, but still illustrates the political culture of New Deal Democrats. In the

Figure 4.2. The Larger the Middle-class Sector in the City, the Smaller the Increase in General Expenditures, 1960–70

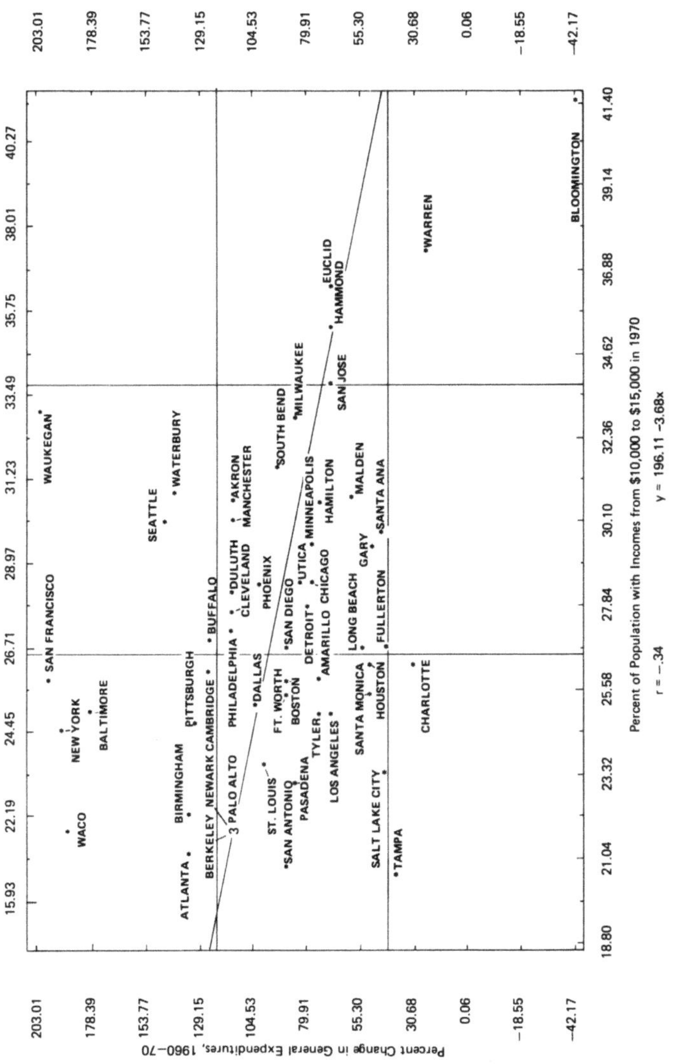

Note: At the base of each scatterplot are simple correlations and regressions, although multiple regression results are mainly discussed in the text.

Figure 4.3. The Larger the Black Sector in the City, the Larger the Increase in General Expenditures, 1960–70, but the Relationship is Weak

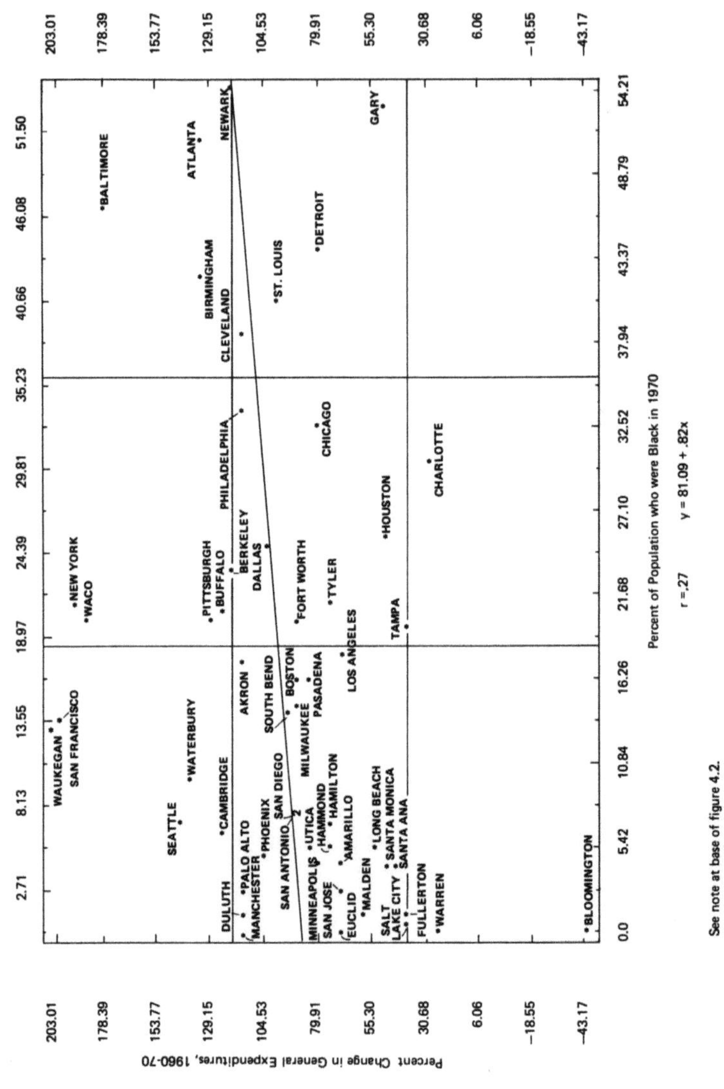

See note at base of figure 4.2.

mid-to-late 1960s, he sought to expand his political base and appeal to poor blacks. If a constituent visited him for a job, he would try to find one in a city agency. Decisions on projects like parks were often made in meetings with active neighborhood groups. Whether or not the city could afford a project was often gauged by asking the city treasurer if cash on hand was sufficient. No one projected revenues or expenditures. This approach continued until the mid-1970s when revenue declines led to deficits, and a new mayor elected.[4]

Consider the other finding for the 1960s: black sector impact. Figure 4.3 plots percentage of black residents against expenditure changes. Many cities are well above or below the regression line, indicating a weak relationship.[5] Eight cities where blacks exceeded 35 percent of the population cluster at the far right. Of these, Baltimore increased spending most, by almost 200 percent. But Gary and Detroit fall well below the line; despite their large black populations, fiscal policy did not respond to black citizen preferences.[6] This documents the potential in these cities for a political entrepreneur to win votes via policies more responsive to blacks—which happened at the end of the decade.

What of organized groups and political leaders? Municipal employee organization was slightly related to general expenditure changes over the 1960s, but insignificant in the regressions. Employee organization did increase compensation, aided in cities like New York by a Democratic political culture—exemplified by Mayor Robert Wagner's direct encouragement of unionization. Business and middle class groups (civic groups, neighborhood associations, etc.) may be important in individual cities, but as they favored more expenditures in some cities and less in others (shown in chapter 7), their effects were insignificant across the 62 cities.

Political leadership appears insignificant to the 1960s in table 4.1. Leaders might still be dynamic in individual cities, but they did not stand out as a national trend. In the Eisenhower and Kennedy years, Republicans and reform Democrats set the national tone. Fiscal policies emerged from party differences, influenced more by individual citizens than by groups. Cities below the regression line like Bloomington, Warren, Fullerton, Charlotte, and Santa Ana had more homogeneous and affluent constituents, and more fiscally conservative policies. Other cities increased expenditures considerably, like Baltimore, New York City, San Francisco, and Waukegan. They generally had Democratic mayors and councils who pursued policies consistent with the Great Society programs nationally dominant in the late 1960s, although when intergovernmental grants were controlled, local processes still prevailed (as discussed below). Traditional Democrats and ethnic politicians were important in these cities, but leaders did not have a distinct impact across the national sample. By the end of the 1960s, however, things changed dramatically. Exact timing varies by city, but from the late 1960s until about 1974, new patterns of decision-making emerged in many American cities.

The Dynamic Political Leader Emerges in the Late 1960s and Early 1970s

In this second period, sector size falls and political leadership rises in importance. Cities with powerful leaders favoring more spending increased expenditures 1970–74 (table 4.1). What led mayors to favor more expenditures? We correlated mayors' campaign statements with many plausible sources, but most were insignificant: size or change of black and poor sectors, median family income, unionization, and most others (table 4.2). Only three black sector activity measures are significant; mayors campaigned for more spending: (1) if their cities suffered severe racial disorders, (2) if "ethnic and religious groups" were powerful supporters of the mayor, and (3) if blacks were active supporters of the mayor. Such activities were found only in cities with significant black sectors, and the larger the sector, the more likely were these three activities. The causal ordering thus runs from a large black sector to black political activities which in turn persuaded leaders to campaign on, and then implement, higher spending programs.

These results recall the urban turmoil of the late 1960s, punctuated by riots, arson, and militant black groups. The mass disorders disturbing this period, for leaders and in terms of our chapter 1 propositions, peaked in the late 1960s.[7] Municipal employee strikes similarly escalated (chapter 6). While these trends are common wisdom, their fiscal impacts are not. Such period effects in urban fiscal policy have not been previously reported.

Table 4.2. Black Protest and Political Activities Are the Major Correlates of Mayor's Campaign Statements Favoring Increased Municipal Expenditure

	Mayor's Campaign Statements Concerning Municipal Expenditure
	MAYRTALK
<u>Sector Size Measures</u>	
Percentage families below federal poverty level in 1969 (LPC70PVIN)	-.03
Change in percentage poor families (below $3,000) from 1959 to 1969 (LPCLC607)	-.03
Percentage black families in 1970 (LPCBLK70)	-.04
Change in percentage blacks from 1960 to 1970 (LPCBL607)	.14
Black families as a percentage of all families below federal poverty level in 1969 (LBLKPV70)	.18
Percentage middle class families ($10 to 15,000 median family income in 1969) (LPC70UMC)	-.18
<u>Sector Activity Measures</u>	
Index of severity of racial disorders (LRIOTSCR)	.30*
Power of ethnic and religious groups supporting mayor in 1967 (IMETHMY)	.29*
Importance of blacks supporting mayor in 1967 (BLKSMY)	.22*
<u>Other Measures</u>	
Index of agreement between mayor and business groups (MYAGREBS)	.03
Business power factor (FBUSL)	.03
Unionization (LPEMP072)	-.11
Median family income (LMD70INC)	-.02
Importance of neighborhood groups supporting mayor in 1967 (IMNBRMY)	.05
Percentage Irish residents (IRISHL70)	-.11
Index of City Wealth (LNTWRT70)	.00

Note: These are simple correlations (r's) between the mayor's campaign statements and each of the other variables. Only the r's carrying an asterisk are significant at the .10 level.

The distinctiveness of the late 1960s and early 1970s is nevertheless clear in several related developments. The civil rights movement, anti-Vietnam war rallies, and political campaigns of McCarthy and McGovern mobilized social protest. Neo-Marxists and other radicals won many campus followers, helping elect radical city officials in college towns like Berkeley, Ann Arbor, and Madison. Ford and other foundations made substantial grants to minority groups to experiment with "community control" of city services, schools, and urban development. The Johnson administration supported black claims of racial injustice and sought change through Great Society programs. These national trends reinforced racial polarization in which "Negroes" became "blacks," and civil rights yielded to black power. The Black Panthers, Black Muslims, and others were portrayed in national news media—sometimes in sit-ins in city halls—as defining a new militant posture. Discussions of black power and pride not only mobilized blacks, but stimulated ethnic symbolism and identity for white ethnics. Intellectuals proclaimed ethnic politics essential for a "cultural pluralism," to transcend "melting pot" assimilation (see Patterson 1977; Novak 1972). Ethnic politicians gained supporters unimaginable a few years earlier. All manner of broadly Democratic groups prospered in a politicized climate. Beck and Jennings (1979) analyzed participation of national samples of young adults and their parents in political campaigns, rallies, letters, and similar activities from 1956 to 1976 and found the late 1960s and early 1970s deviant: the young were then substantially more active, as were Americans young and old on the ideological left. Mayors were urged by many policy advisers to be more dynamic (see Ruchelman 1969; Kotter and Lawrence 1974). Two comparative studies found mayors in the 1960s to have significant effects on public policy (Kuo 1973; Salancik and Pfeffer 1977), and Kuo found that organized groups reinforced mayoral initiatives.

The tumult generated many efforts to refocus political analysis, such as the New Left and New Class interpretations, which saw radicalism expanding across industrial societies (which we dispute in chapter 7). Hundreds of books and articles appeared proclaiming an "urban crisis." Yates (1977) suggested that "street-fighting pluralism" was becoming dominant in city politics. Some theorists proclaimed the dawn of a new era, but only a few years later the era, and its theorists, appeared limited to the "radical '60s."

These national social movements helped increase the explanatory power of organized groups, blacks, and fiscally liberal mayors in our sample cities. A national climate and specific political and fiscal incentives encouraged cities toward ambitious social programs. Consistent with the chapter 1 propositions, in cities and time periods characterized by greater political instability and mobilization of new sectors, organized groups and political leaders become more important determinants of public policy.[8]

Figure 4.4 elaborates these results. Across is the leadership measure from the regression analysis: the mayor's spending preferences (from campaign statements), multiplied by his power. Cities like Gary and Atlanta on the far right thus had powerful mayors who favored more spending. Down is percentage change in expenditures in 1970–74. We see here that Gary reversed its low spending from the 1960s. Why?

Gary is a valuable case, illustrating the dynamics behind the statistical results and thus documenting national trends. From the Depression until the mid-1960s, the Democratic party dominated Gary politics. Whites abandoned the "machine" and its patronage as their prosperity increased. Simultaneously blacks grew to almost half the city's population, providing the machine's principal base. The party backed Martin Katz for mayor in 1963, who lost every white precinct but won thanks to party loyalty in black precincts. Richard Hatcher was elected to the council that year and was expected to cooperate with the machine as had all previous black council members. But he soon demonstrated a new form of black politics. Hatcher was active in civil rights causes and brought the approach to city politics, stressing open occupancy of housing. Initially its sole supporter in the council, he worked skillfully with black activists and mobilized enough pressure for it to pass. In 1967 he ran for mayor against Katz, continuing to stress racial issues. He beat Katz in the Democratic primary with 75 percent of the black vote, and won the election—undermining the machine. The machine still controlled the county-based party organization, and many council members, black and white, stayed loyal to it. Hatcher ran for Democratic county chairman in 1970 and lost, but was reelected mayor by

Figure 4.4. The Greater the Emphasis on Increased Spending by the Mayor in His Campaign Statements, the Greater the Increase in General Expenditures, 1970–74

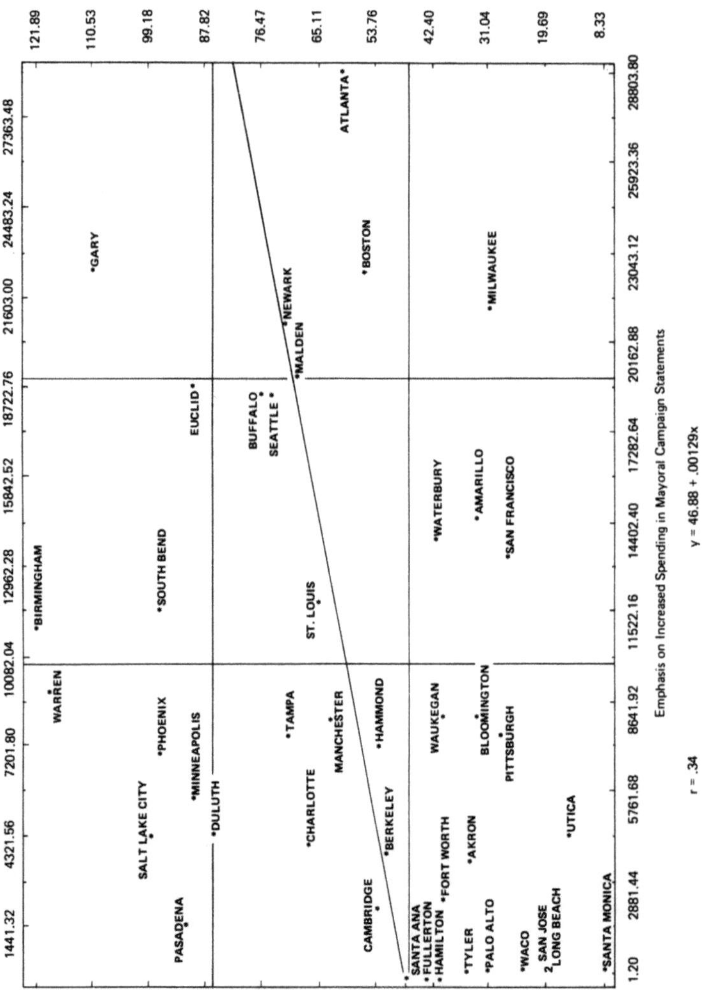

See note at base of Figure 4.2.

a strong margin in 1971, and five blacks pledged to support him joined the council. He previously had to bargain issue-by-issue with council members, but thereafter had much more impact. In the late 1960s, controlling neither party nor council, he built up a coalition of supporters generously funded by Ford and other private foundations and federal grants (sometimes obtained without council approval). Initially opponents kept down Gary's expenditures, but after 1971 manpower programs, housing, and social services rose dramatically. General expenditures grew 112 percent in 1970–74, more than for all but two of the 62 cities. Hatcher became legendary for obtaining outside funds: intergovernmental revenues jumped 307 percent in 1970–74, while the city's own revenues, mostly from property taxes, rose just 60 percent. Richard Hatcher personifies the dynamic political leader. He adapted civil rights activities to city politics by mobilizing on issues involving race, and helped define the political culture of black power. He created a new constituency, raised substantial resources, and gradually consolidated his leadership.

Birmingham increased expenditures even more than Gary, despite a lower leadership score (figure 4.4). Birmingham had many blacks (42 percent in 1970) but unlike Gary blacks and white liberals worked together in important civic groups, which helped mobilize voters behind George Seibels, a white liberal, to elect him mayor in 1967. Less forceful than Hatcher, he still took strong measures to overcome past discrimination. As racial pressures mounted in several incidents, local policies grew more ambitious—and expensive. Major projects included equalizing efforts in neighborhood facilities and service delivery, especially sewers and garbage collection in black areas. Seibels vigorously promoted hiring blacks by the city government. New taxes were passed and bonds floated for these activities. General expenditures rose 121 percent in 1970–74, and intergovernmental revenues 123 percent. Birmingham thus drew more on local revenue than Gary.[9]

Atlanta and Newark also had high leadership scores; Maynard Jackson and Kenneth Gibson were their first black mayors. They increased general expenditures more than the national average, while intergovernmental transfers rose 372 percent in Atlanta and 246 in Newark. Atlanta also borrowed heavily (debt rose 118 percent) for new capital facilities and an airport, such that by 1974 its outstanding long-term debt was $1,175 per capita (surpassed in our sample only by New York's $1,282).

Clearly, intergovernmental revenue was important in these years. But its effects are often overstated. The importance of local processes changes minimally when intergovernmental revenues are added as an explanatory variable.[10]

One should not overlook the many cities in the lower left-hand corner of figure 4.4: Pittsburgh, Utica, Waco, and others. They had more fiscally conservative mayors and spent less. They were less publicized than Gary or Atlanta in the early 1970s, but by the late 1970s the national mood changed, and these cities illustrated a new trend: retrenchment.

Fiscal Retrenchment: 1974–77

Retrenchment began in 1974 quite unobtrusively. When we discussed such results in 1976 and 1977, suggesting a taxpayers' revolt was abroad, listeners often laughed. Only after Proposition 13 passed in 1978 did Americans begin to consider implications of these developments for the welfare state. The role of government has been seriously questioned; debates are illuminated by examining the sources of retrenchment. Consider some widespread interpretations.

1. Early assessments of Proposition 13 saw it specific to California—linked to the state surplus, real estate boom, or kooky politics. This is undercut by our city-level data which show retrenchment *preceding* Proposition 13 in half our cities (table 2.2). Similarly, many other states passed tax and expenditure limits.
2. Recession and the decline of large, old, Northeastern cities were often invoked, specifically via loss of wealth and population. But chapter 3 showed these interpretations insufficient.
3. Another resource interpretation is that cutbacks in federal aid drove cities into difficulty. But cutbacks, we find, began locally, and when intergovernmental revenue is added as an "other variable" to the core model (table 9.1), it does not suppress core variable coefficients, deflating the Washington-centered interpretation.
4. Consider next organized groups. Many Neo-Marxists write of a

crisis of advanced capitalism and the uneven development of capital across cities and regions as generating urban fiscal crisis. One version of this argument leads to a Northeast syndrome interpretation, as considered in chapter 3. Another version stresses business elites as a conservative interest group reducing government spending. We too expected powerful business leadership to suppress spending, but it did not, although we analyzed many different types and combinations of financial and business leaders (chapter 7).

5. Municipal employees are also an important organized group, but again we find that they had no significant impact on increasing expenditures over the 1960–77 period, or in preventing retrenchment at the end of the period. They did increase compensation, but at the expense of numbers of jobs.

6. Individual organized groups had no impact on policy outputs, but a measure combining political activities of all nonpoor groups did. Cities where "special interest groups" contacted the mayor and council members more frequently increased general expenditures and common functions. While social services (welfare, health, and hospitals) were often the fastest growing functions in the late 1960s and early 1970s, by 1974–77 their growth rates declined compared to basic services (see Temporary Commission on City Finances 1977; Merget 1979).

7. What of political leaders? Certainly Edward Koch was blamed for retrenchment by many New Yorkers, as was Peter Flaherty in Pittsburgh, and Pete Wilson in San Diego. But while many mayors were more fiscally conservative than their predecessors, were political leaders distinctly important? We saw that leaders were analytically dynamic in the early 1970s. But for retrenchment in the late 1970s, table 4.1 shows that they were insignificant and thus analytically invisible. This in no way denies that political leaders in many cities had forceful confrontations with employees and service recipients who resisted cutbacks. But it suggests that they acted with conviction because they were not alone. They felt citizens' support behind them.

8. Middle-class citizens emerge as the fundamental explanation of retrenchment in our (table 4.1) analysis. Retrenchment resulted from a taxpayers' revolt. Many factors lead citizens toward fiscal conservatism, but they are insufficient to explain retrenchment; they had to act through citizens, who preferred lower taxes. Chapter 7 details citizen preferences using surveys: the basic result is that most Americans favor lower taxes. The poor and blacks are less conservative, but they too lowered spending preferences on items like welfare over the 1970s.

Catalysts like Howard Jarvis helped, but Jarvis had placed tax reduction referenda on the California ballot for years. Proposition 13 passed with a groundswell of support. Mayors and city council members across the country have similarly adopted more fiscally conservative policies, some reluctantly, others campaigning vigorously and coming to office on these issues. They have succeeded where and when citizens supported them. Cities with larger middle class sectors increased less on all four policy outputs—general expenditures, own revenues, long-term debt, and common functions. Leaders' preferences also significantly affected long-term debt, as in 1960–70. Debt decisions are more "technical," potentially isolated from citizens' pressures on general government, and thus shaped more by leaders.[11]

Considering how selected cities achieved retrenchment illuminates these general patterns. Some cities following the national downtrend in spending had only increased moderately since 1960. For example, Hamilton, Ohio, Hammond, Indiana, and Fullerton, California, represent many cities with large middle-class populations, few minorities, and citizens who consistently seemed to favor Republican leaders and less government. From 1960 onward, they had low spending increases. Given continued political stability, proposition 1 about citizen preferences largely explains low spending in such cities.

San Diego also illustrates consistent low spending. From 1960 to 1974, its expenditures increased modestly, even though it was less small or homogeneous than Hamilton, Hammond, or Fullerton. San Diego has few blacks; Mexican-Americans are the principal minority group, and were less mobilized than blacks in the 1960s. The dominant political culture is that of the large middle (and upper class) population, and for years Republican mayors and council members fared well on low-spending platforms. Under Mayor Pete Wilson, the property tax rate was cut in the early 1970s (facilitated by the real estate boom). A large military and retired population supports honest and efficient government. The press is editorially conservative, but plays down local politics; beaches, parks, and recreation are the salient issues. Political parties and ethnic organizations are weak; leading civic organizations are city-wide in membership and perspective: the Chamber of Commerce and Taxpayers' Association work closely with the city government to promote tourism and controlled development. A respected board of fiscal overseers, chaired by a retired admiral, is used by the council to review important policies. Rumors circulated about favors that Mayor Wilson did for developers, and his predecessor left office after a development-related scandal. But the fact that such favors remain sub rosa and scandalous is clear evidence of their illegitimacy in San Diego's Republican political culture. (In Chicago, by contrast, politicians brag of their "clout," which often means doing favors of just the sort that cause scandals in San Diego.) San Diego's political leaders are not expected to participate in specific policies, but to delegate "administrative details" to professional staff. Political leaders occasionally act as partisan Republicans on issues like a municipal strike—ruling that any strikers would be fired, and enforcing the measure. But they generally convey a low-keyed, nonpartisan concern for "good government" in the American reform tradition. The staff has considerable autonomy, is paid well, and has earned a national reputation for innovations in productivity and financial management. The city well illustrates Republican political culture.

Retrenchment in San Diego was championed not by established organized groups, but by four outspoken council members who came to office in 1977. After they ran in vigorous populist manner on antispending issues, and won, they found enough support with more senior council members to start trimming the budget by about 20 percent, one year before Proposition 13. In San Diego, and many other low-spending cities, retrenchment in the mid-1970s simply reinforced traditional fiscal conservatism. As Howard Jarvis remarked, "If all cities were like San Diego, we would not have needed Prop. 13."

But retrenchment was a revolutionary concept in other cities, like New York. Even though John Lindsay warned of bankruptcy in his 1964 campaign for mayor, once in office he and successor Abraham Beame usually defined New York's problem as too little revenues, not too high expenditures. This changed only after the 1975 fiscal crisis, and considerable federal and state government pressures. Taxpayers too seemed to grow more visible. New York often illustrates disparities between organized group activities and citizen preferences. Apparently no one has surveyed New York citizens on fiscal policy preferences in recent years (or admitted doing so, itself an interesting reflection of its nonpopulist political culture), but most mayoral candidates after the early 1960s ran successfully on programs of fiscal conservatism, at least relative to their predecessors.

John Lindsay was initially elected as a low-spending Republican, and won again only by a plurality when two more conservative opponents split the anti-Lindsay vote. Beame ran initially as the former comptroller who "knows the buck," and the political unknown Edward Koch surprised many experts when, as the most fiscally conservative candidate, he defeated Bella Abzug and incumbent Beame for the Democratic nomination. Yet, once in office, all these mayors increased expenditures, many argue, by capitulating to organized group pressures (see Auletta 1979; Rogers 1971; Haider 1976). Fiscal policies were generated by the same basic processes as elsewhere, but New York's heterogeneity and political instability strengthened organized groups and political leaders who continued the Democratic political culture. By contrast, when Chicago launched major social programs in the 1960s and 1970s, Mayor Daley kept firm control of them and segregated their funds, so that when federal support ended they were terminated, while in New York groups often lobbied successfully to continue their programs at local expense (see Fuchs 1981; Orlebeke 1981).

Both New York and Chicago are large and heterogeneous, which encourages organized groups. But political leadership has been far more stable in Chicago (albeit less under Mayor Jane Byrne), and stability reduces uncertainty for participants and facilitates responsiveness to low tax concerns of middle-class citizens. The many organized groups in New York led political leaders to compromise by giving something to each, while the centralized Democratic party under Daley could restrain spending on more separable goods, like specific housing or neighborhood projects. Patronage in Chicago was controlled and allocated through the party to individuals, while in New York organized groups received blocks of jobs and the mayor little control or credit. After its 1975 fiscal crisis, New York was moved toward Chicago by establishment of the Emergency Financial Control Board which centralized financial control, while after Daley's death, Chicago moved (slightly) toward New York.

These cases illustrate the more general proposition that centralization encourages public goods, but decentralization generates separable goods (see Clark 1975b). For retrenchment, it implies that centralization can help implement cutbacks or achieve public goods like fiscal health (Clark et al. 1976). Other cities have used other means to centralize control for retrenchment, such as San Diego's Board of Fiscal Overseers, or a retrenchment policy committee reporting to the mayor (as in Boston, Cambridge, and elsewhere) to make the hard decisions. Centralization in these cases is largely to shield leaders from special interest group pressures for more spending on specific projects, and to respond instead to the unorganized citizenry which favors lower taxes.

New York's high spending was finally cut back. Does it illustrate a general tendency for high spending to generate cutbacks, a sort of systemic adaptation to the environment defined by expenditures levels of other cities competing for residents, firms, and employees? We considered this by adding a variable to the core: the expenditure level per capita in 1974 (the first year of the downturn). High spending did indeed generate retrenchment (or at least slow growth). Independent of other variables, the higher the 1974 spending, the more likely was retrenchment, for at least some functions.[12] Acute cases were New York and Detroit, which both cut the number of employees 22 percent, and Cleveland, which cut them 19 percent. Other high-spending cities that cut back were Albany, Berkeley, Buffalo, Newark, and Seattle.

As expenditures rose in such cities, political leaders may have been made aware of borrowing costs by banks or financial advisors. But as the trend continued, the mass media, dissenting leaders, and various civic groups helped focus public attention on high spending and taxes, sometimes dramatizing the closing of a local firm or population losses, compared to growth elsewhere. Short-term costs of responding to interest groups eventually rose so high as to generate counterreactions. The most publicized case was New York City, "New Deal liberalism's Vietnam" (Auletta 1979). There and elsewhere middle class residents, as taxpayers, favored less spending. While opposition to taxes and expenditure growth was occasionally noted in the late 1960s, demands escalated in the mid-1970s. Such demands encouraged adapting to the environment through new fiscal policies. More candidates in the mid-to-late-1970s ran and won on fiscal responsibility and conservatism.

For some citizens and leaders, this continues past policies, as in San

Diego where Republican voters were numerous enough to elect mayors and council members who implemented such policies over many years. But in the mid-1970s, only about 22 percent of Americans claimed to be Republicans, and 43 percent Democrats.[13] The Democratic party, after Roosevelt, consistently favored spending. Yet in the mid-1970s some Democrats reversed this position and were elected. Jimmy Carter and Jerry Brown were nationally prominent examples; Mayors Edward Koch in New York and Peter Flaherty in Pittsburgh were other important cases. They were New Fiscal Populists (NFPs), sufficiently new and different from ethnic politicians, New Deal Democrats, and Republicans that their political culture deserves more extended treatment. Middle class citizen preferences were important to explain NFPs' success, so we defer discussion to chapter 7.

Fiscal conservatism may have grown publicly visible in leaders and expenditure changes, but table 4.1 showed that leaders' preferences were not an independent cause of retrenchment in the late 1970s. If leaders grew more fiscally conservative, they still were not "dynamic" like those earlier in the decade; they were "invisible" politicians responding to citizen preferences for lower taxes. The relatively small number of city spending limits (in contrast to state limits like Proposition 13) further indicates that city leaders responded more to citizens.

Expenditure and Debt Levels in 1977

Expenditure and debt *levels* record the cumulative impact of past decisions, including the three periods since 1960. Indeed, most 1977 level findings emerged in one of the three earlier periods. While one process may dominate in one period, effects of several combine to generate the 1977 levels (table 4.1). Most findings have already been interpreted, but a few are distinctive.

As in the first and third periods, cities with large middle classes spent less in 1977, reflecting a consistent low-spending preference by middle class citizens. Yet black sector size was insignificant. Many cities with large black populations are in the South, and traditionally spent less despite recent increases.

Cities performing more functions naturally spent more; this is not per se substantively meaningful, but including the FP Index helps remove its effects from other variables in the model.

The City Wealth Index is similarly important to include, although it affected no changes in the three periods. Yet wealthier cities spent at higher levels in 1977, the result of a long, gradual process, much of which predates 1960. While middle class residents favor less spending, wealthier cities still spend more for reasons analogous to those leading affluent individuals to oppose taxes but still consume more private goods (chapter 7, note 3). These results illustrate the opposing effects of wealth and spending preferences. Most past studies have confused the two.[14]

Another long-term process involves ethnic politics, captured by the percentage of Irish residents. Since the nineteenth century, immigrant and especially Irish residents have supported governments that provided jobs to needy persons. Overt Irish patronage receded by the late 1970s, but effects of past policies were still clear in 1977, as discussed in chapter 5.

Powerful mayors who favored more spending increased expenditures in our middle period. Their legacy, like that of the Irish, was still visible in 1977 levels. By contrast, the 1976 leadership measure was unrelated to 1977 levels, again documenting 1974–77 as a period with more invisible political leaders.

An incrementalist might include the spending level for an earlier year to predict 1977 spending (e.g., Sharkansky 1968). We modeled fiscal feedback for the late 1970s this way, but did not include a lagged level measure in the core. The spending level in one year is obviously related to that of a few years later. But this simply tells us that history is important for the present (see Stinchcombe 1968); it does not indicate what specific aspects of the past, close or distant, generated the fiscal consequences. Core model variables, by contrast, generally do.

Fiscal Strain Analysis

Thus far the chapter has not distinguished fiscal policy outputs from fiscal strain. What changes if we do? Almost nothing. This section thus mainly adds technical details. The same basic analyses were completed for both types of indicators. For strain analyses a variable was added to the core model, the "appropriate" resource indicator which was also in the fiscal strain indicator's denominator. For example, to explain the fiscal strain indicator *Ratio of long-term debt/Median family income 1960–70*, the "appropriate" resource indicator is *Median family income 1960–70*. The fiscal strain core model thus included two private sector resources, the City Wealth Index and an "appropriate" resource indicator.[15] The "appropriate" resource indicator is often strongly related to the fiscal strain indicator simply due to a partial statistical identity (its inclusion as the denominator). One might expect this plus normal intercorrelation to suppress core model variables. But this seldom occurred. Detailed results—direct, indirect, and total effects—are in appendix 2.

We briefly review findings by time period. For 1960–70, the major results again were the smaller the middle class and larger the black sector, the greater the increase. With both fiscal policy outputs and strain indicators, relationships were clearest for general expenditures and long-term debt, while common functions and own revenues sometimes fell below significance. General expenditures include receipts from debt and intergovernmental revenues. As the most complete fiscal expression of city policies, general expenditures should capture basic processes better than more limited measures like common functions. This might be qualified if intergovernmental revenues confounded local processes, but they seldom did; intergovernmental revenues largely act as resources facilitating local processes (tables 5.3 and 9.1). Basic results for this period held in alternative specifications, although multicollinearity suppressed a few coefficients, especially for percent blacks.

Results for 1970–74 were again similar for fiscal policy outputs and fiscal strain; cities increased both if they had powerful liberal mayors. This was clear for general expenditures but fell below significance for other indicators. Black and middle class sector measures were insignificant.

In the third period, 1974–77, cities with large middle class sectors increased fiscal strain less. The leadership measure (spending preferences of mayors and council members weighted by their power) was insignificant for general expenditures and own revenues, but positively related to long-term debt and, less strongly, common functions. In other periods too, debt indicators are more affected than other indicators by leaders' preferences.[16] This suggests that political leaders have more control over debt, but that citizen preferences affect broader decisions more. Cities with high overall liquidity scores (cash and securities divided by general expenditure, LOL74) had smaller middle classes and fewer (just below significance) Irish residents; pressures from these groups for low taxes and high spending may have depleted cash reserves. But problems of comparing cash holdings across cities suggest caution in interpreting these results.

Finally, in 1977 fiscal strain levels were again higher if cities had smaller middle classes, more Irish residents, performed more functions, and were less wealthy. The City Wealth Index is strongly negative simply because it was the denominator for the 1977 strain indicators. To assess stability of results, we also analyzed general expenditures in 1977/median family income; it performed almost identically to general expenditures in 1977/City Wealth Index.

Variables indexing the major processes—the middle class, political leaders, ethnic politics—as well as FP, were of roughly equal importance in some period. And all were about equal for 1977 levels (tables A.2.3 and A.2.4).[17]

Notice the convergence among several findings. Fiscal policy outputs and fiscal strain results differed very little. Second, private resource measures (taxable property value, median family income, population change) were often insignificant: they seldom explained changes in fiscal strain, although they were important (in the City Wealth Index) for 1977 levels.[18] Such weak relationships are consistent with chapter 3 in qualifying the importance of the economic base as generating fiscal strain. Private sector resources are important to explain major differences across cities over the long term (more than a decade). But political processes are more direct sources of fiscal policy over periods as short as four years. Subsequent chapters consider specific political processes.

CHAPTER FIVE

White Ethnics and Black Power

This chapter and the two which follow consider the four political cultures and their distinctive roles in different cities and time periods. The three chapters elaborate the theory from chapter 1 and empirical findings from chapter 4. We begin with ethnic politics, given its deep historical roots. White ethnic politics is initially considered, and how it linked individuals and groups with specific material rewards, like patronage jobs. Rewards were channeled by networks of religious, ethnic, and neighborhood contacts that interpenetrate the political process. Blacks found such patterns difficult to break into, but eventually did, as outlined in the second part of the chapter. Black power emerged as a unique development, although it built on elements of white ethnic politics, Protestant stoicism, and civil rights organization. It had a major impact in the early 1970s, but declined in the late 1970s.

White Ethnic Politics

Why discuss ethnicity in a book on fiscal strain? We did not intend to initially, but when analyses using poverty proved inadequate, we probed further. The importance of ethnic politics for municipal finance emerged a few years earlier in expenditure analyses of our PCS cities. Those with large Catholic and especially Irish populations spent substantially more, and the relationship held strong with numerous control variables (like Democratic voting, wealth, region, unionization, etc.). We were initially skeptical and hesitated to publish the result, but over eight years accumulated substantial supporting evidence (reported in

Clark 1975c). The Irish impact was clear in regression analyses for 1880, 1900, 1930, and 1968. Chapter 4 showed the same for general expenditure and common function changes from 1960–70. But after 1970 the Irish no longer explained changes, although they still affect expenditure levels in 1977. How interpret these results?

A citizen preference hypothesis led us first to citizen surveys. They showed that Irish and Catholic citizens had traditionally supported the Democratic party, and may thus have been fiscally liberal in the distant past. Few surveys are available specifically concerning city government spending preferences. One 1970 survey of citizens in ten cities showed Irish and Catholics no different from Protestants in spending preferences. Similarly, eight spending items in the General Social Survey of the National Opinion Research Center from 1972 to 1980 showed no Catholic-Protestant differences.[1] Catholics were low in education and income in the past, but this has changed; the Irish have even surpassed white Anglo-Saxon Protestants in income (Greeley 1974), which may have weakened their fiscal liberalism. Irish and Catholic citizen spending preferences thus do not explain high spending by cities where they are numerous. What does? Other aspects of ethnic political culture.

In the late nineteenth century Catholic immigrants disagreed with other white Americans over jobs, housing, and politics. Often organized around the Roman Catholic Church, the Democratic party, and neighborhood institutions, immigrants supported "regular" or "machine" candidates, who responded with favors like hods of coal, cash, and patronage jobs. These private, separable goods were critical resources exchanged between candidates and followers. They lubricated a dense network of interpersonal ties, provided inputs for government decisions, and helped allocate public services and contracts to well-connected neighborhoods and organized groups. Near election time, such personal ties would be activated through precinct campaign work, long important in cities with such ethnic political cultures. For example, in 1956, just 10 percent of a national sample of Americans reported that they had been contacted by party workers during the presidential campaign, but twice as many reported contacts in non-Southern cities over 100,000. The number was just 6 percent in nonethnic Seattle and

Minneapolis, but 60 percent in New Haven. New Haven, Chicago, Albany, and Pittsburgh have well-documented ethnic machines which long dominated city politics (e.g., Dahl 1961; Stave 1970; Clark 1975c).

Why are such networks more active in cities with ethnic populations? In part due to citizen values which define these patterns as politically legitimate. Five distinctive value dimensions together comprise "the Irish ethic," or more dryly "non-ideological particularism,"[2] some of which are shared with other Catholic immigrants. *Sociability* measured by items like "would you rather do things with others or by yourself?" showed Protestants less sociable. *Trust and personal loyalty* captured by items like "Do you think most people can be trusted?" yielded scores of 2.5 for Irish Catholics, .24 for white Anglo-Saxon Protestants, and −3.1 for Jews. *Localism*, favoring a local citizen over "the best man available anywhere," is more common for Catholics and less educated persons. *Practicing Catholicism* reinforced social contacts through an important institution. About 90 percent of Irish Catholics reported that they attended mass weekly and sent their children to parochial schools, although the figure has been decreasing. *Social conservatism* has long been a hallmark of ethnic politics, illustrated by the Chicago alderman who, when asked the secret of his long tenure, replied "Don't make no waves, don't back no losers." Daley and his associates were essentially nonideological; they let issues bubble up from organized groups and then only acted if there was little opposition. They made no waves. (See Banfield 1961; Rakove 1975.) The ethnic politician here falls at the opposite end of the spectrum from the ideological reformer who addresses "the issues" in their "own terms." The five are weakened, but not eliminated, as education increases.

These five elements reinforce each other to define legitimate rules of the game distinguishing ethnic political culture. They come together in the famous anecdote about Mayor Daley's press conference: Question: "Why did you give city contracts to your sons' insurance firm?" Answer: "It's a father's duty to help his sons!" This was neither diverting humor nor a unique circumstance; it illustrates the interpenetration of personal friendship and political obligation which are basic rules of the game in cities like Chicago. If Chicago's political machine is unique, patronage and favors are far more widespread.

What does this culture imply for municipal expenditures? Higher spending. Separable goods maintain past political commitments and extend linkages to new groups. From the late nineteenth century until about 1970, ethnic (often Irish) leaders expanded city governments, helping the deprived both as service recipients and city employees. Other chapters show that cities with more Irish residents perform more functions, have more powerful political leaders, and more unionized and numerous (if less highly paid) municipal employees.

Political culture is measured only indirectly in city-level analyses, using the percentage of Irish, foreign stock, Catholics, and Protestants, which are all highly correlated. We included the percentage Irish in the core model because of its greater impact on expenditures, its lower association with other core variables, and our earlier findings that the Irish were so important in maintaining a distinctive political culture.[3]

Recalling our typology of the four political cultures, ethnic politicians are (1) *fiscally liberal*, but this is due to (2) *responding to group pressures* and costs of allocating favors and patronage jobs, rather than to citizen preferences for higher spending. Indeed, ethnic politicans tend (3) *not to respond to populist demands* of citizens per se. They seek to "back no losers," consider only concrete leaders and groups, not abstract issues; concepts like "public opinion" or "the public interest" are instinctively distrusted. Policy emerges instead by slowly waiting for organized groups to aggregate behind an issue, or to redefine it until it can win majority support; only then does the politician endorse it. The major (4) *resources* exchanged in ethnic politics are *private or separable goods* rather than public goods. Specific, material rewards have long been the accepted exchange medium for ethnic politicians and their less educated constituents. Highly educated "amateurs" motivated by the ideology of a candidate or cause are avoided as "morning glories" that will soon fade; patronage workers are preferred who remain more loyal due to dependence on leaders for their jobs and a continuing flow of favors. Finally, (5) *social liberalism* was a subject of no little debate among ethnic intellectuals in the last decade (e.g. Greeley 1974; Novak 1972; Patterson 1977). A central issue was blacks. Were they discriminated against, and if so, how? Greeley (1974) and others stressed that individual Catholics, especially Irish, were not prejudiced toward blacks, or no more than Protestants comparable in education and income. Still, "turf battles" between white Catholic ethnics and blacks have arisen from the nineteenth century to the present. When the abolitionist Protestant North entered the Civil War, anticonscription riots broke out between Irish and blacks in Chicago, New York, and other cities. Tensions continue into the 1980s on issues like forced busing, where Catholic ethnic groups have violently opposed blacks. The Irish ethic helps interpret these collective actions, and reconcile them with low racial antagonism by individual ethnics.

Aggregating individual preferences explains neither city spending nor discrimination against blacks. Leaders are critical in both cases, and those with strong personal interest; majorities seldom act, even if mildly opposing high taxes or racial discrimination. The explanation for both phenomena lies in the network of personal obligations and traditions defining neighborhood boundaries, specific patronage jobs, or contracts for items like road salt as the "property" of a given family or ethnic group. The Irish succeeded in part by their abilities to broker among competing ethnic factions. They helped bring political organization to Polish, Italian, and other European ethnic groups, as well as blacks, who became a political force in Chicago after the 1920s. Still, favors went to new ethnic leaders only when they could deliver their precincts. Outsiders questioning such arrangements—Yankee reformer or black dissenter—are strongly resisted, as illustrated by the reaction of a Chicago Democratic party official when approached for a job by a University of Chicago law student. Question: "Who sent ya?" Answer: "Nobody." Reply: "We don't want nobody nobody sent." To an outsider the response can imply discrimination. Insiders retort that any group regularly supporting the party is properly rewarded.

How liberal ethnic politicans are on social issues besides race varies with their constituency, especially its educational level, although distinctive national patterns persist after controlling for education (see Greeley 1974).[4] If some cultural patterns persist, the significance of ethnic politics has declined for most European immigrants with increasing opportunities outside local government. Irish Catholics still participate in government more than other ethnic groups, but they now may be New Deal Democrats (like Mayor Kevin White in Boston), Republicans (like Pete Wilson in San Diego), or New Fiscal Populists (like

Peter Flaherty in Pittsburgh). The Irish have declined, but not disappeared.

White Catholic immigrants are "ethnics" in general American usage. Yet politics was structured even more rigidly by ethnicity in the South. The major European immigrations were to northern cities, such that most southerners were either white and generally Anglo-Saxon Protestants, or blacks. Traditionally, blacks were slaves and whites the masters, and in politics, despite a few carpetbaggers and others in the 1870s, whites dominated a virtual caste system. Major changes came only in the 1960s, as discussed below.

Given the out-migration of many white Protestants from older, northern cities, and the importance there of white ethnic politicians, as the number of blacks increased in many cities after World War II, conflict between white ethnics and blacks was almost inevitable. Blacks both reacted against and incorporated various aspects of white ethnic political culture, first in the South, then in the North.

Black Politics

Following the chapter 1 framework, we examine impacts of black citizen preferences and organized groups on fiscal policy. Few past studies address these linkages. Urban fiscal analyses rarely study black groups, while work on blacks has usually considered issues like citizen participation or service delivery. Most linkages thus come from our own analyses. The components defining ethnic political culture for blacks shifted over the 1960s and 1970s. While blacks affected fiscal policy in all periods, they did so according to the distinctive political culture of black power for only a few short years, 1970–74 (chapter 4). This chapter concentrates on the rise and fall of black power because of its cultural distinctiveness and powerful fiscal effects.

Black Citizen Spending Preferences

Black citizens prefer more government spending than whites on a range of domestic social issues; results for 1980 are in table 5.1. Black-

Table 5.1. Blacks Prefer More Spending Than Do Whites

	Percentage Who Say Too Little Is Spent On:							
	Welfare	Cities	Education	Health	Improving Condition of Blacks	Crime	Environment	Drug Addiction
Black	38	68	76	76	79	80	69	76
White	11	43	53	55	20	71	49	63

Source: NORC-General Social Survey, 1980.

white differences are not simply an expression of income disparities. Blacks have much stronger prospending views than whites at all income levels (table 5.2).[5] Black-white differences are large concerning welfare, spending to improve the conditions of blacks, health, cities, the environment, and education—many of which are income redistributive. On less redistributive issues like crime and drug addiction, black-white differences are smaller. Results for welfare spending are particularly interesting since welfare is so ideologically salient: it has long been a symbol of big redistributive government and thus used to classify respondents as fiscally liberal or conservative. The 1970s marked a distinct shift in black spending preferences on welfare. From the 1950s through the early 1970s, surveys consistently showed most blacks favoring more welfare spending (see Taylor 1978; Janowitz 1978:160), but by 1980 a majority no longer did. This is not explained by increased income, since blacks at all income levels lowered welfare spending preferences during the 1970s. On other domestic spending issues, however, changes were minimal.[6] Blacks probably moderated their support for welfare for reasons similar to whites, as explored in chapter 7. One distinctive factor, however, may have been enhanced participation in mainstream American society. Most programs were expanding too, so that attitudes referred to changing programs as each year passed. We particularly looked for shifts in spending preferences by middle-class blacks, given the public debate about cleavages between poor and middle-class blacks (Wilson 1978), but found no significant changes from 1973 to 1980 except for welfare. Differences between poor and middle-class black citizens thus seem of more enduring character, but were often politically submerged in the late 1960s commitment to racial unity. Middle class blacks may be more fiscally liberal than their white counterparts, but are still more cautious about public spending than poor blacks.

Black attitudes towards spending in 1980 still indicate racial differences not explained by "class" or income. While many blacks are poor, the majority are above the poverty level; many are clearly middle class. The stereotype that blacks are poor and the poor are black is simply false.[7] Many blacks nevertheless favor redistributive policies even if they might not seem to gain from them. Yet imputing self-interest is complex; some even suggest that middle class blacks gained most from

Table 5.2. Blacks Prefer More Spending Than Do Whites of the Same Income Levels

Total Family Income	Percentage Who Say Too Little Is Spent On: Conditions of Blacks		Cities		Education		Health		Welfare, 1973	
	Whites	Blacks	Whites	Blacks	Whites	Blacks	Whites	Blacks	Whites	Blacks
Under $5,000	21	81	44	56	45	73	48	76	30	68
$5,000-9,999	29	79	47	71	52	76	60	68	15	55
$10,000-14,999	18	90	42	70	59	76	63	71	8	52
$15,000-24,999	17	71	42	81	52	75	52	85	11	35
$25,000 +	17	73	44	73	53	86	53	86	10	40
Number of Respondents	1167	143	1109	126	1223	132	1226	135	1166	159

Total Family Income	Percentage Who Say Too Little Is Spent On: Welfare, 1980		Crime		Environment		Drug Addiction	
	Whites	Blacks	Whites	Blacks	Whites	Blacks	Whites	Blacks
Under $5,000	24	59	67	79	46	65	64	77
$5,000-9,999	14	25	71	72	46	72	63	76
$10,000-14,999	11	25	73	90	51	68	70	80
$15,000-24,999	10	26	71	85	56	71	60	80
$25,000 +	5	33	71	76	43	73	61	66
Number of Respondents	1222	133	1220	134	1205	129	1182	128

Note: NORC-General Social Surveys, 1973 (welfare only) and 1980.

the Great Society programs.[8] Many blacks also feel ties to the past when they were less affluent, and more dependent on welfare-type programs, a feeling heightened by a shared racial heritage.

Whatever the motivation, black citizens show consistent preferences for increased spending. How were such preferences translated into fiscal policy? We consider in turn the number of black citizens, organized groups, and the emergence of black power.

Black Political Activity: Citizens, Groups, Leaders

Black Sector Size. Although blacks comprised only 12 percent of the U.S. population, in many cities they were a third by the mid-1960s and in a few almost half the population. A strict citizen preference model implies that a large black sector will generate responsive policies. But in practice, the linkage is more complex. Blacks had striking effects on fiscal policy in our PCS cities in the late 1960s and early 1970s, but black sector size then showed no direct effects (chapter 4). To explain fiscal impacts of blacks in these years, one must turn to organized groups and political leaders.

From Traditional Organized Groups to Civil Rights Movement Activities. Before the mid-1960s, the active organized black groups were the Urban League and the National Association for the Advancement of Colored People. In many cities, black lawyers, ministers, and other professionals in these organizations worked closely with liberal whites in gradual but persistent efforts toward racial integration. Ministers and church groups were similarly active in linking their members to the national movement. During the summer of 1960 sit-ins swept the South, organized by new civil rights groups, especially the Southern Christian Leadership Conference and Congress on Racial Equality. They helped mobilize national sentiment, the U.S. Congress passed a series of civil rights acts in the mid-1960s, and federal officials began enforcing them. Splinter groups developed in the late 1960s, ranging from ad hoc organizations for housing and jobs to the armed militancy of the Black Panthers. Of course these were the Vietnam years and demonstrations of all sorts grew in number and intensity.

The Political Culture of Black Power. A problem for all groups is how to convert political resources into influence on concrete decisions.

The urban poor were largely unsuccessful.[9] Blacks were slightly more numerous than the poor; still more important was their potential for group solidarity from racial distinctiveness, a vivid history of discrimination, and growing concentration in numerous cities. How to convert these resources into influence?

Many approaches were tried, several with success. Individual leaders disagreed, but most sought to maintain black unity. Symbols were important, especially the "black power" slogan launched by Stokely Carmichael in 1966 (Carmichael and Hamilton 1967). Some black leaders, especially in the South, avoided black power symbols, but it was hard for black leaders in northern cities not to adopt the movement's militant rhetoric and clenched fist symbol.

Four elements came to define the political culture of black power: organized group activities, separable goods as resources, racial independence, and fiscal liberalism. We document each with examples from cities and national surveys.

Organized group activities were highly successful in voter registration drives in the rural South. Urban leaders brought these tactics to cities, initially building on civil rights organizations. The Student Nonviolent Coordinating Committee successfully mobilized support for aldermen in Atlanta after 1965 (Greenberg 1974). In Cleveland, ad hoc and national organizations joined in successful school drives and then sought out a black candidate for mayor. They drafted state representative Carl Stokes after the organization generated 25,000 petitions (Stokes 1973). Great enthusiasm, long hours, and low pay fueled community organizers to mobilize thousands of blacks to register and vote in city after city. Organizers often sought to adopt their constituents' styles: college students donned straw hats and overalls in the rural South; in cities, their dress and speech took on more "streetwise" toughness.

Direct action tactics—sit-ins, pickets, marches, and the like—distinguished these efforts from traditional Democratic or ethnic organizers. Still, violence had often accompanied ethnic succession in urban politics. Italian, Polish, and Czech leaders were routinely threatened and occasionally assassinated in cities like Gary, Chicago, and Detroit; similarly black efforts to overcome discrimination and political repression brought threats of violence (e.g., Suttles 1968; Clark 1975c).

Nevertheless, political violence is taboo for middle-class Americans; in the early 1960s, repressive violence against blacks mobilized white support for civil rights. Violating the norm of nonviolence generated strong reactions. Direct action tactics both defined the black organizing style and rendered it controversial to many Americans, especially as it was unclear to what degree such tactics encouraged the growing civil disorders. The sources of urban disorders, and their relations to organized protest activities, are subjects of continuing research (e.g., Morgan and Clark 1973; Spilerman 1976; Genevie 1978). We note here simply that blacks participating in riots were not politically uninformed or persistent troublemakers. Rioters were generally representative of black residents, and sometimes disproportionately high in income and education (Fogelson 1971; Eisinger 1974; Kilson 1975). While some held that rioters were just out for "fun and profit," others saw riots as clear political protests. Participation in political activities of all sorts was increased by education and income—as it was for whites—as well as by a sense of mistrust (Shingles 1981), leading blacks to higher participation levels than whites of comparable socioeconomic status.

Violence was the essence of black power for some extremists, but few elected officials endorsed this position. For example, on his election night as mayor of Gary, in the mass celebration and dancing in the streets, Richard Hatcher urged "that the outcome of this election will be unmarred by any incident of any kind. . . . If we spoil this victory with any kind of occurrence here tonight, or anywhere in the city, it will be a hollow victory" (quoted in Hadden, Masotti, and Thiessen 1969:21).

A 1971–72 survey of 799 black elected officials by Conyers and Wallace (1976:20) found that of various direct action tactics, petitions and delegations were endorsed by virtually all, mass public demonstrations by many, and actual violence by few.[10] Organized groups were clearly important in the Conyers-Wallace survey: black officials considered election support from "organizations and leaders not in government" substantially more important than a matched sample of their white counterparts.[11]

Separable Goods As Political Resources. The moral fervor of the civil rights leaders was clear in songs and prayers stressing equal treatment for black and white Americans. Martin Luther King's speeches typically appealed to equality irrespective of race, invoking an abstract Protestant and Jewish commitment to universalistic justice. King's stoicism in confronting openly racist whites generated outrage and sympathy among thousands of Americans, helping mobilize national sanctions against local recalcitrants like Governor George Wallace. The civil rights leaders appealed to the white electorate (for votes against racism), elite white supporters (for their time and money), and all blacks (to register and vote their own interests). All three responded to appeals for equal rights irrespective of race from leaders like Martin Luther King. But as the movement succeeded and then generated electoral victories, public sector resources increased, and the private, civil rights groups no longer set the national tone for blacks; black mayors did. They could appeal directly to black voters and ignore whites. Appeals for justice also got nowhere with the Richard Daleys and their constituents, who saw them akin to Protestant reform politics. Nonideological ethnic politics does not reward its followers with justice, however, but with the material good. The universalistic, ideological element in the civil rights movement was transformed as it entered northern cities. The public good of movement ideals receded as material rewards of ethnic politics became accessible. Still the Protestant background of many blacks, and continuing importance of church groups (and some federal officials), encouraged more universalistic appeals than those of white ethnic politicians. Black power leaders could sometimes even merge themes of patronage politics and abstract justice in such policies as "affirmative action" quotas, which implied that jobs were not just payoffs for precinct work, but retribution for past sins by whites. Some rewards came with elective office; the federal government also helped with the War on Poverty. While many felt that funding never justified the label, both the funds and programs were dramatically more ambitious than anything in the history of American cities. In the vanguard were the Community Action Agencies (CAAs), initiated under the Office of Economic Opportunity with the Congressional mandate to encourage "maximum feasible participation." CAAs were either existing or new organizations funded by federal officials who sought out "community leaders," often poor and black. Such direct federal-neighborhood linkages were meant to disrupt the local status quo, and often did. Organizing activities thus continued with more funding than ever before. City halls fought back vigorously, and succeeded in having the CAAs increasingly supervised by locally-elected officials. Model cities and then Community Development Block Grants superceded them, but retained the formal requirement of citizen participation. These programs remained vehicles for significant political input from black citizens in some cities. In others they did not, but still supported careers for emerging leaders and campaign workers.[12]

Racial Independence. This differentiated black power advocates clearly from more traditional blacks. Racial integration had been the preeminent goal of the Urban League, NAACP, and most civil rights activists. This shifted dramatically in the late 1960s. That blacks could do things on their own, without whites, seemed a logical extension of the idea of black pride. Yet despite the Black Muslims who sought to claim and settle an all-black territory, most blacks sought to work within existing institutions. The elected officials survey indicated support for more black leaders in white businesses. Yet most officials also favored more black-owned businesses, and some an all-black political party.[13] Commitment to "community control" and decentralization of social service programs (CAAs, Model Cities, etc.) often reflected concern for racial independence (e.g., Altschuler 1970). Then as black elected leaders came to control jobs, they had the same incentives as white ethnic politicians to allocate them to loyal supporters. Anticipating this, white municipal employees organized against blacks in many cities. The most attractive solution, of course, was not to fire anyone, but to create new jobs. This was a common policy in the early 1970s, consistent with a general fiscal liberalism.

Fiscal Liberalism. We saw that black citizens preferred more government spending than whites. Black leaders shared these views in their campaigns and in office. Stokes stressed improved housing for blacks in Cleveland; his efforts were clear, although success uneven. In Gary, Hatcher stressed housing and job training programs for the poor and unemployed. Similarly, the national survey of black officials showed strong support of government involvement in housing, income, and leisure programs.[14] Even if unemployment and poverty are largely private sector problems affected little by one city government, mayors who speak out on the issues and create a few jobs can still hope for active support from those receiving the jobs, and votes from citizens who share these concerns. Many evaluations in the late 1960s and early 1970s reporting that manpower and other social programs were unsuccessful, underestimated their symbolic and political importance.

Consequences of Black Political Activity

The most important point about the black power movement is that it worked, at least compared to other groups and the past. Blacks came to public office in unprecedented numbers. Between 1970 and 1981 black mayors and council members increased more than threefold (Joint Center for Political Studies 1981; Karnig and Welch 1980).[15] Mayor Hatcher characterized the change: "Blacks still do not control the real power centers in this country. . . . Our major gains so far have been limited to local government. Here we do indeed control terrain that was formerly beyond our group."[16] Carl Stokes in Cleveland, and Richard Hatcher in Gary received extensive coverage in national media as the first black mayors of major cities in 1967. They were tangible evidence that black power was more than a phrase, and more than registration drives or sit-ins which remained activities of political outsiders. The symbolic importance of winning office was clear.[17]

Fiscal Consequences in the Early 1970s

How much did these developments affect fiscal policy outputs? Cities with larger black sectors had more quasi-political activities by black organized groups in the late 1960s.[18] These activities were in turn associated with prospending mayors (table 4.2). Such mayors increased expenditures in their cities from 1970 to 74. Figure 5.1 shows the basic pattern. These results deserve elaboration. If black support encouraged black (and white) leaders to increase spending, did black political activity directly affect fiscal policy? And what role, if any, did intergovernmental grants play? Answers are in table 5.3, which essentially elaborates figure 5.1. The major source of 1970–74 general expenditure increase was clearly the mayor's preferences, weighted by his power:

Figure 5.1. Black Political Activities and Responsive Mayors Were Necessary to Increase Spending in 1970–74

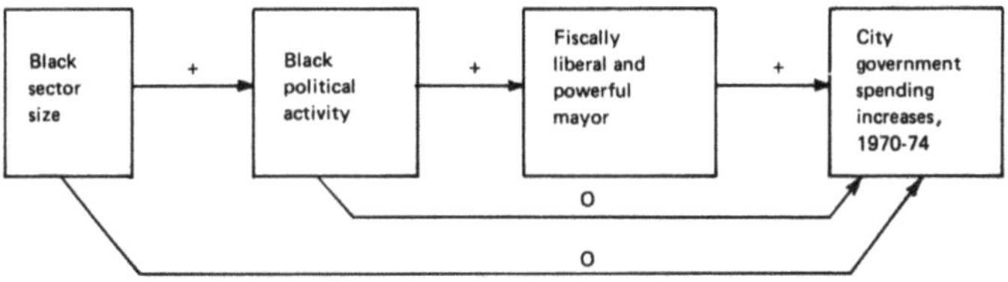

powerful mayors who wanted to spend more did just that.[19] There is no direct effect on general expenditure changes from either black sector size or three measures of black political activity. The fiscal impact of these black political processes thus came via elected leaders (see equations 1 and 2). Interestingly, black sector or political activity measures also have no direct effects on changes in intergovernmental revenue (equations 3 and 4). Again, only leaders' preferences are positively associated with increased intergovernmental revenue, while the percent Irish and size of the middle class depress intergovernmental revenues. Both index competing political processes.

One further and somewhat unexpected result is the insignificance of intergovernmental revenues in equations 1 and 2. This does not imply that federal and state funds were unimportant in increasing general expenditures, but that they in turn were sufficiently explained by the core variables that they had no independent impact. This illustrates a pattern elaborated in chapter 9: federal programs reinforced local processes, but did not create them.

That leaders did not react merely to black sector size supports the organized group argument of proposition 2 and chapter 4: interests must be organized to be effective.[20] Still, the relatively small number of blacks in office in the early 1970s, and responsiveness by white liberal mayors to blacks, suggests that many mayors—like John Lindsay, John Cavanaugh, and Ivan Allen—were ready to champion the black cause once convinced of its political viability. See Kotter and Lawrence (1974), Allen (1971), Ruchelman (1969). The Gary, Birmingham, and Atlanta cases in chapter 4 similarly illustrated dynamic mayors at work.

We can look back on these dramatic effects on fiscal policy, but

Table 5.3. Mayoral Preferences Explain Much of the Increase in General Expenditure and Intergovernmental Revenue, 1970-74

	Dependent Variables			
	Percent Change in General Expenditures, 1970-74		Percent Change in Intergovernmental Revenue, 1970-74	
Independent Variables	(1)	(2)	(3)	(4)
	LGXP7074		LIGRV704	
Sector Size				
Percent middle class (LPC70UMC)	-.25*	-.27*	-.35*	-.35*
Percent black (LPCBLK70)	-.15	X	-.21	X
Functional Performance (LFPDEC4)	-.03	-.03	.06	.11
Political Activity				
Unionization (LPEMP072)	.03	.0007	-.20	-.18
Riots (LRIOTSCR)	X	-.04	X	-.20
Black support for mayor (LBLAKSMY)	X	-.20	X	-.21
Racial and religious group support for mayor (LIMETHMY)	X	.06	X	.13
Leadership				
Mayor spending preferences X Mayor power (LRPNTALK)	.68*	.69*	.24*	.25*
Other				
Percent Irish (IRISHL70)	-.20	-.28	-.33*	-.41*
City Wealth Index (LNTWRT70)	-.05	.10	-.10	-.05
Percent changes in intergovernmental revenue, 1970-74 (LIGRV704)	-.05	-.08	X	X
Multiple R	.60	.61	.53	.58

Note: These are multiple regression results for the 62 PCS cities which show the standardized regression coefficients (betas) and an asterisk if the corresponding F statistic equals or exceeds 1.8 (significant at about the .10 level).

X = Variable not included in the regression (The percent black was excluded when black political activity measures were included to avoid multicollinearity).

Equations 2 and 4 include all three group activity measures to see if they might suppress the effects of leadership. They clearly do not as the leadership coefficients are virtually identical in the first two and last two equations.

should not underestimate difficulties of achieving them, even in cities with black chief executives. Three leading cases—Cleveland, Gary, and Newark—illustrate difficulties from white opposition, fiscal condition of the city, and jurisdictional limitations on service responsibility. In Cleveland, Stokes faced a hostile, white city council, and sought to avoid policies that would further polarize a racially divided city. Increasing public safety expenditures was a compromise acceptable to the council; crime and fire affect blacks and whites alike. In Newark, Mayor Kenneth Gibson also had a recalcitrant white council, and from the outset sought not to offend declining local businesses by disruptive tax increases. Local officials complain, but impacts of state constraints are hard to determine for these years. New Jersey and Indiana limit debt and expenditures more stringently than most states, and closely monitored fiscal activities in Newark and Gary. Newark's 1970 to 74 expenditure increase placed it just on the regression line for our PCS cities (figure 4.4), thus representing the national pattern. In Gary, after Hatcher had a majority on the council, he increased expenditures in areas chosen to help blacks, especially public housing. Gary thus placed well above the national average in figure 4.4. But Hatcher avoided burdening local taxpayers, thanks to his success in acquiring external aid, both private and governmental (Keller 1978). These mayors were also adept at giving old programs a new symbolic twist—"parks and recreation" became "youth services," etc.

Juristictional limitations precluded increases in most redistributive functions: welfare, health, and hospitals are seldom municipal responsibilities (see chapter 9). Black officials could thus infrequently affect these services of concern to many black citizens. Still, the range of services is not fixed. Indeed it relates to black political activity: cities providing more functions, including redistributive services, were more likely to have prospending mayors who depended on black support.[21] And Karnig and Welch (1980) found that cities with black mayors increased spending in the early 1970s on social services, especially education, but not other functions.[22] Over time these variables can reinforce one another—organized black citizens elect prospending mayors who expand social service functions, which in turn mobilize more citizens, etc. But not indefinitely.

Fiscal Retrenchment in the Late 1970s

Victories of the early 1970s were dramatic but brief; the late 1970s saw widespread retrenchment. Reductions were in specific services, personnel, and capital expenditures, as we saw in chapter 2, even though general expenditures kept growing in most cities. Cutbacks came in cities with large black populations and black mayors, even though black citizens in 1980 still felt government spending was too low. Why then were there cutbacks? We begin with more descriptive results, and then assemble the pieces in an explanation.

One might imagine from media coverage that cities with numerous black citizens were poorer, and thus cut back on spending more than other cities. But did they? Consider figure 5.2: across is percent of black residents in PCS cities, and down 1974 to 77 change in general expenditures. Cities with large black populations that cut back expenditures cluster in the lower right-hand corner. Gary is notable for its considerable absolute decrease, and Birmingham low, but Detroit, Atlanta, Baltimore, and Newark were about average. The simple relationship in the scattergram is obviously weak, and in multiple regressions insignificant.[23] The media image is thus correct for Gary, but generally incorrect: cities with numerous black citizens suffered no more and no less retrenchment than other U.S. cities in the late 1970s.

How about wealth? Again, less wealthy cities have been popularly portrayed as suffering greater retrenchment. Cities with more blacks are slightly less wealthy.[24] But the popular view is again wrong: wealth was unrelated to cutbacks in 1974–77 in the chapter 4 regressions. Another common view is that federal and state grant decreases caused local retrenchment. But as table 9.2 shows, intergovernmental revenues were insigificant in changing local general expenditures in 1974–77 (see also chapter 9).

If these widespread views are unsupported, what explains fiscal policy changes in the late 1970s in cities with large black populations? The basic result is that such cities increased overall spending at about the same rate as other U.S. cities. The contrast, of course, is with the situation a few years earlier. What led cities with numerous blacks to resemble other cities over the 1970s? What in particular happened to the black power indicators, so important early in the decade? Did force-

Figure 5.2. Black Sector Size and Fiscal Retrenchment Are Virtually Unrelated in the Late 1970s

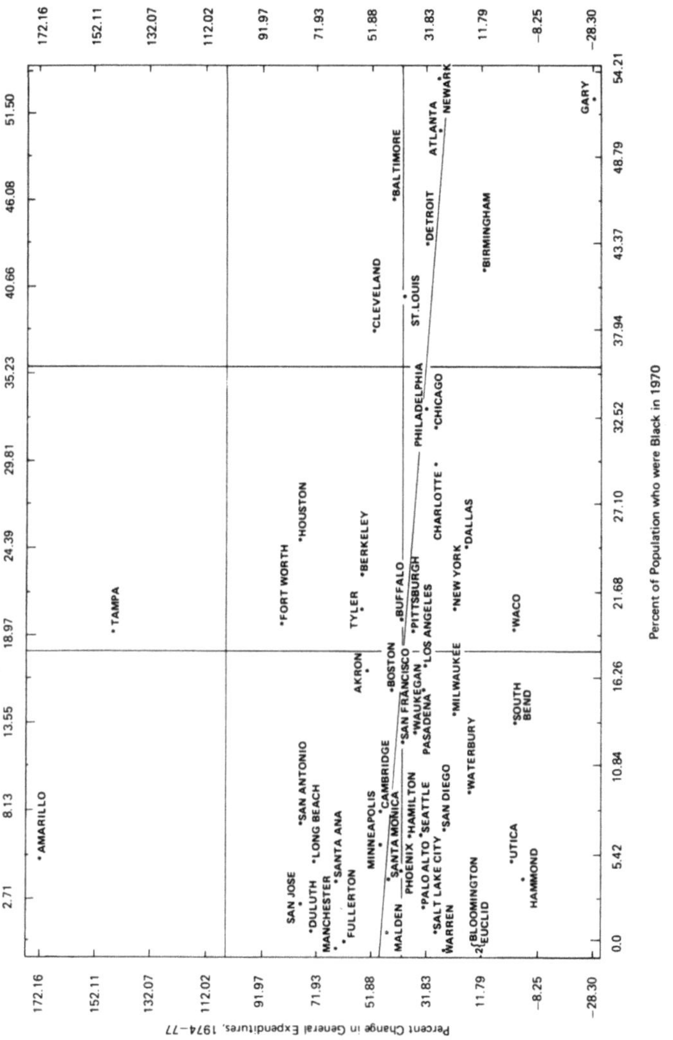

ful conservative mayors lead the way for their constituents? No. In the late 1970s, mayor's spending preferences had insignificant effects on spending. Black organized groups? They were either insignificant or negatively related to spending changes, i.e., cities that cut back more saw *more* group activities. These were probably protests by groups against cutbacks rather than, as earlier, causes of fiscal policy. The black power measures (leaders and organized groups) so important just a few years earlier thus fell to insignificance. Of course, cities with black leaders might shift expenditures across functions, or reallocate specific services within functions differently from other cities. But this was equally true in the early 1970s when their overall expenditures also increased dramatically. These regression results are striking, but useful to explore with other types of evidence.

If the comparative city results dramatically undercut most common explanations, what do some leading cases suggest about changes in political culture? Consider the four cities with more than 25 percent black population and black mayors in this period: Detroit, Atlanta, Newark, and Gary.[25]

Black mayors' constituencies changed over the 1970s. When Richard Hatcher was elected in 1967, he depended heavily on middle and low income black voters. White support was limited to civil rights activitists and some upper-income Jews (Nelson and Meranto 1977:217). He initially worked with civil rights organizations to mobilize black voters, with great success. Gary had long been dominated by a political machine, with patronage and ward organizations accepted traditions as in nearby Chicago. Since the Democratic party remained a powerful threat at the county level, in his early years Hatcher devoted considerable energy and resources to building his own political organization. He helped keep the city calm; Gary was never rent by severe racial disturbances such as troubled Newark and Detroit. Tension among black and white citizens remained relatively low compared to these two other cities (Rossi et al. 1974:59–66). Hatcher worked hard for his poor black constituents in the early 1970s, dramatically raising funds for social services (chapter 4). He was thus a dynamic leader in providing more fiscally liberal politics than the majority of Gary citizens probably favored, but such programs were important, both to build a personal organization and to respond to organized group leaders who helped elect him. After several terms in office, Richard Hatcher was one of the most respected black leaders in America, and within Gary, black power an established tradition. He could thus afford to broaden his electoral base and still retain the loyalty of poorer voters. Cutbacks were reinforced by a freeze on property taxes imposed by the state of Indiana in 1973, but Gary's reductions considerably surpassed those of other Indiana cities. Relations had long been strained with U.S. Steel, Gary's largest employer, and many local merchants and white citizens left the city. Over the 1970s, Hatcher grew increasingly concerned to adapt to an economic base which could erode further if taxes kept rising. Spending was thus trimmed in many areas in the late 1970s, although Gary, like Newark, received particularly generous CETA allocations and hired large numbers of temporary employees at low wages, policies prevented by unions in many other cities.

Ken Gibson in Newark, Maynard Jackson in Atlanta, and Coleman Young in Detroit were also the first black mayors of their cities, but they came to office after the most bitter racial disorders, in 1970, 1973, and 1974 respectively. They were thus less associated with the militancy and riots of the late 1960s, and acted more as peacemakers, seeking to "get their cities moving again." While Newark had a political organization before Gibson, Detroit and Atlanta had been governed by more shifting coalitions. All three mayors followed leadership styles that involved coalition building with whites; they were less pure examples of the political culture of black power than Hatcher had been.

Business groups were also traditionally important in Atlanta and Detroit, and Mayors Jackson and Young worked effectively with them. Young gained support of the "New Detroiters," an urban coalition of blacks, business, and labor leaders including Henry Ford and Leonard Woodcock. He arranged huge fiscal support programs from Washington in the Carter years for the Chrysler Corporation and a new General Motors plant that brought him considerable national attention. A senior statesman with such business leaders and in Washington, Young could also be street-tough enough to recall his background as union organizer. This combination of personal traits and public policies helped him head off more fiscally liberal contenders for the mayorship. Gibson also maintained a coalition with leaders from major banking and insurance industries. From the outset, Young and Gibson sought to further economic development and basic services, playing down more redistributive social services. Still, hiring blacks in city agencies remained a major commitment, even if it generated conflict with white municipal employees (Woody 1975, 1981). Unions were strong in Detroit and Newark, however, and both Young and Gibson generally sought to work with them, at least through most of the 1970s.

Maynard Jackson similarly worked with business leaders, but inherited neither a political machine as in Gary nor such powerful unions as in Detroit or Newark. Elected in 1973 with 59 percent of the vote, Jackson won nine to one in most black precincts, but also captured 20 percent of the white vote. Considered a moderate, he claimed support from many constituencies including municipal employees. When he ran again in 1977, however, the Atlanta branch of the American Federation of State, County, and Municipal Employees (AFSCME) openly opposed him. The union took out radio and newspaper advertisements stridently criticizing Jackson; sanitation workers then went on strike. He chose to tilt policies toward the middle class electorate, white and black, rather than respond to employees. And unlike Detroit, where organized labor was powerful and symbolically important for Young, the former labor leader, Jackson's personal background and the antipathy of many Atlanta citizens toward unions, led him to take the offensive. He insisted that funds were insufficient to meet union demands and dismissed over 1,000 largely black, striking employees. He was returned to office and continued moderate spending policies.

The Declining Significance of Black Power?

What does this lead us to conclude about black power? Consider the basic components of political culture: citizens, organized groups, political leaders, and resources joining them. While many black leaders came to office with support from black organized groups, such groups declined over the 1970s. Civil rights organizations lost much of their membership and support, nationally and in city politics. Spending increases were initially important to symbolize victory in new programs for blacks, to build personal campaign organizations, and to implement affirmative action. But as the comparative city data indicated, these distinctive increases disappeared by the late 1970s.

As organized groups became less critical,leaders appealed to broader electoral constituencies, including whites as well as middle class blacks, who were less visibly united with poor blacks than a few years earlier. This appeal to individual citizens often meant a decline in racial saliency. Debates emerged about the black middle class, its rapid economic gains, materialistic life style, and waning civic involvement. While many blacks remained poor, poverty seems to have declined through the 1970s, and many blacks are following patterns of economic advancement and political integration into the middle class similar to white ethnic groups, although debate on this continues (e.g., Wilson 1978; Patterson 1977; Farley 1977; Katzman and Childs 1979; Sowell 1978). As black leaders grew less visibly militant, whites grew less concerned about leaders' racial identity. Mayors Gibson in Newark and Bradley in Los Angeles could thus become serious contenders for governorships of their states by the early 1980s.

Political resources and public policies similarly shifted. Jobs became harder to create for supporters, and conflicted with other policy goals. The national economy was less buoyant and local economies sometimes seriously in decline, as in Detroit or Gary. While other cities also lost jobs and population, the trends held greater ethnic significance in cities where blacks recently came to power. The wars on poverty fell short of their ambitious goals, but funded jobs for minorities in city governments (via OEO, Model Cities, CETA, and other programs). These hiring policies were often resisted by unions and senior municipal employees. In the late 1970s retrenchment, senior employees clashed with recently hired blacks and Hispanics in Detroit, Atlanta, Newark, and other cities. The rule of "last hired, first fired" often meant that minority employees decreased as a proportion of city work forces.[26]

Nationally, the New Deal coalition of liberals, labor, and blacks fragmented after the 1960s. Problems of fiscal austerity were thus compounded for blacks by loss of past political allies. To a degree that seems unappreciated at the time, the great advances for blacks in the late 1960s and early 1970s depended on support from prospending Democrats. State and federal allies created generous grant programs, and channeled them to appreciative local officials.

President Carter upset traditional Democrats with his New Fiscal Populist leanings, while President Reagan came to office on a clear Republican program of reducing taxes. Congress and state houses similarly shifted toward fiscal conservatism with more Republicans and New Fiscal Populists, and fewer New Deal Democrats of the Teddy Kennedy variety. "Coalition politics" became a common slogan among black leaders to refer to combining black concerns with those of others. But with the Democratic party and national black organizations in decline, it was harder for individual black leaders to join with one another or other leaders. Coalitions were more fragile, short lived, and ad hoc than in the past. If black citizen preferences did not fundamentally shift, their articulation by public leaders became decidedly more pluralistic. Some blacks point to this as a sign of political maturity—who speaks for whites, as a group, is their rhetorical question. The late 1970s were years of ideological reexamination and questioning for Americans, black and white. At least some black leaders moved toward the New Fiscal Populist position with its distinctive governance problems. Many leaders remained fiscally liberal in principle, but felt pressured toward more conservative policies by forces like the taxpayers' revolt (black leaders grew even more fiscally conservative than their white counterparts by 1976—see table 7.2). As Kenneth Gibson put it, his solution to fiscal problems was "not living beyond your means" (Woody 1981).

In terms of political culture, over the 1970s: 1) black organized groups declined in salience; 2) citizens grew more important for policy input and political bases of black leaders often expanded to include more whites; 3) race declined as a political issue, and when it continued was invoked in less militant style; 4) local and national pressures constrained revenues to city governments, and in particular limited jobs and similar separable good resources for supporters; it thus was more important to stress the public good of lower taxes to citizens who would turn out for candidates responsive to such issues; 5) more conservative fiscal policies were the result. But recall that these changes occurred simultaneously with dramatic increases in numbers of black elected officials. By the early 1980s, however, the charisma of political victory had faded. Black leaders increasingly resembled their white counterparts, as they confronted, day-by-day, the harsh problems of meeting constituents' demands with limited means. As blacks grew more politically important, black power declined as a political culture.

CHAPTER SIX

Democrats and Municipal Employees: The End of the Liberal-Labor Coalition

New Deal Democrats are one of our four basic political cultures, distinguished by fiscal liberalism concerning government programs, social liberalism in favoring the disadvantaged and minorities, and emphasis on organized groups rather than individual citizens as sources of policy input. Republicans differ on all four points. We elsewhere analyze individuals, but here consider characteristics of cities where Democratic and Republican parties are respectively powerful. Those with powerful Democratic parties are more likely to have powerful labor unions, ethnic and religious groups, and municipal employees, but weaker chambers of commerce (table 6.1). Further, mayors have held office longer and are more often Catholics. Irish residents are more numerous as are private school students (associated with Catholicism); so are blacks and lower income residents. These correlations capture basic patterns, but many are low, underlining diversity within the parties and within many cities. And the power measures are from 1967; relations are less clear in later years. For this reason we have generally not used Democratic or Republican party power measures at the city level, but instead analyzed specific components critical for fiscal policy, like municipal employee power.

Our four political cultures distinguish ethnic politicians from New Deal Democrats. This distinction is important for labor since it was linked to strains within the Democratic party which mounted over the

Thomas E. Panelas is coauthor of this chapter.

Table 6.1. Democratic and Republican Dominated Cities Differ Somewhat

	Democratic Party Powerful	Republican Party Powerful
	IMDEM	IMREP
Labor unions (private and public sector) powerful	.46	.32
Ethnic and religious groups powerful	.23	.11
City and county employees powerful	.22	.10
Chamber of Commerce powerful	-.07	.20
Number of years mayor in office	.40	.08
Mayor is Catholic	.23	.10
Percentage foreign stock residents	.38	.31
Percentage Irish residents	.33	.19
Percent students attending private schools	.57	.26
Percentage black residents	.07	-.32
Median family income	-.04	.21

Note: Democratic, Republican, and other power measures shown here are closed-end reputational power (CERP) items from the 1967 PCS survey discussed in appendix 1.D.

These are simple r's (Pearson correlation coefficients) for the 62 PCS cities. If $r \geq .21$, $p \leq .10$; if $r \geq .32$, $p \leq .01$.

1970s. One might consider ethnic politicians a Democratic subtype, but they distinctively emphasize ethnicity. Reform Democrats decry such emphasis. Reform and traditional Democrats have long differed on ethnic salience as well as on the use of public goods. Reform Democrats are more committed to abstract, general policies which promote "the public interest," like environmental protection, metropolitan government, and mass transit systems. More highly educated, Protestant and Jewish, they appeal to humanity and social justice. Followers of Adlai Stevenson and (former Republican) John Lindsay have thus disagreed with the Richard Daleys and Abraham Beames, who are more tolerant of mingling ethnicity with politics, and use separable goods to reward specific ethnic groups, neighborhoods, and individuals. Similarly, while Democrats generally view organized groups as providing more legitimate inputs to the political system than do individual citizens, traditional Democrats emphasize organizations more than reformers, although reformers are not as responsive to citizens as New Fiscal Populists. Traditional and reform Democrats have most often joined on state and national candidates and issues where both favored matters like expansive social programs, pollution controls on private firms, and federal subsidies for housing and mass transit. However, in local politics, the two wings more often separate in part because of traditional Democrats' use of patronage and other policies distasteful to reformers. Similarly, while federal and state governments approve general programs, implementing them locally often generates zero-sum conflicts. Jobs and contracts quietly provided to loyal traditional Democrats might be tolerated by reformers. But publicized "corruption," such as exchanging favors for campaign contributions, can break the coalition apart. Compromises are also easier to accept at federal or state levels as they often involve "other people's money"; local costs are scrutinized more carefully and tensions erupt more easily (see Peterson 1981). The two wings often formed a liberal-labor coalition from FDR through LBJ, but split at the Chicago Democratic convention in 1968 where Richard Daley and company defeated the reformers to nominate Hubert Humphrey. But anti-Vietnam demonstrations, women's liberation, and counterculture movements mobilized enough reformers behind George McGovern to win the 1972 presidential nomination.

The Republican party suffered after 1968 from identification with Richard Nixon and the Vietnam war; the scandal of Watergate and subsequent investigations led many would-be Republicans to remain Independents. The party itself had been dominated by the more ideologically committed since the 1964 Goldwater nomination. It was still internally divided between coalitionists and the ideologically committed. Coalitionists included Presidents Nixon and Ford and many upper status persons in the Northeast. While this was the traditional base of the party, Democratic gains here led some to advocate a "Southern strategy" appealing to white southerners. To compete with George Wallace in the late 1960s, Republicans emphasized conservative positions on social as well as fiscal issues, and picked up votes in the South. The West was the strongest Republican area, where an ideological commitment to individual liberty was reinforced by the frontier, vast land areas, and rapid development. After the 1964 Goldwater nomination, many party activists, led from the West, grew more ideological.

Nationally, numerous middle and working class persons grew disenchanted with Democratic leadership in the McGovern era, yet were reluctant to vote for an ideological Republican. Union members in particular fell in this category.

Activists in both parties were absorbed with ideological issues removed from many citizens. In the early 1970s young activist "reformers" attacked party structures and seniority from the Presidency to city councils. Campaign contributions were limited in size and disclosure required, seniority in Congressional committees was abolished, etc. Like the reform movement near the turn of the century, the 1970s reformers weakened the parties. "Special interest groups" then became more important vehicles of policy pressure as the parties could no longer coordinate them. The lib-lab coalition disintegrated as labor groups split from the more ideological reformers and from organized groups like blacks and women who alleged discrimination in union hiring practices. Chapter 4 showed that cities where nonpoor organized groups were more active increased expenditures in 1974–77. These special interest groups are so diverse that looking at a few more closely helps unravel their dynamics. Of the major subgroups that split off from the lib-lab coalition, we treated white and black ethnic groups in the last chapter, and discuss reformers who became New Fiscal Populists in the next. The remainder of this chapter considers municipal employees as the labor group most important for urban fiscal policy.

Municipal Employees

Municipal employees are expensive. They are the largest item in most city budgets, comprising about half of total (general) expenditures. This chapter asks how municipal employees affect expenditures on themselves, and if they affect fiscal strain. The theoretical framework in chapter 1 leads to some basic propositions: in cities where employees are numerous and well organized, they should be more politically active and have more impact on political leaders, who in turn should implement policies responsive to them.[1] What are such "responsive" policies? One measure appealing for its comprehensiveness is per capita expenditures on municipal employees (labeled "personal services" by the Census). New York City tops our 62 cities on this measure, spending $732 in 1977, while Gary, Indiana, was lowest at $89.

Do cities with more organized and politically active employees spend more on personal services? Seasoned *New York Times* readers may smile at the question since the answer appears so obvious. Yet the surprising result is that there is simply no relationship. This negative finding has not to our knowledge been explicitly recognized or addressed heretofore. Yet if municipal employees do not increase personal service expenditures or city fiscal strain, they do affect other policies. Policy makers and researchers should redirect their attention to policies of greater concern to employees, and be more conscious of choices involved. Three components are important to distinguish, which together comprise per capita personal services expenditures, shown in the simple equation:

$$PSCA = CN/P \qquad (1)$$

where

$PSCA$ = personal services per capita
C = compensation (wages and paid benefits) per employee
N = number of municipal employees
P = city population

The three components are important to separate since their causes are distinct. Population is the most general, considered in chapter 3. Compensation and number of municipal employees are important outputs of city government and the major variables analyzed in this chapter.

Employee-related processes are central to the chapter, but we also analyze general processes using the core model. Results underline the distinctiveness of the two sets of processes. One involves political influence by municipal employees themselves. Cities performing more functions have more organized and politically active employees; these in turn encourage proemployee attitudes of elected officials. Employee compensation increased most in such locations from 1960 to 1974. These results appear as solid lines in figure 6.1.

Second are more general political processes. Cities with larger mid-

Figure 6.1. Basic Results of Municipal Employee Analysis

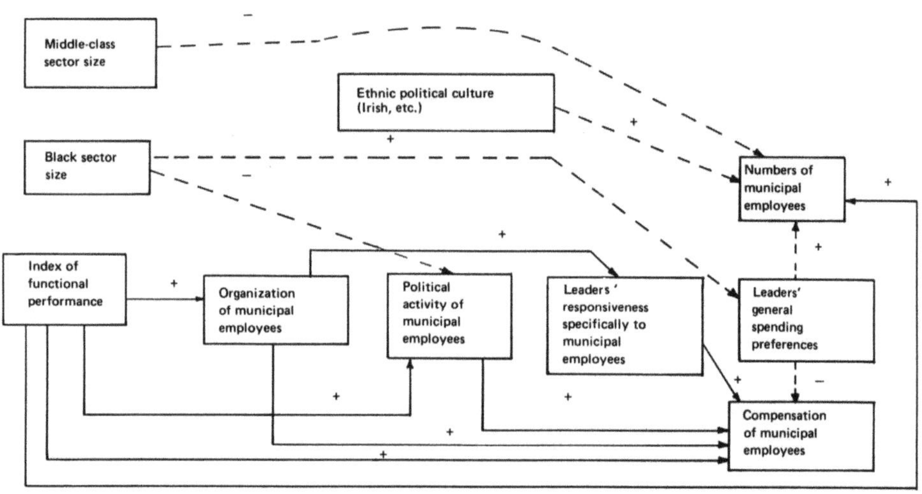

Note: The figure shows two sorts of influences:

——→ = Municipal employee influence

— — → = Broader political influence

These general results vary somewhat by time period.

dle classes have fewer municipal employees. But cities with more politically active blacks have leaders who favored more services and who in turn increased city work forces, while holding down compensation. Activities of blacks in the late 1960s were similar in their effects to earlier political dynamics involving Irish, foreign stock, and Democratic leaders. Cities with ethnic and traditional Democratic political cultures built up the number of municipal employees. This second set of processes is indicated by dotted lines in figure 6.1.

The distinction between the two patterns of influence has important implications for fiscal strain. Organized municipal employees are powerful enough to increase compensation, but as they often are willing to trade off compensation against numbers of employees, they do not drive up total expenditures. At least in this sense they do not increase fiscal strain. This negative result is important. Municipal employees are often blamed for urban fiscal difficulties. Our measures do not capture all political activities of municipal employees, or all their costs to cities. But the measures are more inclusive than those in most studies to date. That we find no relationship between municipal employee activity measures and personal services expenditures suggests that employees are not powerful enough to determine overall spending, but does not imply that they are powerless in policies affecting them. The result shifts attention to specific policies of concern to employees: their compensation and numbers. These, rather than total personal services expenditures, are the chapter's two basic dependent variables.

Most analyses in this chapter were completed for the three periods and 1977 level measures as in chapter 4. The core model was used with occasional variables added. While the three periods were important for the general political processes (dotted lines in figure 6.1), the municipal employee processes (solid lines) did not differ in the first two periods. Most of this chapter thus considers 1960–74 as one period. But the 1974–77 period remains the same as in chapter 4. The chapter considers in turn the basic municipal employee processes, moving from left to right in figure 6.1.

Organization of Municipal Employees

Various professional associations existed for decades, but large scale organization, unions, and collective bargaining of municipal employees were distinctive to the 1960s and 1970s. Long time series are unavailable for municipal employees alone, but for federal, state, and local employees combined, the percentage unionized rose from 12 in 1956 to 20 in 1976. An equal number were members of "associations" performing many union functions, including labor negotiations, so that 39 percent of all public sector workers were thus "organized" by 1976 (see Burton 1979). This trend contrasts markedly with declines in unionization for all private sector nonagricultural workers, from 33 percent in 1956 to 24 in 1976. Many observers have speculated on these trends. The public sector grew faster than the private sector in these years, and some argue that government workers were a major force behind its growth. Others see public employees as rote bureaucrats who essentially do what they did last year, with an incrementally larger budget.[2] Certainly municipal employee styles shifted over this period: the detached civil servant ideal often yielded to that of the self-interested worker, or so it seems (see Nisbet, Mansfield, and Wheeler in Chickering 1976). Such styles changed with the organization of employees.

The national diffusion of municipal employee organization resembled other social movements. Just as national civil rights groups helped organize blacks, national unions and associations guided organization of municipal employees. Some workers were literally unorganized in the early 1960s, but many belonged to professional associations, some local, others national like the Fraternal Order of Police or the National Education Association. Unions, strikes, and collective bargaining were traditionally taboo in the public sector. This changed with the drives of aggressive national unions in the 1960s, both to enlist unorganized workers and to affiliate with independent locals. Pacesetters were the American Federation of State, County, and Municipal Employees (AFSCME) and the American Federation of Teachers (AFT). Fierce competition developed as the national organizations often sought to enlist the same workers. "Raiding" territory staked out by others was common. AFSCME, for example, even had to contend with frequent incursions by fellow AFL-CIO unions, particularly the Service Employees International Union (SEIU), which it fought bitterly in San Diego and Gary (Spero and Capozzola 1973:31–32).

Against this backdrop of escalated unionization, many states passed laws to permit unions to negotiate and sign contracts with local governments. Professional organizers heavily influenced organizing tactics. Fledgling unions often used demonstrations of strength to show new members and city officials that they were fighting for the worker's interests. This coincided in the late 1960s with increasing use of direct action tactics by blacks, by students on college campuses, and dramatized media coverage—strikes and protests make ideal television material. All reinforced the sense of a national social movement. An example duplicated in many (especially Democratic) cities comes from one day's events for Mayor Ivan Allen of Atlanta in 1966:

> At City Hall on the afternoon of Sept. 6, Allen was beset by a series of crises that seemed to summarize the worst problems of all big-city mayors. Firemen

were on strike for more money [a dissident local union, apparently supported by the Teamsters, was seeking to win members away from the AFL-CIO-affiliated International Association of Fire Fighters]. The firemen's pickets and antiwar pickets were crossing paths at City Hall. A walkout of carpenters had halted major construction throughout the city. Aldermen were in session wrestling with the necessity of raising taxes $4 million a year for the lackluster business of building sewers. Then, late in the afternoon, word came that a riot had started at Capitol and Ormond Avenues. . . . It occupied all of Mayor Allen's time until late in the night. . . . Characteristically, he walked the streets attempting to cool the situation. . . . While a one-story frame building had been burned, there had been no looting and no one had been shot by the police. (Phillips 1977:3:33, includes quotation from Cleghorn)

Gradual institutionalization of public sector labor relations in the 1970s reduced internecine feuds among organizations. Most noteworthy was granting exclusive recognition as bargaining agent to the one organization enlisting the majority of employees. The government then bargains only with the organization with exclusive recognition, even if some employees belong to minority organizations. This practice, and nonaggression pacts between rival unions, discouraged raiding (Spero and Capozzola 1973; Stieber 1973).

The rise of municipal employees as an organized group is recorded in membership growth. Another sign is increased direct action tactics, especially strikes. Strikes rose dramatically in 1966 and stayed at a new plateau from 1970 until 1975 when they jumped to their highest point (table 6.2.). These periods parallel the three in chapter 4: the late 1960s disruptions were part of unionization, exacerbated by political instability in many cities, while 1975 saw the onset of retrenchment, often marked by conflict between political leaders and employees.[3]

The degree of organization has attracted more attention than other aspects of employees. Some distinctive points emerge from comparison with the private sector, as it served as a guide for most public employee organizers (Perry 1979). Introducing organized conflict via collective bargaining has troubled many observers concerned with public sector distinctiveness. They often invoked an earlier model: that of the impartial civil servant. With the turn of the century reform movement, civil service boards were established to remove political pressures on employees, encouraging hiring and promotion on purely professional grounds. This often meant strong emphasis on seniority, plus job se-

Table 6.2. Work Stoppages in Local Government, 1958-1980

Year	Number	Workers Involved (in thousands)
1958	14	1.7
1959	21	1.6
1960	33	27.6
1961	28	6.6
1962	21	25.3
1963	27	4.6
1964	37	22.5
1965	42	11.9
1966	133	102.0
1967	169	127.0
1968	235	190.9
1969	372	139.0
1970	386	168.9
1971	304	137.1
1972	335	114.7
1973	357	183.7
1974	348	135.4
1975	446	252.0
1976	352	146.8
1977	367	136.2
1978	435	171.0
1979	536	205.5
1980	493	212.7

Source: U.S. Bureau of Labor Statistics, Work Stoppages in Government, 1976; and Analysis of Work Stoppages, for data on 1977 to 1980.

curity provided by review boards that discouraged layoffs. Such employee protections did not exist in the private sector. Thus when unions were added to existing civil service systems, the result was still further weakening of management.

Another difference between city governments and many private firms is that union organization reaches high up in the administration of many cities. Only the department head and a few assistants are not organized in some city departments. Many department heads thus understandably avoid the role of "bad guy" and support staff pressures for higher wages. This forces decisions up to general city administrators. Yet if work conditions also enter collective bargaining, department heads lose management prerogatives. As general city officials do not know departments as well as their heads, task-specific leadership is weakened (Lewin, Horton, and Kuhn 1979). The net result is often increased compensation and decreased productivity (see Edwards and Edwards 1980). Available data do not specify levels, but the percentage of all employees organized; the two are probably associated.

In cities like Dallas or Tampa, general public opposition discouraged unions. In many others political leaders sensed that citizens did not much care, while militant employees did. Yet leaders perceived that citizens cared about basic services, and thus sought not to interrupt them with strikes (see Wellington and Winter 1971; Stanley 1972). Many leaders in the late 1960s feared that strikes would reflect more on them than the workers; unions thus organized and extracted benefits often by only threatening to strike. This changed by the late 1970s when leaders were more willing to accept strikes. The long San Francisco strikes in 1975 and 1976 marked a national turning point. The mayor and other leaders opposed the unions, campaigned, and won on the issue; citizens thus voted in a manner foreshadowing Proposition 13 (see Katz 1979a). In Seattle, Mayor Wes Uhlman (1976) overcame a recall vote two to one after a confrontation with firefighters. The late 1970s saw many similar developments, such as in Atlanta and San Antonio where entire city departments were fired. Some local officials and union leaders commented that they no longer sensed that "the public" would accept compensation increases but not service interruptions. Still, several surveys suggest that citizens changed their views less than political leaders changed their tactics.[4]

How does the degree of employee organization affect city policies? Since the 1960s the International City Management Association and Bureau of Labor Statistics have conducted several one-time surveys of labor organization which we and others have used. However the best data date from 1972, when the U.S. Census initiated annual surveys of employee organization, which we analyze here. The Census collects data on two aspects of labor-management relations. One is the type of negotiations. For example, in 1976, 62 percent of our sample cities had collective negotiations, 22 percent engaged only in meet and confer discussions, while 17 percent had neither. Similarly, 53 percent had at least one contractual agreement, 22 percent had memoranda of understanding but no formal contracts, and 25 percent had no contracts of any kind.[5] Some studies have used such measures, but we found them less significant than a second type of measure, the percentage of all city government employees organized, shown for our PCS cities for 1972 and 1976 in table 6.3.[6] The average increased from 55 to 61 percent in these years, although by no means consistently. Many were stable or increased, but 23 cities decreased, like San Francisco from 95 to 79 percent organized. Fluctuations indicate the fluid character of organizing activities in these years as well as tactics and personalities: a mayor who appears calm but firm, yet genuinely responsive to employees, is less likely to encourage unionization and conflict than one seen as dogmatic or arbitrary. To buffer the labor-management process from personality conflicts, most observers suggest retaining a negotiations expert. Costs are low compared to those of a poorly negotiated settlement.

The Sources of Organization

Why are employees organized and politically active in some cities, yet inactive in others? The percentage organized was analyzed using the core model. Consistent with our chapter 1 propositions, sector size was significant in that cities performing more functions had more employees organized (see section A, table 6.4).[7] The FP Index was the principal source of organization in several alternative specifications. The rationale seems to be that having more functions implies more potential members, larger city budgets, easier communication among workers (than if some worked for separate local governments), a greater sense of potential power for employees, as well as a more attractive setting for national unions (see Liebert 1976; Clark 1974b). Most other variables were insignificant or are discussed below.[8]

Political Activities of Municipal Employees

Municipal employees are sometimes major participants in city politics. They are usually most active on issues directly affecting them, especially compensation and working conditions, but in some cities also campaign for mayors and council candidates. They can be critical

Table 6.3. Cities Differ Considerably in the Percentage or municipal Employees Organized

Cities	Percentage of Municipal Employees Organized in 1976	Percentage of Municipal Employees Organized in 1972	Cities	Percentage of Municipal Employees Organized in 1976	Percentage of Municipal Employees Organized in 1972
	PCEMPO76	PCEMPO72		PCEMPO76	PCEMPO72
1. Akron, OH	77	87	33. Memphis, TN	55	54
2. Albany, NY	26	22	34. Milwaukee, WI	85	82
3. Amarillo, TX	28	39	35. Minneapolis, MN	100	49
4. Atlanta, GA	19	31	36. New York, NY	78	90
5. Baltimore, MD	53	67	37. Newark, NJ	56	39
6. Berkeley, CA	60	67	38. Palo Alto, CA	76	33
7. Birmingham, AL	73	48	39. Pasadena, CA	68	84
8. Bloomington, MN	33	34	40. Philadelphia, PA	76	76
9. Boston, MA	91	87	41. Phoenix, AZ	44	48
10. Buffalo, NY	82	86	42. Pittsburgh, PA	66	57
11. Cambridge, MA	78	49	43. St. Louis, MO	52	27
12. Charlotte, NC	17	20	44. St. Paul, MN	92	82
13. Chicago, IL	34	33	45. St. Petersburg, FL	60	40
14. Cleveland, OH	84	56	46. Salt Lake City, UT	57	63
15. Clifton, NJ	--	--	47. San Antonio, TX	46	41
16. Dallas, TX	0	30	48. San Diego, CA	72	71
17. Detroit, MI	87	85	49. San Francisco, CA	79	95
18. Duluth, MN	73	54	50. Santa Ana, CA	73	77
19. Euclid, OH	53	69	51. San Jose, CA	93	71
20. Fort Worth, TX	39	0	52. Santa Monica, CA	66	36
21. Fullerton, CA	--	93	53. Schenectady, NY	89	71
22. Gary, IN	42	53	54. Seattle, WA	73	65
23. Hamilton, OH	56	47	55. South Bend, IN	32	45
24. Hammond, IN	65	35	56. Tampa, FL	20	23
25. Houston, TX	80	65	57. Tyler, TX	18	17
26. Indianapolis, IN	48	38	58. Utica, NY	70	88
27. Irvington, NJ	69	78	59. Waco, TX	25	27
28. Jacksonville, FL	82	40	60. Warren, MI	--	--
29. Long Beach, CA	84	89	61. Waterbury, CT	98	56
30. Los Angeles, CA	77	76	62. Waukegan, IL	44	20
31. Malden, MA	80	64			
32. Manchester, NH	62	70	MEAN	60	55

-- indicates data not available.

Table 6.4. Sources of Municipal Employee Organization and Political Activities

Independent Variables	Dependent Variables A Percentage of Municipal Employees Organized	 B Political Activities of Municipal Employees	 C Responsiveness of Mayor and Council Members
	LPEMPO72	LPAME	LLME76
Index of Functional Performance (LFPDEC4)	.46*	.51*	-.09
Percentage Irish stock residents (IRISHL70)	.05	.14	.17
Size of middle class sector (LPC70UMC)	.18	-.02	.05
Size of black sector (LPCBLK70)	-.16	-.33*	-.14
Leaders' spending preferences, 1967 (LRPNTALK)	-.19		
Leaders' spending preferences, 1976 (LLEAD3W2)		-.17	.45*
Organization of municipal employees (LPEMPO76)		-.10	.26*
City Wealth Index (LNTWRT70)	.09	-.11	.07
Multiple R	.49	.59	.57

Note: These are multiple regression results for the 62 PCS cities which show the standardized regression coefficients (betas) and an asterisk if the corresponding F statistic equals or exceeds 1.8 (significant at about the .10 level). Independent variables comprise the core model (see chapter 4 and appendix 2).

when turnout is low. Several case studies report municipal employees as the preponderant force in some issues (see Rubin 1979; Horton 1973; Spero and Capozzola 1973). They reputedly helped increase black voter turnout from 38 to 55 percent in Philadelphia in 1973 (Schick and Couturier 1977:51). Our 1976 PCS survey asked mayors and council members to list the groups "most active in government affairs"; unions or public employee associations were frequently mentioned (table 7.3). The leader was then asked how often they contacted him, or he contacted them.[9] Such frequency of contacts constituted our political activities measure. Municipal employees were more politically active in cities performing more functions (see section B of table 6.4), and in cities with fewer blacks, countering the view that blacks and labor united as New Deal Democrats. If some blacks and unions cooperated nationally in the 1960s, the situation was more complex locally.

Responsive Political Leaders

Political leaders are visibly "antiunion" in some cities, but in others work closely with union leaders, most obviously when a mayor or council member is a former city employee—like Mayors Frank Rizzo of Philadelphia or Abraham Beame of New York. Such variations in political leaders make it misleading to consider them simply "management" and ipso facto opposed to "labor." If a labor-management perspective is appropriate for some cities (see Kochan and Wheeler 1975), in others leaders are so responsive to employees that labor practically is management. To capture such variations in leaders' responsiveness to employees, we asked mayors and council members to "indicate your own preferences [concerning] the development of public employee unions. 1) I oppose this policy; 2) I am neutral about this policy; 3) I support this policy."[10] A city-level average was computed and its sources analyzed (section C of table 6.4). Leaders were more responsive in cities where a higher percentage of employees was organized (although the causal arrow can run both ways here). Leaders favoring more spending for city services were also more responsive to employees.[11]

In general, cities with more foreign stock and Irish residents, more

Democratic voters, and "unreformed" governments also had more organized and politically active municipal employees, with leaders more responsive to them. These political cultural characteristics were associated with the core variables, suppressing some regression results below significance. This was also true of a cost of living measure (results not shown). A larger sample might raise these to normal significance levels. We consider next how the three measures just analyzed—organization and political activities of municipal employees, and responsiveness of leaders—relate in turn to compensation and numbers of employees.

Compensation for Municipal Employees: Variations and Sources

Our compensation measure takes total annual expenditure for wages, overtime, and paid fringe benefits, and divides it by the number of municipal employees (full time equivalents) to generate average annual compensation per employee. Levels vary substantially from Palo Alto's high of $21,907 (in 1977) to Gary's low of $6,208. Growth continued over most of the 1960–74 period, but after 1974 some cities began to reduce numbers and compensation (table 6.5).[12]

An interesting literature has developed on correlates of compensation, largely by urban and labor economists.[13] Like most other studies, we use a national sample of cities analyzed using multiple regression. But two important differences distinguish our study from most others. Past studies usually compare compensation levels cross-sectionally across cities at one time, while we study both compensation levels and changes. Second, we include specifically political measures. These two additions provide a more complete view of the processes at work. Still, to avoid differences just from model specification, we include most important variables from past research.

Results for 1977 compensation levels directly parallel past studies: more organized employees and higher opportunity wages both increase compensation (table 6.6).[14] Compensation is also higher where leaders are more responsive to employees. For compensation changes in 1960 to 74, opportunity wages fall just below, and city wealth moves just above significance.[15] Leaders' spending preferences were also impor-

Table 6.5. Compensation Levels Per Municipal Employee in 1977 and Percentage Changes from 1960 to 1974 and 1974 to 1977

Cities	Percentage Change in Compensation 1960-74	Percentage Change in Compensation 1974-77	Average Annual Compensation per Municipal Employee in 1977	Cities	Percentage Change in Compensation 1960-74	Percentage Change in Compensation 1974-77	Average Annual Compensation per Municipal Employee in 1977
	PSME6074	PSME7477	PSPEMP77		PSME6074	PSME7477	PSPEMP77
1. Akron, OH	126	14	$13409	33. Memphis, TN	126	7	$ 9132
2. Albany, NY	--	--	6557	34. Milwaukee, WI	100	14	13258
3. Amarillo, TX	78	102	14769	35. Minneapolis, MN	99	30	15523
4. Atlanta, GA	153	17	11668	36. New York, NY	170	15	17636
5. Baltimore, MD	118	26	12950	37. Newark, NJ	109	-3	11002
6. Berkeley, CA	100	15	15202	38. Palo Alto, CA	144	44	21907
7. Birmingham, AL	70	38	10061	39. Pasadena, CA	112	47	18910
8. Bloomington, MN	71	35	15994	40. Philadelphia, PA	151	11	13066
9. Boston, MA	143	28	16435	41. Phoenix, AZ	212	1	12562
10. Buffalo, NY	138	12	12951	42. Pittsburgh, PA	105	-2	10747
11. Cambridge, MA	122	36	14664	43. St. Louis, MO	132	6	10383
12. Charlotte, NC	64	17	10376	44. St. Paul, MN	104	15	15289
13. Chicago, IL	151	17	17689	45. St. Petersburg, FL	74	48	9794
14. Cleveland, OH	107	20	13322	46. Salt Lake City, UT	45	45	10256
15. Clifton, NJ	74	28	13564	47. San Antonio, TX	83	29	10394
16. Dallas, TX	124	20	11643	48. San Diego, CA	134	23	15244
17. Detroit, MI	119	40	17639	49. San Francisco, CA	129	15	15583
18. Duluth, MN	103	58	16786	50. Santa Ana, CA	111	0	12191
19. Euclid, OH	94	36	14333	51. San Jose, CA	120	18	15620
20. Fort Worth, TX	120	29	10488	52. Santa Monica, CA	91	9	14124
21. Fullerton, CA	134	13	14690	53. Schenectady, NY	140	33	14282
22. Gary, IN	80	-35	6208	54. Seattle, WA	131	39	17290
23. Hamilton, OH	90	30	13656	55. South Bend, IN	76	31	12155
24. Hammond, IN	44	12	8457	56. Tampa, FL	64	121	12567
25. Houston, TX	124	25	12168	57. Tyler, TX	115	27	8842
26. Indianapolis, IN	113	17	9967	58. Utica, NY	129	-25	6678
27. Irvington, NJ	145	27	17220	59. Waco, TX	89	46	9557
28. Jacksonville, FL	89	11	10378	60. Warren, MI	209	16	17540
29. Long Beach, CA	126	17	16274	61. Waterbury, CT	84	24	11317
30. Los Angeles, CA	123	18	16425	62. Waukegan, IL	79	24	13878
31. Malden, MA	140	18	12411				
32. Manchester, NH	113	31	11156	MEAN	113	23	12970

-- indicates omitted.

Table 6.6. Sources of Compensation Levels and Changes

Independent Variables	Dependent Variables Compensation per Municipal Employee 1977	1960-74	1974-77
	LPSEMP77	LSEM6074	LPSM7476
Index of Functional Performance (LFPDEC4)	.15	.48*	.05
Percentage Irish stock residents (IRISHL70)	-.16	.03	-.25
Size of middle class sector (LPC70UMC)	-.05	.12	-.08
Size of black sector (LPCBLK70)	-.01	.21	-.12
Leaders' spending preferences, 1967 (LRPNTALK)	-.20	-.40*	
Leaders' spending preferences, 1976 (LLEAD3W2)			-.05
Organization of municipal employees, 1972 (LPEMPO72)	.25*	.13	
Organization of municipal employees, 1976 (LPEMPO76)			-.22
City Wealth Index (LNTWRT70)	.21	.28*	-.01
Opportunity wages (LOWSVK67)	.23*	-.02	-.06
Political activities of municipal employees (LPAME)	.12	-.01	.36*
Responsiveness of mayor and council members (LLME76)	.29*	.21	.23
Multiple R	.64	.58	.47

See note to table 6.4.

tant here, as in chapter 4. Leaders preferring more spending increased compensation less, as discussed below. And cities performing more functions increased compensation more than others. In 1974–77, political activities by municipal employees increased compensation.[16]

Our approach helps reinterpret findings from past studies. Note that employee-specific processes are the major sources of compensation. By contrast, measures of general political processes—black and middle-class sector size, and percent Irish—were unrelated to compensation. Citizens may demand more services, or revolt against taxes, but they are generally too distant to affect compensation. Not so for numbers of employees.

Numbers of Municipal Employees

With fiscal austerity, cities can hold the line on compensation, or reduce the number of employees. These should be considered together as competing policies. Our numbers measure includes employees in all municipal functions. Full time equivalents standardize for part-time workers.[17]

Results for the 1977 level involve general political processes and resemble those in chapter 4 for expenditure levels (table 6.7). Cities performing more functions quite understandably have more employees. So do those with more Irish residents, reflecting the legacy of political leaders for whom patronage was a normal and legitimate part of government. Cities with larger middle classes have fewer employees, consistent with earlier results for spending. These three general city characteristics capture longer-term processes and citizen preferences. They contrast markedly with results for compensation, or shorter-term *changes* in numbers of employees, which respond more to organization of employees and leaders' preferences.

Table 6.7. Sources of Numbers of Municipal Employees

Independent Variables	Dependent Variables Number of Municipal Employees per Capita 1977	 1960-74	 1974-77
	LLGM77CA	LLG674CA	LLG747CA
Index of Functional Performance (LFPDEC4)	.64*	.08	-.27
Percentage Irish stock residents (IRISHL70)	.23*	.02	-.07
Size of middle class sector (LPC70UMC)	-.28*	-.08	.06
Size of black sector (LPCBLK70)	-.004	-.04	-.13
Leaders' spending preferences, 1967 (LRPNTALK)	.02	.39*	
Leaders' spending preferences, 1976 (LLEAD3W2)			.09
Organization of municipal employees, 1972 (LPEMPO72)		-.00	
Organization of municipal employees, 1976 (LPEMPO76)	-.12		-.21
City Wealth Index (LNTWRT70)	.04	.08	-.12
Multiple R	.82	.43	.46

See note to table 6.4.

Specifically, only the leadership measure significantly changed the number of employees from 1960 to 74 (table 6.7). This is interesting since the same measure depressed compensation over this period. That is, leaders who campaigned for more public services in the late 1960s implemented these policies by holding down compensation but hiring more employees. Recall that the leaders' spending measure is the mayor's campaign statements multiplied by his power: mayors who increased numbers of employees thus favored more spending and had more power. Gary is a good example, with a mayor strong enough to hold down salaries and increase the number of workers. Trade offs between compensation and numbers are complex; over time, talented employees leave if salaries are low. But in the short-term, policy preferences of these mayors led to increasing numbers. Traditional patronage generated such results in the past. Patronage jobs often rewarded party work, illustrated, for example, by Dan O'Connell in Albany who often gave one full-time position to two or more part-time persons (see Clark 1975c). More recent black politics is less structured by individual favors, and more in the spirit of affirmative action. Both traditional patronage and ethnic hiring were used in manpower programs like CETA (e.g., Johnston 1979; Nelson and Meranto 1977; Altes and Mendelson 1980). A study of 10 California cities by Browning, Marshall, and Tabb (1982) found that cities which incorporated minorities into the political leadership hired more minority employees, even though California cities generally have reform governments with little overt patronage (e.g., Thompson 1975; ch. 6). As both traditional patronage and affirmative action increase numbers and decrease compensation, strong unions resist these policies, sometimes violently, as in Atlanta, Detroit, Gary, and Kansas City in the late 1960s and early 1970s (see Persons 1977; Nelson and Meranto 1977; Levi 1977; Levine 1974; and Wheeler in Chickering 1976). Of course these were the first years of black electoral success. Union representatives, new themselves and concerned to represent members' interests aggressively, clashed with activist black leaders. Several PCS results indicate contrasting responses by blacks and municipal employees in different cities. For example, cities with more disturbances involving blacks in the late 1960s had fewer political activities by municipal employees.[18]

The 1974–77 changes in employee numbers showed two results almost significant: cities performing more functions and with more organized employees decreased their numbers. This contradicts the image of unions favoring "featherbedding," but is consistent with their favoring policies to benefit current members.

Political activities of employees, and leaders' responsiveness to them, generally increase compensation and decrease numbers of employees (tables 6.6 and 6.7). Similarly, employee organization generally increases compensation and decreases numbers, although it sometimes is below significance. In sum, employee organizations seek primarily improved compensation and working conditions for their members. If this reduces active work time, less work may be done and more workers must be hired to maintain service levels. But with limited funds, more workers may not be hired. With retrenchment after the mid-1970s these often became public issues.

Figure 6.2 distinguishes alternative retrenchment patterns by plotting 1974–77 changes in compensation against changes in employee numbers. The negative relationship ($r = -.21$) indicates that trimming compensation or numbers were often competing policies. For example, the fiscally strained cities of Detroit, Cleveland, and New York reduced employees, but still increased compensation as much as most other cities.[19] These were cities with strong unions and relatively weak mayors. By contrast, Gary, Newark, and Utica did the opposite: when they too suffered fiscal strain, they held down compensation increases, but expanded numbers.[20] Other variables affect service levels and numbers of employees, but are often specific to individual functions (see Weicher and Emerine 1973). Several are in appendix 5.

Are Some Cities "Overstaffed"?

The last sections stressed the compensation-numbers trade off; does it follow that political leaders and employees disagree over it? Not necessarily in the short term. But reasonable short-term policies can soon grow unreasonable; cities can become over- or understaffed. Current employee numbers reflect a long historical legacy. Leaders may accept distant past decisions as justifying present policies. Or they can independently assess staffing levels. How might an elected official cut

Figure 6.2. Changes in Compensation and in Number of Workers from 1974–77 are Slightly Negatively Related

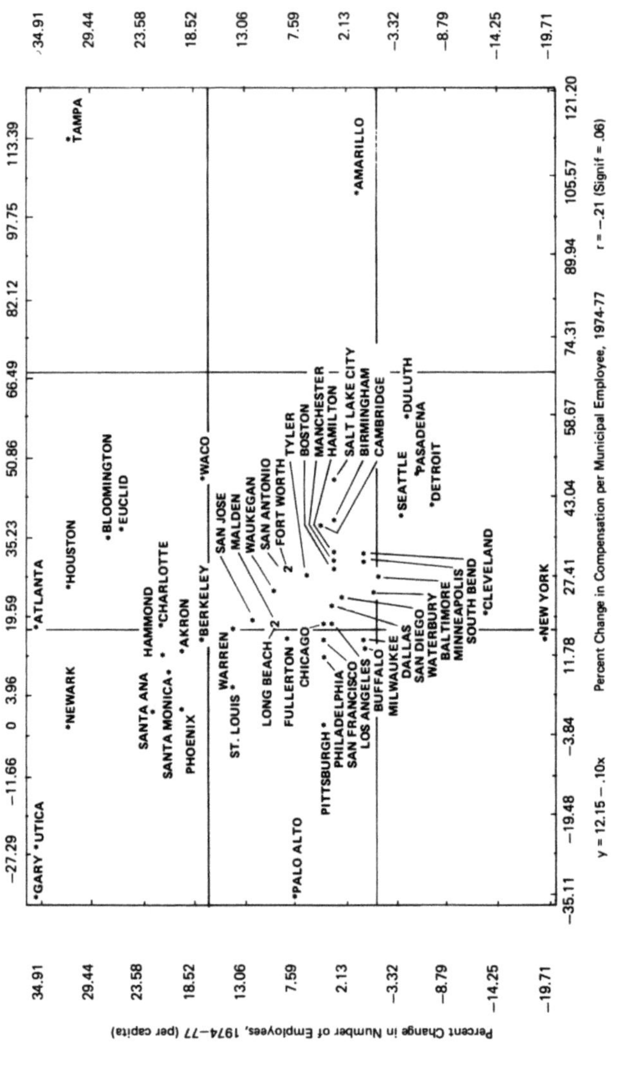

into this process to learn where his city does and should stand? In recent years leaders have often reexamined staffing levels, asking hard questions about the number of "necessary" employees. There are no accepted standards. Responding to inquiries from city officials, we developed an Index of Staffing to approach this problem. Its logic is as follows.

Cities differ in numbers of employees for three basic reasons. First, they vary in functions performed. We handled this in the Index by considering workers in common functions,[21] and including the FP Index as a control variable. Second are city characteristics that generate demands for public services—the number of poor residents, etc. The Index adjusts for effects of several such demand characteristics through a regression procedure explained in appendix 2F. Third, employees may have increased due to inefficient administration, patronage, or other reasons besides one and two. The Index reflects such over- or understaffing. It is computed both for total employees and common function employees. Table 6.8 shows that the Index is simply the difference between the actual number of municipal employees, column (1), and the number expected from the city's demand characteristics, column (2). Column (3) shows the Index in employees per thousand citizens, while column (4) shows the same Index in percentage form. For example, column (3) indicates that Albany has 7.08 more workers per 1,000 residents than one would expect from Albany's demand characteristics and functional responsibilities. Column (4) tells us that this is 29.6 percent over the predicted number. A city with exactly the number of employees predicted by its demand characteristics would score zero on the Index. Cities with negative scores are understaffed by comparison with the national average. The Index of Staffing for common functions correlates only moderately ($r = .56$) with that for total employees. This indicates that cities may be highly staffed in common functions, but not in total municipal employees, or vice versa, and that demand characteristics affecting total employment differ somewhat from those of common functions. For example, Newark was 20 percent understaffed on the common function Index (table 6.9), but 20 percent overstaffed in total employees—matching statements of Mayor Gibson that Newark had not maintained its basic services adequately compared to other programs.[22] But many cities are

Table 6.8. Components of Index of Staffing for Total Municipal Employees per 1,000 Residents

Cities	(1) Actual Number of Municipal Employees	(2) Expected Number of Municipal Employees	(3)=(1)-(2) Index of Staffing (Absolute Numbers)	(4) [(3)/(1)] X 100 Index of Staffing (Percentage)
1. Akron, OH	14.87	14.42	.45	3.02
2. Albany, NY	23.90	16.81	7.08	29.64
3. Amarillo, TX	10.63	9.83	.80	7.50
4. Atlanta, GA	21.26	18.79	2.47	11.60
5. Baltimore, MD	51.25	50.87	.39	.75
6. Berkeley, CA	13.69	18.44	-4.75	-34.68
7. Birmingham, AL	13.95	19.83	-5.87	-42.09
8. Bloomington, MN	5.94	5.50	.45	7.54
9. Boston, MA	40.27	45.07	-4.80	-11.92
10. Buffalo, NY	32.16	33.71	-1.56	-4.84
11. Cambridge, MA	41.39	44.00	-2.61	-6.31
12. Charlotte, NC	13.92	14.53	-.62	-4.44
13. Chicago, IL	15.52	14.72	.80	5.15
14. Cleveland, OH	18.70	20.28	-1.58	-8.43
15. Clifton, NJ	18.09	22.84	-4.75	-26.23
16. Dallas, TX	15.93	11.53	4.40	27.65
17. Detroit, MI	18.57	23.62	-5.05	-27.17
18. Duluth, MN	14.54	11.10	3.45	23.69
19. Euclid, OH	11.72	6.39	5.33	45.51
20. Fort Worth, TX	12.56	10.22	2.34	18.64
21. Fullerton, CA	7.76	8.02	-.26	-3.29
22. Gary, IN	16.75	19.63	-2.88	-17.19
23. Hamilton, OH	11.17	11.53	-.36	-3.27
24. Hammond, IN	10.19	8.80	1.39	13.65
25. Houston, TX	8.83	10.83	-2.05	-23.25
26. Indianapolis, IN	15.97	19.94	-3.96	-24.81
27. Irvington, NJ	19.15	18.71	.44	2.30
28. Jacksonville, FL	20.71	23.51	-2.79	-13.49
29. Long Beach, CA	13.58	15.31	-1.73	-12.70
30. Los Angeles, CA	15.94	12.53	3.41	21.41
31. Malden, MA	28.90	28.06	.84	2.89
32. Manchester, NH	33.45	27.15	6.29	18.82
33. Memphis, TN	34.97	31.35	3.62	10.36
34. Milwaukee, WI	14.15	14.41	-.26	-1.81
35. Minneapolis, MN	14.46	15.65	-1.19	-8.24
36. New York, NY	43.63	42.95	.68	1.56
37. Newark, NJ	55.90	44.66	11.24	20.11
38. Palo Alto, CA	14.26	11.09	3.17	22.21
39. Pasadena, CA	13.50	13.73	-.23	-1.71
40. Philadelphia, PA	20.48	22.12	-1.64	-7.99
41. Phoenix, AZ	12.14	15.06	-2.91	-23.99
42. Pittsburgh, PA	12.98	15.47	-2.50	-19.26
43. St. Louis, MO	27.62	25.71	1.91	6.91
44. St. Paul, MN	13.06	13.30	-.24	-1.84
45. St. Petersburg, FL	13.94	11.17	2.77	19.84

Table 6.8. (Continued)

Cities	(1) Actual Number of Municipal Employees	(2) Expected Number of Municipal Employees	(3)=(1)-(2) Index of Staffing (Absolute Numbers)	(4) [(3)/(1)] X 100 Index of Staffing (Percentage)
46. Salt Lake City, UT	11.99	15.00	-3.01	-25.08
47. San Antonio, TX	15.67	19.61	-3.95	-25.19
48. San Diego, CA	8.68	11.19	-2.50	-28.84
49. San Francisco, CA	33.32	32.50	.83	2.49
50. Santa Ana, CA	8.03	11.69	-3.65	-45.49
51. San Jose, CA	6.79	10.56	-3.77	-55.43
52. Santa Monica, CA	14.03	13.81	.22	1.56
53. Schenectady, NY	10.87	14.09	-3.41	-31.98
54. Seattle, WA	18.14	13.18	4.97	27.38
55. South Bend, IN	14.63	10.94	3.69	25.24
56. Tampa, FL	22.46	15.84	6.62	29.46
57. Tyler, TX	10.94	8.78	2.16	19.74
58. Utica, NY	14.89	15.64	-.75	-5.00
59. Waco, TX	14.53	18.10	-3.57	-24.58
60. Warren, MI	6.84	8.20	-1.56	-23.49
61. Waterbury, CT	30.70	30.37	.33	1.08
62. Waukegan, IL	8.15	9.94	-1.79	-21.93
MEAN	18.69	18.58	0[#]	0[#]

[#]Due to rounding error the computed mean is not exactly zero.

high on both Indexes, like Albany (+29 on total employment and +33 on common functions). New Yorkers may note that the combination of demand characteristics and functional responsibilities are such that New York is near zero on both Indexes. Of course, the New York case reminds us that staffing should be considered along with compensation.

The Index provides a clear measure of where a city stands compared to others. Officials in several cities have used the Index in personnel decisions. Objections can be raised to it. A city may have other reasons for numerous employees besides the demand measures in the Index. Conversely, it can be argued that patronage was most common in cities high on the demand characteristics; if so we are "overadjusting." Similarly, cities like Albany which have openly used patronage are part of the national sample, which elevates the national average. The Index permits reasoned comparison with other cities at the same time. No more weight should be placed on it than it can withstand; it is a rough

Table 6.9. Components of Index of Staffing for Common Function Employees per 1,000 Residen

Cities	(1) Actual Number of Common Function Employees	(2) Expected Number of Common Function Employees	(3)=(1)-(2) Index of Staffing (Absolute Number)	(4) [(3)/(1)] X 100 Index of Staffing (Percentage)
1. Akron, OH	10.59	9.53	1.06	10.05
2. Albany, NY	13.92	9.27	4.66	33.46
3. Amarillo, TX	7.49	7.80	-.31	-4.18
4. Atlanta, GA	13.90	10.21	3.69	26.54
5. Baltimore, MD	16.09	12.57	3.52	21.88
6. Berkeley, CA	9.33	11.13	-1.79	-19.20
7. Birmingham, AL	10.87	11.05	-.18	-1.68
8. Bloomington, MN	3.72	6.07	-2.35	-63.35
9. Boston, MA	13.51	12.74	.77	5.72
10. Buffalo, NY	10.34	11.17	-.84	-8.10
11. Cambridge, MA	11.03	12.54	-1.52	-13.76
12. Charlotte, NC	9.91	9.05	.86	8.67
13. Chicago, IL	10.15	9.75	.40	3.90
14. Cleveland, OH	11.51	11.89	-.38	-3.30
15. Clifton, NJ	6.57	7.43	-.86	13.11
16. Dallas, TX	7.96	7.87	.08	1.04
17. Detroit, MI	10.80	11.59	-.78	-7.25
18. Duluth, MN	7.74	7.86	-.12	-1.53
19. Euclid, OH	8.63	6.72	1.91	22.11
20. Fort Worth, TX	9.23	8.41	.82	8.91
21. Fullerton, CA	5.53	6.98	-1.46	-26.37
22. Gary, IN	8.66	10.65	-1.99	-23.00
23. Hamilton, OH	7.32	9.03	-1.71	-23.42
24. Hammond, IN	7.56	8.03	-.47	-6.23
25. Houston, TX	6.15	7.72	-1.56	-25.41
26. Indianapolis, IN	8.09	7.64	.45	5.56
27. Irvington, NJ	9.10	11.14	-2.04	-22.45
28. Jacksonville, FL	8.28	9.83	-1.55	-18.68
29. Long Beach, CA	7.43	8.75	-1.33	-17.87
30. Los Angeles, CA	9.07	8.65	.42	4.61
31. Malden, MA	10.08	9.80	.27	2.69
32. Manchester, NH	9.83	8.36	1.47	14.99
33. Memphis, TN	9.49	10.00	-.51	-5.35
34. Milwaukee, WI	10.10	8.91	1.19	11.78
35. Minneapolis, MN	9.87	9.40	.47	4.73
36. New York, NY	10.29	11.31	-1.03	-9.99
37. Newark, NJ	13.14	15.82	-2.68	-20.37
38. Palo Alto, CA	8.84	6.28	2.56	29.00
39. Pasadena, CA	8.29	8.90	-.61	-7.37
40. Philadelphia, PA	14.43	10.61	3.82	26.47
41. Phoenix, AZ	7.86	8.70	-.84	-10.74
42. Pittsburgh, PA	10.58	10.74	-.16	-1.52
43. St. Louis, MO	13.42	12.22	1.20	8.97
44. St. Paul, MN	9.67	8.82	.84	8.71
45. St. Petersburg, FL	9.72	8.96	.76	7.86

Table 6.9. (Continued)

Cities	(1) Actual Number of Common Function Employees	(2) Expected Number of Common Function Employees	(3)=(1)-(2) Index of Staffing (Absolute Number)	(4) [(3)/(1)] X 100 Index of Staffing (Percentage)
46. Salt Lake City, UT	8.60	9.60	-1.00	-11.60
47. San Antonio, TX	7.33	10.81	-3.49	-47.62
48. San Diego, CA	5.71	7.98	-2.27	-39.85
49. San Francisco, CA	13.43	11.82	1.60	11.95
50. Santa Ana, CA	6.39	8.63	-2.24	-35.01
51. San Jose, CA	5.45	7.50	-2.05	-37.68
52. Santa Monica, CA	9.04	9.31	-.27	-3.03
53. Schenectady, NY	9.02	8.84	.19	2.07
54. Seattle, WA	11.29	8.43	2.85	25.28
55. South Bend, IN	9.95	8.69	1.26	12.67
56. Tampa, FL	16.00	10.66	5.34	33.40
57. Tyler, TX	8.24	8.68	-.44	-5.35
58. Utica, NY	8.49	9.67	-1.18	-13.87
59. Waco, TX	8.00	10.18	-2.18	-27.20
60. Warren, MI	5.40	6.48	-1.08	-20.08
61. Waterbury, CT	11.34	8.87	2.46	21.71
62. Waukegan, IL	6.28	7.94	-1.66	-26.46
MEAN	9.45	9.45	0[#]	0[#]

[#]Due to rounding error the computed mean is not exactly zero.

benchmark to help direct further investigation of why individual cities are high or low, but cities with negative scores may well have lessons for others.[23]

Municipal Employees and Fiscal Strain

Widespread beliefs to the contrary, we find that organization and political activities of municipal employees have minimal effects on general fiscal policy outputs or fiscal strain. For municipal employees to increase fiscal strain, total expenditures on personal services should increase. But most measures of municipal employee organization or political activity are unrelated to personal services expenditures.[24]

How explain these counterintuitive results? They flow from a seldom recognized relationship: cities that pay employees more have fewer employees. And total personal services expenditures equal compensation per employee times number of employees. Cities where employees are organized, and political leaders responsive to them, pay more but hire fewer workers (controlling the range of functions and other variables). Employees are powerful enough to increase their compensation, but not to drive up total expenditures, which are explained more by citizens and political leaders.

These results have many policy implications. Employees may have impaired service delivery, but have not increased tax burdens and fiscal strain. This illuminates debates over stimulation-substitution effects of federal grants by showing that cities differed in their responses to grants and why. By helping cut the budget pie to reduce the number of jobs, municipal employees helped redirect manpower and employment aspects of certain federal grants. But general city characteristics were more critical for decisions on the size of the budget pie, and thus whether stimulation or substitution resulted. In particular, politically active blacks, and powerful mayors who were fiscally liberal increased city government jobs in 1960–74. Then in 1974–77, cities with large middle classes reduced spending on employees along with other cutbacks. The blame frequently assigned to municipal employees for general fiscal difficulties of cities thus appears exaggerated. But number and compensation trade offs deserve more careful analysis.

CHAPTER SEVEN

Faces of the Middle Class: New Fiscal Populists, Republicans, and the Taxpayers' Revolt

Chapter 4 showed that cities with large middle classes pursued more conservative fiscal policies, especially in the late 1970s. But paradoxically, business groups had no effects. This chapter interprets these and other findings using data for middle-class citizens to explain why the "taxpayers' revolt" surfaced in the late 1970s, and how it affected urban fiscal policy. Our interpretation stresses fragmentation of traditional Democrats and Republicans, and the emergence of New Fiscal Populists.

Traditional Democratic and Republican leaders are in trouble, and know it. Electoral turnout has declined. Confidence in leaders has dropped. The percentage of self-declared Independents keeps rising, in 1980 up to 38 percent, equal to Democrats, while Republicans numbered 22 percent.[1] Many leaders continue past ideological commitments, but the New Deal coalitions are over. Perhaps the most striking political development is a new type of political leader, the New Fiscal Populist. He is fiscally conservative but socially liberal: examples are Jimmy Carter, Jerry Brown, and Peter Flaherty. Such leaders remain poorly understood, but are critical in redefining the agenda for government in America.

The Beginnings of Political Realignments: The Taxpayers' Revolt and the New Class

New Fiscal Populism emerged from a combination of the liberal social movements of the late 1960s and taxpayers' revolt of the late 1970s.

The 1960s witnessed important movements for liberal causes: civil rights, the women's movement, counter culture groups supporting "post-materialist" policies. These mobilized behind George McGovern for President in 1972, defeating traditional labor and blue-collar groups within the Democratic party. Some observers like Irving Kristol, Seymour Martin Lipset, and Aaron Wildavsky interpret such developments as shifting the direction of American society, and suggest that a college-educated New Class influenced government toward more liberal policies (see Bruce-Briggs 1979). This New Left or New Class interpretation is reasonable for many social issues, but off the mark for government spending and taxes.[2] It implies continued growth in spending, but spending was curtailed in the late 1970s.

Why was spending curtailed? The "taxpayers' revolt" is a common answer. Proposition 13 and related limits in more than half the states have been interpreted as a "New Conservatism" (Irving Howe 1978) or "New Negativism" (Vernon Jordan); others speak simply of a "New Right." This New Right is portrayed as conservative across a range of issues, including racial intolerance, religious orthodoxy, traditional morality, and less government. Moral Majority campaigners for Ronald Reagan are cited as a vanguard driving American society to the Right. The youthful energy and excess of the New Right poses dangers to some (left of center) observers just as great as those posed by the New Left to (right of center) observers a few years earlier.

Who does the future belong to? The New Left or New Right? Or are both interpretations overblown? Both New Left and New Right interpretations imply a shift in policy for the whole society—albeit in opposing directions. If we consider not the general interpretations, but the specific social movements they sought to explain, are they really so contradictory? We suggest not, but that they are manifestations of two fundamental and continuing trends. The New Left interpretation is reasonable in identifying a growing social liberalism, but wrong for fiscal liberalism. The New Right view does capture a more salient fiscal conservatism, but is incorrect in generalizing it to social issues. The New Fiscal Populist incorporates the social liberalism of the New Left, but the fiscal conservatism of the New Right. These apparently conflicting tendencies can indeed combine; only the New Deal ideology held they could not. New Fiscal Populists (NFPs) have been widely misunderstood because they do not fit the traditional (New Deal) categories of left or right. But if political commentators and competitors have lamented the arrival of NFPs, voters have sent increasing numbers of NFPs to elective office. How has this come about?

The Distinctiveness of New Fiscal Populism

Many leaders lost touch with their citizens in the 1970s, as indicated by passage of Proposition 13 and similar measures and defeat of established leaders by "unknowns"—like Hubert Humphrey by Jimmy Carter or Mayor Abraham Beame by Edward Koch. Leaders lost touch in part because they misunderstood two simultaneous changes in citizen preferences. First, citizens grew more fiscally conservative and/or more vocal about their conservatism in the 1970s. But, second, they remained liberal on many social issues (concerning race, civil liberties, sexual permissiveness, etc.). The *combination* of these two changes went unrecognized by most political leaders.

By the 1970s, fiscal liberalism diverged from social liberalism for many American citizens, but the ideological commitment of most Democratic leaders to liberal causes (social and fiscal), and conservative preferences on both by Republicans, kept leaders in both parties from recognizing such changes. A new type of leader thus emerged, the New Fiscal Populist, more in tune with this combination of citizen preferences. The New Fiscal Populist position is clear if we chart the two major components of political ideology:

		Fiscal Issues	
		Conservative	Liberal
Social Issues	Conservative	1. New Deal Republicans	2. Ethnic Politicians
	Liberal	3. New Fiscal Populists	4. New Deal Democrats

New Deal Republicans and Democrats demand little comment. Ethnic politicians favor more government, but are conservative on race and often other social issues. Just as New Deal Democrats found ethnic politicians like Frank Rizzo troublesome, so they find New Fiscal Populists disturbing. These two "off diagonal" positions are typically considered ideologically confused—by traditional Republicans and Democrats.

Are civic and business leaders less bound by such ideological blinders? Indeed—to a degree unappreciated in practically all past research; civic and business leaders varied enormously across our PCS cities in policy preferences. Stereotypes to the contrary, business groups were not consistently conservative.

With elected officials and civic groups often unresponsive, many citizens grew disenchanted. This created the potential for a Howard Jarvis to mobilize support for tax reduction, or for new candidates unbound by ideological barriers. Both increasingly emerged in the late 1970s. Yet these changes remain barely described by political observers, and virtually unanalyzed using serious research tools. This chapter helps fill the gap by offering a more coherent interpretation and assessing it with several large-scale data sets.

We begin with surveys which show that citizens have grown more fiscally conservative and socially liberal. Next we outline characteristics of the New Fiscal Populist (NFP) leader and consider them with data for 227 mayors and council members. We then turn to conversion of citizen preferences into fiscal policies, specifically via organized groups and the taxpayers' revolt. The chapter closes with a case study of Pittsburgh illustrating how Mayor Peter Flaherty implemented New Fiscal Populist policies with remarkable success. Pittsburgh illustrates the more abstract ideas of the chapter in a particular setting, documenting how at least one old, northeastern city with declining population used forceful local policies to reduce its fiscal strain.

Fiscal Policy Preferences of American Citizens

Few Americans have sharp views on public policies (see Converse 1975). This troubles any analysis, using surveys, voting, or other procedures, but surveys provide the best preference measures across categories of citizens and over time. We thus analyze citizen surveys to document changing patterns of fiscal and social liberalism. Still, deductive reasoning about interests and taxes leads to similar results.[3] Three generalizations summarize the major survey findings.

1. *The nonpoor prefer lower expenditures and taxes for government at all levels (federal, state and local). Opposition to social welfare activities is especially strong.*

For example, 67 percent of Americans responded to a NORC-GSS item in 1980 that income taxes were "too high."[4] Just after Proposition 13 passed in 1978 a nationwide survey showed that 57 percent of Americans favored a similar measure.[5] Asked where spending might be cut, most citizens mention welfare and social services.[6]

2. *The nonpoor have preferred lower taxes for many years, but this preference grew stronger in the mid-1970s.*

Responses that income taxes were "too high" increased from 46 percent in 1961 to 67 percent in 1980.[7] People oppose taxes in part because they consider government inefficient: the number of Americans who feel that "people in the government waste a lot of money" increased from 45 percent in 1958 to 79 percent in 1978.[8]

Preferences about specific programs have shifted less. Eight programs included in NORC-GSS surveys from 1973 to 1980 showed few changes in spending preferences for the environment, crime, or education, but slight decreases (for whites) in support for health and drug addiction, "improving the condition of blacks," and "solving the problems of big cities." The sharpest decrease was for welfare (table 5.2).

Citizens thus support many programs, but also want lower taxes. These two preferences have conflicted for years, but leaders responded more to the spending preferences in the late 1960s and early 1970s. More persons came to support lower taxes over the 1970s, but even more important was the increased *salience* of taxes. Such "intensity of preference" is hard to measure but important to consider here.[9] When the economy slowed in the early 1970s, government growth did not. Consequently, the "tax bite" increased.[10] The rise in saliency of taxes and economic concerns over the 70s is clear in responses to the question, "what is the most important problem" (see figure 7.1). Attitudes vary with economic trends, but attitudes are still important intervening variables leading to less government spending.

Proposition 13 set off debates as to what citizens "really" wanted. Some initial observers suggested that citizens preferred near-current spending levels (e.g., Lipset and Raab 1978; Citrin 1979; Mushkin 1979). But these conclusions usually came from survey items on spending, not taxes. Most spending questions generate upwardly biased re-

Figure 7.1. The Economy Has Come to Dominate All Other Problems in the 1970s. Question: "What do you think is the most important problem facing the country today?"

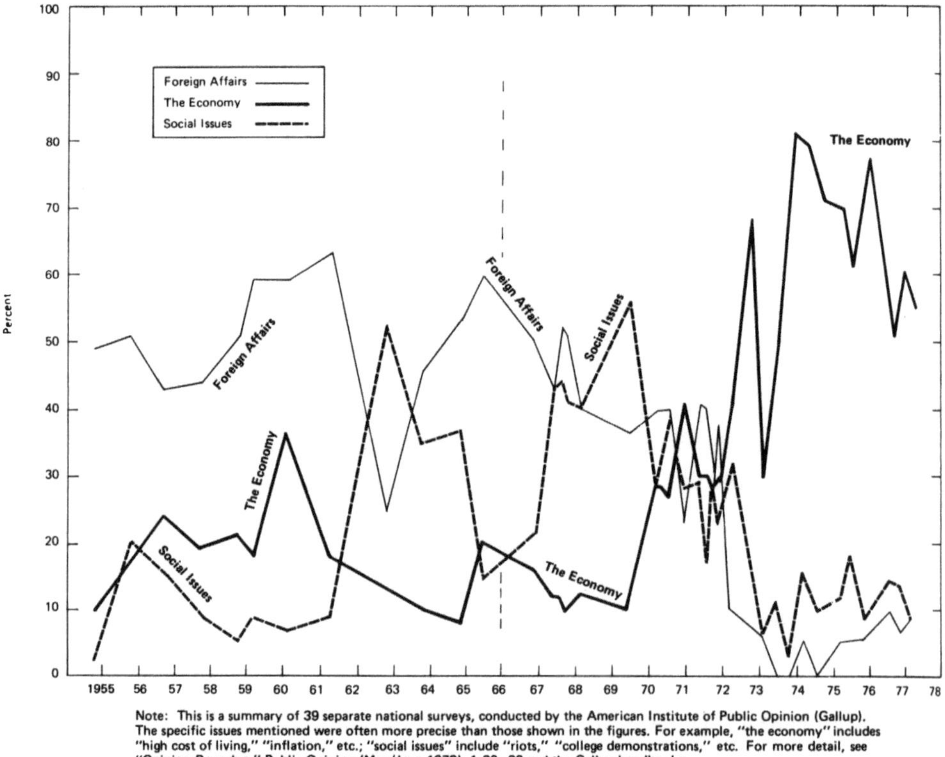

Note: This is a summary of 39 separate national surveys, conducted by the American Institute of Public Opinion (Gallup). The specific issues mentioned were often more precise than those shown in the figures. For example, "the economy" includes "high cost of living," "inflation," etc.; "social issues" include "riots," "college demonstrations," etc. For more detail, see "Opinion Roundup," Public Opinion (May/June 1978), 1:30–32 and the Gallup handbooks.

sults since respondents are not held within a budget constraint or otherwise forced to reveal their willingness to match taxes to specific service levels—a classic issue in public finance theory (e.g., Tideman 1976). Procedures exist to address this issue, often variations of budget pies (see Clark 1974), but have not been used in national surveys. However, the available results imply that even if citizens want more services and lower taxes, the low tax concern is often stronger. Consider figure 7.1, note 11, and referenda like Propositions 13 and 2½ where citizens were told that services would be cut, but still voted to cut taxes. Many citizens also feel governments could be made more efficient, and thus permit both lower taxes and the same services. But most citizens prefer to let elected officials decide how to increase efficiency, or if necessary reduce services.

3. *In general, the more affluent the citizen, the less government spending he prefers, especially for poor-oriented services. However, some studies suggest that the most affluent are less opposed to spending than middle income persons.*

The more affluent prefer less spending, overall and for welfare. But in some areas like public schools and environmental services, spending preferences are unrelated to income (figure 7.2). Similarly, income is weakly related to spending preferences on six of eight NORC-GSS spending items; the exceptions are welfare and income taxes which the more affluent oppose. Figure 7.3 also shows the same relationship for welfare as well as consistency across time: respondents at all income levels increasingly opposed welfare spending from 1973 to 1977. Other studies concur that the more affluent prefer less government spending.[11]

But do the most affluent feel *noblesse oblige* and support *more* spending? Clearly, established citizens are sometimes active in charitable and civic groups benefiting the poor (e.g., Allen 1971; Baltzell 1979). Is this widespread enough to appear in mass surveys? Evidence is mixed. Persons earning over $25,000 supported more welfare in 1973–74, but not in later years (figure 7.3).[12]

Besides income, what explains expenditure preferences? Blacks prefer more spending than whites, as discussed in chapter 5. Jews tradi-

Figure 7.2. Spending Preference for Five Policy Issues by Income Level

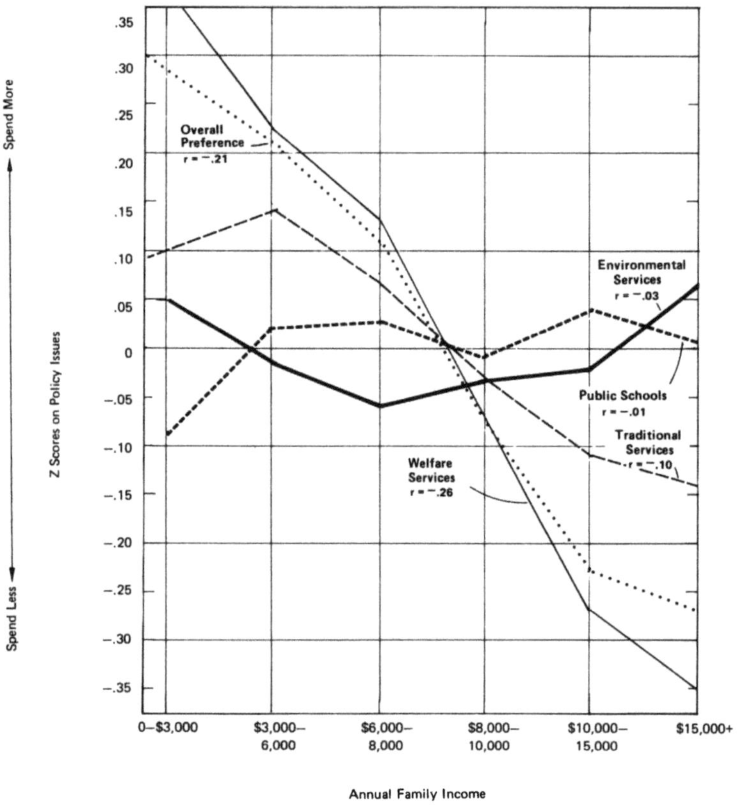

Note: These are responses to an item which asked "whether you think the local agencies should spend more money, less money, or about as much money as is now spent on those services and problems." "Environmental services" included controlling pollution and mass transit; "traditional services" were police, street lighting, street repair and trash collection; "welfare services" were low-cost housing, medical care, welfare, and AFDC. "Overall preference" was a sum of all others. Z scores of the items were summed in each area. The survey was administered to 4,266 citizens in 10 cities in 1970. See Hoffman and Clark (1979).

tionally preferred more spending than Protestants and Catholics, but the NORC-GSS welfare and tax items showed no differences between Jews, Protestants, or Catholics. Most other individual characteristics are inconsistently related to general spending preferences, although users of specific services prefer more spending on them (Hoffman and Clark 1979). Some city and neighborhood effects are also important, but are mentioned primarily to indicate that when they are controlled, income results remain strong.[13] Various attitudes like opposing cor-

Figure 7.3. The Higher the Respondent's Income, the More He Opposes Welfare Expenditures

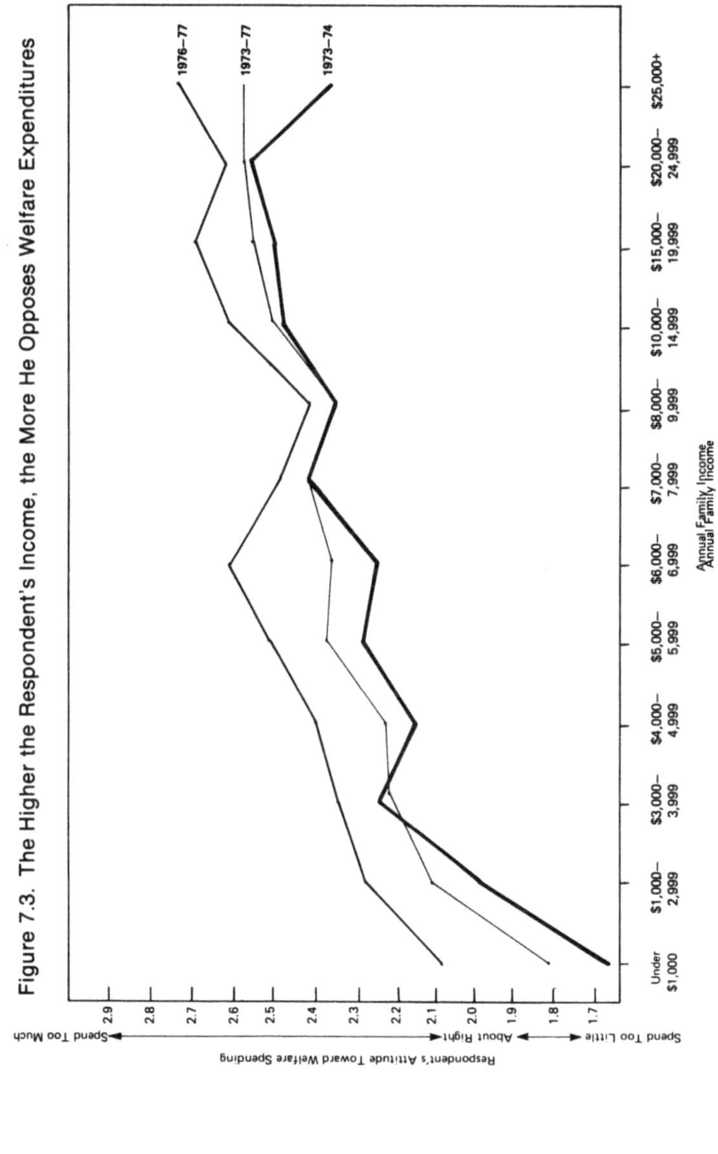

Source: Computations from NORC–GSS, 1973–77.

Note: The item is in chapter 5, note 8. Responses were coded: 1 = spend too little, 2 = about right, 3 = spend too much on welfare. The bottom line is a two-year average for 1973-74; the middle line the average for 1973-77; the top line the two years of 1976-77. Data are for whites only.

ruption are related to spending, but difficult to disentangle from spending preferences themselves. One attitude is the dramatic loss of confidence in government and other institutions since the 1960s (Miller 1979), which seems partially explained by unresponsiveness to citizen preferences.

Americans revolt against taxes when the tax bite is still lower than in many other countries. National factors reinforce fiscal conservatism for Americans: the absence of a feudal past, the correspondingly egalitarian ideology, individualistic Protestantism, the frontier with vast areas for individual farming (reinforcing isolation), abundance of natural resources, isolation from other countries, and few wars. Such factors are hard to weight; other countries have nevertheless experienced reactions against the welfare state for reasons apparently similar to those in the United States (see Rose and Peters 1978; Flora and Heidenheimer 1981).

Social Liberalism

The basic social liberalism finding is simply stated: *Most Americans have become socially liberal on issues of personal liberty and tolerance.* The classic civil liberties issues have been won by the "liberals." Battles continued for decades against intolerant school boards, Senator McCarthy's anti-Communism, and discrimination against blacks in schools, restaurants, etc. But by the 1970s, most Americans were liberal on these and similar personal liberties issues.[14]

There are still a few major exceptions. One concerns crime and law enforcement: Americans have moved toward support for tougher police and harsher sentencing since the 1960s. Another area is the grey one involving both social and fiscal issues, such as having the federal government help a particular "special interest group"—veterans, the handicapped, union members, or minorities—in ways that everyone pays for. One might hold that such issues do not imply social liberalism, but they were often presented in terms of commitment to the disadvantaged by the "liberal-labor" core of the Democratic party. In debates over the 1972 platform, however, the Democratic party itself fragmented, so that many of these groups pursued their own "special interests" over the 1970s. And if we look specifically at the 1970s, changes in social attitudes are few. The major shifts were earlier, with changes on most items leveling off in the 1970s.[15]

These results are also for the whole U.S. population; specific subgroups are more volatile, such as elite college students. In dress, career plans, use of drugs, and support for political candidates, their changes have often been dramatic, from the drugs-rock-lib of the late 1960s to the more conservative tone of the early 1980s. The mass media, looking for "news," understandably seek out extremes and publicize changes: Gloria Steinem has obviously been superceded by Moral Majority activists. But such dramatic changes for specific subgroups should not obscure sea changes for the whole U.S. population. So few Americans ever endorsed the "social extremes" of the late 1960s, that most can move in a slight liberal direction, or not change on most social issues, without foresaking past commitments.

Do Civil Libertarians, Black Supporters, and Feminists Favor More Government Spending?

The two general trends—toward fiscal conservatism and social liberalism—combine as follows: *By the late 1970s, there was a low relationship between fiscal and social liberalism.* This virtually eliminates a general left–right continuum for the U.S. population. Fiscal liberalism items—like support for a Proposition 13-type limit in your state, federal taxes are "too high," and federal taxes should be cut by a third—are virtually unrelated to social liberalism items—those concerning civil liberties, school integration, affirmative action, women's rights, abortion, and ERA.[16] This directly contradicts the New Deal ideological assumption of Democrats, Republicans, New Left, and New Right groups, that social and fiscal liberalism "go together." There are some persons of each of these four types, but they no longer adequately summarize the American population. The major change is an increase in New Fiscal Populists. NFPs have emerged from the two major trends in attitudes in American society. Increasing education generates more social liberalism. Higher income, especially combined with a constant or growing tax bite, generates more fiscal conservatism. Until these more general trends are halted, or somehow shifted in their effects, NFPs are likely to grow in number.

The New Fiscal Populist Leader

Traditional Democratic and Republican leaders failed to appeal to New Fiscal Populist citizens on these issues, which opened the way for NFP leaders to emerge. Jimmy Carter, Jerry Brown, Peter Flaherty, and Edward Koch illustrate six characteristics of most NFP leaders: fiscal conservatism, social liberalism, populism, a new ideology and style, Democratic party affiliation, and distinctive policies.

1. *Fiscal Conservatism.* NFP leaders differ most from New Deal Democrats in their fiscal conservatism. Cautious about government growth, the NFP is skeptical of expensive programs of recent decades. He shares the tax burden concerns of the modest homeowner and small businessman. His fiscal conservatism can lead Republicans and Independents to support him, despite his other positions. There are many ways to articulate fiscal conservatism, however, and NFPs have difficulty outdoing Republicans on their classic issue. Republicans led the taxpayers' revolt, while most NFP's were more cautious, albeit supporters. The 1980 landslide that brought Ronald Reagan and many Republicans to office partly derived from the too cautious fiscal conservatism of Jimmy Carter and other NFPs. If traditional Republicans were more socially conservative than many Americans in 1980, they could still win thanks to the salience of fiscal over social issues.

2. *Social Liberalism.* NFP leaders are socially liberal, although what this specifically means varies by leader. What is clear is that NFPs obviously avoid the sorts of anti-minority, anti-tolerance symbols and issues that George Wallace or Spiro Agnew vigorously invoked just a decade ago, or Jesse Helms continues in the 1980s. Times have simply changed, and most candidates (including the "new" George Wallace) recognize that they cannot succeed on their earlier positions. Some American citizens are still openly racist and intolerant on social issues, but they are too few to encourage many ambitious political leaders to champion their causes. The few leaders who do are usually conservative Republicans.

NFP leaders seek support from traditional Democratic voters, including racial, ethnic, and religious minorities. Some NFPs are very liberal socially—as in Jerry Brown's leanings toward the counterculture. In more socially conservative areas, like Peter Flaherty's Pittsburgh, tolerance of minorities, but opposition to issues like pornography and violent protest movements, are more likely. Yet to win votes, an NFP leader has to be more than tolerant; he must convince racial minorities and the poor that he is more concerned with them than other candidates. Or an NFP leader may leave them to ethnic politicians and Democrats, and seek to win some traditional Republican votes. Tactics shift with opposing candidates, and strong incumbents many convince others not to run; in their second elections, Peter Flaherty and Edward Koch were endorsed by both Republican and Democratic parties.

If Koch was criticized for ignoring blacks, this seems to have derived largely from his fiscal conservatism and brusque personal style (see Auletta 1980). Some feel Koch wavered from his liberal past and used ethnic symbolism against blacks in the early 1980s. Yet if he was branded a conservative by New Yorkers, his liberalism on most social issues would be clear if he moved to a traditional Southern town. As Americans have grown more socially liberal, socially conservative groups have lost ground. Moral Majority activism in the 1980 elections was a vigorous minority effort. Republican candidates like Ronald Reagan had difficulty eluding such enthusiastic campaigners, but were cautious about endorsing their issues. President Reagan and his Congressional allies read the polls and astutely placed almost total emphasis on fiscal issues in their first year, achieving remarkable success while deferring action on social issues.

Fiscal conservatism combined with social liberalism defines the NFP leader in a policy space. Other NFP characteristics follow from difficulties of embracing these policies in the 1970s. If the two major parties accommodate NFPs, and this is happening somewhat, the other characteristics may fade.

3. *Populism.* Because traditional parties avoided NFP issues in the 1970s, NFP leaders emerged as distinctly populist.[17] They appealed to citizens by disagreeing with established parties and interest groups. That they attracted many Democratic and Republican voters suggests that they adapted to citizen preferences faster than other candidates.

They are thus quintessential "invisible politicans"; they seek to represent citizen preferences, not a leader defined party program.

But if populist chiefly means responding to citizen preferences, it also suggests a distinctive personal style. The post-Watergate exposure of intimate lifestyle, religious practice, and personal fortune are standard for NFPs. Informal clothes, driving one's own car or bicycle, jogging, and similar breaks with established protocol set off the NFP from traditionalists.

Populist leaders often have little support from organized groups and parties. Lacking endorsements and campaign work by traditional groups means greater dependence on the individual voter. As the NFP distrusts traditional vehicles which convey constituents' priorities, a sharp sense for the public mood is essential. The populist may meet with citizens in the streets, use sophisticated polls, or other means to "test the water." He must also show potential critics (especially council members or other leaders) that he embodies the popular will—easier near election time and on more publicized issues. Using the media effectively is critical to reach citizens and convince critics and himself of his broad public support. Indeed the rise of television debates and campaign advertising seems to have weakened organized groups that could at least claim to "deliver" more voters in earlier years. Still, like Max Weber's charismatic leaders, NFPs are unstable over time given their lack of support from traditional and bureaucratic organizations. They are better at winning elections than governing, which involves dealing with groups more than citizens.

4. *New*. New Fiscal Populist leaders are new in ideology and style: they became nationally important only in the late 1970s. Unresponsiveness of traditional Democrats and Republicans opened the door for NFPs. Some long-term incumbents moved toward NFP policies, but NFPs often succeeded precisely because they were "new faces." If not always younger and literally new, it was new for them to win as many offices as they reached in the 1970s.

5. *Democratic*. Obviously one need not be a Democrat or social liberal to implement fiscally conservative policies. Electing Republicans might seem simpler. But while a one-dimensional preference analysis deemphasizes social liberalism and Democratic affiliation, these remain important for many voters. Most NFP leaders are Democrats,

in part simply because most voters in the mid-1970s were too. Republicans could doubtless represent the same issues, but had more negative associations with the electorate. Mayor Kathy Whitmire of Houston spoke for many NFPs when she identified herself to the *Washington Post* as a "fiscal conservative and social progressive—I guess that's neo-something," and "wondering at this point which party is ultimately going to identify itself more with that combination. . . . I find it disadvantageous to be partisan." But if NFP leaders are temperamentally independent, reaching high office is hard as an Independent. Only 22 percent of Americans considered themselves Republican in the mid-1970s, and 43 percent Democrats in NORC-GSS surveys. By 1980 Democrats fell from 43 to 38 percent, but Republicans held a steady 23 percent; Independents rose to 38 percent. Some NFP Republicans, like Congressman John Anderson of Illinois, faced problems inside the Republican party similar to those of NFP Democrats within their party.

6. *A Search for New Policies*. Reconciling these tendencies leads to avoiding or repackaging traditional issues: large social programs are hard to continue while easing the tax burden. New issues more consistent with NFP policies include symbolically important but inexpensive actions which appeal to the poor or minorities but do not alienate the affluent. Examples are (sometime NFP) Mayor Jane Byrne moving into a dangerous public housing project, or Peter Flaherty visiting the scene of urban disorders. Blacks and women can be appointed to visible positions. But the primary means to such seemingly contradictory ends is through greater productivity. The NFP leader thus tries hard to make government more efficient, or at least visibly demonstrate that he is trying. Carter thus stressed zero base-budgeting.

Openness to new technologies is moderated by pragmatic readiness to use what works. The lesser dependence on unions and patronage than traditional Democrats or ethnic politicians facilitates policies that may have been previously obvious but politically infeasible (like replacing expensive staff with new machinery). Public goods benefiting citizens generally are stressed as these can be emphasized in open meetings and the media. They follow from criticisms of inefficiency and patronage which reward entrenched groups at the cost of the public. "Sound" fiscal management, or its appearance, is essential. So is reducing, or not increasing, taxes (chapter 10).

Mayors and Council Members: Are NFPs Emerging?

We next examine political cultural characteristics among 227 mayors and council members from the 1976 PCS survey. Party affiliation remains important, but NFP tendencies are also clear. Fiscal liberalism was measured with items on eleven functional areas—police, fire, etc. Officials indicated if they preferred more, the same, or less spending. Social liberalism was measured by summing eight social items. (Appendix 1 has details.)

We compared first term officials with those serving two or more terms. Contrary to our NFP hypothesis, first term officials were not more fiscally conservative or socially liberal, although other data support this trend.[18] However, the connection between fiscal and social liberalism does vary by term of office. Second term fiscally conservative Republicans are also socially conservative. By contrast, first term officials, especially those "responsive to citizens," fit the NFP characterization—fiscal and social liberalism are unrelated for them (table 7.1).

Consider specific correlates of fiscal liberalism. More affluent citizens were more fiscally conservative (above). Income was too sensitive to ask leaders, but education and occupation were asked. For officials serving two or more terms, those higher in occupation were less fiscally liberal. But party was the critical factor, reflecting the New Deal schism (table 7.2).[19] First term officials are less bound by traditional cleavages: party importance falls, as does the explanatory power of the whole model (shown by the R).

Leaders also reported on preferences of local citizens and organized groups in the same 11 spending areas. If not fully objective, leaders document well their political cultures. Democrats report agreement with organized groups on more spending, while Republicans are closer to citizens and favor less spending.[20]

Organized Groups, Especially Business Groups

Many studies point to business as fiscally conservative, implying conflict with citizen preferences. This is a major theme of community

Table 7.1. Fiscal and Social Liberalism Are Strongly Related for Republicans, Second Term or More, but Moderately Related for Newer Officials

	Strength of Correlation (r) between Fiscal and Social Liberalism
Republicans, second term or more	.45
All Republicans	.28
Republicans, first term	.11
All respondents	.25
All Democrats	.16
Democrats, second term or more	.16
Democrats, first term	.17
First term Democrats scoring more responsive to citizens than average#	.06

Note: All r's are significant at the .10 level except that for first-term Democrats responsive to citizens.

#The citizen responsiveness score came from an item asking how often the leader voted against the dominant opinion of his constituents. See appendix 1.F, item #9 (VOTOPIN).

Table 7.2. Causes of Spending Preferences for Two Subgroups of Mayors and Council Members

Independent Variable	Dependent Variable: Fiscal Liberalism (SPEND11) First-Term Officials	Officials Serving Two or More Terms
Citizen responsiveness	-.05	-.09
Democrat	.28*	.44*
Independent	.19*	.10
Race (RACE)	-.19*	-.08
Immigrant (IMMIG)	-.03	-.01
Education (EDUC)	.04	.17*
Occupational prestige (OCCUPRES)	.13	-.19*
Multiple R	.40	.47

Note: This table shows standarized coefficients (betas) from a multiple regression analysis. An asterisk indicates that the F statistic exceeds 1.8, or significance at about the .10 level. N=98 for first term officials; 129 for those serving two or more terms. See table 7.1 note on citizen responsiveness.

power studies in the elitist tradition from Hunter (1953) to Domhoff (1978). The theme continues with O'Connor (1973:87): "[in some cities] the dominant private interests (particularly the leading industries) predetermine the volume of state spending and the major budgetary priorities." In New York City in particular banks were often blamed for the 1975 fiscal crisis: "Ultimate power over public policy in New York is invisible and unelected. . . . The most powerful circle is composed mostly of banking and international finance" (Newfield and DuBrul 1977:74, 77). How do our findings relate to such assertions?

Business leaders are clearly important in American cities. In our 1967 PCS survey, business leaders were mentioned as important more often than any other organized group (Clark 1975a). Groups reported by mayors and council members as "most active in city government" in the 1976 survey appear in table 7.3. Business organizations still led with 18.5 percent of the mentions. To see if business leaders have conservative effects on public policy, we included several power and influence measures for four types of business groups in our city-level regressions.[21] Their impacts on fiscal policy outputs were consistently zero (table 4.1, appendices 1 and 5). How reconcile high influence with no policy impact? By considering the chapter 1 propositions about "invisible" leadership, here applied to organized groups. Business leaders serve on civic boards and marshall resources for activities like United Funds. But they are seldom "dynamic" leaders in independently affecting decisions. They participate actively in community discussions and come to share the views of many other participants. On this point we agree with Marx when he criticized as "Benthamismus" the idea that capitalists must narrowly represent their interests. More recent structuralist-Marxists like Castells (1972) have similarly deemphasized business elites, stressing more general structures within which they operate. This links with the "non-decisions" argument that powerful interests suppress undesired policies (Bachrach and Baratz 1970). The critical issue in such analyses is isolating the "deep structure" which drives other variables. For some it is capitalism. As Newfield and DuBrul announce: "The city's crisis is a reflection of a much larger national and international crisis affecting the entire capitalist system . . . a vast complex struggle over who will control the limited capital resources of mankind in the decades to come" (1977:35–36). Others

Table 7.3. Groups and Organizations Most Active in Governmental Affairs

Public Employee Associations	4.3
Teachers' Associations	.6
Policemen's Associations	1.1
Firemen's Associations	.9
Sanitation Workers' Associations	.2
Social Workers' Associations	0.0
Public Employee Unions	6.7
Teachers' Unions	.4
Policemen's Unions	1.2
Firemen's Unions	1.1
Sanitation Workers' Unions	.4
All Public Employee Associations and Unions	16.8
Political Organizations	2.4
The Local Republican Party	.8
The Local Democratic Party	2.8
Church Organizations	1.6
Businessmen's Organizations	8.5
Retail Merchants Associations	.8
The Chamber of Commerce	5.3
Downtown Businessmen's Associations	2.5
Bankers	.7
Industrialists	.4
All Business Organizations	18.5
Professional Organizations	.4
The Bar Association	0.0
The Medical Association	0.0
Clients of City Services	4.3
Welfare Recipients	.2
Users of Public Health Services	0.0
Parents of School Children (the PTA, etc.)	.8
Users of Low-Income Housing	.9
Civic and Charity Groups	5.4
League of Women Voters	3.0
Community Service Organizations (e.g., Rotary, the Optimists)	.3
Neighborhood Groups	15.3
Civil Rights Organizations	.7
Environmentalists	4.1
Unions in the Private Sector	2.2
Taxpayers Associations	1.6
Ethnic or Racial Organizations	3.9
Community Action Organizations	7.3
Other	6.5

Note: These results derive from a question which asked the mayors and council members to list the five groups and organizations most active in government affairs in their city. The above list was used by the respondents. (See appendix 1.F.)

The table shows percentages of total mentions given to each of the above groups and organizations by the mayors and council members in all the cities combined. For example, 4.3 percent of all mentions went to Public Employee Associations. The total mentions for all types of public employee associations and unions was 16.8 percent. Public employee associations differ from unions which have a bargaining agent recognized by city officials.

see capitalism as driving the "social accumulation of capital" or "uneven development of capital" across cities and regions (Alcaly and Mermelstein 1977). But the problem with blaming the banks for refusing a city credit, or capitalism for shifting investments across regions, is that these are not inherently capitalist processes. In socialist societies like Yugoslavia banks play visible roles, and Yugoslavs in cities refused credit complain like New Yorkers.[22] Except that they seldom label Yugoslav bankers capitalist tools.

What then is the deep structure? Answers vary with what one seeks to explain, but for fiscal policy differences across cities, citizen preferences and rules of the game about organized groups are strong candidates. They drive the regressions in table 4.1 while business leaders do not. We can explore this interpretation further with PCS data for organized groups. A major problem with past analyses of business elites is that they measured power, not policy preferences, and usually just imputed conservative interests to business (Morlock 1974; Aiken 1970; Walton 1970; Turk 1977). We could not find a single comparative city study of business interests. Yet interests are critical, and sometimes surprising. Consider table 7.4 which shows how much each group favored redistributive policies (helping the poor) compared to all groups in all cities. Look down the Business Organizations column. In 16 cities business opposed helping the poor, but in 13 others favored helping the poor. In one city they scored 0, i.e., just at the national average. When we see that business leaders thus supported the poor in 43 percent of the cities, it becomes clear why they had no impact in city-level analyses: business groups take different positions in different cities.[23] The table also shows that in this regard business groups are not the exception but the rule. Most groups are pro-poor in about half of the cities, and anti-poor in others. The major exception is the two political parties, the only groups with consistent ideology across cities (boxed for emphasis). By contrast, other organized groups take on policy preferences dominant in their respective cities. For example, in Amarillo, all groups opposed poor-oriented activities, but in Malden all supported such activities. Citizens in Malden thus had no organized spokesmen for low taxes. This explains why many local groups, and business groups in particular, do not hold down expenditures in cities where they are influential.

Do group patterns vary with the city's political culture? Our characterization of the four political cultures implies more organized groups in Democratic and ethnic cities, and fewer in Republican and NFP cities. Municipal employees and black groups were discussed in earlier chapters. Considering all types of organized groups, we and others (e.g., Turk 1977) have used the number of different voluntary associations in a city as a measure of organizational density. If the number of association headquarters is simply correlated with the percentage of Republican votes in Presidential elections, we find a strong correlation in the expected direction, $r = -.44$ (for the 62 PCS cities, see Zimmermann 1979). Recall too our chapter 4 finding that cities where all nonpoor groups were more active increased expenditures from 1974 to 1977. Most organized groups favor more spending on themselves; especially where groups are numerous and legitimate sources of policy input, leaders compromise by giving more to all. Business groups sometimes act in this way, seeking more parking lots or neighborhood renovation. But only the measure for all nonpoor groups significantly increases expenditures.

Some results from the 1967 PCS survey clarify the interpretation of business as an invisible group. It identified business leaders via power and influence measures. The power measures asked respondents to indicate groups whose support was *essential* for mayoral elections, urban renewal, and similar issues. Business leaders were seldom mentioned. By contrast, the influence measures asked which groups actively participated in such decisions; business leaders often did (Clark 1975a). We pursued these issues in case studies of two PCS cities, Waukegan and South Bend, both of which had active business elites. They participated actively in urban renewal and school desegregation decisions, but when conflicts escalated, they were on the losing side in every case (Clark 1973b). Business leaders may seem powerful if they do not challenge the local political culture. If they do it is harder to win.

Business is not always invisible, of course; a major factor weakening local involvement was the rise of national public corporations after the 1920s. As many local firms are now absentee-owned, managers advance within the corporation by changing cities. Middle managers of such firms typically participate in charitable and civic activities of their cities, but seldom in partisan, conflictual issues (Aiken and Mott 1970; Appleton 1981). This pattern also reflects the NFP and Republican political cultures of most business leaders, which consider political inputs from civic associations representing the "entire community" as more legitimate than self-interested individuals or firms.

Another type of business participation is similarly invisible: private loans for municipal bonds. As links in national credit markets, banks provide information about nearby local governments to institutions elsewhere such as Moody's and Standard and Poor's rating agencies,

Table 7.4. Redistributive Interest Orientations of Eight Local Community Organizations (Including Business Groups) Relative to the Grand Mean over All Organizations in All Cities

Cities	Municipal Bureaucracy	Democratic Party	Republican Party	Business Organizations	Newspapers	Labor Unions	Civic Groups	Ethnic, Religious, & Racial Groups
1. Gastonia, NC	-.3	3.2	--[a]	-1.5	-1.2	--	-3.5	1.5
2. Dothan, AL	-.5	3.7	-1.8	-1.4	-.9	-1.8	-.7	-1.8
3. Chelsea, MA	.9	-5.1	3.2	1.2	1.3	.4	1.9	-1.8
4. Superior, WI	5.7	.4	-1.8	.2	-.1	-.9	1.2	4.9
5. Orange, NJ	1.8	1.5	1.5	2.0	.8	2.8	1.5	1.2
6. Eau Claire, WI	-.5	.4	-2.6	-1.0	-1.2	-1.3	-.9	--
7. Grand Forks, ND	2.0	1.5	-1.8	.9	1.5	1.5	1.5	--
8. Wyandotte, MI	1.5	1.5	-1.8	-.3	.2	1.5	1.2	2.6
9. Middletown, OH	-.9	-.1	-.1	-1.1	-.6	-.5	-.5	-1.1
10. Highland Park, IL	.7	.7	-2.9	.6	1.2	--	.5	1.5
11. Malden, MA	2.9	4.9	4.9	2.8	3.0	4.9	2.6	1.5
12. Manchester, NH	.3	1.1	1.5	.5	.3	-.1	-.3	1.5
13. Hamilton, OH	-1.8	1.5	-2.6	-1.4	-2.2	-2.3	-2.4	-1.8
14. Tyler, TX	-1.5	.9	-1.1	-.9	-.6	-5.1	-1.5	-1.0
15. Waukegan, IL	1.1	2.6	-3.9	0.0	.1	2.9	.1	0.0
16. Warren, MI	.5	1.5	--	1.5	.5	2.9	2.0	.4
17. Clifton, NJ	-1.1	-.7	-2.6	.1	-.8	-.1	0.0	1.5
18. Bloomington, MN	-.3	-.1	-1.6	-.8	-.3	-.1	-.5	1.5
19. Santa Monica, CA	-.2	2.4	-3.5	-2.6	-.3	-1.1	-.9	-1.8
20. Palo Alto, CA	-.1	--	.4	-.9	.6	--	1.3	1.5

21. Jacksonville, FL	-.2	.1	-3.5	-2.0	-2.0	-.3	-2.3	-1.8
22. Utica, NY	1.7	2.1	-1.8	.9	1.0	.4	.6	4.9
23. St. Petersburg, FL	-.7	1.5	-2.9	-1.1	.1	-1.8	-1.4	-.1
24. Gary, IN	1.1	1.2	3.2	.2	0.0	0.0	-.6	.7
25. Charlotte, NC	0.0	-2.9	-5.1	-2.0	-2.0	--	-.6	-1.8
26. Cambridge, MA	-.1	.2	-1.8	.4	-.6	-3.5	-.8	-2.9
27. South Bend, IN	-1.6	3.2	1.1	-.3	-.3	0.0	-.3	1.2
28. Amarillo, TX	-1.6	-5.1	-5.1	-1.0	-2.9	-5.1	-2.4	-.1
29. Salt Lake City, UT	2.6	4.9	.4	1.9	1.5	1.5	4.5	4.0
30. Pasadena, CA	.3	1.5	-1.0	-1.4	-1.1	1.5	-1.8	-1.3
Percentage of cities where group favorable to poor[b]	50%	79%	29%	45%	45%	42%	41%	56%

Source: This table is drawn from Zimmermann (1979) and Williams and Zimmermann (1981) which describe the procedure used to infer the orientations toward poor-oriented policies of each group and organization. These specific data were collected in conjunction with the International Studies of Values in Politics in 1967, and are available only for 30 cities, 20 of which are in our basic PCS sample of 51. Ten smaller cities were added for international comparisons.

Note: The Grand Mean is 5.145 and the standard deviation 1.23.

[a]Scores could not be estimated due to missing data.

[b]This is the percentage of cities with a +score. Example: 45 percent for business = (13/29) X 100 = 45%

banks and bond houses selling municipal bonds, and law firms and accountants who verify the city's bond prospectus and financial statement. Banks regularly perform these functions for cities that use the credit market. After the 1930s depression these functions were usually ritualistic since the risk that a city would default was low. But this changed in 1975 for New York City; the normally routine functions then became critical. Like the Shakespearian messengers, the banks were castigated for announcing the bad news. Yet banks have the sad job of reminding others that resources are not infinite; even rich cities must respect budget constraints. Cities compete for funds with other investments; if a city becomes less desirable, fewer investors will purchase its bonds, and borrowing may eventually become impossible. The argument by Mayor Beame and Controller Goldin that New York City banks were charging interest rates "unfair, unwarranted, and outrageously high," (see Newfield and DuBrul 1977:41; Beame 1972), is hard to reconcile with the refusal of many out-of-town banks to buy City bonds. If New York banks were profiteering, public officials would not have had to pressure them to buy more City paper.

These activities occasionally lead banks to more direct involvement in fiscal policy making. In past depressions, banks often advised defaulting cities and private corporations on day-to-day decisions to help them return to fiscal viability. Similar functions were performed by Emergency Financial Control Boards in New York City and Yonkers after 1975, and the Chicago School Finance Authority after 1979. Business and banking officials on such boards are expected to apply basic principles of fiscal management, matching revenues with expenditures, and asking hard questions about priorities if no one else does.[24] But when this perspective was reintroduced into New York City in 1975, it was greeted by many as grand tragedy, captured by Newfield and DuBrul: "It was the bankers who did the hoodwinking—lying to thousands of hapless investors, to the press, and even to the City Hall sharpies who were left holding the bag after a full-fledged market panic had commenced. The true story has taken almost three years to emerge: New York didn't jump: it was pushed" (1977:35–36). Similar rhetoric was common at the time among Democratic political leaders and union officials like Abraham Beame, Albert Shanker, and Victor Gotbaum. But as time passed, NFP Edward Koch was elected on a program of repairing his predecessors' mistakes, the first three-year bail-out was renewed for three more years, more facts about New York's high spending were published and gradually accepted, and it became less common for New York media and leaders to blame the banks.[25]

Organized groups, including business, are thus often on stage, but usually remain analytically invisible. What then shifts more fundamental policies across cities and time? Propositions 13 and 2½ are strong candidates.

The Taxpayers' Revolt as a Social Movement

Was the taxpayers' revolt channeled by taxpayers' associations like those of Howard Jarvis? Our mayors and council members gave such associations a paltry 1.6 percent of mentions in table 7.3. In a few cities (like Lakewood, Colorado) local groups actively coordinated the taxpayers' revolt, but our table 4.1 regressions showed that the only consistent depressor of spending was the size of the middle class. Its impact was still heightened by the national taxpayers revolt.

After Proposition 13 the taxpayers' revolt took on the character of earlier social movements: it was new and exciting, a few colorful spokesmen received great publicity, the news media sought out local instances of the national trend, polls were taken showing broad citizen support. When the popular base grew clear, many leaders sought to respond. This was hardest for traditional Democrats and ethnic politicians, but New Fiscal Populists and especially Republicans made the most of it.

If not via local groups, the taxpayers' revolt still exerted distinct local impact as a social movement, sharing some characteristics with black and municipal employee movements discussed above. Like past movements it offered newsletters, conferences, and speakers for local events. Howard Jarvis provided supporting letters to selected candidates, with dramatic effects in several California races.[26] Direct mailings by the Republican Party and ad hoc organizations like the American Tax Reduction Movement emphasized similar themes, requesting contributions, and endorsing local candidates (Jacob 1979).[27] One group hired a jet, baptized the "Tax Clipper," to transport speakers and lobbyists. With turnout well under 50 percent in most local elections, such efforts can nudge a few nonvoters toward their ballot booths. The movement's effect was not to enhance influence of local organizations, but of middle-class taxpayers. Rather than generating strikes or protests, it encouraged leaders to listen for soft murmurs by their silent majorities—perhaps letters to the newspaper or comments at a council meeting. Such "murmurs" sometimes seemed unfocused or irrational. But the national movement provided careful analyses for those interested, and bumper stickers for others seeking one-line slogans. If effects on citizens were modest, elected officials' fears that taxpayers might revolt were important. Across the country, local officials invoked the taxpayers' revolt to explain their more conservative spending policies. If they felt the movement was significant, then it was.

Peter Flaherty As a New Fiscal Populist: Pittsburgh As "An Anti-New York"

We now consider how earlier points in the chapter—fiscal conservatism among voters, NFP policies of a new mayor, and opposition by organized groups—come together in a case study of Pittsburgh. Since NFPs are often criticized as impractical, considering a specific city permits illustrating how NFP political culture, implemented in specific policies, helped a political system adapt to its changing private sector environment. Peter Flaherty was one of the first and most successful NFP mayors, in part because Pittsburgh was ready sooner. It experienced many problems common to old, northeastern cities, but in some respects earlier or more acutely than Boston, New York, or Philadelphia. Pittsburgh lost more jobs and residents in the 1960s than most cities, and increased its percentage of poor, nonwhite, and welfare supported residents. The steel mills traditionally employed Pittsburgh's blue collar immigrants, although many had moved into other occupations and improved their neighborhoods. Since the depression, most mayors had governed with support from the Democratic party "machine," as well as, especially after the late 1940s, with support from civic and business leaders.

Peter Flaherty, born in Pittsburgh in 1924, was the son of an Irish Catholic streetcar conductor and shopkeeper. After serving in the Air Force in World War II, he attended Carlow College (Pittsburgh) and Notre Dame Law School. He rose slowly, supported by the Democratic party, to Assistant District Attorney, and then City Council member from 1966 to 1970. Although a Democrat, he grew increasingly critical of the "machine," less on ideology than because it had simply grown rusty and inefficient. His views were popular with voters, and when he campaigned for mayor in 1969, Flaherty's slogan was "Nobody's Boy." He ran as an unendorsed, independent Democrat against Democratic and Republican candidates and won in most wards.

His independence continued in office; he relied minimally on organized groups. He discontinued several dramatic projects involving civic and business leaders that had defined the Pittsburgh "Renaissance." After the first six months he ignored many inquiries from journalists and newspaper publishers. He openly scorned the Democratic party and City Council which it still controlled. He fired leading party officials from patronage jobs, and began appointing young, aggressive department heads who looked for more efficient procedures. Municipal workers and union leaders sought to ignore or subvert these efforts. Tension mounted. A major critic was Teamster leader Thomas Fagan, important spokesman for municipal employee unions and active City Council member. Pittsburgh had numerous highly paid drivers and chauffeurs due in part to Fagan. As an austerity measure, the new mayor and department heads gave up their chauffeurs, and asked the water meter installers to give up theirs too. The Teamsters refused to accept this loss of jobs and called a strike joined by about half of all city employees. The issue was made to order for an NFP leader, and Flaherty made the most of it, denouncing excesses of municipal employees. The strike's message was clear: if water meter installers demand chauffeurs, how much fat must there be elsewhere? The newspapers were on strike but television stations publicized the issues, and many observers felt that citizens were generally outraged at the workers. After two weeks of pickets and court battles, the clear victor was Mayor Flaherty: from the 1971 strike until he left office in 1977, he had his way in all significant issues with nonuniformed municipal employees—and usually the council. From 1970 to 1974, the work force was cut by 18 percent, more than any of our other 62 cities; the average city expanded 10 percent. Work force reductions should be compared to Pittsburgh's population decline: 13 percent from 1970 to 1975. But many other cities lost population; Pittsburgh just adapted sooner. Few workers were fired; reduction was mainly by attrition.

In collective bargaining and labor relations, Flaherty was firm but reasonable (Campbell 1975). After the strike, he was in clear command. Compensation generally rose consistently with the private sector. But the administration was firm on staffing and work conditions, and thus reduced and reorganized the work force. Committed workers who improved productivity were promoted, whereas in the past, personal and political contacts were more important. These wage and staffing policies resulted in a modest 18 percent increase in personal service expenditures per capita from 1970 to 1974, when the mean for our 62 cities was 50 percent.

There was obviously room for improving productivity, although Flaherty's chief administrator, Bruce Campbell, claimed "we could do the same thing in most big cities east of the Mississippi." The mayor and department heads would arrive unannounced at work sites and police stations, asking questions, and subsequently redefining tasks and reassigning hundreds of employees. Unnecessary jobs like cuspidor cleaner were eliminated, sleeping policemen were given citations, a fire boat sold, jobs titled "deputy to" cut out. Crew sizes were reduced and complete divisions merged or given new tasks. The dissatisfied left; those who stayed adjusted to the new style. Without systematic performance data, service quality changes are unclear. Municipal employees claimed that staff reductions impaired services. And some citizens complained of potholes. But few service declines were significant enough to be seriously criticized. The press and political opponents looked hard for failures, but found few.

On social issues, Flaherty was sensitive but nonideological. Urban disturbances are a good litmus paper for mayors. A major disturbance in Pittsburgh followed the shooting of a black youth by an elderly white woman. Police circled the predominantly black neighborhood and were ready to break up the black crowd with clubs. Flaherty said no. He came in person, visiting homes of several black leaders to confer. They jointly agreed simply to let the crowd continue until it dispersed. No demands or concessions were made. Crime is another volatile racial issue. Its sources are poorly understood, but some observers credit Flaherty's calm handling of race relations as helping Pittsburgh's drop in crimes in the early 1970s.

Flaherty's fiscal conservatism was clear. He reduced the property tax rate three times and abolished a wage tax (subsequently reinstated). He kept debt at past lows. Major capital projects were few, but some, including maintenance, were later increased with federal funds. Flaherty was cautious about federal and state programs. He declined to participate in those initially involving small local contributions, but which might increase in a few years; he instead emphasized one-time capital projects. When Governor Shapp sought to marshall support for a state tax increase by promising funds to cities, Flaherty sent a well-publicized telegram: keep the funds and hold down taxes.

Flaherty's independence from the Democratic party, City Council, media, civic and business elites, and municipal employees was clear. How could he govern? The basic answer was his success in responding to preferences of Pittsburgh citizens. When first elected as an Independent, observers may not have believed his campaign statements about efficiency. But four years later, he won nominations from both Democratic and Republican parties, 65 percent of the popular vote, and most wards—the exceptions were a few lower-status areas still controlled by the Democratic machine and reform Democratic areas near the University of Pittsburgh. He served as mayor until 1977 when he assumed a high position in the Justice Department with the Carter administration. His successor Richard Caliguiri had opposed many Flaherty policies as city council president. But over time, popular support for the policies grew clearer, so that when Caliguiri ran for mayor, he reversed his earlier position, pledged to continue NFP policies, and won.

Flaherty and Pittsburgh illustrate many NFP themes, and contradict the common wisdom about the New York fiscal crisis and Northeast "syndrome." Flaherty turned the situation around by sheer "political muscle," as his staff put it. Flaherty acted forcefully because he felt the support of citizen preferences. Despite apathy or opposition from most organized groups, he excelled at the ballot box. Citizen preference surveys are unavailable, but his success in two elections and adoption of similar policies by his successor, are strong evidence that he captured basic citizen concerns. Although an "invisible politician" in chapter 1 terms, his forceful style was clear.

Flaherty illustrates well how NFP characteristics reinforce each other. His (1) fiscal conservatism appealed to the middle class, but (2) social liberalism concerning blacks and the disadvantaged, and his own modest origins and Democratic background helped average citizens identify with him. He captured their imagination in taking on traditional elite groups, as well as confronting and winning against the Teamsters. His (3) populism made (4) organized groups appear barely legitimate, while citizens were the major source of Flaherty's policies. He emphasized (5) new policies involving public goods, increasing efficiency via creative use of staff, and lowering taxes and manpower to adapt to the declining population. He was elected, reelected, and converted opponents to his policies. Altogether a suggestive case to study.[28]

If Pittsburgh were alone, it would stand as one dramatic illustration of which might be done elsewhere. Because Flaherty was "ahead of his time," he received little national attention as mayor. Yet by the mid-1970s, other cities began to recognize similar problems: a clearly declining private sector resource base, generating fewer city government revenues, yet a growing public sector. How adapt an expansive political system to its declining environment? NFP leadership is one of the most viable options. Republicans are unlikely candidates in cities with long and strong Democratic and ethnic traditions. The number of socially disadvantaged voters implies that leaders must respond to them as well as the middle class electorate. NFP leaders can succeed if they continue appropriate policies of social liberalism, especially concern for minorities and the disadvantaged. Yet they must also invoke the public interest to counter pressures from militant municipal employees and other organized groups resisting cutbacks. NFP political culture, channeled by a strong leader, can redefine the rules of the game in such cities, and help the political system make the adaptations necessary for it to survive in a more austere environment. This path was followed by the increasing numbers of NFP leaders who came to power after the mid-1970s. Mayors Edward Koch in New York, William Green in Philadelphia, and Diane Feinstein in San Francisco are just some of the best known. Like Peter Flaherty, they struggled to do more, or at least the same, with less. Specific lessons they suggest for other cities are reviewed in chapter 10.

CHAPTER EIGHT

Migration and Fiscal Policy: Are They Clearly Related?

Earlier chapters analyzed how citizens affect fiscal policies through "voice"—via referenda, organized groups, or political leaders. But these are slow and marginal compared to migration (Hirschman 1970; Orbell and Onu 1972).

Most migration research omits public policy variables, especially local expenditure patterns. Yet most local expenditure research omits migration. This chapter joins these two traditions by studying the linkage between migration and urban fiscal policy. Feelings can run high in this area. Some suggest that more fortunate citizens move to suburbs and the Sunbelt to avoid their social responsibilities. The debate over "white flight" from school integration has been particularly intense (e.g., Coleman, Kelley, and Moore 1975; Frey 1979), and zoning also assessed for its segregating effects (e.g., Shlay and Rossi 1981). Others lament that minorities are "locked in" to cities by place-specific grant programs, and call for a negative income tax or other measures (see Kasarda 1980). Still others deny that migration by either the more affluent or minorities is affected by local fiscal policies. Despite strong ideological overtones of these discussions, and the major policy implications of alternative assumptions, little research has focused on migration effects of fiscal policies.

Citizen preferences were analyzed above using surveys; migration is another preference measure, one of "revealed preference" manifested in actual behavior. Migration rates thus identify cities that citizens find variously attractive. Migration can also change sector sizes,

Thomas P. Bonczar is coauthor of this chapter.

if persons leaving a city differ from those who remain or migrate to it. Citizen preferences and sector composition are joined in our basic migration proposition (proposition 4 in chapter 1):

The more urban policies are consistent with sector members' preferences, the greater the expansion of that sector through migration.

This general idea informs analyses of two fiscal policies that may influence migrants: welfare benefits and tax burdens. It suggests that the closer fiscal policies are to preferences of citizens in a sector, the more the locality attracts such citizens. Similarly, as fiscal policies deviate from sector preferences, sector size declines.[1] Still, before any reaction occurs, dissatisfaction must transcend a threshold due to (1) incomplete information among citizens concerning public policies, (2) low salience of these policies and hence their limited role in migration decisions, (3) greater importance of other factors (jobs, housing and site characteristics, etc.), and (4) costs of moving. Thus, public policy shifts may not have visible or immediate migration effects.

Should local leaders conclude that their policies seldom affect migration? Some have. Elected officials must generate results in less than four years, and the public's memory is often shorter. Is it better to consider service requests and raise taxes, or consider migration and reduce taxes? In the early 1970s officials responded more to service requests. Migration was seldom a political issue, given its slow and silent workings. Our distinction between changes and levels is important here too: with New York City's per capita tax burden of $1,549 compared to $719 in San Antonio (in 1977), New York officials might understandably not try to compete. Working for changes is hard for citizens too; moving is simpler. Tax burdens are political decisions, but include residues of past decades, hard to undo in four short years. Civic and political leaders often ask if they should even try. The question is clarified by analyzing impacts of tax burdens and welfare benefits on migration.

For theoretical background, we partially build on Tiebout (1956), but differ on some important points. He assumed that citizens sort themselves into cities providing public policies with which they agree, such that within a city citizens come to share policy preferences. Such a long-term equilibrium assumption facilitates analysis, but ignores some important issues. By contrast, we do not assume homogeneity, but introduce the sector concept to distinguish citizens by policy preference. Sector size can then change as policies depart from sector members' ideals. This implies that if citizens differ in policy preferences, so will their satisfaction with current policies, and in and out migration continue. Our shorter-term perspective than Tiebout isolates fiscal policies as a source of such migration. Tiebout's paper was purely theoretical, and generated much discussion but little empirical analysis. Most empirical work on migration has simply ignored Tiebout. In a time perspective shorter than necessary for Tiebout's equilibrium, what impacts are visible, and how do they differ by sector?

The sectors used in this chapter are nonwhites and whites as Census migration data are available primarily for them. The periods generally correspond to those elsewhere in the book: 1960–70 and 1970–75. Migration is considerable in just five years. Forty-four percent of Americans changed residences 1970–75. Of central city residents moving in these years, about 50 percent stayed in the same city; the others move to suburbs, another metropolitan area, or a nonmetropolitan area. But since almost as many persons moved in as out, central cities averaged only a 3 percent net loss in 1970–75 (U.S. Bureau of the Census 1975). We analyze such net migration. Because appropriate fiscal data are available only by county, the migration analysis uses counties overlapping with the 63 PCS cities. (There were only 57 since more than one city often fell in the same county.)[2]

Do High Tax Burdens Discourage Migrants?

The chapter 7 surveys imply that in-migrating, nonpoor citizens should reveal their low tax preferences by avoiding cities with high tax burdens. Do they? Our measure is the tax burden born by residents from all overlapping units of local government.[3] Most of the book considers city governments. But for migration, tax burdens from all local governments are important since city governments often generate well under half the total local tax bill. Many local governments are not coterminous with the city government, complicating analysis. Appropriate data are compiled by county every five years in the Census of Governments. Our tax burden measure thus sums revenues collected by all city, special district, school district, and county governments in the county area in 1967 and 1972. To this is added a per capita share of the state tax burden. All local revenues (taxes, charges, etc.) are included, but intergovernmental transfers and state trust funds excluded.

Figure 8.1 is a scatterplot of 1970–75 net migration against the 1972 tax burden. Consider San Francisco. The horizontal axis shows that the average San Francisco resident paid almost $1,200 to local governments and the State of California in 1972. On the vertical axis is San Francisco's net migration rate 1970–75, about −9 percent. By contrast, Houston's net migration rate was +11 percent, and its tax burden only about a third that of San Francisco: $455.[4]

The downward sloping regression line indicates that cities with high tax burdens generally lost population. Cities above the line, like Phoenix, gained more residents than one would expect from their tax burdens. Those below the line—St. Louis is the most extreme—are losing residents even faster than predicted by their tax burdens. Brooklyn is slightly below the regression line, while Richmond County (Staten Island) grew as fast as Houston. That all cities do not fall on the regression line shows that other variables affect migration.

Other variables are omitted from the scatterplot, but included in regression analyses and discussed below. Tables 8.1 and 8.2 report multiple regressions for 1960–70 and 70–75. The top row of each indicates total tax burden effects. They are significant and consistent in magnitude considering even effects of many variables used in past research. While no study used a comprehensive tax burden measure like this one, those including some tax measure generally found it negatively related to migration.[5]

The tax burden may be consistently significant, but how large is its effect? Using standard regression procedures and assumptions, our estimates of tax burden effects from the table 8.1 and 8.2 models indicate that a 10 percent tax burden increase would decrease net migration for whites by 1.48 to 3.12 percent in 1960–70, and decrease net migration of the total population in 1970–75 by .46 to 1.16 percent. A 10 percent tax burden increase thus led about two more white persons

Figure 8.1. The Higher the Tax Burden, the Lower the Net Migration from 1970–75

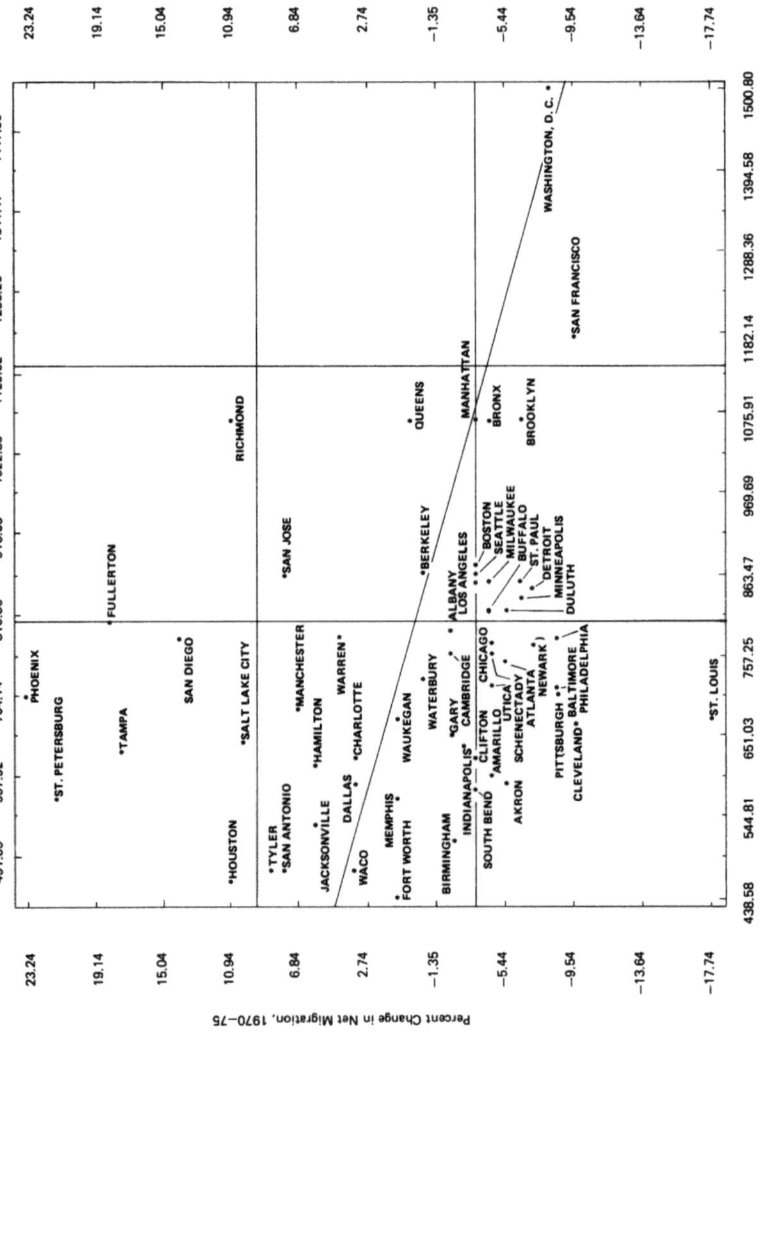

Table 8.1. Regression Results with Net Migration for Whites, 1960-1970, as Dependent Variable

Independent Variables	Equation Number (1)	(2)	(3)	(4)	(5)	(6)	(7)
Total tax burden	-.30*	-.34*	-.30*	-.47*	-.43*	-.22*	-.26*
Median family income	.30*					.11	
Median school years completed	.21*	.25*	.28*	.25*	.20*	.14	.15
Mean January temperature			.40*				
Mean July temperature			.05	.12			
Temperature index	.46*	.37*			.29*	.49*	.45*
Percent housing unsound		-.28*	-.30*	-.32*	-.30*		-.14
Population size	-.19*	-.15	-.15	-.07	-.13	-.10	-.10
Percent black population						-.36*	-.34*
Prevailing wages, manufacturing		.05	.10	.25*	.18		.04
Net change in employment				.34*	.22*		
Multiple R	.63	.65	.67	.62	.66	.69	.70

Note: These are multiple regression results for the 57 PCS counties. They show standardized regression coefficients (betas) and an asterisk if the corresponding F statistic equals or exceeds 1.8 (significant at about the .10 level).

per hundred to leave in 1960–70 and one more person in 1970–75. This is not small. Obviously, such results depend on the specific model estimated, but tax burden coefficients in tables 8.1 and 8.2 are relatively stable.[6]

Other variables are important enough that one should not overstress the tax burden, especially for cities in the middle range. But for those high or low, taxes often become salient to citizens and firms. The few hundred dollars in tax burden differentiating Gary from Berkeley is small compared to other factors, but New York's reputation for high and irresponsible spending is a factor local leaders have to work hard to overcome. Conversely, Texas cities have developed low tax reputations, and gained population. Some commentators explain growth in cities like Houston by their Sunbelt climate. Perhaps, but part of the "climate" is a low tax burden. This critical point is illustrated vividly

Table 8.2. Regression Results with Net Migration for Total Population, 1970-1975, as Dependent Variable

Independent Variables	Equation Number						
	(1)	(2)	(3)	(4)	(5)	(6)	(7)
Total tax burden	-.36*	-.34*	-.16	-.14	-.19*	-.33*	-.32*
Median family income	.03					-.07	
Median school years completed	.38*	.39*	.43*	.27*	.27*	.22*	.20*
Mean January temperature			.46*				
Mean July temperature			.18*	.09			
Temperature index	.47*	.47*			.21*	.55*	.57*
Percent units without plumbing		-.17*	-.14*	-.13*	-.15*		-.11*
Population size	-.17*	-.19*	-.18*	-.05	-.11	-.06	-.10
Percent black population						-.42*	-.39*
Prevailing wages, manufacturing		-.09	-.02	-.03	-.06		-.11
Net change in employment				.62*	.53*		
Crude birth rate, 1970	.19*	.14	.04	.22*	.24*	.19*	.16*
Multiple R	.71	.73	.78	.80	.81	.78	.79

See note to table 8.1

by exceptions within each region (see Clark and Fuchs 1977b). For example, San Francisco and Atlanta are more like the "old, declining, northeastern cities" in their tax burdens than they are like Houston. And San Francisco and Atlanta are losing population. By contrast, Manchester, and the whole state of New Hampshire, are booming in jobs and population—and New Hampshire is the one New England state with a tax burden resembling Sunbelt cities.[7] These specific cities are more than casual examples; comparative analysis similarly indicates important variations within regions (see chapter 3 and Clark et al. 1976). Clearly, many factors affect migration, which may differ by migration streams (new households forming, older persons retiring, middle-age persons seeking better jobs, etc.). Our results simply suggest the importance of the tax burden above and beyond other variables. High tax burden cities attract fewer new residents and lose more old residents than those with lower tax burdens.

Jobs and People

A classic argument in migration theory is that people move to jobs. This was the traditional urbanization pattern of European peasants moving to cities, and of blacks leaving southern farms for northern cities after World War I. Jobs influence migration, but how much and in what manner? We and others have analyzed these questions in several ways.

To explain net migration of individuals, we used data concerning prevailing wages in manufacturing and services, and net changes in employment. They were included both to assess their importance and to remove their effects from the tax burden and other independent variables. Changes in jobs were closely related to net migration for whites (1960–70) and the total population (1970–75), but unrelated to black net migration (tables 8.1, 8.2 and 8.3).

Second, we analyzed net change in nonagricultural employment 1970–75 as a dependent variable, using the same independent variables as for migration of individuals. Cities with higher tax burdens increased jobs less (results not shown).

These results show consistent tax burden effects. We completed these analyses since most research on net employment and migration omits the tax burden. Two results from research by others are interesting here as they both question traditional wisdom and dovetail with our work. One is a series of papers by Muth (1971) and Greenwood (1975b) using simultaneous equations to estimate effects of changes in jobs on changes in population, and vice versa. To the surprise of many, Muth found that the effect of changes in population on changes in jobs was *larger* than that of changes in jobs on changes in population, although both effects were present. Others using similar methods differ on the magnitudes, but generally conclude that the effect of migration on jobs is important (see Greenwood 1975a, 1975b). This suggests that many people move to cities like Phoenix and San Diego, and once there, find or create jobs for themselves. While other persons are attracted

Table 8.3. Regression with Net Migration for Nonwhites, 1960-1970, as Dependent Variable

Independent Variables	Equation Number										
	(1)	(2)	(3)	(4)	(5)	(6)	(7)	(8)	(9)	(10)	(11)
Welfare payments/recipient	.19*	.31*	.15	.15	.18*	.19*	.26*	.23*	.19*	.20*	.31*
Median family income	.46*										
City income per capita 1960								.09		-.05	
Median school years completed	-.14	.01	-.03	-.04	-.04	-.04	-.02	-.10	.04	.05	.02
Mean January temperature					.23*						
Temperature index	.28*	.18*	.19*	.17*		.19*	.15	.15	.19*	.21*	.19
Percent housing unsound			-.26*	-.27*	-.27*	-.29*	-.34*	-.30*	-.29*	-.27*	
Percent housing owner occupied	-.13	-.05									-.05
Population size	.08	.30*					.24*	.18*			.30*
Population density			.21*	.20	.21*	.32*			.32*	.35*	
Percent black population	-.34*	-.45*	-.38*	-.38*	-.40*	-.41*	-.34*	-.34*	-.41*	-.41*	-.45*
Prevailing wages, services			.16	.17	.19						
Prevailing wages, manufacturing		-.02				-.08	-.10		-.08		-.04
Net change in employment				.03				.04		-.03	-.04
Multiple R	.70	.64	.71	.71	.72	.71	.70	.69	.71	.70	.64

See note to table 8.1.

to these same cities by jobs, the causal arrow is sometimes stronger from population to jobs than vice versa. This pattern may be related to earlier retirements, more mobile youths, greater affluence and attention to amenities, and similar factors which may grow in importance over a more job-centered past. Specific results no doubt differ by SMSA and capture myriad motives of separate individuals, but for city officials they underline the importance of amenities for citizens qua residents, in contrast to citizens qua employees.

A second result comes in good part from research by David Birch and his MIT associates (e.g., Birch 1979, 1980). They have done detailed analyses of job changes in cities, isolating patterns by firm size, neighborhood, etc. From 1969 to 1976, 80 percent of new jobs in cities were in small firms (under 100 employees). And firms with under 20 employees created 66 percent of all new jobs. But these small firms are born and die off rapidly. Differential birth and death rates of small and medium sized firms thus explain most changes in jobs in a city.

These results provide a sharper sense of job and population movement. They suggest that the stereotype of the large corporation "moving" from New York City to Houston is inadequate. Some large firms do move, but most growth is in new, small firms, and people starting them can be attracted by factors which lead them as residents to choose the Houstons and San Diegos. Once there, many start new firms. There is such continual movement of persons, and birth and death of firms, that cities should be careful not to give too many tax breaks or other advantages to large firms, or the shift in tax burdens will discourage new residents and smaller firms, and thus generate net losses in jobs and population.

Welfare and Nonwhite Migration

Cities providing policies more consistent with blacks' preferences should attract and retain more black migrants than those which do not. As black citizens have lower incomes than whites and prefer more government spending (chapter 5), we would expect cities with more public services, especially redistributive services, to attract blacks. The effects of welfare payments on attracting migrants have been much debated. New York's generous welfare benefits are often cited as a source of both its fiscal strain and its growing minority population. Others suggest that migration is primarily due to jobs and related economic opportunities. Do welfare benefits significantly affect nonwhite migration when other variables are controlled?

We related 1960–70 nonwhite net migration to welfare benefit levels to address this question. Net migration data for nonwhites include some Hispanics, Orientals, and others, but the majority are black. The welfare measure included all expenditures in the county area classified by the Census as "public welfare."[8] Other variables were considered using multiple regression procedures. Nonwhite net migration was indeed higher in counties with higher welfare benefits (table 8.3). For 1970–75, migration was available only for the total population, which one might expect to be decreased by high welfare payments; it was (results not shown).

Interpretation is complicated by possible differences in in-and-out migration, but the same methodology as for the tax burden indicates that a 10 percent increase in welfare payments in 1962 raised nonwhite net migration by .44 to .93 (just under 1) percent for 1960–70.

The finding should still be placed in the context of other studies on black and nonwhite migration. Studies are of two basic types. One is comparative studies like this one of counties or SMSAs, four of which have related black migration to some welfare benefit measure. All four (listed in table 8.4) confirmed our results: nonwhite migration was higher in jurisdictions with higher benefit levels. Of course, this by no means implies that other variables, like job opportunities, were not also significant sources of nonwhite migration. Nor does it specifically indicate that nonwhites move for welfare benefits. Jobs may be a primary attraction to a city, but once there, welfare benefits help retain nonwhite residents.[9]

A second research tradition studies individuals: their decisions to migrate to cities and behavior upon arrival (Abt 1970; Price 1969; Petersen and Sharp 1969; Fried et al. 1971). Two findings are of interest. First, migrants rarely cited welfare or other support programs as an attraction for in-migrating, although the stigma of welfare discourages such a response. More frequently stated causes were job opportunities or "general economic advancement." Second, recent migrants found

Independent Variables \ Study / Dependent Variables	Cebula (1974): Net mig., by race, 1965-70 SMSAs	Hinze (1977): Net mig., age, sex, race, 1960-70 SMSAs	DeJong & Donnelly (1973): Net mig., nonwhites 25-29 1950-60 SMSA counties	Pack (1973): Gross in-mig., by race, 1955-66 Central cities	Blanco (1963): Net mig., total 1950-57 States	Lowry (1966): Net mig., total 1950-60 SMSAs	Mazek (1966): Gross mig., age, sex, race, occupation 1955-60 SMSAs
Taxes/capita				X			
Property taxes/capita	X						
General expenditure/capita	X			X			
Educational expenditure/capita				X			
Welfare payments/recipient	X	X	X	X			
Population		X		X			
Population nonwhite (%)		X	X	X			
Natural increase					X	X	
Age structure index		X					
Armed services personnel					X	X	
Mean January temperature		X					
Mean July temperature		X					
Possible sunshine	X				X		
Pollution	X						
Population density		X	X				
Income/capita	X						X
Median family income		X	X	X		X	
Change in median family income				X			
Unemployment rate		X		X	X		X
"Prospective" unemployment					X		
"Potential" unemployment							X
Change in non-ag. employment			X		X	X	
Change in mfg. (value added)		X			X		
Change in service ind. rcpts.		X					
Change in wholesale ind. rcpts.		X					
Change in farm products sales		X					
Housing, unsound (%)				X			
Housing, owner occupied (%)				X			
Median education				X	X		
Change in college enrollment					X		
Population in college (%)		X					
Population in high school (%)		X				X	

jobs rather quickly and did not join the welfare rolls in any larger proportion than nonmigrants.

How reconcile these survey results with city-level findings? By distinguishing in- and out-migration. Job opportunities seem to encourage in-migration, which in the 1960s was often in areas with higher welfare benefits. Welfare may have had some independent impact, but was often associated with general economic opportunity. Welfare benefits thus seem to affect in- less than out-migration. This interpretation is supported by findings of higher net nonwhite migration to larger northern and western SMSAs, but no relationship for smaller northern or western SMSAs, or southern SMSAs (DeJong and Donnelly 1973). Other studies report that a common pattern was that southern-born migrants would find work in the first few years in the North, but over the longer term turn to welfare (Petersen and Sharp 1969; Fried et al. 1971). Once dependent on welfare, the migrant was reluctant to move; out-migration from northern, urban areas was thus low. Studies in Chicago have shown that AFDC support continued longest for women who were the most southern in origin, most rural, oldest, and who have the most children, worst health problems, and lowest levels of employability (Mayo 1975; Ensminger 1978). As cities growing most in jobs and population are no longer those with the highest welfare benefits, it is important to reassess these patterns as newer data become available.

Conclusion

Consistent with our theory, two fiscal policies affected migration by selected types of citizens. County areas with higher tax burdens had lower net migration rates for whites in 1960–70, and all residents in 1970–75. Counties with high welfare benefits had more net migration by nonwhites in 1960–70, although welfare benefits seem less important for in- than out-migration. These migration results fit with surveys of individuals in earlier chapters. Fiscal policies of cities thus significantly affect migration patterns of their residents, although they are by no means the sole determinants of migration.

We estimated migration impacts of changes in each fiscal policy. A 10 percent increase in tax burden decreased net migration by about 2 percent, while a 10 percent increase in welfare decreased nonwhite migration by just under 1 percent. Such results can help public officials assess how much their fiscal policies may affect migration. These results also imply that "place-specific" grants affect migration in ways that "people-oriented" grants would not.

The results for population and jobs reinforce others identified above. Americans marry less and later than in past years, divorce more, have fewer children, pursue more education, join unions less—and more often work in small, service firms, and frequently change residence. The "post industrial" economy of small service firms permits persons to achieve more individualistic life-style preferences than do larger firms. Small firms are attracting graduates of leading business schools as well as middle-aged persons dissatisfied with the more unionized, regulated, and bureaucratized large corporations. These patterns both reflect and reinforce the individualistic political culture which has long impressed foreign observers (Lipset 1979), and has traditionally implied limited government. Combined with the increased social tolerance associated with education and exposure to diverse life styles, via changes in residence and jobs, these patterns reinforce the trends identified in chapter 7 toward New Fiscal Populism.

Addendum: Other Variables Affecting Migration

To provide unbiased estimates of fiscal policy effects, related variables should be controlled. To this end we reviewed the migration literature, beginning with two major overviews by Shaw (1975) and Greenwood (1975a) and all issues of the *Social Sciences Index* and *Social Sciences and Humanities Index* from 1970 to 1977. These generated some 75 articles and books which we inspected, especially studies of substate units (counties, cities, SMSAs) using large, preferably national samples, multicausal statistical procedures, and including local fiscal policies among explanatory variables. Table 8.4 lists major studies; other studies suggested further explanatory variables.

Twenty-two explanatory variables were constructed for each period, of six types: fiscal policy, socioeconomic characteristics, amenities, housing, population, and economic activity.[10] As several were similar (e.g., income per capita and median family income), multicollinearity was a problem with just 57 cases. A series of models was thus specified such that correlations between any two independent variables did not exceed $r = \pm .5$. For those more highly correlated, the one with the higher simple correlation with the dependent variable was retained, and a variable substituted similar to the one omitted. The procedure was repeated until all variables had been included in several equations, with a maximum of about 10 explanatory variables. Tables 8.1, 8.2, and 8.3 show the basic results. The 1960–70 dependent variables were white and nonwhite migration, while for 1970–75 only migration for the total population was available. Results are briefly reviewed by type of independent variable.

Fiscal Policy Measures. Two alternatives to the total tax burden were used, largely to replicate earlier work. *General expenditures, excluding education and welfare* (for all local governments in the county area) generated the expected negative coefficients for white net migration in 1960–70 and total population 1970–75. *Educational expenditures per capita* are sometimes thought to attract residents. They showed a positive coefficient with white net migration in 1960–70, but the sign became negative in 1970–75, matching the increasing disapprovals of school bond referenda in these years.

Socioeconomic Characteristics. We expected cities with higher average income and education to attract more migrants. *Median family income* generally did for both whites and nonwhites in 1960–70, but not in 1970–75. Similarly, *median school years completed* positively affected migration for whites 1960–70 and total migration 1970–75, but not nonwhite migration. *Income per capita* was insignificant. The *unemployment rate*, only available for 1970–75, was negatively related to migration, as expected, but only marginally significant.

Amenity Variables. Following earlier work (e.g., Karp and Kelly 1971) we expected a high *mean January temperature* to attract migrants. It did in both periods, although less for nonwhites than whites in 1960–70. *Mean July temperature* was insignificant in 1960–70, but marginally positive in 1970–75. A *temperature index* divided mean January by mean July temperature; a warmer winter or cooler summer would increase the ratio—indicating a more moderate climate. It was positively related to 1960–70 migration for whites, as expected, but fell below significance for nonwhites; by 1970–75 it was strongly significant for total net migration. *Possible sunshine* (percent sunshine hours in recent years) similarly increased net migration for whites in 1960–70, but not nonwhites, then strongly increased total migration in 1970–75.

Housing Variables. The *percent of owner-occupied housing* was weakly related to 1960–70 migration, but positively related to total migration in 1970–75. Nonwhites moved toward areas with higher *population density* from 1960–70. *Percent housing unsound* we expected to discourage migrants, and it generally did for whites and nonwhites in 1960–70. A similar measure, *percent units without plumbing*, discouraged total migrants in 1970–75.

Population Measures. The classical migration trends involved industrialization and urbanization—movement toward larger population centers. But later flight to suburbs and exurbs would lead one to expect a negative coefficient. *Total population* was virtually always insignificant in our regressions, indicating a decline in importance of population size and/or that most of its correlates were included in other variables. *Percent black population*, in the traditional "migration stream" hypothesis, suggests that personal contacts help migrants find new locations. Instead we found a negative relationship for nonwhite migration in 1960–70, and for total migration 1970–75, reflecting movement of blacks to suburbs and other areas with relatively few black residents.

Economic Activities. The simultaneous equation studies of Muth, Greenwood, and others imply declining importance of jobs for attracting migrants. Our results fit this pattern. For 1960–70, the *prevailing wage rate in services* was insignificant for whites, although sometimes positive and significant for nonwhites, while for 1970–75 it was usually insignificant. The *prevailing wage rate in manufacturing* was insignificant for whites but weakly negative for nonwhites in 1960–70 and insignificant in 1970–75.[11] *Net change in nonagricultural employment*, 1970–75, showed coefficients generally positive and strong, indicating simply that areas growing in jobs also grew in population.

PART IV

Reducing Fiscal Strain: What Works?

CHAPTER NINE

Strategies That Often Failed: Intergovernmental Grants and Legal Reforms

Many laws have been passed to redirect local fiscal policies, but they have seldom had their intended effects. Legal structures include intergovernmental grants, functional responsibilities of cities, state fiscal controls on city finances, and legal responsibilities of local officials. This chapter considers each in turn, and using our chapter 1 framework, indicates how they affect fiscal policy.

Many observers suggest that current legal-fiscal arrangements seriously undermine local autonomy. One legal specialist writes: "The radical transformation that has occurred in the structure of our federalism in nearly two centuries of existence has . . . replaced it with the frank recognition of the legal hegemony of the national government" (Monaghan 1980: 92). Many conclude on similar notes.[1] Such statements convey three overlapping meanings:

1. local autonomy has decreased over time
2. there should be more local autonomy
3. little local autonomy remains

It is hard to disagree with #1. And most local officials subscribe to #2, although debate continues. But #3 is most central to this chapter: how much autonomy remains? How fully are local processes dominated by federal and state constraints? Without denying such constraints, we consider legal and fiscal structures as resources. They facilitate goals for some participants, and constrain others. They are not direct causes, but interact with the processes generating fiscal policy.

Why should there be local concern about state or federal laws? Primarily because they may conflict with local preferences. Past laws may no longer correspond to current preferences; "blue laws" are thus obeyed in the breach. Second, voters in a larger jurisdiction (nation or state) may differ from those in any one locale over political culture: fiscal or social liberalism, responding to organized groups or citizens, and use of public or separable goods. Third, chapter 1 suggests that leaders in larger jurisdictions with more heterogeneous citizens have more difficulty responding to citizens' diversity. Consequently, organized groups are more successful at increasing expenditures.[2] It follows that growth of higher-level governments should increase citizen dissatisfaction. The next sections elaborate these ideas to consider how specific legal structures affect fiscal policy.

Two Models of Intergovernmental Revenue

Intergovernmental grants are often discussed with terms like "rifle shot," "targeting," or "implementation" to imply that local officials execute policies from above. Discrepancies between federal or state intent and local practice then become technical problems of insufficient knowledge, time, or expertise (Pressman and Wildavsky 1973; Pressman 1975). A second view assigns a more active role to local participants who obtain intergovernmental revenues to implement local preferences. Figure 9.1 contrasts these two conceptions. This chapter emphasizes dynamics of Model II. Model II fits traditional philosophies of American government which stress federalism, checks and balances, and decentralization, and is esteemed by many local officials and citizens.[3] Model I is preferred more in Washington, especially in the executive branch, and by some economists analyzing intergovernmental fiscal flows.[4] Philosophical issues behind these conceptions are many, but our main concern here is the empirical appropriateness of each.

Do Federal Grants Shift Local Priorities?

We first consider support for Models I and II with our PCS cities. Combined effects of paths a, b, and c are estimated using a variation

Figure 9.1. Two Types of Intergovernmental Relations

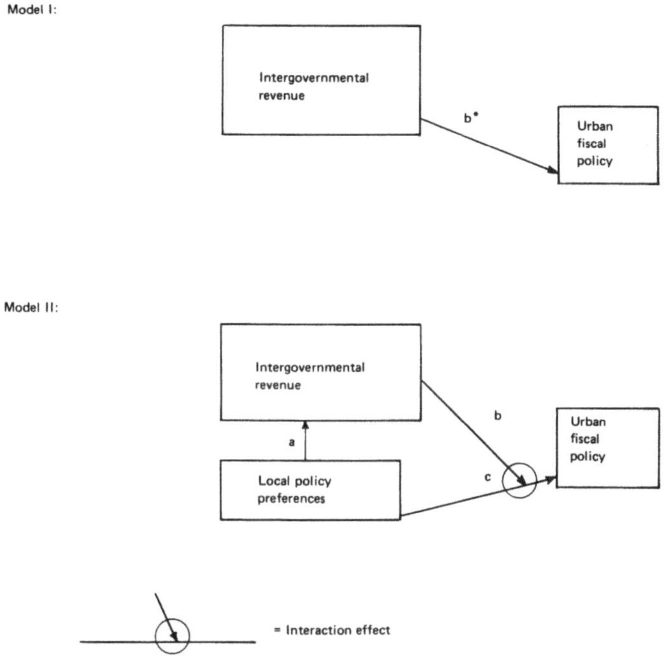

of the seven variable core model (see chapter 4), with federal and state intergovernmental revenues added as an eighth explanatory variable. If intergovernmental revenues affect local priorities, cities receiving more revenues should differ in policies from those receiving less. Do we find such effects? Remarkably few.

Results are in table 9.1: equations 1, 3, 5, and 7 are the basic core, while 2, 4, 6, and 8 add intergovernmental revenues. Only one core variable coefficient (of $7 \times 4 = 28$) changes across a significance level with addition of intergovernmental revenues, and then just from $-.20$ to $-.23$. Insignificant intergovernmental revenue coefficients in two of the four models (second to bottom row) suggest that the core variables include the major sources of intergovernmental transfers.[5] The intergovernmental coefficients drop in later years, when grant autonomy increased. The results are striking evidence that intergovernmental revenues do not fundamentally alter local processes. Nonlocal rev-

Table 9.1. Adding Intergovernmental Revenues to the Core Model Minimally Changes the Results

Independent Variables	Dependent Variable: General Expenditures							
	(1) 1960-70	(2) 1960-70	(3) 1970-74	(4) 1970-74	(5) 1974-77	(6) 1974-77	(7) 1977	(8) 1977
Middle class sector size (LPC70UMC)	-.20	-.15	-.20	-.23*	-.43*	-.42*	-.32*	-.32*
Ethnic political culture (IRISHL70)	.24*	.22*	-.25	-.27	-.02	-.01	.18*	.15*
Unionization of municipal employees (LPEMP072)	.06	.15	.009	-.006	-.04	-.02	.04	.01
Percentage blacks[a] (LPCBLK70)	.29*	.26*	-.18	-.19	-.46*	-.44*	-.15*	-.21*
Leadership measure[b] (LRPNTALK)	.012	.03	.68*	.70*	-.08	-.10	.06	-.002
Functional Performance Index (LFPDEC4)	-.20	.15	.02	.04	.10	.13	.73*	.50*
City Wealth Index (LNTWRT70)	-.03	.007	.10	.09	-.09	-.10	.18*	.14*
Intergovernmental revenues[c]		.33*		-.06		.18		.37*
Multiple R	.62	.69	.61	.61	.43	.46	.88	.91

Note: This table is similar to those in chapters 4 and 6, based on multiple regressions of the 62 PCS cities. It shows the standardized regression coefficients (betas) and an asterisk if the corresponding F statistic equals or exceeds 1.8 (significant at about the .10 level). Equations 1 through 6 are for percentage changes in general expenditures per capita; 7 and 8 are for the 1977 level per capita.

[a] The black political activity measure (LBLAKSMY) is used for the 1970-74 period.

[b] The 1976 leadership measure (LLEAD3W2) is used for the 1974-77 period.

[c] This measure is the percentage change in intergovernmental revenues per capita in 1960-70, 1970-74, 1974-77, and the level per capita in 1977.

enues essentially reinforce existing local influences. Related analyses are in appendix 5, which reports effects of intergovernmental revenues on other fiscal policy and fiscal strain indicators, and table 5.3 which analyzes local causes of intergovernmental revenues. These results counter so much common wisdom that we review several other studies to illustrate how cities can adapt intergovernmental revenues to local concerns.

Growth in Intergovernmental Revenues from 1960 to the Late 1970s

Before the 1960s, intergovernmental revenues to cities were few, but by 1981 they were over half of total revenues for some cities. Cities report the bulk of intergovernmental revenue as coming from state governments (59 per cent in fiscal 1977) rather than the federal government (37 percent). But much federal aid is "passed-through" state governments.[6] Intergovernmental grants may ease immediate pressures, but seem not to reduce fiscal strain. Fiscal strain increased simultaneously with increased intergovernmental dependence of all U.S. cities in the last 15 years; high dependence of cities like New York is not a strong argument for more assistance. A study of several European countries found that those with central governments providing the most assistance had the most fiscally strained cities (Newton 1980). Effects still vary by grant type.

Four Types of Intergovernmental Revenue Programs

As intergovernmental assistance has increased, its forms have differentiated. Tensions between Models I and II changed the types of grants. Two dimensions of grants concern (1) distribution via formula or competitive bidding, and (2) local discretion in administration. Cross-classifying these dimensions yields the four types in figure 9.2. In the 1960s, categorical grants addressed specific projects from Urban Renewal to Community Action Programs. Mayors complained that such piecemeal programs diverted basic services; the New Federalism of the early

Figure 9.2. Types of Intergovernmental Aid to Cities

Method of Distribution	Local Discretion in Administration: Low	Local Discretion in Administration: High
Competitive	Project Categoricals e.g. Urban renewal	Discretionary Block Grants e.g. Model cities program Community action program
Formula	Formula Categoricals e.g. Public assistance	Entitlement Block Grants and Revenue Sharing e.g. Community development block grants, comprehensive employment and training act, general support from state government

1970s thus provided grants with more local discretion. Grants then shifted rightward on figure 9.2 as well as down from competitive bids to formulas.[7] Special interest groups, which helped create many categoricals, shifted tactics in the 1970s to press for regulations. The autonomy of block grants was thus undermined by enhanced regulation of all grants.[8] Mayors often testify on these issues. Frequent program changes and rigid federal agencies are common complaints. Some mayors imply that Model I characterizes most intergovernmental grants, but elements of Model II often lie just below the surface.

"Grantsmanship" and Its Converse, "Fiscal Selectivity"

Local preferences encourage pursuing some grants and avoiding others. This is path a in Model II, most obvious for grants via application. Considerable choice is possible with over 500 programs for state and local governments in the early 1980s. Activities may be funded under

Table 9.2. Many Cities Receive More or Less Intergovernmental Revenue than Expected on the Basis of the Functions They Perform

Cities	Intergovernmental Revenue FP Residual#	Cities	Intergovernmental Revenue FP Residual#
	IGVREVFP76		IGVREVFP76
1. Akron, OH	4.25	33. Memphis, TN	-74.50
2. Albany, NY	88.81	34. Milwaukee, WI	75.26
3. Amarillo, TX	-34.89	35. Minneapolis, MN	43.01
4. Atlanta, GA	28.93	36. New York, NY	223.27
5. Baltimore, MD	117.23	37. Newark, NJ	230.01
6. Berkeley, CA	88.19	38. Palo Alto, CA	-7.77
7. Birmingham, AL	-.43	39. Pasadena, CA	34.86
8. Bloomington, MN	8.14	40. Philadelphia, PA	-46.13
9. Boston, MA	-35.10	41. Phoenix, AZ	4.01
10. Buffalo, NY	189.47	42. Pittsburgh, PA	23.17
11. Cambridge, MA	-248.43	43. St. Louis, MO	-57.50
12. Charlotte, NC	59.60	44. St. Paul, MN	51.79
13. Chicago, IL	-52.81	45. St. Petersburg, FL	7.50
14. Cleveland, OH	-9.43	46. Salt Lake City, UT	-25.48
15. Clifton, NJ	-228.44	47. San Antonio, TX	-69.62
16. Dallas, TX	-6.75	48. San Diego, CA	28.60
17. Detroit, MI	43.62	49. San Francisco, CA	168.91
18. Duluth, MN	109.81	50. Santa Ana, CA	23.27
19. Euclid, OH	-22.82	51. San Jose, CA	-3.50
20. Fort Worth, TX	12.91	52. Santa Monica, CA	-14.00
21. Fullerton, CA	17.15	53. Schenectady, NY	-3.95
22. Gary, IN	-11.19	54. Seattle, WA	29.62
23. Hamilton, OH	7.76	55. South Bend, IN	24.97
24. Hammond, IN	11.70	56. Tampa, FL	111.71
25. Houston, TX	-32.90	57. Tyler, TX	-43.96
26. Indianapolis, IN	-103.78	58. Utica, NY	39.92
27. Irvington, NJ	-105.88	59. Waco, TX	-9.44
28. Jacksonville, FL	-105.97	60. Warren, MI	-9.18
29. Long Beach, CA	-27.72	61. Waterbury, CT	-243.36
30. Los Angeles, CA	-30.27	62. Waukegan, IL	-11.89
31. Malden, MA	-202.67		
32. Manchester, NH	-27.67	MEAN	0

#This measure indicates how much a city receives in intergovernmental revenue above or below the amount predicted on the basis of its functional responsibilities. The computation procedure uses the residual approach of appendix 4.

several headings—like swimming pool repairs under neighborhood youth, park maintenance, or public works. "Grantsmanship" links local concerns to existing programs. In the 1950s and 1960s a few cities excelled at it: New Haven in urban renewal (Dahl 1961), federal housing and highway grants in New York via Robert Moses (Caro 1974), demolition and rebuilding over 50 acres in Boston (Fried 1973).

If grantsmanship stands in bricks and mortar, the often ignored converse is that many cities do not apply for grants—"fiscal selectivity" is a real option. Many cities opposed all federal grants until the 1970s. Urban renewal was defeated in some because of "creeping socialism" (Clark and Greer 1967; Anderson 1964). Pittsburgh and Dallas often avoided service programs because of uncertain continued funding (Clark 1978a; Bradley et al. 1980). Of 97 California cities, 33 received no federal categoricals from 1970 to 1974 except for emergency public employment, and two city councils explicitly prohibited seeking categoricals (Lovell and Korey 1975:92–94). The alternative strategies of grantsmanship and fiscal selectivity still imply a minimally knowledgeable staff. Small cities have sometimes not participated due to incomplete knowledge; preserving their autonomy, they lost out on federal largesse.

Provocative Findings from Comparative Studies of Grants

Combined effects of grantsmanship, fiscal selectivity, and lack of knowledge generate uneven distributions of federal funds. One telling finding has somehow been widely ignored: distribution of categorical grants in the 1960s and 1970s was unrelated, or weakly related, to unemployment or poverty.[9] This violation of the public finance principle of horizontal equity—treat equals equally—casts doubt on project categoricals as redistributive vehicles. Related findings are that 21 percent of U.S. cities received no federal or state grants in FY1970–71, just before enactment of General Revenue Sharing, and those first receiving funds in the mid-1970s were distinctly low on several wealth measures (Stein 1981). These results undercut the common arguments that grants should be targeted from Washington to preserve responsiveness to the poor, and that formula grants like GRS go to the more affluent.

Grant allocation discussions are troubled by cross-city differences in functional responsibility. Some 70 percent of the variance in intergovernmental revenues across cities is explained by differences in functions performed. Our FP approach permits adjusting for such differences, and examining those which remain, in table 9.2. Results are interestingly patterned. With one exception, all Texas cities received less intergovernmental revenue than expected, and all New York cities, save one, more than expected. Local preferences help explain these patterns (see table 5.3).

The Dynamics of Local Autonomy in Allocation of Funds

Does use of grant formulas reduce local autonomy? Yes, in terms of grant applications (via path a), but autonomy is preserved by adapting outside funds to local preferences (paths b and c). This is most difficult with formula categoricals, like welfare or Medicaid, whose administration is governed by detailed regulations. Despite exceptions—like the massive and successful drive to expand welfare rolls in New York City in the late 1960s (see Jackson and Johnson 1974)—the core of these programs is closer to Model I than II. Still, one should not forget the basic force leading local officials to intergovernmental grants: grants help constituents. Whatever the funding source, local officials receive credit (or blame) for most programs they administer. Depending on the political culture, programs may involve organized patronage or more public goods like major parks. John Lindsay, Ivan Allen, Richard Hatcher, and other mayors built local reputations on their success as Washington fundraisers. Disparity of goals between programmatic federal officials (or subsequent evaluators) and politically sensitive local leaders explains disagreement over many categoricals. What is "just throwing money around" to one is building a constituency to the other.

Local autonomy is less obvious in categorical programs. By contrast, General Revenue Sharing (GRS) and block grants openly encourage local initiatives. GRS was minimally constrained, permitting direct substitution and tax reductions—as in Chicago and Worcester. Other cities like Cincinnati, cautious about GRS continuation, segregated the funds and used them for one-time capital projects (see Anton 1975; Schoch 1978).

Another block grant, the federal Economic Stimulus Package, including Countercyclical Revenue Sharing (ARFA), Emergency Local Public Works (LPW), and Public Service Jobs (CETA) was launched partially for macroeconomic policy reasons in the 1975 recession. But many cities, including Detroit, Boston, New York, and San Francisco, were locally pressed, and used CETA funds for basic services like police and fire (Reischauer 1978). These local "diversions" of federal goals fueled discussion about the legitimacy of Models I and II (e.g., Vaughan 1976). Normative debate continues, but empirically Model II remains strong.

Responsibility for Redistributive Functions: Welfare, Health, and Hospitals

Redistributive functions are controversial. New York officials argued that without them their fiscal crisis would be solved. Dissatisfied taxpayers cite welfare as a program to trim, often implying that cities control social services. But few cities pay for social services. We try to clarify misunderstandings by asking: how many cities are responsible for redistributive services, and how much of a fiscal burden are they? Services considered are welfare, public health, and public hospitals.[10]

Does City Government Have the Responsibility? Where welfare, health, and hospitals are city provided, expenditures are large: 38 percent of general expenditures in New York, and 39 percent in San Francisco. Intergovernmental transfers reimburse about 40 percent of these expenditures. Still, as a percentage of the city's own source revenues, the figures are still large in some cities; four spent over a quarter of own revenues on these services (table 9.3).[11]

Local Autonomy in Welfare, Health, and Hospital Services. Welfare includes federally aided cash assistance, including Aid to Families with Dependent Children (AFDC), Supplemental Security

Table 9.3. City's Own Expenditures for 13 Cities on Welfare, Health and Hospitals as a Proportion of General Expenditures and City's Own Revenues

Cities	As a Proportion of: General Expenditures, 1974	Revenue from City's Own Sources, 1974
Baltimore, MD	6.2%	15.1%
Berkeley, CA	4.8	6.5
Birmingham, AL	13.7	21.1
Boston, MA	13.0	17.8
Cambridge, MA	17.3	19.8
Detroit, MI	8.2	10.9
Indianapolis, IN	18.4	30.5
Irvington, NJ	35.7	35.7
Jacksonville, FL	15.5	22.0
New York, NY	13.7	26.4
Philadelphia, PA	7.6	10.5
St. Louis, MO	20.2	23.9
San Francisco, CA	19.4	26.3

Note: These figures are reported for the 13 cities where welfare and related services exceed 10 percent of general expenditures.

Income (SSI); Medicaid (for the "medically needy,"); and General Assistance (a state-local program with no federal reimbursements). Expenditures vary because of the number and level of benefits, eligibility criteria, and size of the dependent population. Most decisions are made within broad federal guidelines by state governments which can add federal options, supplement federal payments, and require local contributions. California, Minnesota, New Jersey, New York, and North Carolina require local contributions to all major welfare programs, although these vary from 25 percent of the nonfederal share of AFDC in New Jersey to 50 percent in New York and Minnesota. Cities thus have relatively little local discretion over welfare policies.[12]

They have far more control over public health, but expenditures are small, seldom exceeding 3 percent of general expenditures. Only 13 of the 62 PCS cities support public hospitals, but for them expenditures were substantial. Eight spent more than 10 percent of general expenditures on public hospitals, 33 percent in Irvington and 20 in St. Louis.

Differences in Functional Responsibilities Across Cities. Funding arrangements are disputed for these three and other "noncommon"

functions which only some cities perform. What kinds of cities perform more functions? Cities with more functions—as measured by the FP Index—have more foreign stock and black residents and more poverty. Spending pressures are reinforced by more Democratic voting, and more active blacks and municipal employees. Leaders in these cities favored more spending, and nonpoor and business groups were low in influence, especially in 1967. The cities were higher in density and had more old housing, but insignificant population loss. Fiscal strain levels were higher (table 9.4). We previously saw that cities with more functions had mayors favoring more spending in the late 1960s (chapter 4). Such mayors were often supported by black political activists (chapter 5), and municipal employees were more active (chapter 6).

These results indicate past and current spending pressures. Most programs were approved by local officials, albeit often in expansive times. In retrenchment after 1975, state and federal maintenance of effort requirements and matching fund provisions deterred cutbacks on noncommon functions ranked low in priority by local citizens (Wolman 1979). Special interest groups often pressed for continuation. Transfer of noncommon functions to a higher-level government is thus often proposed as a solution.

Functional Transfers and Fiscal Strain

A few careful studies consider transfer of local functions to metropolitan, state, or federal levels. Some use national data and simulation techniques (Maxfield and Edson 1978), others data for several states (Bahl 1976; Bahl and Vogt 1975), while others concentrate on selected cities, especially New York (Hamilton and Rabinovitz 1977; Gifford 1978). Despite differences in approach, they consistently contradict normal arguments for takeover. The main reason is that in transferring up, it usually is necessary to raise service levels for all local units toward the highest levels. This upward-ratcheting has been mandated for many programs, and occurred "spontaneously" for most others (see Hamilton and Rabinovitz 1977; Bahl and Vogt 1975). The paradoxical result follows that "tax-base sharing" *increases* the tax burden on residents in poorer jurisdictions, since they contribute to raising services elsewhere. For example, New York City residents would bear

Table 9.4. Relationships between Functional Performance and Selected City Characteristics

City Characteristics	Index of Functional Performance
Socio-Economic Characteristics	
Median family income	-.26
Percentage black	.27
Percentage middle class	-.10
Percentage Irish	.54
Percentage native-stock American	-.44
Percentage owner-occupied housing	-.48
Percentage in poverty	.34
Percentage native-stock American/Republican (WCWPL)	-.54
Index of City Wealth (see chapter 2)	-.28
Political Process Measures	
Percentage voting Democratic	.42
Black mayoral support, 1967	.30
Black riots	.22
Ethnic group mayoral support, 1967	.35
Black political activity, 1976	.28
Poor political activity, 1976	.33
Nonpoor political activity, 1976	-.23
Municipal employee organization (LPEMP072)	.32
Business influence, 1967 (DCINBUS)	-.20
Business influence, 1976 (BUSGROAV)	-.34
Leader's spending preferences X resources, 1967 (LRPNTALK)	.43
Leader's spending preferences X resources, 1976 (LLEAD3W2)	.21
Fiscal Measures	
Index of staffing	.08
Compensation per employee, 1977	.11
Percentage change in general expenditures,	
1960-70	.47
1970-74	.13
1974-77	.01
Percentage change in long term debt,	
1960-70	.22
1970-74	.18
1974-77	.43
Common functions/net worth, 1977	.53
Other Variables	
City density	.44
Percentage old housing	.48
Change in population	
1960-70	-.17
1970-75	-.20

Note: These are simple r's (Pearson correlation coefficients) for the 62 PCS cities. If $r \geq .21$, $p \leq .10$: if $r \geq .32$, $p \leq .01$.

FP scores by city are in table 2.4.

a heavier tax burden if forced to contribute to providing services at New York City levels throughout the metropolitan area, state, or nation. Such benefits may be socially desirable, but not of fiscal advantage to central cities. If the transfer may help the city government, it still could raise total central-city tax burdens on residents. These results seriously undercut the normal equity argument that tax base sharing would benefit less affluent central city residents. Alternatively, it would be very hard to transfer welfare responsibility from New York City to the federal government and fund New York welfare at Mississippi levels. But movement in this direction is necessary to avoid increasing New York City tax burdens. Or New Yorkers could try to convince Mississippi taxpayers to transfer their funds to New York City to support welfare at current levels, but not increase benefits for Mississippians—a hard political feat. One can understand enthusiasm of agency officials to transfer functions up and increase service levels everywhere. But this is not what most citizens or elected officials prefer.

A few cities like New York and San Francisco provide social services because they are joint city-counties. But they also receive state revenues to counties which most cities do not. If county responsibilities are transferred, probably revenues would be too. From the New York and San Francisco cases, many infer that cities with broad service responsibilities are doomed to fiscal strain. But recall the table 2.3 result which showed that this was not the case for Baltimore. Its expenditures were below average after adjusting for services performed.

Clearly the fiscal incidence of a specific transfer depends on benefit levels, revenue types, and program extension to other jurisdictions. But in considering reasonable combinations of these, the studies cited conclude that costs and tax burdens generally increase. Several authors of these studies initially supported functional transfers, but shifted their views after more careful examination.

Metropolitan Government: A Meaningful Policy Option?

A related solution proposed for fiscal strain is consolidating central city and suburbs into a single metropolitan government. A reform plank for decades, "metrogov" has found minimal implementation (e.g.,

ACIR 1976a). What issues does it raise? The demographic background is the relative increase in total population, income, and percentage white in all U.S. suburbs (e.g., Berry and Dahmann 1977; Alonso 1978). These national trends still hide local variations. The Census defines suburbs as all city governments outside a central city but inside the metropolitan area. Some are farmland, while others have high-rise buildings; they vary equally in socioeconomic character. Annexing suburbs thus would not increase wealth or change the ethnic composition in areas where suburbs resemble central cities. Metrogov also implies dramatically increased size of government and fewer local options. These multiple changes have seldom been carefully assessed (see, however, Ostrom 1972; Greene and Parliament 1980).

One argument for metropolitan government is that suburbs "exploit" central cities. Some have sought to determine if central cities spend more due to suburban public service users who do not pay city taxes (see Hawley 1951; Kasarda 1976). But there are also fiscal benefits, such as increased central city sales taxes from suburban shoppers, and increased land value due to the presence of suburbs. Varying research designs generate sufficiently divergent results that who is "exploiting" whom is no longer clear (see Weicher 1972; Neenan 1972).

Political dynamics oppose metropolitan government. Affluent and white citizens often resist consolidation with the less affluent and minorities (e.g., Dye and Hawkins 1967; Downes 1971). But as proportions of blacks and Hispanics grow, so do opportunities for their political leaders (see Rakove 1975). More control, many black leaders have argued, means more minority jobs and contracts. They point to isolated poor and blacks in rural or affluent areas who lack spokesmen and public programs. Views also shifted in the late 1960s as racial integration goals were displaced by black power. White ethnic leaders use similar arguments. More generally, tensions emerge between abstract, public interest arguments of reformers, which might sway some NFPs and Republicans, and more circumscribed interests of ethnic politicians and traditional Democrats.

A "public interest" argument is that metropolitan consolidation increases efficiency in service provision (e.g., Hawley and Zimmer 1970). With economies of scale, larger units should generate less expensive public services. This argument is undercut by the available evidence:

larger units are generally more costly for similar services (see Ostrom 1972; Ostrom et al. 1978), apparently through less efficient employees, although possibilities for scale economies exist in services like public transportation (see Peterson 1976). Economies of scale are also reduced by the tendency of consolidation to raise service levels, as discussed in the last section.

Capturing suburban population growth was another consideration. But in the 1970s, most growth was in the South, West, and nonmetropolitan areas (Fugitt and Zuiches 1975). By contrast, many *entire* metropolitan areas lost population (ACIR 1980a). For example, the New York metropolitan area lost about 9 percent of its population from 1970 to 1978. If New York annexed its suburbs, this would probably exacerbate population decline.

The above are points that citizens and leaders often consider apropos metropolitanization. But whatever the rationales, most metro efforts have failed (see Campbell and Dollenmayer 1975). More successful is metropolitan coordination of specific services, especially via contracting (Zimmerman 1975; Ostrom et al. 1975). Economies of scale are present for some services, and at some levels. "Incorporating externalities" is also sometimes important, such as for "fresh pursuit" of criminals. Service-specific agreements respond to these issues.

State Fiscal Controls on Local Governments

Dillon's Rule, the nineteenth-century legal interpretation, holds that authority over local government resides in the states. Most legal arrangements affecting cities (constitutions, laws, mandates) are creations of states. American municipalities suffered fiscal difficulties in most depressions, which since the nineteenth century have been followed by reforms; limits like Proposition 13 build on a long tradition. Yet legal reforms seldom work as intended. Some make a difference; they change some rules of the game, and strengthen one or another player. We do not suggest that laws never have been nor could be devised to affect fiscal policy; the United States is loosely administered by comparison with Western European societies or totalitarian regimes.[13] We distinguish legal structures from policy preferences (of leaders, organized groups, and citizens). Legal structures embodying policy preferences are often effective. But if disparities arise, preferences usually prevail.[14]

A common legal concept in local autonomy discussions is "home rule" (Grad 1970). But if clear in one state, it varies so across states as to lose meaning. We focus on fiscal components of home rule: debt limitations, revenue and expenditure limitations, overall financial monitoring, and mandated activities.

Debt Limitations

Default in the 1930s seemed exacerbated by large debt (see Hempel 1971; Hillhouse 1936). By the late 1970s most states limited local debt to a proportion of taxable property value. About half also required a local referendum to issue general obligation bonds. Do these legal controls reduce debt? ACIR (1965) and Pogue (1970) reported lower borrowing in states with debt limits, while Mitchell (1967), Cho (1972), and Hickam, Berne, and Stiefel (1981) suggest that limits are circumvented. Results differ as studies include different explanatory variables besides the legal limits. Why are limits ineffectual? Due to spuriousness: they work if they reflect local preferences, but otherwise are circumvented. How? Most simply by exceeding the limit, often by special permission from the state legislature or agency responsible. But this is unnecessary for cities below the limit, and few cities approach the limits for general obligation (g.o.) bonds that pledge the "full faith and credit" of the city to support debt payment. Even Cleveland used only 66 percent of its limitation in the late 1970s.[15] Some cities do not reach their limits because they want to avoid state officials, and many dislike referenda. They may thus issue "revenue bonds" for facilities like water lines which generate revenues earmarked for debt payment.[16] This avoids pledging the city's full faith and credit, but increases borrowing costs as g.o. interest is usually less. Some states also limit revenue bonds. A common solution is then to create a special district controlled by local officials. It can build facilities and lease them back to the city.[17] Revenue bonds increased dramatically in 1970–1980, from 30 percent up to 72 percent of all debt issued.[18] This hardly reflects the sober spirit of state debt limits.

Tax, Revenue, and Expenditure Limitations

Fashionable in the 1930s, debt limits resembled blue laws by the 1970s. But continued expenditure growth encouraged taxpayers to impose numerous limits, usually on taxes, revenue, or expenditure. Limits on property tax rates and levies were most common, yet often ineffective. When property taxes in California decreased by about half after Proposition 13, many localities made up the loss via fees, charges, and transfers from the state. This outraged many citizens, mobilized the next year (1979) by Paul Gann, cosponsor of Proposition 13, to pass Proposition 4. It limited all spending, not just debt or property taxes, but also fees and charges. New Jersey and Massachusetts also adopted spending limits. While the laws imposed dramatic cuts, responsive leaders could achieve similar results; many did.

More traditional limits restrict the revenue structure of cities to specific sources, like property taxes and charges. Some observers, like Mayor Kevin White, hold that such restrictions generate fiscal difficulties: "The property tax is the real problem of the Boston economy. . . . If the Governor and Legislature do not act to revise the state tax structure, Boston and other Massachusetts cities will continue to pay the price" (*Boston Globe*, "Special report on fiscal plight of Bay State Cities," January 11, 1977). But defining the problem as inadequate revenue rather than high expenditures did not convince most Massachusetts citizens. They elected Governor King on a tax reduction platform, and in 1980 passed Proposition 2½, more drastic than previous measures in any state.

The taxpayers' revolt struck like lightning on many cities. But practically every state permitted localities to surpass state limits via referendum, or a majority, or two-thirds of the council. That few cities exercised such options indicates the degree to which the limits reflected citizen preferences. Sources of the taxpayers' revolt will be studied for years, but it, the thunderstorm, deserves the attention.[19] The lightning rods of legal limits only carried the charge.

Overall Financial Monitoring

Practically all states had an agency supervising local finances in the late 1970s (Petersen et al. 1977). Most helped cities borrow. Some regulated financial reporting (see National Council on Governmental Accounting 1981). Agencies actively supervised city finances in a few states like New Jersey and Indiana, for example forcing Gary to trim its budget by $5 million in 1978. Clearly state supervision could limit local expenditures and taxes, but to date it has only rarely.

State Mandates

A widespread mandate prohibits strikes (in 37 states in 1975). But not only is it honored in the breach, it counters other mandates tending to increase wages. An ACIR (1978c) survey identified 77 mandates with local expenditure repercussions. Most affect personnel (43 of the 77), via wages, work conditions, and fringe benefits. Local officials often point to such mandates as fiscally detrimental: the New York Public Employee's Fair Employment Act (Taylor Law) was "an irresponsible sellout of local governments by state government in that it will result in substantial costs being imposed upon the taxpayers of local governments." (Resolution No. 2, Annual Meeting of New York Conference of Mayors and Municipal Officials, 1974). But a multicausal analysis of binding arbitration effects on local wage settlements in New York state found arbitration generally insignificant (Kochan et al. 1979). This is a strong test case as New York arbitration procedures are considered among the most favorable in the country to municipal employees.

The 1975 PCS survey included 12 items on state laws governing municipal employees; we correlated them with the percentage of municipal employees organized and found only one of the 12 significant.[20]

Burton and Krider (1975) similarly report few effects of state laws on strikes. However heated the rhetoric, prounion legislation is more often a consequence than a cause of strong unions. Still, state and federal mandates in some areas like environmental protection and the handicapped seem to have significantly increased local expenditures (see Lovell and Tobin 1981 and chapter 10).

Reform Government

Cities today differ in general government structures thanks largely to the turn-of-the-century reform movement. It opposed machine politics in cities with large immigrant populations. The reformers sought to replace a patronage system of exchanging votes for personal favors with a neutral political system responsive to the "whole community." Basic legal reforms included a professional city manager, at-large constituencies, and nonpartisan elections—all designed to reduce the influence of organized groups and encourage "efficient and honest" city government. These were adopted in many American cities formed after the turn-of-the-century. Older cities largely retained the unreformed mayor-council structure with partisan elections by ward.

The reform movement remains strong today in many cities, often encouraged by city managers and their professional organization. The core professional elements are administrative; a leading concern is efficiency, as for New Fiscal Populists. The reform administrative style shares with NFPs and many Republicans a commitment to the public interest and public goods. Reformers conflict with Democrats and ethnic politicians who use political criteria to allocate jobs or contracts; the professional seeks the best at the least cost. But as reformers stress administrative autonomy from politics, they do not have strong views on other components of political culture. They hold elected officials responsible for general policies, who may thus be fiscally and socially liberal or conservative, and responsive to either citizens or organized groups.[21] Separating politics from administration is easiest in homogeneous communities with consensual politics. Elections are nonpartisan in reform cities, but voters are often Republicans, NFPs, or reform Democrats. In more heterogeneous cities with predominantly ethnic or traditional Democratic leaders, politics permeates administration, and as Richard Daley put it, "good government is good politics." The emphasis in such cities on separable goods and rewarding organized groups causes political leaders to resist delegation to professional staff.

Reform structures are thus resources that help shift rules of the game and policy outputs. Cities with managers have legally "weak" mayors, often the council member receiving the most votes, or elected indirectly by the council. Weak mayors make few appointments to positions like city attorney or treasurer, have no veto over the council, and are not responsible for administration: the city managers' bailiwick. Such items are summed in an index of mayoral and council authority used in the core model (see appendix 1). Research on reform structures suggests that they buffer government from citizens and organized groups, centralizing authority in administrators who can become more dynamic and less invisible (e.g., Lineberry and Fowler 1967; Lyons 1978).[22] Appendix 5 adds reform government to the core model, which suppresses about 5 percent of the core variable effects. This modest result is consistent with past research and the rest of the chapter. Reform administrators exert impact by increasing efficiency more than by changing general fiscal policies.

Conclusion

Intergovernmental revenues and legal characteristics are resources helping those with access to them. Intergovernmental revenues help cities do more, but cities seek out grants consistent with local preferences. Our core model thus changes minimally by adding intergovernmental revenues. There is similarly little evidence that legal characteristics directly affect debt or expenditures. Legal and other characteristics are often interrelated, complicating interpretation. For example, state mandates favoring municipal employee unions appear primarily where unions were already influential. Moreover, maneuverability within legal restrictions has meant that laws like debt limits are often circumvented.

External "reforms" seldom affect cities as intended. Legal structures are not unrelated to fiscal policy, but they promote or retard policies generated by local political processes. Taxpayers seeking to limit expenditures in the late 1970s imposed legal limits on taxes, revenues, and expenditures to constrain spending by elected officials. But without active voters, interest groups, or especially political leaders committed to the laws, they soon become ignored.

CHAPTER TEN

Strategies That Work for Local, State, and Federal Officials

This chapter has two parts. Part I concerns local options for mayors, council members, managers, and others concerned with major local policy commitments. Part II addresses state and federal policies affecting cities. Many policies can reduce fiscal strain; macroeconomists prescribe macroeconomic policies, accountants better accounting, etc. We consider mainly policies building on earlier chapters in the volume.

Part I. Options for Local Officials, Emphasizing Retrenchment Strategies

The problem variously labeled cutback management or adapting to retrenchment or budgeting under fiscal stress is today's number one issue for most American governments. But it is so new that little analysis specifically addresses it. Most public management discussions prior to the late 1970s assumed continual government growth. It is thus important to reexamine past tools and perspectives. The few writings to date explicitly addressing retrenchment share a weakness limiting their generality. They assume, usually implicitly, that all governments are fundamentally similar. Some suggest general principles without considering how they apply to different situations. For example, general checklists of cost-cutting ideas are presented (e.g., Illinois Department of Commerce and Community Affairs 1981) or an approach like contracting out recommended (Nelson 1980). A second approach still assumes that governments are basically similar but that they vary in their degree of severity of retrenchment. Decisions then differ primarily as a function of available resources; as stringency increases, decisions are expected to move down an ideal-typical list of options (e.g., Levine, Rubin, and Wolohojian 1981:48ff).

We suggest that policy options become more useful if their appropriateness for different types of cities is indicated. Twelve options are reviewed for adapting to fiscal strain; these emerge largely from discussions with local officials. Throughout the volume we showed how policies differ by political culture, each of which is right for its proponents. Most options could be adapted to virtually any city by a creative leader, but we still assess them for responsiveness to each political culture. To make the political cultures more concrete, the reader might consider as examples: Boston for the Democrats, Gary for ethnics, San Diego for Republicans, and Pittsburgh under Peter Flaherty for New Fiscal Populists. Note that Democrats refers more to traditional than reform Democrats, as the latter sometimes resemble NFPs below. Most cities and leaders are not pure types, but the four types are well known and useful bases for development of your own combination of strategies.

1. GENERAL POLICY

Democrats	*Ethnics*	*Republicans*	*NFPs*
Find new revenues, increase taxes, borrow, defer hard retrenchment decisions, cut capital expenditures if necessary, cut employee compensation last.	Similar to Democrats but with emphasis on retaining ethnic group members on city staff, and symbolically important services and projects for the dominant ethnic group.	Cut taxes, reduce services if necessary, make no special effort to protect specific service recipients or employees; cut poor-oriented programs most; perhaps pursue productivity improvement program.	Emphasize productivity improvement; maintain symbolic responsiveness to disadvantaged; then make cuts similar to Republicans.

Democrats	*Ethnics*	*Republicans*	*NFPs*

COMMENT: These patterns follow primarily from the fiscal and social liberalism positions of the four types. Obviously those listed for Democrats and ethnics include many that avoid retrenchment, but they are widely used in conjunction with retrenchment strategies.

2. DECISION-MAKING PROCESSES

Major inputs from mayor and council members, municipal employees, Democratic party leaders, neighborhood groups, organized groups of service recipients.	Similar to Democrats but weighted toward those elected officials, employees and organizations that most represent the dominant ethnic group.	Individual citizens as taxpayers define budget constraint; specific programs set more by professional staff than extra-governmental groups. Business groups and general civic leaders may provide some input.	Similar to Republicans, but stress more the populist legitimacy of individual citizen over professional staff; leaders thus use polls, public meetings, etc. to solicit citizen input; professional consultants and other sources of productivity ideas likely to be stressed.

COMMENT: These patterns follow from characteristics of each political culture as outlined above, and are not distinctive to retrenchment decisions. For personnel decisions, the power of municipal employees may be as critical as the type of political culture.

3. ADOPT LOW VISIBILITY REVENUE-RAISING DEVICES

Yes	Yes	No	Sometimes

COMMENT: This strategy follows from the view that visible taxes are the problem, rather than general citizen resistance to taxes and spending. After Proposition 13 limited property taxes, many California cities adopted or increased other revenue sources.

Low visibility revenue sources include value-added taxes and long-

Democrats	*Ethnics*	*Republicans*	*NFPs*

term debt, especially as revenue bonds issued by subordinate special districts (housing authorities, etc.) rather than by the city government. Specific fees may also be imposed on private sector activities, such as those of construction companies, gas stations, accountants. Exceptions can be made for political supporters or disadvantaged groups. Many new forms of borrowing are discussed in U.S. Conference of Mayors (1982). Special districts are covered in Walsh (1978) and Davidson et al. (1977).

4. USER CHARGES

No	Slowly	Yes	Selectively

COMMENT: Citizens much prefer charges to other revenue vehicles.[1] User charges differ from fees under #3 in that charges are imposed on recipients of specific government services. They reduce consumption of the service by increasing its cost, and permit gauging intensity of preference for the service by observing use levels under different charges. The principle of full cost recovery is analogous to having the service provided by the private sector in that it is not subsidized. Calculating full cost recovery is sometimes complex; concentrated heavy usage can be captured by a charge schedule with peak-load pricing, such as higher charges for electricity at midday. See Mushkin (1972) and Aronson and Schwartz (1981). User charges may be imposed selectively by ethnic and NFP leaders to protect their own or the socially disadvantaged. For example, seniors or the less affluent may be given lower rates, or a free day can be declared for museums and certain swimming pools, etc.

5. PUBLICIZE SERVICES

High	High	Medium-Low	High

COMMENT: This is less a retrenchment strategy than a means of reallocating staff activities, but has been stressed in many cities to help legitimate service delivery and thus ward off citizen retrenchment pressure. The basic idea is to move staff out of central administrative positions to publicly visible places. For example, firefighters can do home and office inspections instead of waiting in a firehouse; police can do more patrols and school visits, etc.

This may be a generally good idea, but can still be adapted to different leadership styles. For example, services may be publicized

Democrats	*Ethnics*	*Republicans*	*NFPs*

more to politically important citizens. Some Democratic leaders have thus reallocated garbage pickups to neighborhoods critical for forthcoming elections. Black political leaders have often publicized their improvement of services to black neighborhoods, especially those previously deprived. NFPs may appeal more to the general citizenry, and Republicans do the same if with less populist zeal than NFPs. Publicizing services and other populist-oriented activities may be resisted by influential unions or professional staffs.

6. MAKE VISIBLE EFFORTS TO IMPROVE PRODUCTIVITY AND FISCAL MANAGEMENT

Low	Low	Often High	High

COMMENT: Productivity improvement can resolve the apparent conflict between low taxes and high services. Virtually every city can be made more productive. Pittsburgh and San Diego made impressive efforts and succeeded. Pittsburgh's Mayor Flaherty spearheaded the effort, arriving personally unannounced on worksites, observing, and looking for improvements in work practices. The style was openly critical, tough, and led personally by top staff. In San Diego, productivity was initiated with a management consulting firm which used cautious, detailed analyses. Time and motion studies were combined with organizational development techniques to encourage staff to participate. The two cities differed in methods, but results were similar: expenditure reductions of 10 percent or more in areas studied, with no apparent service loss (Clark 1978; Clark and Ferguson 1978. Other guides: Washnis 1980; Kellar 1979; Poole 1980; Illinois Department of Commerce and Community Affairs 1981).

Good fiscal management can improve information and thus productivity. More serviceable accounting and budgeting systems, revenue and expenditure forecasts, and a multi-year capital program are important if only to help employees accept multi-year policies rather than bargaining for cash on hand. Monthly or quarterly statements of important revenues and expenditures help monitoring. Clear and meaningful budgets, financial statements, and bond prospectuses build support with citizens, investors, and organized groups. So do accounting procedures which permit reporting service costs over time and compared to other cities. More efficient fiscal management can come from encouraging talented staff, new management ap-

Democrats	*Ethnics*	*Republicans*	*NFPs*

proaches, new systems and technology, better bond marketing procedures, an outside auditor's management letters, professional associations, and consulting services (see Aronson and Schwartz 1981; Steiss 1975; U.S. Conference of Mayors 1982).

To demonstrate a continual commitment to productivity may be as important as actual improvements, since seldom can people outside government assess most changes. Publicizing improvements is thus essential. So is introducing tools that symbolize efficiency, like computers and other hardware to demonstrate and photograph. Fiscal management tools like program budgets, performance indicators, cost of service data, and revenue forecasting models suggest that top management is in control and improving services. The tools may in fact help improve productivity, but their vigorous development is itself important for NFPs and Republicans. The tools symbolize an administration responsive to citizens in general. Democratic and ethnic leaders are less inclined toward such symbols as they may conflict with responsiveness to organized groups and particular constituents. Democratic and ethnic leaders can still use these tools to good effect, but simply not publicize them. Many hybrids are possible, such as Mayor Daley who stressed advanced technology and productivity, as well as patronage politics. But Democratic political culture did not lead him toward productivity.

7. PRIVATIZATION

No	Little	Yes	Selectively

COMMENT: Their positions on fiscal liberalism lead Democrats to oppose and Republicans to favor privatization, i.e., terminating government services and leaving the private sector to supply them. Ethnic leaders may favor terminating programs unresponsive to their constituents, and NFPs programs with high costs relative to their visibility. Democrats tend not to terminate programs due to employee resistance.

8. USE VOLUNTEERS

No	Little	Somewhat	Yes

COMMENT: Few cities use volunteers beyond limited areas such as libraries. Volunteers compete with regular jobs. As the staple of patronage politics, jobs reward supporters and maintain campaign

Democrats	*Ethnics*	*Republicans*	*NFPs*

workers. Traditional Democrats and ethnic politicians rely on patronage or at least affirmative action and avoid volunteers. By deemphasizing patronage, NFPs can more easily involve volunteers. Republicans may too, but occasional patronage considerations, and professional staff concerned to maintain positions and standards, discourage volunteers. Republicans often use volunteers in areas where private charity was important in the past, like high culture and social services, while the more egalitarian NFPs are more likely to encourage self-help activities of neighborhood groups, clean-ups, park maintenance, etc.

Examples: In New Orleans, volunteers work free for part of a day, but are paid some wages. Volunteered time is recorded and treated as a contribution to the city for the record. In the wake of Proposition 13, one park had its budget cut by half; it developed an "Adopt-a-Park" program and raised $15,000 from Kaiser Aluminum (*Tax Revolt Digest*, March 1979). Many private firms have facilities and equipment—swimming pools, trucks, etc.—which they can donate for favorable publicity, or lease for a special fee. Banks and commercial firms have talented staff they can loan. Chambers of commerce and similar organizations have developed national networks of information to help locate such assistance. Universities can provide faculty and student interns. New York, Pittsburgh, and Waukegan have thus used volunteers for fiscal management, secretarial support, and other tasks (Rogers 1978; Burns 1981).

9. PUBLIC VS. SEPARABLE GOODS AS SERVICES

Separable	Separable	Public	Public

COMMENT: Cities can provide services that approximate pure public goods in being shared by most citizens and with access hard to restrict, like clean air and fluoridated water. Or separable goods can be emphasized, like patronage jobs for specific individuals. All services can be scored on a continuum from public to separable goods. Programs may have both public and separable aspects, like a public works project to clean the air which also provides jobs. Still, an overall ranking is possible, and aspects important for our four types distinguished. Democrats and ethnics tend toward separable goods to reward specific supporters, while Republicans and NFPs prefer more public goods (Clark 1975b; Knoke 1981).

Democrats	*Ethnics*	*Republicans*	*NFPs*
10. CONTRACTING OUT			
Little	Little	Yes	Yes, but selectively

COMMENT: Republicans lean toward contracting with private service providers on principle as the private sector seems more efficient. The commitment of NFPs to productivity should lead toward the best service at the least cost. They may conduct service cost studies and create nonprofit firms or contract with other governments as well as with private firms. Professional staff in Republican cities follow similar tendencies. Democrats in principle trust private firms less—leaders from concern with loss of patronage, employees from concern with their jobs; ethnic leaders have similar misgivings. Democratic and ethnic leaders may still contract with campaign contributors, ethnic firms, and in situations generating political benefits. Such political motivation is not inherently more costly; competitive bidding can keep contracts with political supporters at a reasonable cost. Still, Democrats and ethnics often limit contracting to new construction, office supplies, and other items traditionally provided by contract, while NFPs and Republicans may contract basic services, up to 80 percent of all city services in some small towns.

Examples: Fire protection is provided to nine municipalities and fire districts in the Scottsdale, Arizona area by a private firm using as part-time employees, city staff who work in various city departments. Employees receive a monthly salary plus an hourly fee for answering calls. Cost savings since it began in 1948 are dramatic (Ahlbrandt 1973). Lakewood, California and many other Los Angeles-area governments regularly contract for services. In 1978, San Francisco even contracted out its finance department, albeit with a firm headed by the former finance director. San Diego set up a nonprofit firm providing data processing, thus solving the common conflict between civil service regulations and highly paid programmers. (See Nelson 1980; Fisk et al. 1978; Savas 1977.)

11. CAPITAL VS. LABOR TRADEOFF			
Labor	Labor	Capital	Capital

COMMENT: With reasons similar to those for contracting out, Democrats and ethnics tend toward labor-intensive technologies, while Republicans and NFPs have fewer commitments to large staffs. This

Democrats	*Ethnics*	*Republicans*	*NFPs*

should lead the last two to whatever mixture is most efficient, and by comparison with the first two should involve more capital (Huckins and Tolley 1981).

12. COMPENSATION VS. NUMBER OF EMPLOYEES

High Compensation High Number	Low Compensation High Number	Market Compensation Low Number	Market Compensation Low Number

COMMENT: Cities vary considerably on this continuum. Democratic and ethnic leaders concerned with patronage favor larger numbers of employees. Municipal employees and their unions, however, are concerned more with compensation than numbers. Where strong employee unions and patronage-based leaders are found together, both high compensation and numbers are likely. Strong ethnic leaders have patronage considerations, but need not pay high compensation unless employees are powerful (as in Detroit where the average wage was $17,639 in 1977, while in Gary, where unions were weak relative to Mayor Hatcher, it was $6,209. See chapter 6). Republican leaders tend to hold down wages, but Republicans and NFPs often delegate such decisions to management, whose professional standards usually raise wages. Republican or NFP leaders themselves are likely to move toward a market-defined standard.

Table 10.1 summarizes the various strategies.

Part II. Policy Recommendations for Federal and State Officials (Which Local Officials May also Seek to Influence)

A direct solution to urban fiscal strain is more funds from higher-level governments. Common in the past, it is unlikely in the early 1980s. In time of austerity, the "system" of intergovernmental relations is especially important to reassess. Never designed as a system, it emerged from incremental additions for specific problems, like environmental protection or street curb repair. If such programs once made sense, priorities change, especially with retrenchment. In under a decade, sound programs can become absurd luxuries, yet the burden of the past was clear in the early 1980s in over 500 federal categorical

Table 10.1. Retrenchment Management Strategies by Type of Political Culture

	Democrats	Ethnic Politicians	Republicans	New Fiscal Populists
Adopt low visibility revenue-raising devices	Yes	Yes	No	Sometimes
User charges	No	Slowly	Yes	Selectively
Publicize services	Yes	Yes	Sometimes	Yes
Make visible efforts to improve productivity and fiscal management	Low	Low	High	High
Privitization	No	Little	Yes	Selectively
Use volunteers	No	Little	Somewhat	Yes
Public versus separable goods as services	Separable	Separable	Public	Public
Contracting out	Little	Little	Yes	Selectively
Capital versus labor tradeoff	Labor	Labor	Capital	Capital
Compensation versus number of employees	High compensation High numbers	Low compensation High numbers	Market compensation Low numbers	

grants, thousands of pages of federal and state regulations, busy auditors, and lawsuits concerning all of these. From the President to governors and mayors, no one feels responsible for this complex system of which all have become prisoners. When elected officials are burdened with regulations, government works more slowly, citizens become frustrated and in turn organize as "special interest groups." Their successes, publicized in further regulations, again testify to the weakening of general government. Left out of this process are the unorganized—like middle-class taxpayers and the poor, who, as we saw in earlier chapters, have been relatively neglected.

These problems would be eased if (1) more funds were available through general grants, and (2) relatively fewer via categorical grants, (3) regulations were simplified, (4) more technical assistance to cities were available, and (5) bond market access were facilitated. Each would strengthen general government.

Underlying our five recommendations is the view that most important is not some new technology or legal mechanism, but simplifying basic processes. Local officials can solve many problems if given adequate authority. Our recommendation to strengthen general government is based in part on the observation that where organized groups are less active, governments can respond more to citizen preferences. Special interest groups often implant their concerns in a court case or bureaucratic regulation, with support from perhaps a few elected officials. Seldom do they have full support of the general government. Some feel that government should be reduced in size to be more responsive to citizens. We carry the logic one step further to suggest that whatever the size of the federal budget, allocating spending decisions to lower levels is likely to increase responsiveness to citizen preferences. Clearly, involvement by organized groups and leaders will vary with the local political culture, but in most cities in the early 1980s, moving federal and state policies closer to local (and usually) citizen preferences is a widely shared concern.

Increase General Grants

If money can help, unrestricted funds help most. Only about 10 percent of federal funds to cities in 1981 were for General Revenue Sharing, and block grants about 10 percent more. If such programs were increased and categoricals decreased, savings in administrative costs would be enormous. This would also reduce the distrust which has grown so pervasive in intergovernmental relations. Categoricals have *not* gone to cities with greater poverty or related distress, but like intergovernmental assistance generally, they reinforce local processes (chapter 9). It is thus naive to think that outside officials are overly important to cities or beneficial to the disadvantaged.

Make Allocation Formulas Fairer

Many grants are primarily allocated by formula. Most federal and state formulas are simple, using such elements as population size, percentage poor, per capita income, and unemployment (Ellett 1976). These follow the rationale that "needy people" define "needy cities." But chapter 3 showed this assumption largely incorrect. Social, economic, and fiscal distress are not the same; fiscal strain is often distinct from distress indicators in grant formulas. And helping needy people is not the goal of every program.

Our ratio approach to fiscal strain suggests using social and economic indicators only if affecting these is a goal of the grant. Most such grants—for unemployment compensation, welfare, etc.—do not go to cities, however, but to individuals. For grants aimed at fiscal problems, fiscal characteristics should be used. To this end a basic element for broad formula grants should be the range of functions performed by the local government. It is currently ignored in most grants; cities performing education, for example, receive no more than other cities. Grants should be adjusted by service responsibilities.[2]

Categorical Grants

Categorical grants are complicated to apply for and expensive to administer. If not replaced by Revenue Sharing, they could at least be streamlined and periodically regrouped as block grants. Categoricals may be appropriate, but it is important to give more consideration as to just when they are suitable. Examples of criteria: issues that require long-term commitments, or where spillover benefits are considerable, such as clean air and water. (See the papers by Steiner, Arrow, Dorfman and others in U.S. Congress, Joint Economic Committee 1969.)

If categoricals are to alleviate fiscal strain, funding should address this problem. Still, we recommend federal aid based on functional responsibilities, revenue-raising capacity, and user characteristics—not fiscal difficulties per se. For intervention in a local crisis, states are better placed than the federal government. They can marshal substantial funds if they so choose, and are close enough to confront the hard political decisions. Differences in local politics and culture are so great that federal efforts are condemned in advance as "administrative bungling" by those assisted, and "partisan favoritism" by those not.

General "urban development" programs, like most of the Carter Urban Policy, are inefficient means to help city governments. Major trends of population and job movement are not diverted easily or inexpensively. In time of fiscal austerity, outside funds could be better used to help local governments maintain basic services, capital infrastructures, and hold down tax burdens. Future national urban policies should seek to work with rather than against the fundamental processes in the private sector.[3]

Regulation and Administrative Policies

Mandated costs imposed by higher governments have become huge. They have seldom been dramatized by the mass media, but the mayors of New York and Los Angeles have forcefully argued that mandates generate some of their most urgent fiscal problems (Bradley 1979). Mandates have often been enacted without understanding their consequences and are often enforced inflexibly, as stressed by former congressmen and state legislators like Edward Koch of New York and Coleman Young of Detroit. For example, New York City officials pleaded with the Department of Transportation about adapting their 255 subway stations for the disabled, estimating the average cost for a disabled passenger to be $38 per trip while for the general public it was about 85 cents. The City could offer the disabled private taxi service more inexpensively. A compromise solution, combining buses and paratransit, was rejected as inconsistent with DOT regulations (Koch

1980). Similar conflicts arose in other cities. Simultaneously, many mass transit systems are cutting services and on the verge of bankruptcy.

Pending federal and state legislation can be monitored for local consequences, and "fiscal notes" appended. Reimbursements are now made in California if local governments can document mandated costs. Many options for addressing mandated costs are available and in use in some states (see Walzer 1978; Lovell and Tobin 1981).

Limits on City Revenue, Expenditures, and Debt. The late 1970s saw referenda to limit spending in many states. But these varied in form and focus; sensitive leaders did not have to be bludgeoned. Both citizens and leaders are better off if general government can proceed without tying officials' hands. State limits are particularly crude for cities. Policies satisfactory to an entire state are inevitably dissatisfying to some cities. Encouraging city-level solutions permits policies closer to local citizen preferences. Stringent controls can require *local* referenda for major debt offerings or spending increases exceeding inflation that would permit citizens to obtain more locally satisfactory policies.[4]

Grant Administration. Many policies here could assist cities. Examples:

—*Tax collection and fiscal year schedules could be integrated.* In some states, cities must collect property taxes at the end of the summer (after the harvests, once upon a time) while the fiscal year ends in June. This commonly generates short term borrowing; interest costs could be reduced by revising the state law (see Moak and Hillhouse 1975).

—*Federal and state governments could settle their accounts more expeditiously.* Some agencies are exemplary, but others, like the Economic Development Administration and Environmental Protection Agency, have required cities to complete construction of sewerage and other facilities before initiating reimbursement, which has dragged on for months or even years. State reimbursements of Medicaid are also classically troublesome. Providing some funding at outset would eliminate borrowing in anticipation of reimbursement (see Congressional Budget Office 1977).

—*Standardize accounting and reporting requirements for different federal and state agencies.* Compounded by requirements for different grants from different federal and state agencies, accounting efforts have grown voluminous. They could be considerably reduced by standardization. Efforts in this direction could be extended.

—*Increased predictability of funding* would enormously facilitate local revenue estimation and budgeting. Cities like San Diego, with sophisticated revenue estimation procedures, must await federal and state decisions to finish their budgets. More federal and state items could be budgeted for two or more years, as with some block grants and General Revenue Sharing.

Research, Development, and Technical Assistance in Fiscal Matters

Some activities are more cost-effective for the federal government than for individual states or cities. Research and development is a classic example. For a few years after the New York fiscal crisis, research and technical assistance on urban public finance increased.[5] The federal government can and has aided: by sponsoring development of new accounting systems, performance indicators, and helping cities improve productivity. Innovations are often best undertaken initially by a few cities; generalizable results can then be diffused. Information diffusion about new practices is inexpensive but useful—through handbooks, workshops, newsletters, etc. The Census and other agencies could collect and report data in ways more responsive to cities (instead of by SMSA).

While the federal government can help, local officials remain dubious about its intervention. For example, many local officials agree that a standardized accounting system for government would be desirable, but resist federal legislation of such practices. Still, HUD and NSF have usefully aided local officials in pursuing these goals.

Facilitating Bond Market Access

States can help cities considerably in borrowing.

Better Financial Reporting. Many cities have looked for ways to improve financial reporting since the 1975 New York difficulties. Several states have required uniform reporting by their cities. States often monitor local finances to help preserve a healthy investment climate for other local governments and private investment (e.g., Florida ACIR 1980). The most compelling argument is still that better reporting is in the city's own interest. Investors, elected officials, and some citizens will read and use clear and meaningful reports. States can help with model formats, visiting technical staff, consultants available by telephone, workshops on new or complex matters, and preparing fiscal data from federal and state sources for city reports. Some do each of these (see Peterson, Cole and Petrillo 1977).

Financial statements and bond prospectuses are important preparation for market access. So are combining and timing of capital projects, selection of debt instruments, and finding investors to purchase bonds. Banks and consulting firms can help, but states are specially suited to facilitate debt management. Two kinds of cities distinctly benefit: smaller cities (and other local governments and agencies) that seldom borrow and thus lack experience, and cities with difficulty borrowing at all, because of fiscal strain or other reasons.

Six Mechanisms. Six mechanisms follow which states have used to facilitate market access and lower interest rates. If not required of all local governments, they can help some.

1. *State Bond Banks*, as in Maine and Vermont, borrow from the private market and lend in turn to cities, thus increasing the size of offerings and making operations more economical. If they generate administrative costs and possible liabilities for the state, their advantages may be considerable for smaller localities. To reduce its involvement, the state can provide only "moral" rather than general obligation support.

2. *State Agency Ratings*. State agencies may rate cities by risk level, or simply give their approval to bond offerings. But investors have seldom been impressed with such procedures.[6]

3. *State Guarantees of Bonds*. If a state guarantees payment, the credit risk becomes virtually that of the state. This means reduced borrowing costs for most cities. But few states find this acceptable on a continuing basis, although it has been used since 1975 for New York City.

4. *State Moral Obligation Bonds*. Some bonds are issued with state "moral," but not legal, obligations to cover debt service not paid by the issuer, but these are not very compelling to investors.

5. *Maintain a Separate Bond Fund.* States can maintain bond funds from which city debt service is paid, using funds from the city or intergovernmental revenues which the state would otherwise pay the city.

6. *Earmark State Aid for Bond Payments.* State aid to the city can be legally pledged for bond payments if the city cannot meet them from other sources. This is a variation of #5 but ties up less cash. No state funds beyond normal intergovernmental revenues are guaranteed, but this is almost as compelling to investors as #5. Its use in New Jersey has helped cities like Newark borrow at reasonable cost (Leone 1979).

These mechanisms are variations on a general theme. With others in part II of this chapter, they provide more leeway for local officials. Higher-level governments are better placed to tap certain resources, but no one can better solve problems of cities than cities themselves.

APPENDIX ONE

Data Sources, Sampling, and Measurement

A. The Permanent Community Sample

The Permanent Community Sample (PCS) was initiated in 1966 by the National Opinion Research Center (NORC) at the University of Chicago to overcome the noncumulativeness of one-time surveys. It has become the most extensive data file for American cities with a focus on political processes and fiscal policy. Use of the file eliminates basic data collection for each new study, and over time generates time series for plotting changes. Data come from private sources, the Census and other federal agencies, and especially from original data collection by NORC. Certain series are updated annually by coding reports or merging tapes. More extensive data are collected in specific projects. This appendix provides examples of the thousands of variables in PCS archives. Data are stored on magnetic tapes, most of which are available through NORC or the Interuniversity Consortium for Political and Social Research, Ann Arbor, Michigan, 48106. Several hundred reports have been completed using the PCS. Research reports and information are available from Library, National Opinion Research Center, 6030 South Ellis Ave., Chicago, Illinois 60637.

Sampling Frame. The PCS was designed as a sampling frame representative of the cities of residence of urban Americans. (A representative sample of *cities* would overpresent smaller cities relative to the proportion of Americans residing in them.) NORC's sampling frame for interviewing the American population was adapted for the PCS. This brought the advantages of a national fieldstaff and data available from citizen surveys (Rossi and Crain 1968).

Specifically, the PCS sampling frame emerged as follows. A simple random sample of 200 cities, stratified by size, was drawn from the population of 312 cities with 50,000 or more residents in 1960. Table A.1.1 shows sampling weights and cities by size category. Funding and other considerations have led to studying subsets of the 200, chosen as follows. NORC uses Primary Sampling Units (PSUs) selected proportionate to their population size from all U.S. metropolitan areas and nonmetropolitan counties. PSUs are updated with each decennial census to reflect population change, usually by adding or deleting individual PSUs if they have grown or decreased in population relative to the rest of the country. Within each PSU, localities were ordered by cities with block statistics, other urban places, and urbanized and nonurbanized Minor Civil Divisions. The largest city within each PSU was selected (normally the central city of the SMSA) and the remaining localities selected randomly. This list of localities included 60 cities with populations over 50,000 (see Johnstone and Rivera 1965).

The first PCS study in 1967 used 51 of these 60 cities; the nine with populations over 750,000 were excluded because of uncertainty about access for elite interview (Clark 1968a). Cities below 50,000 were excluded due to nonavailability of some Census data. Subsequent PCS studies used the 51 and special samples of 100 (Vanecko 1970) and 95 cities (Kirby et al. 1973). This volume mainly uses 62 (or 63) cities, which includes the 51 supplemented by the 11 (or 12) largest cities. (The 12 include Washington, D.C., excluded from some analyses for its administrative distinctiveness.) The 63 include the original 60 from the NORC PSU's plus three cities that surpassed 1 million residents in the 1970 Census, added since the original sampling design included all cities over 1 million. The list of 62 cities appears in chapter 2. The PCS was thus designed as a self-weighting sample of the places of residence of the American metropolitan population in cities over 50,000. Metropolitan is the Census term for central cities and suburbs which comprise Standard Metropolitan Statistical Areas; nonmetropolitan areas are outside SMSAs. The PCS was built mainly using the 1960 Census, which led HUD staff to inquire in 1975 as to its current representativeness. We thus computed means for several social, economic, and legal-structural characteristics for the PCS cities, and compared them to those for: (1) the total U.S. population, (2) U.S. met-

Table A.1.1. Sample Design for Permanent Community Sample Cities (N = 200, 63, and 51)

City Population	Universe: Total Number of U.S. Cities[a]	PCS-200 Sampling Percentage[b]	PCS-200 Number of Cities	PCS-63 Sampling Percentage[b]	PCS-63 Number of Cities	PCS-51 Sampling Percentage[b]	PCS-51 Number of Cities
1,000,000+	5	100%	5	100.0%	5	0 %	0
500-999,999	16	100	16	87.5	14	43.7	7
250-499,999	30	100	30	40.0	12	40.0	12
150-249,999	30	100	30	20.0	6	20.0	6
100-149,999	49	76	37	22.5	11	22.5	11
75-99,999	61	56	35	9.8	6	9.8	6
50-74,999	121	40	47	7.4	9	7.4	9
TOTAL N	312		200		63		51

[a] Based on 1960 Census of Population.
[b] Percentage of universe as of 1960.

ropolitan population, (3) U.S. central city population, and (4) U.S. nonmetropolitan population. Scores for the PCS cities corresponded closely to (2) the U.S. metropolitan population (Clark 1975a:103–6).

Still, we seldom simply report means or similar characteristics for the entire sample. Our major emphasis is rather on how variables covary across cities. Similar concerns lead some other researchers to draw new samples stratified on variables they are studying. This is reasonable if one knows in advance all variables to be analyzed. But seldom is this realistic, and seldom can a study collect all potentially important data. A permanent sample provides data from numerous surveys and variation on most variables of research and policy interest. Many urban phenomena are so interrelated that a convincing analysis is difficult with less than about 10 independent variables, near the maximum for a sample of about 50. Larger N's are statistically desirable, but increase costs. The rich data for the 62 PCS cities led us to use them for most of the present volume.

Three characteristics frequently used in sampling and reporting results are region, population size, and central-city or suburban status. Similarly, we are sometimes asked if our results apply only to certain types of cities. The PCS cities are both large and as small as 50,000. They fall into all major regions, and include both central cities and suburbs. Nevertheless, we seldom focus on these three variables, since they usually explain little when other, more analytically appropriate variables are included. This point is elaborated in appendix 1.C for population size, in chapter 3 for region, and chapter 9 for suburban status. We next include a brief summary of each PCS survey used in the present volume.

The 1967 Survey. This first PCS survey included general questions about political processes and policy outputs. Personal interviews were conducted in the 51 cities by NORC fieldstaff with 11 informants: mayor, newspaper editor, chairmen of Republican and Democratic parties, head of the chamber of commerce, president of largest bank, bar association president, labor council leader, urban renewal director, health commissioner, and director of last major hospital fund drive. An important difference between most earlier research and the PCS surveys was present here: informants occupying identical positions were posed identical questions to maximize comparability of responses. Further documentation is in Clark (1971, 1975a). Data were used in the core model in chapter 4 and elsewhere.

The ISVIP Study. The International Studies of Values in Politics were conducted in India, Yugoslavia, Poland, and the United States, in the late 1960s and early 1970s. These involved case studies of two cities in each country, survey interviews with leaders in PCS cities, and in-depth interviews with selected PCS city leaders, especially concerning values (see Jacob 1971). The case studies were used in chapters 4 and 7 and the value measures of business and group leaders in chapter 7.

The 1975 Survey. Paul Schumaker and Russell Getter, Department of Political Science, University of Kansas, conducted this mailed questionnaire survey (see Schumaker and Billeaux 1978; Schumaker and Loomis 1979) in the 51 cities and 10 Urban Observatory cities (three of which were in the 51). High-level officials were surveyed in several agencies: public housing, public health, environmental protection, community development, welfare, schools, and police. Of 250 administrators contacted, 54 percent responded. Questions dealt with community groups, their agency contacts, and administrative responses. Another questionnaire went to mayors, League of Women Voters' presidents, and city editors of newspapers. At least one response came from 48 of the 51 cities. Questions concerned activities of civic and political groups, including civil rights organizations and municipal employees (used in chapter 9).

The 1976 Survey. Schumaker and Getter again conducted this mailed questionnnaire survey (see Schumaker, Getter, and Clark 1979). It was sent to all mayors and council members in the 51 cities and focused on organized groups which influenced them. Two waves of mailings were used. If after the first, the response rate for the city was low, nonrespondents were telephoned, asked to participate, and sent another questionnaire. Because several items from this survey were used, the full questionnaire is in appendix 1.F, and response effects analyzed in appendix 1.B.

The 1977 Survey. Public Administration Service staff conducted personal interviews for this study of municipal personnel policy. In 42 cities they interviewed from three to six of the following informants: urban chief executive, chief of police, city personnel director, civil service official, police personnel officer, police association/union leader. Laws and labor contracts were collected and a supplementary questionnaire left for the police department. The 42 were not significantly different from the 51 cities in basic socioeconomic characteristics (Greisinger, Slovak, and Molkup 1979). This survey is used in chapter 6.

B. Methodological Problems of Surveying Urban Elites[1]

General Methodological Issues Raised by the 1967 PCS Survey. The first PCS survey of urban elites was conducted in a frankly experimental atmosphere. Virtually all studies of political leadership to date had been of no more than four cities; a survey of 51 was seen as enormously ambitious. Many observers were skeptical of a study with less than full immersion in the style of the best case studies like Dahl (1961) and Banfield (1961). They expected that a low number of informants would generate superficial and biased results, and/or that a hidden power structure might emerge from more detailed fieldwork (e.g. Polsby 1969). So many urban and other elite studies have subsequently been conducted that the skepticism seems dated, but it is still useful to review briefly the major procedures used to assess data validity.

Concurrent Case Studies. One approach was to conduct detailed case studies in cities also surveyed by NORC fieldstaff, and compare results. Waukegan, Illinois and South Bend, Indiana were selected as accessible from Chicago and sites of completed or on-going case studies by others. We compared fieldnotes and draft reports with these researchers, subscribed to local newspapers, and interviewed many more local informants than the NORC interviewers. In reinterviewing those contacted by NORC fieldstaff, we asked about the interview itself and more general issues. Urban renewal and public education decisions were studied in each city, and results compared with those from NORC fieldstaff.

Younger researchers with fieldwork interests were involved for each city. Ann Lennarson Greer was a lifelong resident of Waukegan who completed a B.A. thesis using a Hunter-type reputational survey, an M.A. thesis growing out of courses on field methods with Howard Becker and Scott Greer, and a Ph.D. thesis combining several procedures including working as a secretary to the mayor for a year. Each contributed to a cumulative picture. NORC fieldstaff results, while abbreviated, were consistent with the others (Greer 1974; Clark and Lennarson 1967; Clark 1973b). In South Bend, William Kornblum conducted most fieldwork, although we compared results with studies by Notre Dame social scientists D'Antonio (1966), Liu (1967), and Kommers (1967). Methodological conclusions resembled those in Waukegan: we learned far more through detailed fieldwork, but found no significant biases in the NORC-PCS results (Clark and Kornblum 1967; Clark 1973b). (As time went by, we also learned that even many outstanding case studies have used less than 11 informants per city.)

Inter-Informant and Inter-Item Comparisons. As most items were posed to several informants, it was logical to compare agreement among them, and inter-informant reliability across items. Phillips (1977) thus used covariance analysis to assess the magnitude of informant and item effects. Burt (1981) found that differences across issues and informants within communities, on closed-ended issue-specific reputational format (CERP) items described below, were distributed as if they were random. In a confirmatory factor analysis assessing the relative magnitudes of informant bias, issue bias, and reliability, reliability was the dominant effect; collective effects of informant and issue bias were negligible. Still, not all items generated equally reliable results. Those with low reliability scores were not interpreted as conveying objective information, but as the respondents' values or personal assessments, and therefore were analyzed only in these terms.

Explanatory Power of Models Estimated. To help consolidate earlier research, results for 166 cities studied in case studies (by Hunter, Dahl, Banfield and others) were coded. Centralization of decision making as measured by the original researchers was analyzed with a regression model, generating an R^2 of .10 (Clark et al. 1968). A similar model was estimated for a centralization measure computed from PCS data, based on asking identical questions of identical informants in each city; the R^2 was .54 (Clark 1971), indicating less noise in the PCS data.

Original PCS questionnaires remain on file and have been recoded several times. With accumulation of such substantively and statistically robust results, including reanalyses by various skeptics (especially new research assistants), the survey approach has become established in comparative urban research.

Personal versus Telephone Interviews and Mailed Surveys. Surveys using telephone rather than personal interviews have increased; methodological comparisons suggest near identical results for most types of items. Mailed surveys have also been frequently used; their major weakness is low response rates. (See the symposium in *Public Opinion Quarterly*, Summer 1979, vol. 43, and Bradburn and Sudman 1979.) Each method continues to be used for the PCS. Concern about response rates led us to analyze their effects using the 1976 PCS survey.

Response Rate Effects in the 1976 PCS Survey. Responses to the 1976 survey were typical of mailed questionnaires to city officials,[2] but posed possible problems when individual responses were aggregated to the city level.[3] The overall response rate was 43.5 percent; individual cities ranged from 10 to 85 percent. Since low response rates are assumed to increase response bias (unrepresentative results for a city[4]) and measurement error (unstable sample estimates[5]), the response rate variation suggests that some city scores may include considerable measurement error. Theoretically, the most error should occur in "poorly measured" cities, with the lowest response rates and scores the most unstable (i.e., with the greatest variability as indicated by large standard errors). Conversely, "well measured" cities, with the most stable and least biased scores, should have the highest response rates and the least variability (smallest standard errors).

To assess the magnitude of this type of error,[6] subsets of "well measured" and "poorly measured" cities were compared.[7] Correlations (r's) for relationships with survey measures (e.g., mean scores on group activity, spending preferences, and so forth, in appendix 1.E) were recalculated for well measured and poorly measured cities. Results for the two types were then compared with those for all cities. Differences among the three were few, but in the expected direction: relations were attenuated for "poorly measured" cities. This suggested including all cities in the analysis, but that measurement error attenuates some relationships.

C. Comparisons of the 51 and 62 City Samples

Most city-level analyses used 62 cities, but some data were only available for 51. Were results for the 51 similar to the 62? We addressed this in two ways. Correlation and regression analyses for our core models were performed separately for 51 and 62 cities.[8] Coefficients were compared along with distributional characteristics and scatterplots.[9] Relations were generally very similar. Second, did the 62 cities adequately meet regression analysis assumptions, especially homoscedasticity,[10] which might be violated by increased dispersion (variance) for the large cities? Residuals (standardized) from several basic regression equations were plotted against predicted values for dependent variables (standardized), against independent variables (standardized), and against city population size (logged and standardized). The plots revealed no serious differences in variation for the large cities. Specifically, estimates (predicted values) for the largest cities were as good as those for the 51 cities, and no differences could be attributed to city size or other independent variables in the analyses.

D. Measures Constructed From the 1967 PCS Survey

We analyzed several measures of leaders' importance, as discussed in appendix 2. Two operationalized power: open-ended (OERP) and closed-ended (CERP) issue-specific reputational formats. For the OERP series the interviewer asked: "Is there any single person whose opposition would be almost impossible to overcome or whose support would be essential if someone wanted to . . ." followed by five different (issue-specific) endings: "run for/be appointed to the school board in (city)?; organize a campaign for a municipal bond referendum in (city)?; get the city to undertake an urban renewal project?; . . . establish a program for the control of air pollution in (city)?; run for mayor in (city)?" For "no" answers a probe followed: "what person comes closest to this description?" Responses to the OERP format were coded for 72 positions such as newspapers, present mayor, etc. In the CERP version, the informant was handed a card listing 15 positions. The interviewer stated: "Here is a list of groups and organizations. Please tell me for each whether their support is essential for the success of a candidate for the school board, whether their support is important but not essential, or whether their support is not important." The same format was then repeated, substituting for the school board "a municipal bond referendum," "an urban renewal project," "a program for air pollution control," and "a candidate for mayor." Essential was scored 3, important 2, and not important 1.

Influence, conceived as participation in actual decisions, was operationalized using our decisional (DEC) approach, which consisted of five basic questions:

1. Who initiated action on the issue?
2. Who supported this action?
3. Who opposed this action?
4. Who mediated and was involved in negotiating an outcome?
5. Who prevailed? Which participants were most successful in obtaining their stated goals?

These decisional items were repeated for four issue areas: an urban renewal project, the last mayor elected, an antipoverty program, and an air pollution control program.

The mayor was the most important participant mentioned in the OERP series; RPINMAYR was the proportion of all mentions for the mayor. From the CERP series, the mean response score for the city was constructed for the importance of private and public sector labor unions (IMUNMY), city and county employees (IMCOMY), ethnic and religious associations (IMETHMY), heads of city government agencies (IMLOCMY), and neighborhood groups (IMNBRMY). Scores for all 15 participants were factor analyzed; four loaded highly on a business factor FBUSL.[11] From the DEC series for the most general and critical issue area—the mayoral election—measures were constructed of the importance of business groups (BSNESMY), labor unions (LLABORMY), lower class persons (LOCLASMY), blacks (LBLKSMY), and news media (LNEWSMY) (see Clark 1975a). The total number of participants mentioned in each city in the DEC series served as an Index of Decentralization of decision making (INDEXDEC), (Clark 1971). LHDIFF measured the degree to which the single most powerful leader stood out above others, operationalized by computing the mean score (from all informants) in the city on the CERP index (summed for five issues) for the most powerful leader on the list of 15, and subtracting from it the mean score for the second most powerful leader (see Phillips 1977).

The mayor and chairmen of the Republican and Democratic parties were asked: "What were the most important issues that you stressed in your last campaign?" (party chairmen variant: "stressed by the mayor in his last campaign.") Responses were coded:

1. Direct increase in city government spending through a specific program
2. Indirect increase
3. Unspecified direction
4. Insignificant or no increase
5. Indirect decrease
6. Direct decrease

The mean city score on these was MAYRTALK, the mayor's fiscal policy preferences. An analogous measure for the mayor's opponent was OPPOTALK.

Agreement between the mayor and business leaders (MYAGREBS) was measured from an item posed to the mayor: "Would you say there is a great deal of agreement, a moderate amount, or almost no agreement between yourself and the business leaders of (city) on (a) the urban renewal program (b) the community action aspect of the poverty program (c) the role of the municipal government in the control of air pollution, and (d) the question of the municipal government's role in the organization of community resources for the provision of adequate hospital facilities?"

E. Measures Constructed from the 1976 PCS Survey

Numerous items used the survey instrument in appendix 1.F.

1. Individual—(City Official) Level Measures

Variable	*Survey Question*	*Coding or How Computed*
TERMS	Part I, Q1	1,2,3,4 terms
RACE	Part I, Q11	0 = black, 1 = white

Variable	*Survey Question*	*Coding or How Computed*
IMMIG	Part I, Q12	1 = immigrant, 0 = non-immigrant
EDUC	Part I, Q13	number of years of schooling
OCCPRES	Part I, Q14	Duncan Occupation Prestige Scale, two digits

(Other individual variables similar to those in section 2.b below were analyzed in chapter 7.)

2. City-Level Measures

a. Group activity measures. Each respondent was asked to name up to five groups active in city government. Group activity was the proportion of times a group was mentioned. Each mention of a group was also weighted (multiplied) by an impact score (Q11), an influence score (Q6), and a contacting activity score (Q1); the weights (from the Part II items) were 1, 2, 3, 4, 5. City level averages were used for these three items (no mention was scored zero). Groups were municipal employees (associations and unions), businessmen, and those with considerable poor, middle class (nonpoor), or black membership. Two types of poor and black organizations were used in preliminary analyses, but changes in cutting points (using Q3 and Q4) affected few results. Groups with lower class members were classified as POOR1, lower middle class members as POOR2. Those with middle class or upper class members were nonpoor (NP1), and lower-middle-class members were NP2. Groups with memberships over 20 percent black were designated BLCT20, and those with over 50 percent black BLCT50. Resulting measures were:

Variable	*Definition*
TPAMEAV	Average political activity (using contacting activity weight) of municipal employee groups.
BLCT20A	Average political activity (using contacting activity weight) or organizations representing blacks.
LBUSGRAV	Log of the average number of mentions of politically active business organizations.
LPANP2	Log of the ratio of the political activity of nonpoor groups (excl. lower-middle class) to that of poor groups (incl. lower-middle class).

LPAPOOR1	Log of the ratio of political activity of poor groups (lower class only) to that of nonpoor groups (incl. lower-middle class).
LPAME	Log of political activities of municipal employee organizations.
SIPOORP1	Ratio of the sector impact of poor groups (lower class only) to that of the nonpoor (excl. lower-middle class).

b. Indexes of leaders' spending preferences and social issue preferences. These came from city averages.

Variable	*Survey Question*	*Coding or How Computed*
VOTOPIN	Part I, Q9	Populism Scale, 1 to 5, 1 = never, 5 = most of the time
DEM	Part I, Q6	1 = Democrat, 0 = Non-Democrat
REP	Part I, Q6	1 = Republican, 0 = Non-Republican
SPEND11	Part III, Q3 (all of Col. 3)	Average of scores on the 11 spending preference items (coded 1, 2, 3)
ISSUE8	Part IV, Q3 (all of Col. 3)	Average of scores on the 8 social issue items (each coded 1, 2, 3; the last item on pornography was recoded in the opposite direction).
LLPR176	Part III, Q3 for social welfare, public health, hospitals	Average of scores on the 3 spending items (coded 1, 2, 3)
LLPR276	Same as LLPR176 plus low-income housing	Same as LLPR176
LME76	Part IV, Q3 for public employee unions	Same as LLPR176

c. Leaders' resources. Two measures were computed of leaders' resources. SPEN11SB was the standard deviation of SPEND11, measuring dissensus among elected officials (multiplied by −1 and a constant added to make all scores positive.) LEADRES3 summed the z scores of 11 resource measures of mayors and council members, including mayor's term, council members's term, years served by incumbent mayor and council members, number of officials appointed by mayor and council, percentage of incumbents winning reelection bids, and (weighted negatively) number of nonopen council meetings, degree to which city records are made public, number of council members, number of city officials directly elected, number of recalls and referenda, and their success. These came from a tape supplied by Stanley Wolfson of the International City Management Association. (See Boynton 1976 for most items.) A multiplicative interaction term was then created multiplying leaders' spending preferences by the two resource measures: LLEAD3W2 = LN ((SPEND11Z) (SPEN11SB) (LEADRES3)). SPEN11Z was the transformed z score of SPEND11 with mean 0 and standard deviation 1.

F. *Text of 1976 PCS Survey Questionnaire*

PART I. In this part of the questionnaire, we would like you to provide us with some information about yourself. For the multiple choice questions, please check the most appropriate answer. For the open-ended questions, please fill in the blank.

1. How many terms have you served on the city council (commission)?
____ a. one (this is my first term)
____ b. two
____ c. three
____ d. more than three

2. In the last *general election*, how many candidates (including yourself) were on the ballot for your office?
____

3. Of all votes cast for your office, approximately what percentage of the vote did you receive? ________

4. During the last general election to the city council (commission), did voters also cast ballots for state or federal offices?
____ a. for state offices
____ b. for federal offices
____ c. for state *and* for federal offices
____ d. for local offices only

5. During the last general election to the city council (commission), approximately what percentage of the eligible adults in your city cast ballots? ________

6. What political party, if any, do you identify with?
____ a. Republican
____ b. Democratic
____ c. none (independent)
____ d. other (please specify ________)

7. Overall, how conservative or liberal would you say that you are?
____ a. very conservative
____ b. somewhat conservative
____ c. middle of the road
____ d. somewhat liberal
____ e. very liberal

8. In general, how satisfied are you with the performance of the municipal bureaucracy in your city?
____ a. very dissatisfied
____ b. moderately dissatisfied
____ c. neutral
____ d. moderately satisfied
____ e. very satisfied

Sometimes elected officials believe that they should take policy positions which are unpopular with the majority of their constituents. About how often would you estimate that you vote against the dominant opinion of your constituents?
____ a. never or almost never
____ b. only rarely
____ c. occasionally
____ d. frequently
____ e. most of the time

10. While New York City has approached bankruptcy, the municipal governments in other cities appear to be much more financially solvent. If there are no major changes in the levels of federal and state aids to cities, how likely do you think it is that your city's government will be *unable to pay some of its bills* during the next ten years?
____ a. almost certain
____ b. very possible
____ c. about a 50-50 chance
____ d. not likely, but possible
____ e. almost no possibility

11. What is your race?
____ a. white
____ b. black
____ c. other ________

12. Were you *or* your parents immigrants to the United States?
____ a. no
____ b. yes

12a. If you answered "yes" to question 12 below, would you please specify the country or countries from which you or your parent(s) emigrated. ________

13. How many years of schooling were you able to complete? ________

14. What do you consider to be your major occupation in addition to being a city councilman (commissioner)?

If you wish to receive the results of this questionnaire, please fill in your name and address below.

Name ______________________________
Address ______________________________

____

Would you mind being contacted again by phone in order to provide us with additional information about your city? YES NO If YES, what is your phone number?

____

THANK YOU FOR YOUR COOPERATION

No. __________

PART II. In this part of the questionnaire, we would like to know about the groups or organizations which are most frequently in communication with you in your role as an elected official. We have listed below a number of types of groups which are frequently active in city governmental affairs. Please examine this list and select from it the *five* types of groups or organizations which, in your judgment, are most active in city government. You will note that this list of organizations includes both very general types of groups (indicated by capital letters, such as BUSINESSMEN'S ORGANIZATIONS and PUBLIC EMPLOYEES UNIONS) and more specific types of groups (indicated in noncapital letters—for example, retail merchants, bankers, downtown businessmen's associations, etc.). In selecting the five types of organizations you may choose from among the general and the specific types of organizations, as is most appropriate to your situation.

LIST OF GROUPS AND ORGANIZATIONS FREQUENTLY ACTIVE IN MUNICIPAL GOVERNMENTAL AFFAIRS

*PUBLIC EMPLOYEE ASSOCIATIONS
- Teachers' Associations
- Policemen's Associations
- Fireman's Associations
- Sanitation Workers' Associations
- Social Workers' Associations

*PUBLIC EMPLOYEE UNIONS
- Teachers' Unions
- Policemen's Unions
- Firemen's Unions
- Sanitation Workers' Unions

POLITICAL ORGANIZATIONS
- The Local Republican Party
- The Local Democratic Party

CHURCH ORGANIZATIONS

BUSINESSMEN'S ORGANIZATIONS
- Retail Merchants Associations
- The Chamber of Commerce
- Downtown Businessmen's Associations
- Bankers
- Industrialists

PROFESSIONAL ORGANIZATIONS
- The Bar Association
- The Medical Association

CLIENTS OF CITY SERVICES
- Welfare Recipients
- Users of Low-Income Housing
- Users of Public Health Services
- Parents of School Children (the PTA, etc.)

CIVIC AND CHARITY GROUPS
- League of Women Voters
- Community Service Organizations (e.g., Rotary, the Optimists)

NEIGHBORHOOD GROUPS

CIVIL RIGHTS ORGANIZATIONS

ENVIRONMENTALISTS

UNIONS IN THE PRIVATE SECTOR

TAXPAYERS ASSOCIATIONS

ETHNIC OR RACIAL ORGANIZATIONS

COMMUNITY ACTION ORGANIZATIONS

*Note that the difference between public employee unions and associations is that unions have a bargaining agent which is recognized by city officials.

Please indicate the five most active groups in the place provided in the grid below. List the most active group first, the second most active group second, etc.

ANSWER GRID TO PART II

PLACE NAMES OF GROUPS THAT YOU THINK ARE MOST ACTIVE HERE	PLACE YOUR RESPONSES TO EACH OF THE QUESTIONS (Q1–Q12) LISTED BELOW HERE (Be sure to answer each question for *each* of the five groups which you have listed)											
	Q1	Q2	Q3	Q4	Q5	Q6	Q7	Q8	Q9	Q10	Q11	Q12
1.												
2.												
3.												
4.												
5.												

INSTRUCTION. In the answer grid above indicate with the appropriate number the answer to each of the following questions for *each* of the groups you have listed above.

Q1. Approximately how often does each of the five groups which you have listed above *contact you* to express their preferences or provide information regarding city policies?

1. almost never
2. once or twice a year
3. about once a month
4. about once a week
5. almost every day

Q2. Approximately how often do *you contact* each of the groups in order to learn their policy positions or attain information useful to you in making public policy?

1. almost never
2. once or twice a year
3. about once a month
4. about once a week
5. almost every day

Q3. What would you say is the social class to which most members of each of the five groups you have listed belong?

1. lower class
2. lower-middle class
3. middle class
4. upper-middle class
5. upperclass

Q4. Approximately what percentage of each group's membership is composed of black Americans?

1. none
2. less than 5 percent
3. 6 to 20 percent
4. 21 to 50 percent
5. more than 50 percent

Q5. About what percentage of each group's membership is composed of first or second generation Americans?

1. none
2. less than 5 percent
3. 6 to 20 percent
4. 21 to 50 percent
5. more than 50 percent

Q6. In your judgment, how influential is each of the five groups in your community?

1. almost no influence
2. little influence
3. some influence
4. a lot of influence
5. one of most influential groups in town

Q7. Approximately how long has each group been active in the governmental affairs of your community?

1. less than one year
2. between one and three years
3. between three and five years
4. between five and ten years
5. more than 10 years

Q8. As you most certainly recognize, some groups tend to be active on behalf of policies which benefit only their group ("group minded") while other groups tend to be more community-minded. How would you rate each of the five groups you have listed in regard to to their community-mindedness?

1. very community-minded
2. moderately community-minded

3. a mixture of group and community-minded
4. moderately group-minded
5. very group-minded.

Q9. Approximately how many citizens in your city would you estimate are active members in the organizations of each group you have listed?
1. 25 or less
2. 26 to 100
3. 101 to 500
4. 501 to 1000
5. more than 1000

Q10. About how conservative or liberal would you say is each group that you have listed?
1. very conservative
2. moderately conservative
3. middle-of-the-road
4. moderately liberal
5. very liberal

Q11. In your judgment, how often has the city government responded favorably to the requests or policy preferences of each of the groups which you have listed?
1. almost never
2. less than half of the time
3. about half of the time
4. more than half of the time
5. almost all of the time

Q12. Approximately how often do you personally agree with the aims or purposes of each of the groups you have listed?
1. almost never
2. less than half of the time
3. about half of the time
4. more than half of the time
5. almost all of the time

PART III. Listed in the grid below are a number of policy areas in which city governments frequently spend available revenues. We would appreciate your supplying answers and judgments to the following four questions regarding *each* of these policy areas. Please circle the appropriate answer in the grid below.

Q1. In column 1, we would like you to circle the response which best indicates whether or not your municipal government has jurisdiction in the policy areas listed below.
N. The municipal government has *no* jurisdiction
Y. The municipal government has jurisdiction

Q2. In column 2, we would like you to indicate your judgment about the spending preferences of the *active groups and organizations in your community* (such as those listed in Part II). For each policy area, circle the number which best summarizes the *overall* opinions of the groups and organizations active in that policy area in your city.
1. Most groups want *reduced* spending
2. Most groups want to *spend the same* as is currently being spent in this policy area
3. Most groups want *increased* spending

Q3. In Column 3, we would like you to indicate *your own preferences* about spending in each of the policy areas. In the grid below, circle the number which best approximates your own preference.
1. Spend less
2. Spend the same
3. Spend more

Q4. In column 4, we would like you to estimate the preferences of the *majority of all voting adults in your community*. For each policy area, circle the number which is your best estimate of majority preferences in your community.
1. Spend less
2. Spend the same
3. Spend more

ANSWER GRID TO PART III

QUESTION NUMBER

Policy Area Where City Governments Typically Expend Revenues	Col. 1 (Q1) Jurisdiction		Col. 2 (Q2) Group Preferences			Col. 3 (Q3) Your Preferences			Col. 4 (Q4) Majority Preferences		
Primary and Secondary Education	N	Y	1	2	3	1	2	3	1	2	3
Social Welfare	N	Y	1	2	3	1	2	3	1	2	3
Streets and Parking	N	Y	1	2	3	1	2	3	1	2	3
Mass Transportation	N	Y	1	2	3	1	2	3	1	2	3
Public Health	N	Y	1	2	3	1	2	3	1	2	3
Hospitals	N	Y	1	2	3	1	2	3	1	2	3
Parks and Recreation	N	Y	1	2	3	1	2	3	1	2	3
Libraries	N	Y	1	2	3	1	2	3	1	2	3
Low-Income Housing	N	Y	1	2	3	1	2	3	1	2	3
Public Safety	N	Y	1	2	3	1	2	3	1	2	3
Environmental Protection	N	Y	1	2	3	1	2	3	1	2	3

PART IV. Listed in the grid below are a number of policy concerns, or issues, which are primarily of a non-fiscal character, but which are frequently discussed in the governmental affairs of local communities. We would appreciate your supplying answers and judgments to four questions—which are similar to the four questions in PART III above—regarding each of these issue areas.

Q1. In column 1, we would like you to circle the response which best indicates whether or not your municipal government has jurisdiction in the policy areas listed below.

N. *No* jurisdiction

Y. Municipal government has jurisdiction

Q2. In column 2, we would like you to indicate your judgment about the policy *preferences of the active groups and organizations in your community*. For each policy area, circle the number which best summarizes the *overall* opinions of those groups and organizations concerned with the policies listed below.

1. Most groups oppose such policies
2. There is an even mixture of support and opposition
3. Most groups support such policies

Q3. In column 3, we would like you to indicate *your own preferences* about each of the policy concerns listed below. In the grid below, circle the number which best approximates your own preference.

1. I oppose this policy
2. I am neutral about this policy
3. I support this policy

Q4. In column 4, we would like you to estimate the *preferences of the majority of all voting adults* in your community. For each policy area, circle the number which is your best estimate of majority preferences in your community.

1. Most voters oppose this policy
2. There is even division of opposition and support among voters
3. Most voters support this policy

ANSWER GRID FOR PART IV

Issue or Policy Area	Col. 1 (Q1) Jurisdiction		Col. 2 (Q2) Group Preferences			Col. 3 (Q3) Your Preferences			Col. 4 (Q4) Majority Preferences		
	QUESTION NUMBER										
Strict Firearms Regulation	N	Y	1	2	3	1	2	3	1	2	3
Strict Regulation of Industrial Polluters	N	Y	1	2	3	1	2	3	1	2	3
Involuntary School Busing	N	Y	1	2	3	1	2	3	1	2	3
Compulsory Sex Education in Schools	N	Y	1	2	3	1	2	3	1	2	3
Relaxation of Laws Controlling Marijuana	N	Y	1	2	3	1	2	3	1	2	3
Development of Community Live-in Treatment Facilities for Delinquents	N	Y	1	2	3	1	2	3	1	2	3
Development of Public Employees Unions	N	Y	1	2	3	1	2	3	1	2	3
Increasing Control of Pornography and Public Nudity	N	Y	1	2	3	1	2	3	1	2	3

THANK YOU VERY MUCH FOR YOUR COOPERATION!

G. Documentary Sources

Fiscal data came primarily from U.S. Bureau of the Census, *City Government Finances in (19XX)* (annual). The Annual Survey of Governments tape (see appendix 6) was used for the liquidity measure (chapter 2) and locally supported noncommon functions (chapter 9). The overlapping county tax burden was computed from the 1972 and 1977 Census of Governments, *Compendium of Government Finances*. Total locally-assessed property values were adjusted using assessment-sales price ratios, from the 1972 Census of Governments, vol. 2, part 1, *Taxable and Other Property Values*, and part 2, *Assessment-Sales Price Ratios and Tax Rates*. The number of employees came from the Census annual *City Employment in (19XX)*. Government structure measures (city manager, etc.) were from *The Municipal Yearbook* (annual). Socioeconomic characteristics of cities (owner occupied housing, density, etc.) came from the *County and City Data Book*, 1957 and subsequent years, with most data for the core model from the 1970 Census of Population. City age was the decade when the city reached 20,000, according to earlier Census reports. Irish stock came from the 1970 Census of Population (city data from state reports). Percentage Catholic and Protestant came from Douglas W. Johnson, Paul R. Picard, and Bernard Quinn, *Churches and Church Membership in the United States*. Washington, D.C.: Glenmary Research Center, 1974. Republican voting was for the 1964 and 1968 presidential elections, from Richard M. Scammon, ed. *America Votes*. Washington, D.C.: Governmental Affairs Institute, 1964, 1968. Variables and sources are often explained in the text and notes. A full listing of variables and acronyms is available from the authors.[12]

APPENDIX TWO

Model Specification and Statistical Methods

A. Specification of the Core Model

The chapter 1 theory led to a structural equation:

(A) $$FPO_i = \gamma S_j^a OG_j^b L^c FP^d PC^e W^f \epsilon$$

where superscripts a to f are coefficients indicating the importance of each term, γ a constant, and ϵ an error term. (A) explains fiscal policy outputs (FPO_i's) in terms of sector j's size (S_j), organized group activities (OG_j) of sector j, and leaders' policy preferences, following propositions 1 to 3. Resources interact with preferences (proposition 4). Leaders' preferences are weighted by their resources (formal and informal powers); the leadership term (L) is thus the product of leaders' preferences and resources. National movements reinforce coefficients of organized group activities of black and municipal employee sectors. Private sector wealth (W) strengthens the tax base available to all community residents, so it appears as a separate term. The range of municipal responsibilities (FP) both indicates the size of the municipal employee sector and adjusts for functions on which the city spends. The five components of political culture are included as follows. Fiscal liberalism is the basic dimension along which sectors, groups, and leaders are analyzed. Social liberalism is important to channel citizen and group support to some leaders more than others and is reflected in the magnitude of the black sector and group coefficients (chapter 5). The relative salience of citizens or groups for political inputs is reflected in the importance of S_j and OG_j. The political culture term (PC) indicates emphasis on public or separable goods. The four basic sectors considered are the poor, blacks, municipal employees, and middle class; organized groups correspond to each. A multiplicative functional form is used since many variables are reinforced by others in the model. For example, if leaders prefer higher spending, they can more readily increase programs if a larger black sector exists to define social problems, and black organized groups support specific programs. A smaller middle class is less able to resist such measures, but a wealthy city is seen as able to afford more.

This structural equation was simplified as discussed at the outset of chapter 4 and summarized in table A.2.1, which led to our core model,

Table A.2.1. Variables Used in Developing the Core Model

	Sector Size Measures	Organized Group Activity Measures	
		1967	1976
Poor	LPC70PVN	LOCLASMY	LPAPOOR1 LPAPOOR2
Blacks	LPCBLK70	LBLAKSMY LIMETHMY	LBLCT20A LBLCT50A
Middle Class	LPC70UMC See also appendix 2 on other measures	LBSNESMY LNEWSMY LIMNBRMY LFBUSL	LPANP1 LPANP2 LBUSGRAV
Municipal Employees	LFPDEC4	LIMLOCMY LIMUNMY LPEMP072# LIMCOMY	LPAME LPEMP076

Political Culture	(1) Leadership Policy Preference Measures 1967	1976	(2) Leadership Resource Measures 1967	1976	(1) X (2) Multiplicative Interaction Terms 1967	1976
IRISHL70 LWCWPL70	LMYTALK OPPOTALK MYAGREBS	SPEND11 LLME76 LLPR176 LLPR276	RPINMAYR	LEADRES3 SPEN11SB	LRPINTALK	LLEAD3W2

Note: Acronyms are defined in appendix 1.
#Data from 1972 Census survey, explained in chapter 6.

a reduced form of (A):

$$(1) \qquad FS_i = \gamma PSR_k{}^a L^b OM^c IR^d MC^e FP^f BL^g W^h \epsilon$$

$$(2) \qquad FPO_j = \gamma L^a OM^b IR^c MC^d FP^e BL^f W^g \epsilon$$

where

FS_i = fiscal strain indicator i
FPO_j = fiscal policy output j
PSR_k = private sector resource k
L = leadership interaction term, leader's preferences times leader's power
OM = organization of municipal employees
IR = percentage of Irish stock residents (legitimating separable goods)
MC = percentage middle class families ($10,000 to $15,000 median family income in 1969)
FP = Index of Functional Performance
BL = percentage of black residents (used for all FPOs except 1970–74 changes, when black political activities used)
W = Index of City Wealth
a to h = coefficients to be estimated
γ = constant
ϵ = error term

(Logged acronyms of these terms appear in equations 3 and 4.)

The core model was occasionally expanded. Wage-related variables were added for the compensation equation in chapter 6, and intergovernmental revenues in chapter 9. Sixteen fiscal policy outputs (FPO_i's) were computed using four fiscal measures—general expenditures, long-term debt, city's own revenues, and common functions—each analyzed as a level per capita for 1977 and as a percentage change in 1960–70, 1970–74, and 1974–77. Change measures for other periods were also constructed—1960–65, 1965–70, 1968–70, 1970–72, 1968–72, 1968–74—to isolate turning points for the three periods discussed in chapter 4. Results differ slightly by measures, but the distinctive periods remain basically (1) the early to late 1960s, (2) the late 1960s to about 1974, and (3) 1974–77.

Twenty-two fiscal strain indicators (FS_i's in equation 1) were analyzed using changes in the same four basic fiscal measures divided by changes in median family income for 1960–1970, and changes in population for 1960–70, 1970–74, and 1974–77. The 1977 levels of the four basic fiscal measures were divided by our City Wealth measure to generate fiscal strain level indicators. The "appropriate" private sector resource measures (PSR_k's in equation 1) were denominators of the corresponding fiscal strain indicators: change in median family income, change in population, or the City Wealth index (see last section of chapter 4).

B. Level and Change Measures

Both level and change measures are important for processes in the book. The appropriateness of each is often clear; we comment here briefly on general issues. For migration decisions, most individuals are more concerned about major differences across cities than relatively smaller changes. Hence the migration analyses use levels of tax burdens and welfare benefits. For processes that generate fiscal policy, participants are usually interested in change as well as levels. For example, municipal employees are concerned with how political leaders *change* their compensation, although past decisions which generated current *levels* are important too. A similar rationale holds for political leaders, middle class citizens, and blacks, so we analyzed both levels and changes of fiscal policy outputs, and fiscal strain, in processes involving these groups.

If participants in fiscal policy making in each city acted the same as past participants, cross-sectional analysis of levels at one time would suffice to estimate effects. But participants and fiscal policies change over time, which calls for analysis of time-specific change patterns. Leaders' policy preferences can change over just a few years; we thus use leaders' preferences and organized group activities to analyze fiscal changes. Sector size measures change slowly; percentages of middle class, black, and poor citizens are thus analyzed primarily as levels. Changes in percentage poor and black from 1960 to 1970 are *negatively* related to expenditures because cities most increasing these sectors had smaller sector sizes (levels). An increase in the poor or black sector in a single city may increase expenditures, but such changes are much smaller than differences across cities. This example illustrates the inappropriateness of seeking to explain all changes with other change measures, and levels with levels. Instead, we seek to include for each equation the most appropriate types of measures based on specific reasoning for each term. Specifics are often in notes.

Most methodological discussions consider related issues by contrasting time series with cross-sectional procedures. Our change analyses are a hybrid adapted to these specific processes and data. Given changes in dynamics of the processes by period, pooling data across periods was inappropriate (see Hannan and Young 1977). We have generally used Ordinary Least Squares (OLS) regression of cross sections of levels, and of cross sections of changes, to simplify interpretation and presentation.

Incrementalists focus on annual changes in individual cities, which leads to emphasis on continuities with the past (Crecine 1969; Meltsner 1971). But if either levels or changes are compared across cities, results differ markedly (chapter 2). Insufficient attention to these issues has led most urban fiscal research into one of two molds: cross-sectional comparison of expenditure levels for numerous cities, or changes over time for an individual city. Indeed, the only studies we know of besides this one to analyze changes for numerous cities are Bloom, Brown, and Jackson (1975) and Lyons (1978). These methodological limitations narrow substantive thinking, and deserve correction as the Introduction suggests.

We measure most changes as percentage differences. Gain scores were not used as they treat gains equally irrespective of level. To consider a $10 per capita increase equally in two cities, one of which was spending $60 and the other $130, understates the magnitude of the first. Residualization or first difference procedures, regressing the expenditure level on a lagged version of itself, avoids this problem as well as ceiling and floor effects which sometimes trouble percentage measures. We have chosen percentage changes, however, since city expenditure changes are not constrained to a range of 0 to 100; changes in our data could be negative or positive and often exceed 100 percent. Residualization would thus generate results similar to percentages (and was used in chapter 8.) We generally use percentages since policy makers often consider fiscal changes in percentage terms, and they are simpler to communicate. (See Bohrnstedt 1969; Cronbach and Furby 1970; van Meter 1974.) The major exception is the fiscal strain indicators in chapter 2, where ratios were used. Despite earlier controversy over ratios including common components (e.g., Schuessler 1974), they are reasonable when substantively meaningful (Long 1980; Bollen and Ward 1979).

C. Data Preparation and Significance Levels

While most core variables included 62 cases, the 1967 and 1976 PCS surveys were for only 51. Certain cases were also deleted from fiscal change measures (appendix 4). Pairwise deletion of missing cases was used to maximize the N in calculations.

Basic statistics and frequency distributions were computed for all variables to check for skewness, kurtosis, and outliers. Outliers exceeding three standard deviations from the mean were assigned a value equal to three standard deviations. The mean and standard deviation were then recomputed and the procedure iteratively repeated until no case exceeded three standard deviations from the mean. This normally reduced skewness and kurtosis scores below 3. Other approaches to transformation and outliers are in use (e.g., Barnett and Lewis 1978; Anscombe 1968; Kruskal 1968), but given the small N, these procedures seemed reasonable.

Unusual cases were identified from distributional characteristics of the data, and original sources checked. We used financial statements and other reports from cities and telephoned city officials. This led to correcting a few Census results for personal service contributions and number of municipal employees, mainly due to cities changing their reporting procedures (Duluth and Palo Alto).

We sought to be consistent in significance levels for testing hypotheses, but using different data sets, different statistics, and different computation programs made this sometimes impossible. We sought to report .10 and/or .05 significance levels, or if a relationship was obviously strong, its very high significance level.

D. Three Alternative Modeling Procedures[1]

Three alternative models were estimated. The first estimated direct effects of all core variables on fiscal policy outputs and fiscal strain indicators. The second distinguished direct, indirect, and total effects using path analytic techniques. The third used a reduced form version of the core omitting all organized group and leadership variables. Given the limited cases and occasional multicollinearity, using slightly different models and considering other variables (appendix 5) provide useful tests for consistency.

Direct Effect Estimates for the Core Model. Equations 1 and 2 were log transformed as

$$(3)\quad LFS_j = \log\gamma + a\ LPSR_k + b\ LL + c\ LPEMPO72 + d\ IRISHL70 + e\ LPC70UMC + f\ LFPDEC4 + g\ LPCBLK70 + h\ LNTWRT70$$

$$(4)\quad LFPO_i = \log\gamma + a\ LL + b\ LPEMPO72 + c\ IRISHL70 + d\ LPC70UMC + e\ LFPDEC4 + f\ LPCBLK70 + g\ LNTWRT70$$

where terms are logged versions of those in equations 1 and 2:

LFS_i = logged fiscal strain indicator i
$LFPO_j$ = logged fiscal policy output j
$LPSR_k$ = logged "appropriate" private sector resource k
LL = logged leadership interaction term, LRPNTALK or (for 1974–77 changes in FPO or FS) LLEAD3W2
LPEMPO72 = logged organization of municipal employees
IRISHL70 = logged percentage of Irish stock residents
LFPDEC4 = logged Index of Functional Performance
LPC70UMC = logged percentage of middle class families ($10 to $15,000 median family income in 1969)
LPCBLK70 = logged percentage of black residents (used for all FPO's except 1970–74 changes, when

LBLKSMY, the 1967 black political activities measure, used)

LNTWRT70 = logged Index of City Wealth ("net worth")

a to h = coefficients to be estimated

γ = constant and error term

This functional form, that of a Cobb-Douglas production function, considers both direct and interaction effects in estimating a single effect for each term (see Goldberger 1964:213ff.). Linear rather than log-log versions of these equations were estimated with similar if less strong results. Table A.2.2 reports OLS regression estimates.

Path Analysis: Decomposition into Direct and Indirect Effects. The decomposition into direct, indirect, and total effects is summarized in a path diagram for Models B and F (figure A.2.1) and corresponding recursive equation system for all models (eqs. 3a to 8d). The models differ in that for 1970–74 black political activity (LBLAKSMY) is substituted for black sector size, consistent with the importance of black political activities in this period (chapter 4). The fiscal strain equations add an "appropriate" resource measure as an independent variable, identical to the denominator of the fiscal strain indicator in the same equation. Leadership measures change by time period. These combinations generated six models labeled Models B, F, D, H, L, and J (missing letters were for slightly different specifications). All terms are as defined above except that

$LFPO_j$ = log of percentage change in fiscal policy outputs for 1960–70 and 1977 level

$LFPO_k$ = log of percentage change in fiscal policy outputs for 1974–77

$LFPO_m$ = log of percentage change in fiscal policy outputs for 1970–74

LFS_j = log of fiscal strain change indicators for 1960–70 and 1977 level

LFS_k = log of fiscal strain change indicators for 1974–77

LFS_m = log of fiscal strain change indicators for 1970–74

All terms are logs.

The decomposition procedure used path analysis algorithms in Dun-

Model			
B	(3a)	$\log \gamma$ + a LPCBLK70 + b LPC70UMC + c LFPDEC4 + d IRISHL70	= $\widehat{\text{LPEMPO72}}$
	(3b)	$\log \gamma$ + a LPCBLK70 + b LPC70UMC + c LFPDEC4 + d IRISHL70 + e LPEMPO72	= $\widehat{\text{LRPNTALK}}$
	(3c)	$\log \gamma$ + a LPCBLK70 + b LPC70UMC + c LFPDEC4 + d IRISHL70 + e LPEMPO72 + f LRPNTALK + g LNTWRT70	= $\widehat{\text{LFPO}}_j$
F	(4a)	$\log \gamma$ + a LPCBLK70 + b LPC70UMC + c LFPDEC4 + d IRISHL70	= $\widehat{\text{LPEMPO72}}$
	(4b)	$\log \gamma$ + a LPCBLK70 + b LPC70UMC + c LFPDEC4 + d IRISHL70 + e LPEMPO72	= $\widehat{\text{LLEAD3W2}}$
	(4c)	$\log \gamma$ + a LPCBLK70 + b LPC70UMC + c LFPDEC4 + d IRISHL70 + e LPEMPO72 + f LLEAD3W2 + g LNTWRT70	= $\widehat{\text{LFPO}}_k$
D	(5a)	$\log \gamma$ + a LPC70UMC + b LFPDEC4 + c IRISHL70	= $\widehat{\text{LBLKSMY}}$
	(5b)	$\log \gamma$ + a LPC70UMC + b LFPDEC4 + c IRISHL70	= $\widehat{\text{LPEMPO72}}$
	(5c)	$\log \gamma$ + a LPC70UMC + b LFPDEC4 + c IRISHL70 + d LBLKSMY + e LPEMPO72	= $\widehat{\text{LRPNTALK}}$
	(5d)	$\log \gamma$ + a LPC70UMC + b LFPDEC4 + c IRISHL70 + d LBLKSMY + e LPEMPO72 + LRPNTALK + g LNTWRT70	= $\widehat{\text{LFPO}}_m$
H	(6a)	$\log \gamma$ + a LPCBLK70 + b LPC70UMC + c LFPDEC4 + d IRISHL70	= $\widehat{\text{LPEMPO72}}$
	(6b)	$\log \gamma$ + a LPCBLK70 + b LPC70UMC + c LFPDEC4 + d IRISHL70 + e LPEMPO72	= $\widehat{\text{LRPNTALK}}$
	(6c)	$\log \gamma$ + a LPCBLK70 + b LPC70UMC + c LFPDEC4 + d IRISHL70 + e LPEMPO72 + f LRPNTALK + g LNTWRT70 + h LPSR	= $\widehat{\text{LFS}}_j$
L	(7a)	$\log \gamma$ + a LPCBLK70 + b LPC70UMC + c LFPDEC4 + d IRISHL70	= $\widehat{\text{LPEMPO72}}$
	(7b)	$\log \gamma$ + a LPCBLK70 + b LPC70UMC + c LFPDEC4 + d IRISHL70 + e LPEMPO72	= $\widehat{\text{LLEAD3W2}}$
	(7c)	$\log \gamma$ + a LPCBLK70 + b LPC70UMC + c LFPDEC4 + d IRISHL70 + e LPEMPO72 + f LLEAD3W2 + g LNTWRT70 + h LPSR	= $\widehat{\text{LFS}}_k$
J	(8a)	$\log \gamma$ + a LPC70UMC + b LFPDEC4 + c IRISHL70	= $\widehat{\text{LBLKSMY}}$
	(8b)	$\log \gamma$ + a LPC70UMC + b LFPDEC4 + c IRISHL70	= $\widehat{\text{LPEMPO72}}$
	(8c)	$\log \gamma$ + a LPC70UMC + b LFPDEC4 + c IRISHL70 + d LBLKSMY + e LPEMPO72	= $\widehat{\text{LRPNTALK}}$
	(8d)	$\log \gamma$ + a LPC70UMC + b LFPDEC4 + c IRISHL70 + d LBLKSMY + e LPEMPO72 + f LRPNTALK + g LNTWRT70 + h LPSR	= $\widehat{\text{LFS}}_m$

Figure A.2.1. Path Diagram for Causes of 1960–70, 1974–77, and 1977 Levels of Fiscal Policy Outputs (Models B and F)

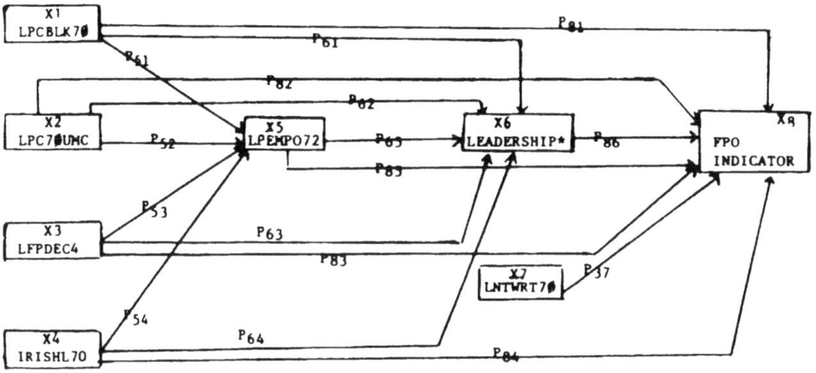

*LEADERSHIP variable is LRPNTALK when the fiscal policy outputs are for 1960-70 and 1977 levels (= Model B). LLEAD3W2 is used when fiscal policy outputs are for 1974-77 level (= Model F)

can (1966), illustrated in table A.2.3, which shows decomposition of effects of all variables in Model B leading to LGXP6070. The total association (column A) is the simple Pearson correlation between each variable and the fiscal policy output. The direct effect (B) is estimated by the standardized regression coefficient (beta) for the path shown; for example in line 1, $P_{81} = a =$ the coefficient for LPCBLK70 in equation 3c. Indirect effects (C) are obtained by multiplying path coefficients (betas from equations 3a, b, and c). For example $p_{61} = a$ in equation 3b, and $p_{86} = f$ in equation 3c. The two other indirect paths from LPCBLK70 to LGXP6070 (column C, line 1) are estimated by multiplying appropriate path coefficients, and products summed to generate total indirect effects of LPCBLK70 on LGXP6070. Direct and indirect effects are summed in D. Finally E shows the unanalyzed effect, the difference between columns A and D, due to spurious association and common causes.

This procedure was followed for all 16 fiscal policy outputs and 22 fiscal strain indicators. The total effects column (D) is the single most interesting result of table A.2.3; the corresponding total effects for all fiscal policy outputs and fiscal strain indicators appear in tables A.2.4 and A.2.5. Using the same example, the first line of table A.2.4 shows

Table A.2.2. Direct Effects, Estimates of Equations (3 and 4)

Standardized Betas - Direct Effects for Model B

Dependent Variables	Independent Variables							Multiple R
	X_1	X_2	X_3	X_4	X_5	X_6	X_7	
	LPCBLK70	LPC70UMC	LFPDEC4	IRISHL70	LPEMPO72	LRPNTALK	LNTWRT70	
LPEMPO72	-.21*	.12	.34*	.08	--	--	--	.45
LRPNTALK	.16	.39*	.52*	-.06	-.17	--	--	.56
LGXP6070	.29*	-.20	.20	.24*	.06	.01	-.03	.62
LONRV607	.14	-.21	-.05	.17	.00	.33*	.05	.43
LFS08607	.02	-.14	-.05	.30*	-.10	.17	.17	.36
LFS01607	-.10	-.43*	.01	.03	.02	.27*	-.13	.47
LGENXP77	-.03	-.29*	.60*	.22*	.11	.11	.10	.86
LONREV77	-.07	-.31*	.49*	.34*	.05	.13	.29*	.83
LFS08477	.14	-.33*	.22	.18	.24*	.07	.25*	.63
LFS01Y77	.06	-.15	.36*	-.09	-.06	.30*	-.02	.58

Table A.2.2. (Continued)

Standardized Betas - Direct Effects for Model D

Dependent Variables	Independent Variables							Multiple R
	X_1	X_2	X_3	X_4	X_5	X_6	X_7	
	LPC70UMC	LFPDEC4	IRISHL70	LBLAKSMY	LPEMPO72	LRPNTALK	LNTWRT70	
LBLAKSMY	-.15	.61*	-.61*	--	--	--	--	.53
LPEMPO72	.23*	.19	.21	--	--	--	--	.43
LRPNTALK	.29*	.38*	.01	.36*	-.05	--	--	.57
LGXP7074	-.20	.03	-.25	-.18	.00	.68*	.10	.61
LONRV704	-.17	.22	-.21	-.19	-.04	.23	.31*	.34
LFS08704	-.04	-.05	-.24	-.30*	-.01	.09	.15	.47
LFS01704	.03	.07	-.13	-.15	.10	.39*	-.11	.44

Standardized Betas - Direct Effects for Model F

Dependent Variables	Independent Variables							Multiple R
	X_1	X_2	X_3	X_4	X_5	X_6	X_7	
	LPCBLK70	LPC70UMC	LFPDEC4	IRISHL70	LPEMPO72	LLEAD3W2	LNTWRT70	
LPEMPO72	-.21*	.12	.34*	.08	--	--	--	.46
LLEAD3W2	.21	-.02	.13	.03	-.02	--	--	.30
LGXP7477	-.46*	-.43*	.10	-.02	-.04	-.08	-.09	.43
LONRV747	-.57*	-.49*	.15	-.06	-.05	-.14	.02	.52
LFS08747	-.68*	-.34*	.18	-.27*	-.12	.19	-.06	.52
LFS01747	-.27*	-.19	.43*	.01	-.07	.30*	-.05	.57

Table A.2.2. (Continued)

Standardized Betas - Direct Effects for Model H (w/o Intervening Dependent Variables)

Dependent Variables	Independent Variables X_1	X_2	X_3	X_4	X_5	X_6	X_7	X_8		Multiple R
	LPCBLK70	LPC70UMC	LFPDEC4	IRISHL70	LPEMPO72	LRPNTALK	LNTWRT70	Appropriate	Resource	
LLDMI607	-.28*	-.43*	.20	-.08	-.08	.26*	-.04	-.40*	LMDFI607	.62
LLTPO607	-.10	-.24*	.21*	-.11	-.02	.23*	-.15*	-.59*	LPOP6070	.83
LGXMI607	.19*	-.10	.40*	.06	-.12	-.02	.05	-.62*	LMDFI607	.81
LGXPO607	.12*	-.04	.29*	-.08	-.00	.04	-.10	-.76*	LPOP6070	.95
LCFMI607	-.02	-.05	.15	.17	-.25*	.08	.25*	-.62*	LMDFI607	.63
LCFPO607	.04	.00	.08	.05	-.06	.08	.02	-.80*	LPOP6070	.86
LORFI607	.10	-.20	.03	.08	-.04	.30*	.06	-.40*	LMDFI607	.60
LORPO607	.14	-.05	.04	-.03	.08	.19*	-.10	-.57*	LPOP6070	.76
LCFNTW77	-.06	-.36*	.32*	.01	.12	.11	-.43*	--	LNTWRT70	.77
LGENET77	-.11	-.21*	.52*	.23*	.01	.08	-.29*	--	LNTWRT70	.85
LORNTW77	-.12	-.24*	.45*	.42*	-.08	.09	-.19*	--	LNTWRT70	.86
LLTNET77	-.16	-.24*	.38*	-.21*	-.05	.32*	-.33*	--	LNTWRT70	.68
LGXMFI77	.02	-.27*	.52*	.22*	.09	.11	-.02	-.02	LMD70INC	.83

Table A.2.2. (Continued)

Standardized Betas - Direct Effects for Model J (w/o Intervening Dependent Variables)

Dependent Variables	X_1	X_2	X_3	X_4	X_5	X_6	X_7	X_8		Multiple R
	Independent Variables									
	LPC70UMC	LFPDEC4	IRISHL70	LBLKSMY	LPEMPO72	LRPNTALK	LNTWRT70	Appropriate Resource		
LLTPO704	.11	.22	-.22*	-.11	.06	.07	-.09	-.79*	LPOP7074	.85
LGXPO704	-.05	.14	-.21*	-.08	-.02	.26*	-.05	-.80*	LPOP7074	.92
LCFPO704	.01	.07	-.12*	.13*	-.06	-.06	.02	-.92*	LPOP7074	.95
LORPO704	-.01	.23*	-.20*	-.01	-.16*	-.01	.21*	-.84*	LPOP7074	.87

Standardized Betas - Direct Effects for Model L (w/o Intervening Dependent Variables)

Dependent Variables	X_1	X_2	X_3	X_4	X_5	X_6	X_7	X_8		Multiple R
	Independent Variables									
	LPCBLK70	LPC70UMC	LFPDEC4	IRISHL70	LPEMPO72	LLEAD3W2	LNTWRT70	Appropriate Resource		
LLTPO747	-.33*	-.24*	.43*	.00	-.05	.31*	-.04	-.05	LPOP735C	.59
LGXPO747	-.19	-.33*	.14	-.10	.01	-.07	-.10	.44*	LPOP735C	.57
LCFPO747	-.50*	-.25*	.15	-.35*	-.04	.22*	-.03	.02	LPOP735C	.47
LORPO747	-.42*	-.39*	.13	-.17	.01	-.13	.04	.31*	LPOP735C	.60
LOL74	.03	-.32*	.08	-.21	.02	.03	.17	No Resource		.62

Note: Models B, D, and F include certain non-fiscal dependent variables important for the structural equations below. Acronyms of fiscal policy outputs (dependent variables for Models B,D,F) are labeled in table 3.2 of chapter 3, except that here LGENXP77 is general expenditures per capita in 1977, LONREV77 is own revenues per capita in 1977, and LFSO1Y77 is long term debt per capita in 1977. These differ from the table 3.2 variables only in that these are not FP-adjusted (since FP is an independent variable here). Acronyms of fiscal strain indicators (Models H,J,L) are explained in table 2.11 of chapter 2. Slight differences between acronyms here and those in 2.11 are due to omitting FP adjustments here. Acronyms of independent variables are below equations (3) and (4). Models H, J, and L list the acronym of the specific resource corresponding to each dependent variable in the column beside its coefficient.

These are mulitiple regression results for the 62 PCS cities which show the standardized regression coefficients (betas) and an asterisk if the corresponding F statistic equals or exceeds 1.8 (significant at about the .10 level).

-- indicates omitted.

Table A.2.3. Example of Decomposition of Association for One Fiscal Policy Output: LGXP6070 (Model B)

Independent Variable	A Total Association	B Direct Effect	C Indirect Effects	D Total Effects C+B	E Unanalyzed Effects A-D
X_1=LPCBLK70	r_{81}= .42829	P_{81}= .29322	$P_{61}P_{86}$ = .00201 $P_{51}P_{65}P_{86}$= .00049 + $P_{51}P_{85}$ = -.01494 sum = -.01244	.28078	.14751
X_2=LPC70UMC	r_{82}= -.36598	P_{82}= -.20469	$P_{62}P_{86}$ = .00500 $P_{52}P_{65}P_{86}$= -.00029 + $P_{52}P_{85}$ = .00879 sum = .01350	-.19119	-.17479
X_3=LFPDEC4	r_{83}= .47618	P_{83}= .20455	$P_{63}P_{86}$ = .00659 $P_{53}P_{65}P_{86}$= -.00079 + $P_{53}P_{85}$ = .02405 sum = .02985	.23440	.24178

Table A.2.4. Total Effects Explained by Core Model for 16 Fiscal Policy Outputs (Models B, D, and F)

Total Effect Explained by Model B

Dependent Variable	Independent Variables						
	X_1	X_2	X_3	X_4	X_5	X_6	X_7
	LPCBLK70	LPC70UMC	LFPDEC4	IRISHL70	LPEMPO72	LRPNTALK	LNTWRT70
LGXP6070	.28	-.19	.23	.24	.06	.01	-.03
LONRV607	.21	-.08	.09	.14	-.05	.33	.05
LFSO8607	.08	-.09	-.01	.28	-.13	.17	.17
LFSO1607	-.05	-.32	.15	.01	-.02	.27	-.13
LGENXP77	-.03	-.23	.70	.22	.08	.11	.10
LONREV77	-.05	-.25	.58	.33	.03	.13	.29
LFSO8Y77	.10	-.27	.34	.20	.23	.07	.25
LFSO1Y77	.14	-.04	.47	-.12	-.12	.30	.02

Total Effect Explained by Model D

Dependent Variable	Independent Variables						
	X_1	X_2	X_3	X_4	X_5	X_6	X_7
	LPC70UMC	LFPDEC4	IRISHL70	LBLAKSMY	LPEMPO72	LRPNTALK	LNTWRT70
LGXP7074	-.02	.33	-.28	.06	-.02	.68	.10
LONRV704	-.10	.23	-.15	-.11	-.05	.23	.31
LFSO8704	.02	.19	-.45	.34	.01	.09	.15
LFSO1704	.16	.23	-.10	-.00	.08	.39	-.11

Total Effect Explained by Model F

Dependent Variable	Independent Variables						
	X_1	X_2	X_3	X_4	X_5	X_6	X_7
	LPCBLK70	LPC70UMC	LFPDEC4	IRISHL70	LPEMPO72	LLEAD3W2	LNTWRT70
LGXP7477	-.47	-.43	.08	-.02	-.03	-.08	-.09
LONRV747	-.59	-.49	.11	-.07	-.05	-.14	.02
LFSO8747	-.61	-.36	.16	-.27	-.12	.19	-.06
LFSO1747	-.19	-.21	.44	.01	-.08	.30	-.05

Note: Acronyms of fiscal policy outputs (dependent variables) are labeled in table 3.2 (chapter 3) except that here LGENXP77 is general expenditures per capita in 1977, LONREV77 is own revenues per capita in 1977, and LFSO1Y77 is long term debt per capita in 1977. These differ from the table 3.2 variables only in that these are not FP-adjusted (since FP is an independent variable here). Acronyms of the independent variables are in appendix 2 under equations (3) and (4).

Table A.2.5. Total Effects Explained by Core Model for 22 Fiscal Strain Indicators (Models H, J, and L)

Total Effect Explained by Model H

Dependent Variables	X_1	X_2	X_3	X_4	X_5	X_6	X_7	X_8	
	LPCBLK70	LPC70UMC	LFPDEC4	IRISHL70	LPEMPO72	LRPNTALK	LNTWRT70	Appropriate Resource	
LLDMI607	-.21	-.34	.30	-.11	-.13	.26	-.04	-.40	LMDFI607
LLTP0607	-.05	-.16	.31	-.13	-.06	.23	-.15	-.59	LPOP6070
LGXMI607	.21	-.13	.34	.05	-.12	-.02	.05	-.62	LMDFI607
LGXP0607	.13	-.03	.31	-.08	-.01	.04	-.10	-.76	LPOP6070
LCFMI607	.04	-.05	.10	.14	-.26	.08	.25	-.62	LMDFI607
LCFP0607	.07	.03	.10	.03	-.08	.08	.02	-.80	LPOP6070
LORFI607	.17	-.10	.15	.05	-.09	.30	.06	-.40	LMDFI607
LORP0607	.16	.03	.16	-.04	.05	.19	-.10	-.58	LPOP6070
LCFNTW77	-.06	-.30	.41	.01	.10	.11	-.43		
LGENET77	-.09	-.18	.56	.23	-.04	.08	.29		
LORNTW77	-.09	-.21	.46	.40	-.09	.09	-.19		
LLTNET77	.09	-.12	.51	-.24	-.11	.32	-.33		
LGXMFI77	.02	-.21	.61	.22	.07	.11	-.02		

Total Effect Explained by Model J

Dependent Variables	X_1	X_2	X_3	X_4	X_5	X_6	X_7	X_8	
	LPC70UMC	LFPDEC4	IRISHL70	LBLKSMY	LPEMPO72	LRPNTALK	LNTWRT70	Appropriate Resource	
LLTP0704	.16	.20	-.15	-.09	.06	.07	-.09	-.79	LPOP7074
LGXP0704	.00	.24	-.22	.01	-.03	.26	-.05	-.80	LPOP7074
LCFP0704	-.03	.10	-.20	.10	-.06	-.06	.02	-.92	LPOP7074
LCFP0704	-.04	.19	-.22	-.01	- 16	-.01	21	- 84	LPOP7074

Table A.2.5. (Continued)

Dependent Variables	Total Effect Explained by Model L — Independent Variables X_1	X_2	X_3	X_4	X_5	X_6	X_7	X_8	
	LPCBLK70	LPC70UMC	LFPDEC4	IRISHL70	LPEMPO72	LLEAD3W2	LNTWRT70	Appropriate Resource	
LLTPO747	-.25	-.26	.45	.01	-.06	.31	-.04	-.05	LPOP747
LGXPO747	-.21	-.33	.13	-.11	.01	-.07	-.10	.44	LPOP747
LCFPO747	-.44	-.26	.16	-.35	-.05	.22	-.03	.02	LPOP747
LORPO747	-.45	-.39	.12	-.18	.01	-.13	.04	.31	LPOP747
LOL74	.04	-.32	.09	-.20	.01	.03	.17	None	

Note: Acronyms of the fiscal strain indicators (dependent variables) are explained in table 2.11 of chapter 2; those of independent variables are in appendix 2, under equations (3) and (4). The acronym of the specific appropriate resource corresponding to each dependent variable is listed in the column beside its coefficient. Slight differences between dependent variables here and those in table 2.11. are mainly due to omitting FP adjustments from these (since FP is an independent variable here).

for LGXP6070 the total (direct plus indirect) effects of each independent variable. For example, .28 is the total effect of LPCBLK70 on LGXP6070. F statistics were computed to assess significance levels for the direct effects, but are not appropriate for summed direct and indirect effects. Still, as a rule of thumb, total effects less than about ±.20 should not be considered significant.

Reduced Form of Core Regressions

The reduced form of the core regressions included only variables on the far left of figure A.2.1, those exogenous to the equation system. When intermediary variables are omitted, the reduced form equations estimate total effects of these exogenous variables on the final dependent variable (see Alwin and Hauser 1975). Reduced form results were very close to those for the full core (equations 3 and 4) and path analytic decomposition (equations 3a through 8d). Results were omitted to save space.[2]

E. Delimiting the Middle Class Sector: City-Level Analyses

What are the implications of different boundaries for the "middle class"? Data were analyzed for annual income by family in 1969, since city-specific data for residents' income are collected only in the decennial census.[3] Five middle class sector measures were considered. Obviously we use "middle class" broadly, following general American usage. Table A.2.6 shows generally strong correlations among the five measures.

The five are correlated in part because of their association with city wealth. This is clear in table A.2.7 where the five are correlated with median family income, (market equalized) taxable property value, and the City Wealth Index (a weighted sum of the first two, explained in chapter 2). Again, most r's exceed .6. The one exception is the $10,000 to $15,000 sector.

The association of middle class sector size and wealth is troublesome since the two variables have theoretically opposite effects on expend-

Table A.2.6. The Five Middle-Class Sector Size Measures Are Generally Strongly Interrelated

Income Group	Income Group: Above Poverty Level	Poverty Level to $10,000	$10,000 to $15,000	$15,000 to $25,000	Over $25,000
Above Poverty Level (LPC70PVO)	1.00				
Poverty Level to $10,000	-.26	1.00			
$10,000 to $15,000	.72	.01	1.00		
$15,000 to $25,000	.78	-.74	.57	1.00	
Over $25,000	.46	-.77	-.04	.67	1.00

Note: These are simple r's (Pearson correlation coefficients) for the 62 PCS cities. If $r \geq .21$, $p \leq .10$; if $r \geq .32$, $p \leq .01$.

itures. Ceteris paribus, a large middle-class sector should decrease expenditures, but wealth should increase expenditures. Yet given the association between wealth and sector measures, disentangling their separate effects proved difficult. Most appealing for this purpose was the $10,000 to $15,000 measure, as it was least correlated with the three

Table A.2.7. Most Middle-Class Sector Size Measures Are Strongly Related to Median Family Income, Taxable Property Value, and the City Wealth Index

Income Category	Median Family Income	Taxable Property Value	City Wealth Index
Above poverty level	.84	.42	.54
Poverty Level to $10,000	-.66	-.64	-.69
$10,000 to $15,000	.64	.13	.28
$15,000 to $25,000	.97	.64	.76
Over $25,000	.62	.66	.70
Median Family Income		.60	.74
Taxable Property Value			.95

See note to table A.2.6.

wealth measures. It included from 18 to 41 percent of all families in our 62 cities.

If the five sector measures are generally correlated with each other and with wealth, how do they affect fiscal policy outputs? In simple correlations, the $10,000 to $15,000 measure was the most clearly (negatively) related to fiscal policy outputs, especially for 1960–70 and 1974–77 changes and 1977 levels, as discussed in chapter 4. But simple correlations are biased by colinearity with wealth.

To seek to disentangle middle class sector effects from wealth and other variables, the core regression model was reestimated iteratively using each of the five middle class sector measures, including and excluding the Wealth Index. Coefficients for middle class sector measures in the model excluding the Wealth Index resembled the simple correlations. But middle class sector coefficients were often insignificant in the model including the Wealth Index. The important exception was the $10,000 to $15,000 measure, which showed generally negative relationships with spending.

These results illustrate classic problems of multicollinearity with limited cases. Collinearity between most middle class sector measures and wealth suppresses effects of both when both are in the same equation. Their effects are weakened further by moderate relations with percent of black residents (about .5 for most). Three solutions are possible. (1) Consider altogether different data sources for cleaner estimates of critical relations. This was done using survey data for citizens in chapter 5, which showed a generally linear, negative relationship between income and spending preferences. Consequently, in analyzing the city-level data, we were less concerned about delimiting the middle class sector at any particular income point. (2) Consider studies by others using different samples or methods. We reviewed several studies using survey data for individuals in chapter 7 with results generally similar to ours. But we found virtually no comparative city-level studies including measures of both wealth and of middle class sectors. Most studies included just one measure like taxable property value or median family income. (3) Replicating the relationship with a larger number of cities is desirable for future work. Although interview data are expensive, a simplified model could use only Census data.

Is the $10,000 to $15,000 measure the most appropriate? Survey data for citizens suggests that in their opposition to taxes, citizens in this income category resemble others slightly higher or lower in income. The low relationship between this sector measure and wealth measures in the city data suggest that it is the best to distinguish sector and wealth effects.

F. The Index of Staffing[4]

The General Approach. The Index of Staffing analyzes characteristics of cities related to demand for municipal services. Characteristics important in research to date are included in a demand equation to generate estimates of the number of employees that one would expect in each city based on its socioeconomic makeup. This expected number is then subtracted from the actual number of employees to generate the Index of Staffing. Cities with high positive scores are overstaffed compared to other American cities; those with high negative scores are understaffed. A city scoring zero has the number of employees implied by its particular mix of socioeconomic characteristics (tables 6.8, 6.9).

The Demand Models. The demand equations were specified by reviewing the basic literature on determinants of municipal expenditure and especially employment.[5] The principal measures of citizen demand for public services were included. Measures of supply (e.g., unionization of municipal employees), or political processes (e.g., organized group activity, voting, leaders' preferences) were omitted as we did not seek to explain actual employment levels, only citizen demands along with community characteristics, like population size and density, that may act as "taste shifters" or affect the technology of service delivery. We do not present detailed arguments for each variable for reasons of space, and because they have been so frequently discussed in the sources cited. What is important is that standard variables are included. Variables in the demand equations appear in table A.2.8. The Index of Functional Performance (FP) is unnecessary (and insignificant) in the common function equation, but is important for total employment. Intergovernmental revenues are highly correlated with general revenues and total staff size. Yet we exclude intergovernmental

Table A.2.8. Demand Equations for Total Municipal Employees and Employees Working in Common Functions

Independent (Demand) Variables	Dependent Variables: Total Municipal Employees 1978	Dependent Variables: Common Function Employees 1978
Population density, 1970[a]	.00013	.00015*
Total population size, 1975	-.00216	-.00043*
Percent of families in city below federal poverty level, 1969[a]	.96191*	.29272*
Equalized taxable property value per capita, 1972[b]	.00014	-.00009
Serious crimes per capita, 1970[a]	.05767*	.02966*
Cost of living in SMSA[c]	.29936*	.06534
Index of Functional Performance[d]	.06123*	--
Multiple R	.94	.70

Note: These are OLS regression estimates. The unstandardized regression coefficients (b's) are shown with an asterisk if the relationship was significant beyond the 0.1 level as measured by the F statistic. N = 62.

[a]U.S. Bureau of the Census, County and City Data Book, 1972.

[b]U.S. Bureau of the Census, Census of Governments, 1972. The assessed property value was divided by the assessed/market ratio to generate equalized taxable property value.

[c]U.S. Bureau of Labor Statistics, Handbook of Labor Statisitics. For SMSAs missing in this source, the cost of living was estimated from a regression equation calculated from SMSAs without missing data, including region, population size, and median family income as predictors.

[d]Computed as described in appendix 4. Data from Annual Survey of Governments, 1974 (magnetic tape used to generate City Government Finances series).

-- indicates omitted.

revenues from the model as they are not exogenous, but influenced by local policies to seek or avoid them (chapter 9). They relate to differences across cities in functional responsibilities, but these are measured by our FP index. Previous studies lacking an FP-type measure often included intergovernmental revenues as a partial substitute. For this analysis these seem reasonable procedures, although for other purposes the demand equations could obviously be modified.

APPENDIX THREE

Correlation Matrix

We include here a correlation matrix for the most important variables used throughout the book. Variables shown are the nine used in different versions of the core (equations 3 and 4 in appendix 2), major private sector resource measures (chapter 2 and table 3.1), and fiscal policy outputs (table 3.2). Acronyms appear at the places cited.

The table reports Pearson product-moment correlation coefficients (r's). Most variables are for the 62 PCS cities, but the N is sometimes lower due to missing data. The asterisks, one for .01 and two for .001 significance levels, are computed using the N for each variable. With $N = 62$, if $r \geq .21$, $p \leq .10$.

	IRISHL70	LPC70UMC	LPCBLK70	LPEMPO72	LFPDEC4	LNTWRT70	LLEAD3W2	LRPNTALK	LBLAKSMY	LNEAST
IRISHL70	1.0000	0.0583	-0.1373	0.3099*	0.5420**	0.0118	0.0763	0.1621	-0.2752	0.7752**
LPC70UMC	0.0583	1.0000	-0.5472**	0.2127	-0.1076	0.2832	-0.1552	0.2120	-0.3037	0.0756
LPCBLK70	-0.1373	-0.5472**	1.0000	-0.2020	0.2734	-0.3494*	0.2599	0.1310	0.6410**	-0.1017
LPEMPO72	0.3099*	0.2127	-0.2020	1.0000	0.3207*	0.0920	-0.0121	0.0198	-0.2751	0.2613
LFPDEC4	0.5420**	-0.1076	0.2734	0.3207*	1.0000	-0.2879	0.2118	0.4308**	0.3094	0.5301**
LNTWRT70	0.0118	0.2832	-0.3494*	0.0920	-0.2879	1.0000	-0.3720*	-0.1288	-0.1767	-0.2334
LLEAD3W2	0.0763	-0.1552	0.2599	-0.0121	0.2118	-0.3720*	1.0000	0.1813	0.0237	0.1218
LRPNTALK	0.1621	0.2120	0.1310	0.0198	0.4308**	-0.1288	0.1813	1.0000	0.2883	0.2386
LBLAKSMY	-0.2752	-0.3037	0.6410**	-0.2751	0.3094	-0.1767	0.0237	0.2883	1.0000	-0.2104
LNEAST	0.7752**	0.0756	-0.1017	0.2613	0.5301**	-0.2334	0.1218	0.2386	-0.2104	1.0000
LEASTCEN	0.4499**	0.5711**	-0.1556	0.1596	0.2547	-0.1160	0.0654	0.4174*	-0.1699	0.5296**
LPOP75T	-0.0336	-0.2455	0.5442**	0.1882	0.4413**	0.0000	0.0274	0.2673	0.5869**	-0.1110
LPOP6075	-0.3023*	0.1620	-0.2533	-0.0995	-0.2008	0.2617	-0.0591	-0.3085	0.0472	-0.3099*
LCITDE70	0.5969**	0.0458	0.1610	0.4458**	0.4459**	-0.0075	0.0164	0.1710	-0.0807	0.4781**
LCITYAGE	0.3466*	-0.2788	0.5577**	0.1828	0.6368**	-0.4082**	0.3511*	0.3721*	0.3104	0.3844*
LPC70OLH	0.4741**	-0.1642	0.3407*	0.2017	0.4867**	-0.4041**	0.2084	0.3168	0.0806	0.4672**
LPC70NW	-0.1428	-0.5731**	0.9862**	-0.1629	0.2617	-0.2701	0.2593	0.0874	0.6435**	-0.1521
LPC70PIN	-0.1011	-0.7359**	0.8080**	-0.1263	0.3442*	-0.5441**	0.2855	0.0807	0.5303**	-0.0068
LMED70IN	0.0691	0.6489**	-0.5733**	0.1998	-0.2614	0.7424**	-0.2669	-0.1095	-0.3583*	-0.1132
PRSV70LA	0.0177	0.1302	-0.2999*	0.0906	-0.2600	0.9539**	-0.4133*	-0.1202	-0.0752	-0.2249
LMDFI607	-0.0851	0.2976	-0.2701	-0.2457	-0.1291	0.3923*	-0.0198	-0.1104	-0.1592	-0.0977
LFS27072	0.2240	0.0538	0.0462	0.1596	0.0783	0.1345	-0.1797	-0.0413	0.0606	0.0787
LFS01607	0.0878	-0.3486*	0.2089	-0.0364	0.2206	-0.2586	0.1633	0.2007	0.2469	0.2365
LFS01704	0.0458	0.1331	0.0429	0.1307	0.1885	-0.1481	0.4268*	0.3855*	0.0044	0.1367
LFS01747	0.2701	-0.1742	0.0652	0.0707	0.4391**	-0.2572	0.3777*	0.3633*	-0.0167	0.2212
LFS08607	0.2591	-0.0724	0.0324	-0.0424	0.1229	0.1129	0.0896	0.1467	-0.2172	0.1933
LFS08704	-0.3380*	0.0088	0.1696	-0.1371	-0.0946	0.1124	0.0554	0.1132	0.3442*	-0.3548*
LFS08747	-0.1114	-0.0839	-0.2441	-0.0485	-0.0742	-0.0759	0.0902	-0.1069	-0.3236	-0.2023
LONRV607	0.1631	-0.1860	0.2442	-0.0255	0.2262	-0.0784	-0.0819	0.3054	0.1815	0.0245
LONRV704	-0.0281	-0.0293	0.1485	0.0087	0.0580	0.1957	0.2234	0.1555	0.0119	-0.0940
LONRV747	0.0376	-0.1776	-0.2913	-0.0098	-0.0448	0.0943	-0.2049	-0.2067	-0.3257	0.0074
LGXP6070	0.3241*	-0.3660*	0.4283**	0.1040	0.4762**	-0.2482	0.0549	0.1411	0.1973	0.2873
LGXP7074	-0.0794	0.0036	0.0624	-0.0289	0.1339	-0.0271	0.3388	0.5500**	0.1389	-0.0230
LGXP7477	0.0546	-0.2169	-0.1729	-0.0198	0.0113	-0.0589	-0.0804	-0.1925	-0.2861	-0.0127
LGXP77FP	0.0177	-0.2426	0.1931	0.1548	-0.2042	-0.0005	0.0848	-0.0960	-0.0535	-0.1689
LFS177FP	-0.1533	-0.2314	0.3119*	-0.0704	-0.1194	-0.1954	0.1012	0.0490	0.2123	-0.2632
LORV77FP	0.1868	0.0275	-0.2090	-0.0191	-0.2847	0.3424*	0.0762	-0.0345	-0.3987*	0.0933
LFS0RY77	0.3625*	-0.2860	0.2322	0.3037*	0.4407**	0.0637	0.1860	0.1239	0.0438	0.0981

	LEASTCEN	LPOP75T	LPOP6075	LCITDE70	LCITYAGE	LPC70OLH	LPC70NW	LPC70PIN	LMED70IN	PRSV70LA
IRISHL70	0.4499**	-0.0336	-0.3023*	0.5969**	0.3466*	0.4741**	-0.1428	-0.1011	0.0691	0.0177
LPC70UMC	0.5711**	-0.2455	0.1620	0.0458	-0.2788	-0.1642	-0.5731**	-0.7359**	0.6489**	0.1302
LPCBLK70	-0.1556	0.5442**	-0.2533	0.1610	0.5577**	0.3407*	0.8862**	0.8080**	-0.5733**	-0.2999*
LPEMP072	0.1596	0.1882	-0.0995	0.4458**	0.1828	0.2017	-0.1629	-0.1263	0.1998	0.0806
LFPDEC4	0.2547	0.4413**	-0.2008	0.4459**	0.6368**	0.4867**	0.2617	0.3442*	-0.2614	-0.2609
LNTWRT70	-0.1160	0.0000	0.2617	-0.0075	-0.4082**	-0.4041**	-0.2701	-0.5441**	0.7424**	0.5539**
LLEAD3W2	0.0654	0.2274	-0.0591	0.0184	0.3511*	0.2084	0.2593	0.2855	-0.2669	-0.4133*
LRPNTALK	0.4174*	0.2633	-0.3085	0.1710	0.3721*	0.3168	0.0874	0.0577	-0.1085	-0.1202
LBLAKSMY	-0.1699	0.5869**	0.0472	-0.0807	0.3104	0.0806	0.6435**	0.5303**	-0.3583*	-0.0752
LNEAST	0.5296**	-0.1110	-0.3099*	0.4781**	0.3844*	0.4672**	-0.1521	-0.0368	-0.1132	-0.2249
LEASTCEN	1.0000	-0.1323	-0.4142**	0.4189**	0.2344	0.4568**	-0.2307	-0.2800	0.1492	-0.2018
LPOP75T	-0.1323	1.0000	0.0331	0.2292	0.5474**	0.0739	0.5667**	0.4982**	-0.2423	0.0219
LPOP6075	-0.4142**	0.0331	1.0000	-0.5127**	-0.4958**	-0.8061**	-0.2287	-0.2276	0.2922	0.1978
LCITDE70	0.4189**	0.2292	-0.5127**	1.0000	0.3810*	0.5327**	0.1717	0.0662	0.0015	-0.0051
LCITYAGE	0.2344	0.5474**	-0.4958**	0.3810*	1.0000	0.7478**	0.5264**	0.6507**	-0.5553**	-0.3344*
LPC70OLH	0.4568**	0.0739	-0.8061**	0.5327**	0.7478**	1.0000	0.3010*	0.3781*	-0.3976**	-0.3509*
LPC70NW	-0.2307	0.5667**	-0.2287	0.1717	0.5264**	0.3010*	1.0000	0.7834**	-0.5064**	-0.2205
LPC70PIN	-0.2800	0.4982**	-0.2276	0.0662	0.6507**	0.3781*	0.7834**	1.0000	-0.8693**	-0.4198**
LMED70IN	0.1492	-0.2423	0.2922	0.0015	-0.5553**	-0.3976**	-0.5064**	-0.8693**	1.0000	0.6068**
PRSV70LA	-0.2018	0.0219	0.1978	-0.0051	-0.3344*	-0.3509*	-0.2205	-0.4198**	0.6068**	1.0000
LMDFI607	-0.0715	-0.0712	0.5914**	-0.3092	-0.4205**	-0.6029**	-0.2812	-0.3780*	0.3976*	0.2768
LFS27072	0.0746	0.0472	-0.0914	0.4367**	-0.0326	0.0540	0.0953	-0.1085	0.2095	0.1122
LFS01607	-0.0871	0.0534	-0.1968	-0.0045	0.4489**	0.2882	0.2189	0.4208**	-0.4312**	-0.1633
LFS01704	0.2256	0.1835	-0.2039	0.0979	0.2333	0.1960	0.0027	0.0539	-0.1805	-0.1445
LFS01747	0.0507	0.2231	-0.2433	0.1268	0.4881**	0.3812*	0.0432	0.3018	-0.3866*	-0.1730
LFS08607	0.0913	0.0296	-0.4206**	0.3008*	0.1653	0.1766	0.0671	0.0050	0.0027	0.1096
LFS08704	-0.0228	0.2429	0.1639	-0.2880	0.0377	-0.1510	0.1705	0.0586	0.0602	0.1016
LFS08747	-0.2194	0.0071	0.1649	-0.2027	-0.1318	-0.2225	-0.2401	-0.0915	-0.0539	-0.0746
LONRV607	0.0624	0.0650	-0.4273**	0.0634	0.3252*	0.3903*	0.2402	0.2691	-0.2332	-0.0456
LONRV704	0.0462	0.1014	-0.1450	0.0078	0.0743	0.0978	0.1604	0.0043	0.0667	0.1707
LONRV747	-0.3747*	0.0490	0.2571	-0.1617	-0.0716	-0.2458	-0.2740	-0.0832	-0.0072	0.1206
LGXP6070	0.0563	0.2159	-0.4788**	0.2916	0.5894**	0.6278**	0.4311**	0.4407**	-0.3420*	-0.1861
LGXP7074	0.1963	0.1073	-0.1482	-0.0221	0.0619	0.1141	0.0362	0.0785	-0.1420	-0.0297
LGXP7477	-0.3016	0.0847	0.1458	-0.0222	0.0369	-0.0978	-0.1677	0.0277	-0.0973	-0.0516
LGXP77FP	-0.1183	0.1233	-0.1366	0.1178	0.0926	0.0381	0.2166	0.2748	-0.1420	0.0483
LFS177FP	-0.1676	0.3237*	0.0082	-0.1669	0.1861	-0.0552	0.3095*	0.3490*	-0.2590	-0.0437
LORV77FP	0.1113	-0.1222	-0.0412	-0.0056	-0.1401	-0.0291	-0.1926	-0.1908	0.1501	0.3867**
LFS08Y77	0.0100	0.3966**	-0.3620*	0.4462**	0.3899**	0.3308*	0.2926	0.1862	-0.0329	0.5993

	LMDFI607	LFS27072	LFS01607	LFS01704	LFS01747	LFS08607	LFS08704	LFS08747	LONRV607	LONRV704
IRISHL70	-0.0851	0.2240	0.0878	0.0458	0.2701	0.2591	-0.3380*	-0.1114	0.1631	-0.0281
LPC70UMC	0.2976	0.0538	-0.3486*	0.1331	-0.1742	-0.0724	0.0088	-0.0839	-0.1860	-0.0290
LPCBLK70	-0.2701	0.0462	0.2089	0.0429	0.0652	0.0324	0.1696	-0.2441	0.2442	0.1485
LPEMP072	-0.2457	0.1596	-0.0364	0.1307	0.0707	-0.0424	-0.1371	-0.0485	-0.0255	0.0087
LFPDEC4	-0.1291	0.0783	0.2206	0.1885	0.4391**	0.1229	-0.0946	-0.0742	0.2262	0.0580
LNTWRT70	0.3923*	0.1345	-0.2586	-0.1481	-0.2572	0.1129	0.1124	-0.0759	-0.0784	0.1957
LLEAD3W2	-0.0198	-0.1797	0.1633	0.4268*	0.3777*	0.0896	0.0554	0.0962	-0.0819	0.2234
LRPNTALK	-0.1104	-0.0403	0.2007	0.3855*	0.3633*	0.1487	0.1132	-0.1069	0.3054	0.1555
LBLAKSMY	-0.1592	0.0606	0.2469	0.0044	-0.0163	-0.2172	0.3442*	-0.3236	0.1815	0.0119
LNEAST	-0.0977	0.0787	0.2365	0.1367	0.2212	0.1933	-0.3548*	-0.2023	0.0245	-0.0940
LEASTCEN	-0.0715	0.0746	-0.0871	0.2256	0.0507	0.0913	-0.0228	-0.2194	0.0624	0.0462
LPOP75T	-0.0712	0.0472	0.0534	0.1835	0.2231	0.0296	0.2429	0.0071	0.0650	0.1014
LPOP6075	0.5914**	-0.0914	-0.1968	-0.2039	-0.2433	-0.4206**	0.1639	0.1649	-0.4273**	-0.1450
LCITDE70	-0.3092	0.4367**	-0.0045	0.0979	0.1268	0.3008*	-0.2880	-0.2027	0.0634	0.0078
LCITYAGE	-0.4205**	-0.0328	0.4489**	0.2333	0.4881**	0.1653	0.0377	-0.1318	0.3252*	0.0743
LPC70OLH	-0.6029**	0.0540	0.2882	0.1960	0.3812*	0.1766	-0.1510	-0.2225	0.3903*	0.0978
LPC70NW	-0.2812	0.0953	0.2189	0.0027	0.0432	0.0671	0.1705	-0.2401	0.2402	0.1604
LPC70PIN	-0.3780*	-0.1085	0.4208**	0.0539	0.3018	0.0050	0.0586	-0.0905	0.2691	0.0043
LMED70IN	0.3976*	0.2095	-0.4312**	-0.1805	-0.3866*	0.0027	0.0692	-0.0539	-0.2332	0.0667
PRSV70LA	0.2768	0.1122	-0.1633	-0.1445	-0.1730	0.1096	0.1016	-0.0746	-0.0456	0.1707
LMDFI607	1.0000	-0.1326	-0.2842	-0.0177	-0.0443	0.0503	0.1053	0.0637	-0.1332	0.1202
LFS27072	-0.1326	1.0000	-0.1078	-0.1019	-0.1605	0.1383	-0.0598	-0.2817	-0.0540	-0.0430
LFS01607	-0.2842	-0.1078	1.0000	-0.1744	0.1215	0.1504	-0.0361	-0.1956	0.1580	-0.0012
LFS01704	-0.0177	-0.1019	-0.1744	1.0000	0.2470	0.1894	0.1198	0.2208	0.2827	0.3011
LFS01747	-0.0443	-0.1605	0.1215	0.2470	1.0000	0.1553	-0.0737	0.2590	0.1899	-0.0178
LFS08607	0.0503	0.1383	0.1504	0.1894	0.1553	1.0000	-0.2920	0.0904	0.4319**	0.1791
LFS08704	0.1053	-0.0598	-0.0361	0.1198	-0.0737	-0.2920	1.0000	-0.1091	0.1082	0.2530
LFS08747	0.0637	-0.2817	-0.1956	0.2208	0.2590	0.0904	-0.1091	1.0000	-0.1178	-0.0162
LONRV607	-0.1332	-0.0540	0.1580	0.2827	0.1899	0.4319**	0.1082	-0.1178	1.0000	0.1376
LONRV704	0.1202	-0.0430	-0.0012	0.3011	-0.0178	0.1791	0.2530	-0.0162	0.1376	1.0000
LONRV747	0.0325	-0.1968	0.0548	-0.0158	0.1298	0.0797	-0.0485	0.7146**	-0.0828	-0.2377
LGXP6070	-0.3915*	0.0521	0.2429	0.0747	0.0994	0.3989*	-0.0274	-0.0887	0.5233**	0.1741
LGXP7074	0.0109	-0.1287	0.0326	0.4196**	0.2141	0.1325	0.2338	0.0368	0.1684	0.5479**
LGXP7477	-0.0192	-0.1527	0.0053	0.0055	0.1962	0.0410	-0.0527	0.7255**	-0.0888	-0.2122
LGXP77FP	-0.1387	0.0657	-0.0474	0.0833	0.2845	0.2009	0.0718	0.1371	0.0474	0.1927
LFS177FP	0.1493	-0.0757	-0.1792	0.4769**	0.4053*	0.0856	0.2214	0.1665	0.2922	0.2455
LORV77FP	0.0575	0.0047	-0.0592	0.1327	0.0935	-0.0067	-0.0464	0.0870	0.0367	0.1363
LFS08Y77	-0.1826	0.2486	-0.0699	0.1511	0.3410*	0.4258**	0.0553	0.2949*	0.1558	0.1609

	LONRV747	LGXP6070	LGXP7074	LGXP7477	LGXP77FP	LFS177FP	LORV77FP	LFS08Y77
IRISHL70	0.0376	0.3241*	-0.0794	0.0546	0.0177	-0.1533	0.1868	0.3625*
LPC70UMC	-0.1776	-0.3669*	0.0030	-0.2169	-0.2426	-0.2314	0.0275	-0.2869
LPCBLK70	-0.2913	0.4283**	0.0624	-0.1729	0.1931	0.3119*	-0.2090	0.2322
LPEMPO72	-0.0098	0.1040	-0.0289	-0.0198	0.1546	-0.0704	-0.0191	0.3037*
LFPDEC4	-0.0448	0.4762**	0.1339	0.0113	-0.2042	-0.1184	-0.2847	0.4407**
LNTWRT70	0.0943	-0.2482	-0.0271	-0.0589	-0.0005	-0.0954	0.3424*	0.0637
LLEAD3W2	-0.2049	0.0549	0.3388	-0.0804	0.0848	0.1012	0.0762	0.1860
LRPNTALK	-0.2067	0.1411	0.5500**	-0.1925	-0.0960	0.0490	-0.0345	0.1239
LBLAKSMY	-0.3257	0.1970	0.1389	-0.2861	-0.0530	0.2123	-0.3987*	0.0438
LNEAST	0.0074	0.2873	-0.0230	-0.0127	-0.1689	-0.2632	0.0933	0.0981
LEASTCEN	-0.3747*	0.0563	0.1963	-0.3016	-0.1183	-0.1676	0.1113	0.0100
LPOP75T	0.0490	0.2159	0.1073	0.0847	0.1233	0.3237*	-0.1222	0.3966**
LPOP6075	0.2571	-0.4788**	-0.1482	0.1458	-0.1366	0.0082	-0.0412	-0.3620*
LCITDE70	-0.1617	0.2916	-0.0221	-0.0222	0.1178	-0.1669	-0.0056	0.4462**
LCITYAGE	-0.0716	0.5894**	0.0619	0.0369	0.0926	0.1861	-0.1401	0.3899**
LPC70OLH	-0.2458	0.6278**	0.1141	-0.0978	0.0381	-0.0552	-0.0291	0.3308*
LPC70NW	-0.2740	0.4311**	0.0362	-0.1677	0.2166	0.3095*	-0.1926	0.2926
LPC70PIN	-0.0832	0.4407**	0.0785	0.0277	0.2346	0.3490*	-0.1808	0.1862
LMED70IN	-0.0072	-0.3420*	-0.1420	-0.0973	-0.1420	-0.2590	0.1501	-0.0329
PRSV70LA	0.1206	-0.1861	-0.0297	-0.0516	0.0483	-0.0437	0.3867**	0.0997
LMDFI607	0.0325	-0.3915*	0.0109	-0.0192	-0.1387	0.1493	0.0575	-0.1826
LFS27072	-0.1968	0.0521	-0.1287	-0.1527	0.0657	-0.0757	0.0047	0.2486
LFS01607	0.0548	0.2429	0.0326	0.0053	-0.0474	-0.1792	-0.0592	-0.0699
LFS01704	-0.0158	0.0747	0.4196**	0.0055	0.0833	0.4789**	0.1327	0.1511
LFS01747	0.1298	0.0994	0.2141	0.1962	0.2845	0.4053*	0.0935	0.3410*
LFS08607	0.0797	0.3989*	0.1325	0.0410	0.2009	0.0856	-0.0067	0.4258**
LFS08704	-0.0485	-0.0274	0.2338	-0.0527	0.0318	0.2214	-0.0464	0.0557
LFS08747	0.7146**	-0.0887	0.0368	0.7255**	0.1371	0.1665	0.0830	0.2949*
LONRV607	-0.0828	0.5233**	0.1684	-0.0888	0.0474	0.2922	0.0367	0.1558
LONRV704	-0.2377	0.1741	0.5479**	-0.2122	0.1927	0.2455	0.1363	0.1609
LONRV747	1.0000	0.0305	-0.2148	0.8598**	0.3109	0.1276	0.1407	0.2076
LGXP6070	0.0305	1.0000	-0.0028	0.0531	0.1578	0.0451	-0.1428	0.3725*
LGXP7074	-0.2148	-0.0028	1.0000	-0.2180	0.0517	0.2358	0.0394	0.1055
LGXP7477	0.8598**	0.0531	-0.2180	1.0000	0.4261**	0.0355	0.0491	0.3025
LGXP77FP	0.3109	0.1578	0.0517	0.4261**	1.0000	0.7941**	0.1705	0.3953**
LFS177FP	0.1276	0.0451	0.2358	0.0355	0.7941**	1.0000	0.1473	0.2639
LORV77FP	0.1407	-0.1428	0.0394	0.0491	0.1705	0.1473	1.0000	-0.0440
LFS08Y77	0.2076	0.3725*	0.1055	0.3025	0.3953**	0.2639	-0.0440	1.0000

APPENDIX FOUR

Functional Performance Analysis

The importance of functional responsibilities of city governments was stressed in chapter 2, which outlined our Functional Performance (FP) approach. Chapter 9 considered correlates of the Index with other city characteristics. We have adjusted for FP effects in different ways throughout the volume. A related paper (Clark, Ferguson, and Shapiro 1982) compares the FP approach with 11 others, including combined state-local expenditures, combined overlapping local governments, analysis of cities within a single state, study of a single function, and common functions. These 12 procedures were compared in a matrix on 11 criteria such as: permits overall assessment of fiscal condition of city (not just common functions), available for individual central cities or suburbs, separate functions are weighted differently, etc. The FP approach was superior to most alternatives. Nevertheless, for some purposes, other procedures are simpler or more efficient. We briefly review those we used.

For percentage changes in expenditures or debt, the problem disappears since each city is compared only with its past. But this assumes no FP changes. For our change measures, we thus inspected each city and isolated FP changes—usually assumption or deletion of a function. Nine cities with changes over the 1960–77 period were deleted from all change analyses: Albany, Clifton, Indianapolis, Irvington, Jacksonville, Memphis, St. Paul, St. Petersburg, and Schenectady. Massachusetts cities transferred welfare to the Commonwealth during fiscal year 1969–70; changes in general expenditures, intergovernmental revenue, and number of municipal employees for 1960–70 were adjusted

Robert Y. Shapiro is coauthor of this appendix.

by increasing the 1970 figure by a percentage equal to welfare in 1969: 13.6 for Boston, 10.6 for Cambridge, and 11.3 for Malden. In studying migration (chapter 8), we used county-area data since appropriate data were unavailable for cities; the tax burden and welfare measures summed revenues or welfare expenditures for all local governments in the county area. One of our four basic policy outputs was common functions, which avoids FP problems by including only functions common to most cities.

However, the FP approach is often superior. It includes three basic methods. Several tables in chapter 2 use the FP residual procedure which simply computes

$$R_y = Y - \hat{Y} \tag{1}$$

and

$$\hat{Y} = a + bFP \tag{2}$$

where

R_y = residual or FP-adjusted score (dollars per capita)
Y = actual spending level (dollars per capita)
$\hat{Y}$ = predicted level (dollars per capita)
FP = the Functional Performance Index
a = constant
b = OLS regression coefficient

A second method is to inspect simple correlations between the FP index and other measures. High correlations suggest that some FP control is in order.

Our third and principal method is to include the FP Index as an independent variable in a regression equation:

$$FPO_j = a + bFP + \sum_{i=1}^{n} (c_i OV_i) + e \tag{3}$$

where

FPO_j = any general fiscal policy output j—such as general expenditures per capita
FP = the Functional Performance Index

OV_i = each of n other variables
a = constant
b and c_i = coefficients to be estimated for FP and each OV_i
e = a random disturbance

Thus including the FP Index in the core indicates the magnitude of FP effects and helps remove them from other variables.[1]

The Functional Performance Index: Computational Details

FP weights come from average per capita expenditures for all U.S. cities over 50,000 population. Their precision depends on the disaggregation of subfunctions. For example, welfare includes AFDC, general assistance, and medical reimbursements. A city may be responsible for some but not necessarily all these services. The best extant data source for such disaggregation is the *Annual Survey of Governments*, the tape from which the Census compiles *City Government Finances*. We followed the Census in excluding the nine common functions. The *Annual Survey of Governments* includes twelve noncommon functions, disaggregated into 67 subfunctions, listed in table A.4.1. To develop national averages for each subfunction, the following procedure was used for all cities with a population of 50,000 or more in 1974 (n = 481).

First, a frequency distribution of cities was prepared for per capita expenditures on each subfunction. Cities in the bottom 10 percent were excluded since their commitment was so low. (See note to table A.4.1.) Second, per capita expenditures for remaining cities were summed and divided by the number of such cities. Each city was thus counted equally. The resulting average per capita expenditure was the weight for that subfunction. The 67 weights appear in table A.4.1. The FP Index combines the weights as explained in chapter 2.

Potential Sources of Bias

Three sources of potential bias remain.

1. *Regional effects*. Differences across regions in expenditure levels might seem to make a national weight inappropriate. Weights were

Table A.4.1. For Each of the 67 Sub-Functions:
Functional Performance Weights and Cut-Off Points

Variable #[a]	Description of Sub-Function	FP Weight	Cut-Off Point[b]
V79	Airports-Current Operations	3.95	.464
V80	Airports-Construction	7.27	.284
V81	Airports-Equipment	.39	.014
V82	Airports-Land	2.33	.064
V83	Airports-Payments to Government	1.35	0
V84	Airports-Payments to Local Government	.49	0
V85	Miscellaneous Commercial-Current Operations	1.49	.074
V86	Miscellaneous Commercial-Construction	.31	.004
V87	Miscellaneous Commercial-Equipment	.03	.004
V89	Corrections-Current Operations	5.72	.084
V90	Corrections-Construction	1.13	.014
V91	Corrections-Equipment	.05	.004
V92	Corrections-Land	.53	0
V93	Corrections-Payments to State Government	.76	0
V94	Corrections-Payments to Local Government	.35	.084
V96	Local Schools-Current Operations	219.27	7.00*
V97	Local Schools-Construction	24.53	.85
V98	Local Schools-Equipment	3.02	.30
V99	Local Schools-Land	1.61	.03
V100	Local Schools-Payments to State Government	.85	.002
V101	Local Schools-Payments to Local Government	3.34	.12
V102	Higher Education-Current Operations	58.55	7.00*
V103	Higher Education-Construction	13.41	.01
V104	Higher Education-Equipment	1.35	.03
V105	Higher Education-Land	.432	.01
V115	Employment Security-Current Operations	6.10	0
V143	Health-Current Operations	4.91	.14
V144	Health-Construction	.62	.014
V145	Health-Equipment	.13	.012
V146	Health-Land	.17	.004
V147	Health-Payments to State Government	.89	.027
V148	Health-Payments to Local Government	1.15	.056
V149	Own Hospital-Current Operations	78.94	7.00*
V150	Own Hospital-Construction	5.81	.29
V151	Own Hospital-Equipment	1.71	.06
V153	Other Hospital-Current Operation	10.47	.03
V154	Other Hospital-Construction	2.80	.17
V157	Other Hospital-Payments to State Government	2.37	.02
V158	Other Hospital-Payments to Local Government	1.35	.085

Table A.4.1. (Continued)

Variable #[a]	Description of Sub-Function	FP Weight	Cut-Off Poin
V165	Housing-Current Operations	8.71	.382
V166	Housing-Construction	10.06	.30
V167	Housing-Equipment	.17	.007
V168	Housing-Land	14.52	.964
V169	Housing-Payments to State Government	.38	.02
V170	Housing-Payments to Local Government	2.04	.027
V171	Libraries-Current Operations	5.56	1.144
V172	Libraries-Construction	1.89	1.024
V173	Libraries-Equipment	.41	.014
V174	Libraries-Land	.57	.004
V176	Libraries-Payments to Local Government	3.05	.443
V183	Parking-Current Operations	1.26	.114
V184	Parking-Construction	3.47	.064
V185	Parking-Equipment	.16	.014
V186	Parking-Land	1.69	.009
V188	Parking-Payments to Local Government	.62	0
V201	Cash Assistance-Categorical Program	65.08	7.00*
V202	Cash Assistance-Other	5.86	.058
V203	Vendor Payments for Medical Care	5.77	.11
V204	Vendor Payments-Other	2.41	.03
V205	Public Welfare-Current Operations	5.40	.09
V206	Public Welfare-Construction	.34	.01
V207	Public Welfare-Equipment	.10	.009
V209	Public Welfare-Payments to State Government	4.30	.10
V210	Public Welfare-Payments to Local Government	2.56	.039
V223	Water Transportation-Current Operations	5.41	.009
V224	Water Transportation-Construction	5.83	.144
V225	Water Transportation-Equipment	.36	.014

[a]The variable numbers refer to the categories of expenditures listed on the Annual Survey of Governments tape, 1974. The descriptions of the sub-functions came from the same source.

[b]The cut-off points define the level above which each city must spend to be considered fiscally responsible for the sub-function. Unless indicated by an asterisk, the cut-off point indicates the lowest decile. Four sub-functions, marked by an asterisk, have a higher cut-off point. In these cases there is a clear break point at about the $7.00 level, that separates cities with considerable fiscal responsibility from those with minimal responsibility.

computed for the Northeast, North Central, South, and West, and compared with the national weights. There were no systematic differences in weights across regions. Some regional weights differ from the national weight, but this is as much a city as a regional effect. Moving to the regional level trades one problem for another: so few cities perform some subfunctions that regional weights are easily distorted by one high or low city.

State weights were also constructed, but the smaller N made them even more unstable than regional weights. Variance is often as great within as across states. National weights are still close to most state averages. For example, for the six states where more than five cities provide education, the state average was within 12 percent of the national average.[2]

Across states and regions, cities vary enormously in functions they perform. Older cities perform more functions (Liebert 1976). But once the functions are assumed, expenditure variations are more limited.

2. *The Method of Disaggregating the Functions*. Disaggregation into the 67 subfunctions is somewhat arbitrary, but builds on the considerable Census efforts in data preparation. More discrete categories could increase precision of the weights.

3. *The Problem of Intermittent Capital Outlays*. We used only one year of data (for fiscal 1974). This should not trouble the weights (W_i's in note 4 of chapter 2), since the construction and land expenditures should be stochastically distributed across the 481 cases. But does it trouble defining responsibilities of any individual city (F_i's in equation 1)? A city with zero capital outlays that year would score zero on F_i even if it incurred construction or land expenditures in prior or subsequent years. Yet this bias seems limited. We estimated the maximum likely bias as follows: If a city performed all 67 subfunctions, its total FP weight would be 627.91. If it had no expenditures for land or construction in 1974, but spent on them all the next year, the total FP weight would change by 99.32 (the sum of all weights for land acquisition and construction). The distortion would be 16 percent.

APPENDIX FIVE

Other Variables That Could Affect The Analysis

Throughout the book we mentioned "other variables" that might affect core model processes. We and other observers of fiscal policy have suggested several candidates. Hypotheses below indicate fiscal effects of most, but commentaries are brief. One major result is clear: the other variables do not undermine the core results in the text.

Methods, In Brief

The importance of 22 other variables was assessed by adding them each to the core model, one at a time. Dependent variables were the basic fiscal policy outputs and fiscal strain indicators.[1] Two types of results were considered. First, did coefficients of core variables change with addition of other variables? The null hypothesis was that they would not. F statistics for coefficients were compared in models including and excluding each other variable. Three types of changes appear in columns 1 to 3 of table A.5.1: (1) increases in core variable coefficients from $F \leq 1.8$ to $F \geq 1.8$ when the other variable is added, (2) analogous decreases, and (3) changes in sign.

Second, we asked if other variables had direct effects on fiscal policy outputs and fiscal strain indicators, i.e., whether the regression coefficient of the other variable itself was significant. Column 4 reports the percent of fiscal policy outputs and fiscal strain indicators on which the other variable had a significant direct effect. (Table 9.1 illustrates the analysis using intergovernmental revenues as the other variable.)

The regression procedure did not enter the other variable after the core; no variables were forced, so all variables competed equally.

Do Other Variables Affect the Core Results?

This question is answered by inspecting the first three columns of table A.5.1, which suggest that other variables affected few core results. For example, the top line shows that when population size was added, 2.73 percent of the core coefficients increased, 4.83 percent decreased, and 0 percent changed sign. Results are similar for most other variables. Core variables change 9.09 percent at most, and average about 4 percent. Even these changes are only in significance level; coefficients practically never change sign (column 3). Effects of other variables are thus largely independent of core variables, albeit not entirely orthogonal to them.[2]

Do Other Variables Have Any Direct Effects?

Consider now direct effects. Basic results are in column 4 of table A.5.1: percentages here are higher than the first three columns. The top line, for instance, shows that population size had a significant direct effect on 29 percent of the fiscal policy outputs and fiscal strain indicators. Such effects are largely independent of the core variables. We consider below variables by category as listed in table A.5.1.

Discussion of Specific Effects

Many population size characteristics, especially *population size* and *change*, have been widely discussed. "Large cities, declining in population" have often been labeled strained. Chapter 3 showed that such population measures were sometimes related to fiscal policy outputs, but not very often. The first two lines of table A.5.1 show similar results. Larger cities declining in population do have somewhat higher spending and debt levels. In general, we have not added more than

Table A.5.1. Other Variables Seldom Affect the Core Analyses, but Often Do Have Significant Direct Effects on Fiscal Policy Outputs and Fiscal Strain Indicators

Other Variable	Affected by the Other Variable: Percentage of Core Model Variables: Up (1)	Down (2)	Change in Sign (3)	Percentage of Fiscal Policy Outputs and Fiscal Strain Indicators (4)
Population Characteristics and Sector Measures				
Population size, 1970 (LPOP70T)[a]	2.73	4.83	0	29.16
Population change 1960-75 (LPOP6075)	2.31	5.88	0	27.77
Change in percent poor, 1960-70 (LPCLC607)	4.62	6.51	0	31.94
Percent over 18 in 1970 (LPC18Y70)	3.78	5.88	.21	23.61
Percent over 65 in 1970 (LPC65Y70)[b]	3.40	9.09	0	18.18
Organized Groups and Political Activity Measures				
Political activities of non-poor, 1976 (LPANP2)	2.73	4.41	0	23.61
Power of ethnic and religious groups, 1967 (LIMETHMY)	3.78	5.04	0	31.94
Political activities of blacks, 1976 (LBLCT20A)	6.09	5.25	.21	33.33
Political activities of poor, 1976 (LPAPOOR2)	2.52	3.57	0	26.38
Democratic Party dominance (LDMPRTYP)	2.52	4.83	0	20.83
Power of heads of local government agencies (LIMLOCMY)	2.73	5.04	0	23.61
Centralization of power (LHDIFF)	1.89	3.57	0	26.38

Resource Measures				
Cost of living (LCOLSMSA)	4.83	7.14	.02	43.05
Opportunity wages in service sector (LOWSVK67)	1.47	4.41	0	23.61
Intergovernmental revenues, 1976, per capita (LIGREV76)	4.41	6.30	0	19.44
Intergovernmental revenues, 1976, FP residual (LIGR76FP)	7.56	3.57	0	27.77
Percent own revenues from property tax (LPTXOR74)	4.20	5.67	.18	38.88
Index of reform government (LREFRMGV)	2.52	4.62	.18	15.27
Percent Protestant citizens (LPCPRT52)	4.41	7.56	0	25.00
Miscellaneous Measures				
Population density (LCTYDE70)	2.94	6.09	0	30.55
Crime rate (LCRMPC70)	3.99	3.99	.18	25.00
Index of Staffing (LPCOVSTF)	2.73	4.62	0	22.22
Tax burden (LFS27072)[c]	2.00	3.00	0	3.66
January temperature (LJNTMP70)[c]	4.66	2.66	0	4.66
Percent old housing, 1970 (LPC70OLH)[c]	2.66	4.00	0	8.00
Summary (Means)				
Fiscal Policy Outputs (N=50)	3.08	2.65	.0006	27.75
Fiscal Strain Indicators (N=22)	3.95	9.73	.02	23.34
Fiscal Policy Outputs and Fiscal Strain Indicators (combined) (N=72)	3.56	5.18	.04	27.11

[a] This and all other variables without b or c footnotes are based on 50 fiscal policy outputs with six independent variables and 22 fiscal strain indicators with eight independent variables. The percentage base is thus (50 X 6) + (22 X 8) = 476. See notes 1 & 2.

[b] Based on 22 fiscal strain indicators with eight independent variables; N = 22 X 8 = 176.

[c] Based on 50 fiscal policy outputs with six independent variables; N = 50 X 6 = 300.

one other variable at a time due to the low n, but wanted to here because of arguments about the Northeast syndrome. Population size, population change (1960–1975), and old housing (pre-1950) were added to the core as they have been widely discussed in policy circles and variations used in CDBG formulas. Each was significant with some fiscal policy measures in table 3.2 and in some regressions, especially for common functions 1960–70. Yet including 10 variables in a model (the core of 7 plus these 3) suppressed only 8.9 percent of the core coefficients.

Several *sector size* measures were analyzed for the *middle class*, *poor*, and *blacks*. Most were variations of our basic measures, with different cutting points or multiplied by other characteristics to consider interactions: percent black times percent poor, percent black times the number of municipal employees, and both percent black and percent poor separately multiplied by political activity levels of municipal employees, blacks, and poor. The multiplicative terms followed the hypothesis that more poverty and blacks, as well as more politically active blacks, poor, or municipal employees might generate particularly high spending. A larger black or poor sector might provide votes, or simply serve as a potential force whose case could be argued by organized groups or municipal employees (e.g., Piven 1974; Clark and Ferguson 1981a). However, the interaction terms did not show any clear independent effects due to the limited number of cities and high multicollinearity for interaction terms, their components, and closely related core variables.

Change measures of sector size for 1960–70 were computed, especially for blacks and poor, with the hypothesis that increases would raise spending. They did not, because cities with the largest increases in poor or blacks were those with the fewest in 1960. Hence results were the opposite of those hypothesized.

Cities with more *inhabitants who are young* (under 18)[3] *or old* (over 60) may spend more for schools and services for these age groups who may also generate fewer revenues than middle-aged persons, thus increasing fiscal strain. We find some direct effects, but almost as many positive as negative. The inconsistent results seem due to inclusion of wealth and FP in the core, which in turn are affected by a large young or old population.

Discussing *organized groups and political activity measures*, chapters 4 and 7 indicated that apart from blacks and municipal employees, most organized groups were insignificant. Still, we computed several measures for *business groups*, *nonpoor organized groups*, and others (e.g., LDCINBUS, LBUSGRAV, etc., in appendix 1), generally with no effects on policy outputs. Political activities of nonpoor groups did increase 1974–77 expenditures and debt. Business group measures were generally insignificant. The combined measures were too close to their components to distinguish more than effects of the components.

The basic result for *black organized groups* in chapter 4 was that their activities increased spending in the late 1960s and early 1970s. This also holds for the *power of ethnic and religious groups* in the mayoral election (table 5.3). By contrast, the 1976 measure of *black political activity* was unrelated to fiscal level indicators, and negatively related to 1974–77 changes. Other measures were *urban disturbances* (LRIOTSCR) and *black support for the mayor* in 1967 (LBLAKSMY), but their fiscal effects were mainly via mayors' preferences, as in chapters 4 and 5.

Political activity of the poor had similar effects to blacks, only less strong. Most results for the poor seem to capture those of blacks.

Political activities of municipal employees in 1976 (LPAME) increased compensation in 1974–77 but affected few other fiscal policy outputs, as discussed in chapter 6.

Democratic Party dominance was measured by the percentage of Democratic mayors (since 1945) and council members (in the last two council sessions), computed to see if cities with more Democratic leaders spent more. But the few significant relations were almost equally positive and negative. A related measure was the *percentage of Democratic votes* by residents of the (usually) county election district in two presidential elections (LELECON). It showed positive relations with some expenditure items in simple correlations, but fell below significance in most regressions. Parties, due to numerous Democrats in the South and changes discussed in chapter 7, thus have inconsistent effects on fiscal policy. Components of their political cultures are better analyzed separately.

The *power of heads of local government agencies* was analyzed to consider the hypothesis of Niskanan (1971), Borcherding (1977), and others that aggressive bureau heads increase expenditures by expanding staffs and activities. While 24 percent of the fiscal policy outputs and fiscal strain indicators were related to the measure, cities with powerful bureau heads almost always had *lower* expenditures. Such cities often have weak mayors and councils, and strong city managers; the measure thus partially captures "reform" or professional management. Such management may decrease expenditures, but is also bound up with the political culture in such cities (of more affluent, Protestant, highly educated, whites) which favors public goods and lower spending.

Centralization of power was much debated in the community power literature, initially with the hypothesis that more centralized cities spent less since civic and business elites were fiscally conservative (e.g., Hunter 1953). Contradictory findings led to the subsequent hypothesis that centralization encourages public goods, but decentralization generates separable goods (Clark 1973c, 1975b), thus linking centralization to different types of expenditures, and clarifying earlier discussions of special interest groups. Cities where more groups are powerful should increase separable goods programs. While several studies support this proposition (e.g., Clark 1973c; Smith 1976; Williams 1980; Harris 1982), many variables are associated with centralization which must be controlled to assess such a ceteris parabis proposition. Some other studies thus understandably report weak relationships between centralization and policy outputs (e.g., Grimes et al. 1976; Lyons and Bonjean 1981). Elsewhere we classified specific program expenditures on publicness (Clark 1973c); the more aggregated policy outputs here permit less detailed analysis. Nevertheless, insofar as expenditures reflect higher levels of public services which are less pure public goods than the tax burden supporting them, higher spending implies more separable goods. We would thus expect less spending by more centralized cities. And this we find, especially for debt and capital outlays in the 1960s and early 1970s. The (1967) centralization measure had no impact on *changes* after 1974, although 1977 spending *levels* were higher in more decentralized cities. An interaction term of centralization multiplied by mayor's spending preferences generated effects similar to those of the 1967 leadership term in the core (LRPNMAYR). This is reasonable as centralization is similar to the mayor's power term used in LRPNMAYR. The centralization measure in table A.5.1 was LHDIFF; INDEXDEC was generally insignificant.

Policy preferences of leaders were measured by a 1967 PCS item asking leaders what they felt were major problems facing their city. The item has been widely used (e.g., Verba and Nie 1972) and factor analyzed to assess configurations of leaders' policy orientations (see Clark 1973b), generating three distinct patterns: one for economic development and growth, a second for traffic and related management problems, and a third for public social services (housing, health, poverty, etc.). As a leading component of social services, health (LHEALTH) was added as an other variable to see if it might increase expenditures; it was generally insignificant. Similarly, *agreement between business leaders and the mayor* (MYAGREBS) had minimal fiscal effects.

Cities with higher *costs of living* obtain less per dollar, and must spend more for goods and services. A high cost of living acts as a negative resource. One might consequently expect positive coefficients for the cost of living measure, but results are inconsistent. Of 31 fiscal measures significantly associated with cost of living, 13 were positive and 18 negative. Since the cost of living is related to many other city characteristics, past analyses reporting significant effects probably omitted related core variables.

Opportunity wages, like the cost of living, should increase personnel costs. Chapter 6 showed opportunity wages to increase compensation. Here opportunity wages often increased expenditures and debt.

Intergovernmental revenue was analyzed using our other variable procedure in chapter 9. Cities with higher intergovernmental revenues often had higher local expenditures, although the importance of local variables is clear in tables 5.3 and 9.1.

Local revenue sources vary in salience. Least desirable to most citizens (see chapter 9) are property taxes, suggesting that the greater the city's *dependence on the property tax for local revenues*, the greater the resistance of citizens to it and to local spending. Indeed we find that cities more dependent on the property tax increased expenditures and debt less over most of the 1960 to 1977 period, and spent at lower levels in 1977. While only the 1974 measure appears in table A.5.1, 1960 and 1970 property tax measures generated similar results.

The index of reform government (summing at-large elections, nonpartisan ballots, and presence of a city manager) was discussed in chapter 9 as bound up with other city characteristics, but not necessarily exerting a direct fiscal effect. Indeed, it affects only 8 percent of the fiscal policy outputs, and relations with fiscal strain indicators shift from negative to positive in no clear pattern.

Last are *miscellaneous other variables*. The white ethnic section of chapter 5 discussed several measures (*percent foreign-born, Catholics, Protestants, Irish*) hard to distinguish in city-level analyses. The percentage of Irish residents represents this configuration in the core. The percentage of *Protestants* was added as an other variable. As expected, the more Protestants, the lower the 1977 expenditure level. Like the Irish, Protestants are primarily a background force on expenditure levels, but unrelated to most changes from 1960 to 1977. Besides the standard other variable analysis, percent Protestant, foreign born, and a *composite political culture measure* (LWCWPL70) were substituted for percent Irish in the core. Results were similar to those for Irish, but slightly less often significant.

Population density might increase expenditures if social proximity increased spreading of fires and higher crime rates. A counter-argument suggests economies of scale, especially in mass transportation, construction and maintenance of parks, streets, sewer and water lines, and other capital infrastructures (see Peterson 1976). Where density effects are significant, they generally increase spending, especially for 1977 levels, but are negative for 1977 long-term debt and capital outlays. Sorting out specific dynamics demands more disaggregated analysis.

Cities with high *crime rates* might spend more for police and facilities damaged by vandalism (parks, buildings, etc.). Yet the police department's diligence in recording crimes may increase both reported crimes and police expenditures. We find higher 1977 fiscal policy levels in cities with higher crime rates, but inconsistent effects for most change measures.

The *Index of Staffing* from chapter 6 could have risen at any time in the past, and thus should be related to levels but not necessarily changes. Indeed, cities high in staffing are higher on several 1977 fiscal policy levels, and some 1960–70 increases, but after 1970, change relationships were weak and inconsistent.

The *tax burden*, like staffing, is generated by all past commitments, but also by other governments (school districts, counties, and state). One might hypothesize that cities with higher tax burdens would reduce spending in a time of taxpayer revolt, following the fiscal feedback argument in chapter 4. This holds for the (1972) tax burden: cities with higher burdens increased expenditures and debt less in 1974–77. But before 1974, significant effects were few.

A *low mean January temperature* should increase costs for services like snow removal and street repair that are more extensive in colder areas. The measure may also tap fiscal conservatism of "Sunbelt" cities. Both hypotheses imply less spending in warmer cities, which we find, especially for 1977 level measures.

Percent of housing constructed before 1950 roughly indexes an older capital stock, which should increase capital facilities expenditures; this we found for 1960–70 capital outlays, but not for other periods or the 1977 level. The *percent of owner-occupied housing* might increase salience of property taxes to citizens, dampening their support for government spending. Indeed, cities with more owner-occupied housing had lower 1977 levels of general expenditure and own revenues, but few change measures were affected.

Many further variables were considered in preliminary analyses, but were insignificant or too similar to others for full other variable analysis. Many are in the text or notes. One not mentioned above was whether or not a city had earned the *Certificate of Conformance* (for sound fiscal management) *of the Municipal Finance Officers Association*. It was unrelated to most fiscal policy measures.

APPENDIX SIX

Problems with Municipal Fiscal Data

Urban fiscal data have many weaknesses. But so do all data. What analyses can the fiscal data withstand? Those involving broader categories (like general expenditures, long-term debt) demand less precise accounting than specific items (like sanitation). Major differences, such as the more than $1,000 per capita for long-term debt in New York City compared to $26 for Santa Ana, are not due simply to noise in the data. But there is some noise. Results differ if one consults a city's budget, its financial statement, or adjusted data from the Census. Types of problems differ by data source; each is appropriate for certain purposes. This appendix reviews major issues and available solutions, concentrating on the Census as their procedures are little known or appreciated.[1]

Comparability

Comparability of data across cities and time may not concern an auditor verifying that city officials are not misusing funds. But comparisons are essential for a mayor or credit analyst to ascertain whether the tax rate or indebtedness are high. The Government's Division of the U.S. Census invests considerable resources to render fiscal data comparable. It has a large staff: some 170, which increases by about two dozen for the quinquinnenial Census of Governments. Some 40 percent of staff time goes to municipalities; the remainder to states, counties, and other governments. About a dozen agents spend a ma-

Hai Hoang, Harris Trust and Savings Bank, is coauthor of this appendix.

jority of their time in the field, visiting cities and verifying data. By contrast, Moody's and Standard and Poor's each had staffs of about 16 in the mid-1970s (Petersen 1974:92; Sherwood 1976:25).

Data for cities over 300,000 are compiled by assembling basic documents (especially the annual financial report), coding the data, and posting it by hand onto worksheets under Census categories. For example, some cities report retirement expenditures for police only under retirement and other cities under police; the Census consistently reports it under police. This involves a huge reclassification effort, although repeating mainly identical procedures from past years. Documenting changes and clarifying related ambiguities are thus major activities of Census fieldstaff, often by reviewing partially completed worksheets with local officials.

Several manual and computer checking procedures are applied. Revenue and expenditure flows for the same function, such as sewers, are compared over several years. Current expenditure changes should follow a secular trend. Bond or note proceeds should be reflected in capital expenditures, reduction of debt, or bond funds. Taxes and intergovernmental revenues are intensively reviewed because of their importance for General Revenue Sharing entitlements.

More abbreviated procedures are followed in cities under 300,000. A questionnaire is distributed which city officials complete using Census categories. About 400 such governments are studied in more detail each year, usually nonrespondents the previous year with significant populations. Certain checks are completed with verifications by telephone.

Some 350 categories of debt, revenue, and expenditure for each city are recorded on computer tapes and aggregated to generate the 62 categories published in *City Government Finances in 19XX*. Our FP index was constructed from these tapes (appendix 4).

Data Sources

Census sources thus include primarily financial statements of larger cities, and questionnaires for smaller ones, complemented by audit reports and related documents. Some data come from state agencies, especially for intergovernmental revenues. Personal discussion or unpublished local records are used to interpret these materials. Specific sources and their use in the process are recorded in "jacket" files for each city to permit replication in subsequent years. Changes in reporting procedures are also summarized in the jacket files. Files for recent years are kept at the government's division offices near Washington, and those for earlier years deposited in libraries.

Governments Included

Overlapping local governments create frequent misunderstandings. The Census publishes annual series for finances of cities, special districts, school districts, and counties. Dependent authorities (like housing authorities not classified as independent special districts) issue substantial debt, often omitted from the cities' own financial statements, but they are added to Census figures for the city. An important part of the jacket file is a list of all dependent governments, agencies, and their reports. All local governments are surveyed and reclassified in the quinquinnenial Census of Governments; the list is updated as new agencies are created between censuses (often detected by monitoring the *Bond Buyer*). The classification of governments as dependent or independent is based on standard national criteria rather than local practice.

Accounting Basis

State and local governments use fund accounting with separate funds for revenue sharing or buildings or motor vehicles. Many cities report a combined figure for total funds, but this differs from a "consolidated" income statement of a private corporation which nets out transfers across funds; combined funds totals normally do not. Some have argued that consolidated statements would provide clearer fiscal perspective (e.g., Davidson et al. 1977; Zimmerman 1977), but San Diego is one of few cities that publishes a consolidated statement.

The Census attempts to create consolidated statements in categories like General Revenue and General Expenditure. Many analysts do not appreciate the importance of distinguishing these Census categories from revenues and expenditures in a city's General Fund. The main problem is functional performance: cities differ considerably in what they include in their General Funds. To document this clearly, we computed expenditures and revenues of the General Fund as a percentage of Total Funds for the PCS cities which supplied financial statements for FY 1975. Column 1 of table A.6.1 shows the wide range, from 3 percent in Indianapolis to 70 percent in Pasadena for revenues; figures are similar for expenditures (column 2). Percentages are not even constant across the California cities, although they may be within some states. These percentages netted out reported interfund transfers

Table A.6.1. Differences in Funds across Cities

Cities	Percentage of City's Total Funds Revenues Represented by Its General Fund		Disparity (in Percentage Terms) between Total Fund and Corresponding Census Category	
	(1) Revenues	(2) Expenditures	(3) Revenues	(4) Expenditures
Atlanta, GA	22	26	123	113
Baltimore, MD	40	36	7	7
Bloomington, MN	47	48	7	8
Buffalo, NY	36	37	-4	5
Chicago, IL	21	22	138	158
Dallas, TX	40	44	54	24
Detroit, MI	62	62	26	36
Duluth, MN	54	60	28	-16
Gary, IN	59	58	97	133
Indianapolis, IN	3	3	-39	-38
Los Angeles, CA	23	22	112	181
Memphis, TN	34	24	-8	-7
New York, NY	26	NA	20	28
Pasadena, CA	70	78	12	-3
Philadelphia, PA	57	57	34	27
St. Paul, MN	28	30	98	89
Salt Lake City, UT	61	65	22	20
San Diego, CA	26	30	165	93
San Jose, CA	27	26	88	95
Tyler, TX	46	53	50	74
Waco, TX	39	36	17	17
Warren, MI	18	19	192	187

Note: See text for explanation. This table was prepared by Hai Hoang and N.G. Triet as students at the Graduate School of Business, University of Chicago, and research analysts for the Project on Urban Fiscal Strain.

in creating the Total Funds category. Still, we used only the cities' financial statements, omitting dependent agencies and other Census adjustments. We also computed Total Funds revenues as a percentage of the Census category General Revenue, and Total Funds expenditures as a percentage of the Census' General Expenditures. Results again vary dramatically across cities (columns 3 and 4 of table A.6.1). For Buffalo, the revenue discrepancy is only −4, indicating that revenues reported in Buffalo's Total Fund were only 4 percent less than General Revenues in the Census report. But in Warren, Michigan, Total Funds revenues were 192 percent above the Census figure. We similarly computed intergovernmental revenues as a proportion of General Fund revenues, and compared them to intergovernmental revenues as a proportion of General Revenues in the Census; disparities were even larger than in columns 3 and 4 (results not shown).

All these results illustrate the diversity across cities in reporting separate funds, especially General Funds. For periods when a city's reporting is comparable, time series may be constructed for the General Fund (as in Dearborn 1977, 1978). Such indicators are most interesting in cross-city comparisons, yet differences are often due simply to what the General Fund includes, as well as short-term variations from transfers across funds near the end of a fiscal year, etc. These considerations undermine many cross-city comparisons based on cities' General Funds (e.g., Moody's 1977).

The Census standardizes reporting in other ways where possible, such as using cash rather than an accrual basis, and a 12 month fiscal year ending June 30. No doubt such reclassifications are less than exact for cities that do not systematically record data.

Access to Fiscal Data

As a public institution, the Census must keep its files open—and they are continually reviewed. As General Revenue Sharing entitlements are partially based on local tax effort, local officials regularly protest Census results, with millions of dollars at stake. Mayors visit the Census accompanied by finance staff, congressmen, and attorneys who may pursue disagreements with litigation. This understandably encourages Census staff to document each step and make numerous checks to avoid errors.

By contrast, financial statements for individual cities are hard to obtain, and often omit explanatory notes or ancillary materials critical for a clear picture.[2] The finance director is often the only local official who understands the financial statement. Census reports go back several decades, while even the Municipal Finance Officers Association started an historical file of financial statements only in the late 1970s.

Several financial institutions assemble municipal finance data, including Moody's, Standard and Poor's, and some major banks and brokerage firms. Some claim to be superior to the Census. But most remain closed except for institutional use, so most claims remain unchallenged. Moody's and Standard and Poor's regularly publish data uncomparable across cities because they do not reclassify them as does the Census.[3] These data can be used by analysts of an individual city for commentaries when the city sells bonds. Competition among financial institutions is keen: to be chosen by cities to underwrite bond sales, and to sell bonds in turn to investors. Institutions seek to expand their market share by providing thorough analyses. The traditional style of municipal bond credit analysis (in contrast to much corporate analysis) is "judgmental." Reports may be creative and thoughtful, but their quantitative data are often incomparable across cities. This has been under attack since the New York fiscal crisis and is changing in some institutions.

Weaknesses and Criticisms of Fiscal Data

Noncomparability, for the reasons above, remains the source of many criticisms of municipal fiscal data. The best current solution is to use adjusted Census data.

Timeliness is another criticism by municipal employees and bond investors. City budgets are published as planned expenditures, and may be substantially altered in implementation.[4] Financial statements report actual commitments of funds. Although the National Council on Governmental Accounting recommends issuing the annual financial statement no more than 90 days after the close of the fiscal year, a study of 100 cities found only 62 percent dated under 90 days, with actual publication times somewhat later (Ernst and Whinney 1979:40). Census staff usually begin field and office compilation in July, mail questionnaires in August, work predominantly on tax and intergovernmental revenue data from September through January (reported for Revenue Sharing in February), continue basic finance data from February through June, and release publications in late summer or fall—i.e., 15 to 18 months after close of the fiscal year. This delay means that persons concerned with preliminary results often use budgets or other unadjusted data rather than Census reports. This also explains why data in this volume are not more current. Timely information about cash on hand understandably interests employees in wage negotiations, but it is not clear that fiscal analysts are well served by preliminary and noncomparable data.

Another criticism concerns *dependent agencies and units of government*. Many local officials are unhappy to have debt (especially short term) issued by a legally separate agency assigned by the Census to the city government. They feel it may hurt their bond rating or bond price. But such adjustments are necessary to make cities more comparable. Analysts using local sources must locate and sum data from a dozen or more agencies to generate comparable results.

City officials and others are often dissatisfied that *Census fiscal data differ from those in city financial statements*. Still, in dozens of instances where city officials and analysts have brought complaints about Census data to our attention, almost all have been resolved when Census staff explained their procedures.

Errors trouble any undertaking, and we report corrections to Census data in appendix 1, but they are remarkably few. Municipal fiscal data could obviously still be improved, but most significant improvements must begin at the city level.

Notes

1. A Systems Analysis of Urban Fiscal Strain

1. The main ideas are in the numbered propositions and the transformation rules of figure 1.2. These lead to the structural equation system in appendix 2. Its reduced form is the "core model" in chapter 4 and appendix 2. An earlier mathematical statement of the theory is Clark and Ferguson (1981a).

2. Many others stress citizen preferences, especially sociological theorists like Emile Durkheim, Max Weber, and Talcott Parsons. Our sector concept reflects their basic values. Downs differs from some public choice theorists (see the journal *Public Choice*), who do not qualify conditions leading citizen preferences to cause public policy. Indeed, while the four literatures are distinct, general statements can overlap significantly, especially Downs (1957), Dahl (1956, 1961), and Truman (1951). Empirical work more often diverges.

3. Chapter 7 notes and appendix 1 discuss measurement. In brief, we found a reasonably consistent dimension from high to low government spending across specific policy areas, i.e., persons favoring spending on one issue tend to favor spending on other issues. This implies that use of the general dimension is reasonable although we occasionally focus on preferences for specific issues. We use interest, preference, value, attitude, and related terms, following usage in the area discussed (see Clark 1974a).

4. Obviously others have used related concepts, such as Madison's *Federalist*, No. 10: "the latent causes of faction are . . . a zeal for different opinions concerning religion, concerning government, and many other points. . . . But the most common and durable source of factions has been the various and unequal distribution of property. Those who hold and those who are without property have ever formed distinct interests in society." (Cited in Truman 1951:4–5, which reviews related concepts.)

If sociologists and political scientists frequently use concepts distinguishing collectivities, economists do less often. Yet some economists who normally respect methodological individualism use broader concepts to analyze public goods and collective decisions. For example, Dorfman developed a model consisting of "interest groups formed largely along socioeconomic lines . . . the members of each of which share a common set of preferences as regards public goods" (1969:251–52). See also Rothenberg (1961:315); Arrow (1970:20); and Becker: "Whereas welfare economics has a markedly individualistic 'bias,' any relevant analysis of actual political behavior must be heavily 'biased' toward groups" (1982:31).

Our sector concept is still defined by individuals' preferences. Unlike some organized groups, whose leaders alone may be politically active, practically all (adult) sector members may potentially vote, participate politically, or change residence—via individual decisions. A sector's political impact depends on such individual actions. In this sense we retain the goal-oriented, purposive behavior perspective often associated with economic theory, while identifying interests with sectors. We have sharpened our views here in courses and discussions with James S. Coleman.

5. This refers to absolute dollars per capita in taxes, not adjusted by income. The degree to which nonpoor persons subsidize others is considered for different types of policies in chapter 7, note 3. Poor and nonpoor sectors are used in Clark and Ferguson (1981a).

6. Here and below such propositions should be read as statements of causal relationships with other variables held constant. This *ceteris paribus* assumption is usually operationalized in a multiple regression analysis which controls other variables by including them in the equation. Most propositions are stated as simple linear relations, although arguments could be developed for curvilinearities and threshold effects. We discuss only some of the more critical.

Proposition 1 runs partially counter to Olson's (1965) discussion of difficulties of mobilizing a large group due to free rider problems. If political leaders do their job properly, they may solve the free rider problem without the separable goods Olson stresses. Olson concentrated on voluntary associations, rather than governments, which led to his distinctive results. But in governments, political leaders can use their monopoly powers to tax and deliver services impossible for voluntary associations. Elected officials can thus implement either their own or citizen preferences for public goods without the free rider problems of voluntary associations (see Clark 1975b). The importance of Olson's results has led them to be overgeneralized. Political leaders deserve more attention than is often accorded them by Olson and others building on neoclassical economic theory.

7. This is discussed in chapter 7 for special interest groups, in chapter 5 for middle class blacks, and in chapter 6 for employees who are also taxpayers. We are closer here to Simmel (1955) or Coleman (1957) than to welfare economists who aggregate utility functions (e.g., Samuelson 1969), or Marxists who ignore noneconomic statuses like race.

8. Statistical interaction involves a relationship between two variables such as X and Y, strengthened or weakened by a third, R. It is depicted by a circled arrow intersecting a causal path like this

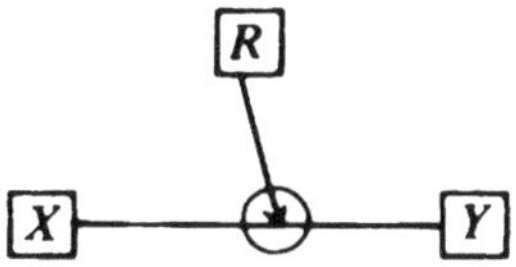

We sometimes estimate interaction effects in regression equations using multiplicative terms, such as $Y = aRX$, corresponding to the above example. Our regressions are specified in log-log form which captures direct, as well as certain interaction, effects.

A lively political science debate concerns the importance of "political" versus socioeconomic characteristics as determinants of fiscal policy. See Hofferbert's (1972) review. Yet, this tradition has considered mainly direct rather than interactive effects. Economists sometimes show wealth as a "budget constraint" on the community utility function or median voter's preferences. This follows our approach in distinguishing resources from preferences. Still, econometric studies seldom use separate wealth and preference measures; income is widely used for both. (See Weicher 1970; Inman 1979; Bahl, Johnson, and Wasylenko 1980; and appendix 2.E.)

9. This model builds on Clark (1968, 1973) and is broadly similar to Hawley and Wirt (1974:259), and Forrester (1969:16), among others. At the core of the "political system" are the formal institutions of government. We use "policy output" to refer to outputs of the political system, although our system is broader than that of Easton (1957) and his followers.

10. We sometimes depict sector size as exerting direct effects on subsequent variables. The careful reader may interpret this as sector interest multiplied by sector size. Note that this assumes sector interests constant across cities. (See chapter 4, note 2.)

11. Past uses of resources can lead users to acquire "reputational power." Resources, reputational power, and influence are each analyzed below. On these concepts and measurement strategies, see Clark (1968b, 1975b), which review previous work, but we mention here that our discussion builds on Dahl (1961), Parsons (1969:part IV), and Coleman (1971, 1973).

12. This proposition is broadly consistent with analyses of "loss functions" of citizens (e.g., Riker and Ordeshook 1973:307ff.), or "policy responsiveness" of government to various types of citizens (e.g., Schumaker, Getter, and Clark 1979). The relationship between policy disparity and resource mobilization may be nonlinear; threshold effects are likely, as stressed by such concepts as "satisficing" (e.g., Simon and Stedry 1968). Rapid and recent increases in policy disparity also seem to generate mobilization. For example, both black and white voter turnout increased to 80 or 90 percent in several cities as the possibility of a black mayor approached. This also suggests that the probability of seriously changing the source of the policy disparity can

assessing changes against the Consumer Price Index, we include the following series:

Year	*CPI*	*Year*	*CPI*
1960	88.7	1975	161.2
1965	94.5	1976	170.5
1970	116.3	1977	181.5
1971	121.3	1978	195.4
1972	125.3	1979	217.4
1973	133.1	1980	246.8
1974	147.7	1981, May	269.0

SOURCE: U.S. Bureau of the Census (1981), table 779.
NOTE: 1967 = 100. Complications in deflating series of this sort are discussed in ACIR (1978a; 1979a).

3. Police, fire, highways, parks and recreation, sanitation, sewerage, financial administration, general control, and general building.

4. Specifically,

$$FP = \sum_{i=1}^{67} (F_i W_i) = F_1W_1 + F_2W_2 \ldots + F_{67}W_{67} \qquad (1)$$

where FP = Index of Functional Performance for the city

$W_i = \dfrac{E_i}{N_i}$ = weight for subfunction i

E_i = per capita expenditures in all cities performing subfunction i

N_i = number of cities performing subfunction i

F_i = performance of subfunction i

where:

$$F_i = \begin{cases} 1 \text{ if city performs subfunction i} \\ 0 \text{ if city does not perform subfunction i} \end{cases}$$

The appropriateness of the procedure depends on the assumption that all cities scored "1" on a subfunction perform the same activities. We recognize that this is not always so, but current data for U.S. cities make it the most reasonable procedure. The Index could obviously be recomputed with more finely disaggregated data should they become available. See appendix 4.

5. Fiscal strain refers to the city government, not its residents. Two cities differing in per capita wealth may be equally strained on our ratios, but the wealthier must collect more revenues per capita to achieve the same "tax effort." (Tax effort = Local Revenues/Local Wealth.) For this reason, the term has been criticized by Oman who argues that low "effort" jurisdictions should not be seen as "somehow shirking their responsibilities" (1978:121). More salient for individual residents than tax effort is the "tax burden" they bear from all overlapping local governments, used in our migration chapter.

6. Own *revenues* (total) were used instead of *expenditures* as intergovernmental revenues cannot be matched to specific expenditure categories.

7. Missing resource data prohibited computing all possible combinations of expenditures and resources. For 1960–70, changes in population and median family income were available, but for 1970–74 and 1974–77, only population change was available from Census estimates. The CWI components were only available for 1969 (median family income) and 1972 (taxable property value). Data are collected more frequently by various local groups, but lack comparability across cities. Both CWI components were per capita and had similar means, so it was unnecessary to convert them to standard scores.

8. We explored other methods including a ratio of percentage change in expenditures over percentage change in resources. But constants must then be added to make all cases positive. The present method was more parsimonious and did not necessitate constants, although the two methods generated results usually correlating .85 or above. Margaret A. Troha devised and computed these indicators.

9. This uses our FP-residual approach, shown in table 2.3. Regressions below use simply general expenditures per capita/City Wealth Index, since the FP index is an independent variable in the core model.

10. The federal government guarantees some long-term debt, but much less than short-term debt. New York consistently issued the most long-term debt of any city guaranteed by HUD, but less than 1 percent of its total general obligation bonds issued in 1974 were HUD-guaranteed public housing bonds. We thus have not subtracted out federally guaranteed long-term debt.

11. In the 1960s, all 34 reported defaults on general obligation bonds involved municipalities with populations under 5,000 (ACIR 1973a).

12. See Clark (1977a), Petersen (1974), and U.S. Congress (1968). Clark (1977a) reviews determinants studies of Moody's and Standard and Poor's ratings, and estimates several models. The basic result is that little correlates with the ratings except the ratings themselves in an earlier year. These results contrast markedly with those for corporate bond ratings by the same firms. Descriptive accounts of the rating agencies' procedures are in Sherwood (1976), Standard and Poor (1979), and W. Smith (1979).

13. These and related issues are considered in Davidson et al. (1977), Zimmerman (1977), Lynn and Freeman (1974), and Peterson, Spain, and Laffey (1978). Some solutions of the Census and others are in appendix 6.

14. In Clark (1977a) funds flow measures were computed for our PCS cities for four years from 1960 to 1974. Many cities showed "deficits" if one interprets the data stringently. But measurement problems are so many that we do not report such funds flow measures here.

15. Dearborn (1977) found similar results for 30 large cities in 1975 and 1976.

16. Our overall cash measure is similar to Dearborn's (1977) in including bond funds, but unlike his, ours includes short-term debt. More refined liquidity measures could divide bond funds by debt outstanding, examine investment patterns, or monthly cash flows. While appropriate for an individual city, such refinements are difficult for a comparative indicator system.

17. Another fiscal management indicator is the percent of uncollected taxes, inappropriate for reasons considered in appendix 6.

18. Clearly many aspects of pensions are not included in these ratios. For example, several cities are high on R because in the late 1970s they were making up low past contributions by rapidly amortizing unfunded liabilities. Actuarial surveys of each fund are necessary to ascertain unfunded liabilities, but since differences in actuarial assumptions generate quite different results, current data are too weak for cross-city comparisons (see Jump 1976, 1980; Ernst and Whinney 1979). Liabilities should be evaluated in light of the age of the pension system and trends in funding levels. The two measures we use do not depend on actuarial assumptions and are comparable. This builds on Nuveen (1976) and ACIR (1973:54–56). They still are troubled by the fact that different pension systems in the same city can vary. Systems for uniformed services are often less adequately funded than general systems (see Fogelson, 1979). This illustrates the more general problem of comparing individual (pension or other) funds across cities.

Components of A and R are from table 8 of *1977 Census of Governments*, vol. 6, Topical Studies, no. 1: "Employee-Retirement Systems of State and Local Governments," which describes sources and limitations.

Assets	= Cash and security holdings at end of fiscal year, including cash and deposits, governmental securities, and nongovernmental securities.
Annual payments	= Benefits and withdrawal payments
Annual receipts	= Employee contributions + government contributions + earnings on investments

19. In the late 1960s San Diego had only 15 disability retirements per year, but in the late 1970s the number jumped to 90, many in the police department. The ratio of disability to regular pension was about 2:1 in 1978 (Clark and Ferguson 1978). San Diego and some other cities have thus tightened disability criteria.

20. Here is an indication of how employee contributions vary:

		Percent Receipts during Fiscal Year 1977 from Employee Contributions
New York—	General	8.3
	Police	12.1
	Fire	10.9
	Teachers	13.1
Chicago—	General	32.2
	Police	30.9
	Fire	23.2
Los Angeles—	General	12.6
	Police and Fire	9.1

SOURCE: *1977 Census of Governments*, table 8.

21. Our results thus diverge from Burchell et al. (1981) and Nathan and Dommel (1981) who suggest consistency across urban distress measures, in part by minimizing fiscal measures.

3. Private Sector Resources and Urban Fiscal Strain: How Tight Are the Linkages?

1. We conducted correlational and factor analyses of the variables in this section and others, and analyzed unweighted indexes, factor weighted indexes, and several individual demographic variables in regressions to explain fiscal strain indicators (see Clark 1977a and memoranda by E. Zimmermann). Inspection of table 3.1 can reveal what more elaborate analyses show: there is no clear single cluster. Several clusters can be extracted depending on the criteria applied. But difficulties in interpreting composite variables are such that results are usually clearer with individual variables, as used here. Clark (1972a) states the methodological background for this analysis.

2. These simple correlations are weakened further when variables from this table are included individually in multiple regression analyses with our core variables in appendix 5. While many of the variables have significant effects on fiscal measures, they do not suppress the basic core results. Bahl and Schroeder (1981:323) suggest finding similarly weak correlations between economic base characteristics and fiscal policy outputs for states, but do not present results.

3. The private-resource / public-expenditure distinction was stressed in Clark et al. (1976), and Clark (1976b, 1977a, 1981a) and has been elaborated by Cuciti (1978), Touche Ross and First National Bank of Boston (1979), U.S. Treasury (1978), and Lovell et al. (1981). More recent discussions by Nathan (1978), and Ross and Greenfield (1980) also pay more attention to this point.

4. Muller asked, "What is the relationship between local fiscal solvency and good economic health?" and answered, "There is little doubt that the most important prerequisite to fiscal well being is a sound local private sector economy," using population change data as documentation (1979:91). See also Sternlieb and Hughes (1975). These authors have expressed more qualified views in other writings. See Muller (1975) and Peterson (1976).

5. The politics of the National Urban Policy, and the three "distress standards" (pre-1939 housing, poverty, and below average population growth), did not escape one Texas observer: this "discriminatory urban package . . . (is) clear evidence that the Administration has associated itself with Massachusetts Speaker Tip O'Neill, New York Senator Jacob Javits and other members of the Frostbelt coalition (which) has been hard at work pushing through discriminatory legislation deliberately designed to let the Northeast raid the federal treasury at our expense" Hoyer (1978). (See also Vernez, Vaughan, and Yin 1979:72–73.)

6. While $r_{GEXP7074 \cdot LPOP7075}$ and $r_{LGEXP747 \cdot LPOP7075}$ are just below significance, $r_{LGEXP7476 \cdot LPOP7075}$ (.228) and $r_{LONRV747 \cdot LPOP7075}$ (.315) reach normal significance levels.

7. Some costs like fixed equipment maintenance are, of course, less susceptible to short term reductions when population declines (Peterson 1976:44).

8. Data are crude as illegal aliens avoid Census takers. U.S. government estimates of illegal aliens vary from 5 to 12 million, although a Mexican government study puts the numbers of Mexicans at only 1 million (Briggs 1975; Gordon 1975; *New York Times*, 10/13/80).

9. The less acute decline in households than in total population, and the persistent growth of the market value of property in many cities declining in population, appear in a table from Riegeluth (1978:8a):

	Population Change		Household Change		Market Value of Property Change
	1960–70	1970–75	1960–70	1970–75	1971–76
San Diego	22%	11%	30%		67%
Denver	4%	– 6%	11%		79%
Los Angeles	14%	– 3%	17%		19%
Baltimore	– 4%	– 6%	5%	– 2%	36%
Boston	– 8%	– 1%	– 3%	– 8%	80%
Buffalo	– 13%	– 12%	– 7%		27%
Detroit	– 10%	– 12%	– 3%	– 7%	– 12%
San Francisco	– 3%	– 7%	0		33%
Minneapolis	– 10%	– 13%	– 3%	1%	21%
St. Paul	– 1%	– 10%	5%	2%	16%
New York	1%	– 5%	7%		43%

For example, Boston lost more households than other cities from 1970 to 1975, yet its property value increased more than San Diego's. Data are from the Census, unadjusted for inflation.

10. The New York fiscal crisis was initially often interpreted, especially in Washington, as due to recession. See the news media and *Congressional Record* for 1975–76.

11. One study of cyclical employment trends found that during the four post World War II contractions (1957–58, 1960–61, 1969–70, and 1973–75), private sector jobs decreased respectively – 4.0, – 1.0, – 0.9, and – 1.4 percent, while state and local government jobs increased 5.1, 4.7, 4.3, and 3.1 percent. This rate of state and local job increase was almost identical to that in periods of expansion. ACIR (1978a, table 2).

12. Revenues raised from own sources were as follows:

	Local	*State*	*Federal*
User charges	15.96	7.75	6.56
Property tax	50.38	1.45	—

	Local	*State*	*Federal*
Individual income tax	3.14	16.36	41.00
Corporate income tax	—	5.89	14.36
Sales, gross receipts	6.92	33.61	6.07
Death, gift, other	2.13	7.58	2.38
Miscellaneous	6.91	4.71	3.85
Insurance	2.35	20.77	25.78
Utility revenue	11.95	0.44	—
Liquor store revenue	0.26	1.44	—
Total (%)	100.00	100.00	100.00
Total millions ($)	$119,626	$155,799	$382,120

SOURCE: U.S. Bureau of the Census, 1977b, tables 1–3.

See note 21 on elasticities of different revenue sources.

13. Certain cyclical federal programs were temporarily administered by local governments in the mid-1970s—especially the Economic Stimulus Package, Countercyclical Revenue Sharing (ARFA), Emergency Local Public Works (LPW), and Public Service Jobs (CETA).

14. An example:

	Federal Government Surplus or Deficit (−)	*State and Local Governments Operating Surplus or Deficit (−)*[a]
1970	−12.1	−4.0
1971	−22.0	−3.8
1972	−17.3	5.6
1973	− 6.7	4.1
1974	−11.5	−2.8
1975	−71.2	−5.1
1976[b]	−58.3	.8

SOURCE: Adapted from Council of Economic Advisors, *Economic Report of the President* (Washington, D.C.: GPO, 1977); cited in ACIR (1979a, table 14).

[a] Operating surplus or deficit excludes social insurance funds

[b] Preliminary

See also Ott et al. (1975); Gramlich (1978).

15. Their procedures are hard to summarize. They disaggregated expenditures and revenues into several components, and assigned each component to a (usually) national price index (mainly the Consumer Price Index, Wholesale Price Index, and Boeck Construction Index). Then they created inflation indexes for each city. Consider the example of inflation for nonlabor expenditures in Atlanta from 1971 to 1974. Expenditures for all nonlabor items (material, supplies, equipment, and contractual services) were disaggregated into 80 categories, and a specific inflation index applied to each, e.g., the Consumer Price Index-Postal Charges was applied to Postage, or the Wholesale Price

large enough to meet our criterion #4 did not appear in the *New York Times*. This series builds on related work by Morgan and Clark (1973); Spilerman (1970); and Genevie (1978).

Charles Perrow and his students at SUNY Stony Brook have coded events involving teachers, women, ecology, welfare rights, peace, farm workers, and Indians, and found that they too generally peaked in the late 1960s or early 1970s. They used the *New York Times Index* and other sources. (Letter of September 16, 1980.)

8. Eckel (1980) analyzed PCS cities using city-specific disturbance measures, and found political leaders more important in cities with more riots and strikes.

9. Information for these and other cities comes mainly from our interviews and NORC questionnaires. See also Nelson and Meranto (1977) on Gary and Levine (1974) on Birmingham. On Atlanta see Phillips (1978) and Kotter and Lawrence (1974).

10. See tables 5.3 and 9.1. Several other variables were similarly added to see if they might affect the results. Few did. See appendix 5.

11. In some cities, certain debt decisions are made by special boards and commissions for housing, airports, etc., partially or fully appointed by local elected officials, and thus less directly responsible to the electorate. Our debt figures include such agencies if classified by the Census as dependent on the city government, but exclude independent special districts.

12. To the core model in note 1 the 1974 per capita expenditure level was added as an independent variable and used to analyze eight fiscal policy outputs. The four used in much of this chapter were supplemented by four used elsewhere in the book and often discussed with retrenchment. The expected negative coefficients were significant only for these four additional variables: capital outlays, property taxes, number of municipal employees, and compensation per municipal employee. We have called this "fiscal feedback" as the high spending feeds back to reduce expenditures in the next period. These analyses included the same *type* of expenditure measure as both independent and dependent variable. For example, the level of capital outlays per capita in 1974 decreased changes in capital outlays from 1974 to 1976. We also analyzed 1974 levels like long-term debt or property taxes to see if they might hold down other fiscal policies, like capital outlays. No such effects were significant. Similarly, 1970 to 1974 increases were poor predictors of 1974 to 1976 retrenchment, although increases from 1960 to 1974 were fair predictors. But the best fiscal feedback predictor was the 1974 spending level. (This analysis used 1974–1976 changes as it was completed before 1977 data were available.) Per capita levels were also graphed for individual cities from 1960 to 1977. Cities spending at the highest levels showed the clearest downturns in later years.

13. By 1980 there were 38 percent Democrats and 23 percent Republicans (Davis, Smith, and Stevenson 1981).

14. See Borcherding and Deacon (1972); Bahl, Gustely, and Wasylenko (1978).

15. See note 1. Two further variations were also estimated. First, just the City Wealth Index, and second, just the "appropriate" resource measure was included in the model. Core variable results were very similar in all specifications.

16. Analogously Salancik and Pfeffer (1977) report that mayors had greater impacts on capital expenditures than most operating expenditures.

17. Several statistical caveats should be added, especially that results depend on measurement procedures for each variable. The FP Index also appears, quite appropriately, stronger in the 1977 level results. And "appropriate" resources often appear strong.

18. This is in part due to greater variance in the numerator than the denominator of the strain indicators. Should one standardize to equalize the variance for each? Not if the finding that there is less variance to be explained in the private sector resources (denominator) is itself substantively interesting. While specific results depend on the metric for each variable, these percentage changes or simple ratios are quite standard.

5. White Ethnics and Black Power

1. These two surveys and specific items are discussed further below and in chapter 7.

2. Several dozen findings are presented in Clark (1975c) supporting these comments, including regressions for PCS cities and for all U.S. cities over 25,000, analysis of Urban Observatory, Boston Homeowners, and National Opinion Research Center (NORC) citizen surveys, coding of names of every municipal employee by national background in Albany, Cambridge, and Minneapolis, and fieldwork in Chicago.

3. Intercorrelations follow for several variables related to political culture:

	1.	2.	3.	4.	5.	6.
1. Percentage Irish (IRISHL70)						
2. Percentage owner-occupied housing (LOWOCH70)	−.58					
3. Percentage Protestants	−.66	.46				
4. Percentage foreign stock	.64	−.36	−.71			
5. Composite Political Culture Measure (LWCWPL70)	−.31	.42	.46	−.33		
6. Percentage Middle Class (LPC70UMC) ($10 to 15,000 income)	.05	.28	−.23	.27	.14	
7. Republican voting (LELECON)	−.52	.32	.41	−.39	.66	−.07

Owner-occupied housing and Republican voting are discussed in appendix 5. The composite political culture measure is WCWPL70 = (Native Stock American − Nonwhites)*(Republican Voting). All these variables were entered iteratively in our core regression model (see appendix 2).

The importance of the Irish has been questioned, especially by Neo-Marxist research assistants, but the basic results hold strong in many reanalyses of these and other data (e.g., Foley 1979; Zimmermann 1979; Morgan and England 1981). Most critics now attack with humor.

Catholic ethnic groups clearly differ; Italians and Poles especially have been contrasted with the Irish (e.g., Gans 1982; Laumann 1973). But Catholics' separate national origins were weakened by conflict with Protestants and integration via the Church. Our concern here is simply to indicate broad distinguishing characteristics of (traditional) Catholic American political culture.

4. Greeley (1981:164ff.) questions our social conservatism characterization, citing citizen attitude data on public policies. As a component of ethnic political cultures, social conservatism is most critical as a rule of the political game, including use of ethnic contacts and criteria in formulating policies, nonideological discussion of issues, willingness to compromise, and strong commitment to seniority as a criterion for selection and promotion. Ethnic (and especially Irish) politicians are distinctive in these respects (Clark 1975c:325ff.).

5. The consistent importance of race independent of income and other variables was also clear in a multiple regression involving these same spending items. When respondent's age, education, job prestige, race (white/black), family income, region of residence (south/nonsouth), and degree or urbanness of current residence were analyzed, race was usually significant. Similarly, Hoffman and Clark (1979) analyze spending preferences in a multiple regression equation with 25 variables (including income, occupational prestige, education, homeownership, years in the city, having children in public or private school, being on welfare, in public housing) and found that net of these variables blacks prefer more spending. The observed racial effects may be cumulative results of these other variables, but over several generations. How fast they may disappear is not clear.

6. Some respondents knowledgeable about welfare may have opposed specific welfare programs due to their publicized criticisms, while still favoring alternatives to help the disadvantaged like a negative income tax. Such responses still imply less support for traditional social service programs that grew out of the New Deal.

Tables 5.1 and 5.2 use the domestic spending items of the General Social Survey: "We are faced with many problems in this country, none of which can be solved easily or inexpensively. I'm going to name some of these problems, and for each one I'd like you to tell me whether you think we're spending too much money on it, too little money, or about the right amount: A. Space exploration program; B. Improving and protecting the environment; C. Improving and protecting the nation's health; D. Solving the problems of the big cities; E. Halting the rising crime rate; F. Dealing with drug addiction; G. Improving the nation's educational system; H. Improving the conditions of blacks; I. The military, armaments, and defense; J. Foreign aid; K. Welfare." Our tables omit the nondomestic issues (A, I, and J).

7. In 1969, 35 percent of black individuals, and 30 percent of black families, were below the federal poverty level. Yet these black individuals comprised only 28.3 percent of all poor; 69.8 percent were white. Twenty-nine percent of black families had incomes over $9,000 per annum, while median family income for the U.S. population was $9,267. U.S. Bureau of the Census, *Census of Population: 1970*, Subject Reports—Final Report PC(2)-1B: Negro Population, table 9 and Characteristics of the Population, U.S. Summary, I, part 1, section 2, table 95. The situation slightly improved by 1980 when the percent of black persons who were poor was 29 percent and the percent of poor who were black was 26 percent. U.S. Census, *Provisional Estimates of Social, Economic, and Housing Characteristics, Supplementary Report*. PHC80-S1-1, March 1982.

8. Peterson and Greenstone (1977) concluded that a major effect of Model Cities, the Community Action Program, the Elementary and Secondary Education Act, and manpower training programs was to increase the numbers of middle class blacks employed by local governments. Kilson (1975) and Borjas (1980) document this for the federal government.

We analyzed GSS spending items to see if persons employed by governments gave more prospending responses. This was not the case for whites, but black government employees were slightly more prospending on several items than other blacks, although more antispending on welfare.

Anderson (1978) argues that the poor have in fact benefited considerably from government programs and sums the many in-kind contributions to suggest that the percentage of the population actually below the federal poverty level was close to zero by the late 1970s.

9. The low importance of the poor was clear in many ways. They received less than 3 percent of the mentions as participants in four issue areas studied in the 1967 PCS survey, thus ranking less important than at least eight other types of participants (Clark 1975a:23). Low rankings for poor-related organizations in the 1976 survey appear in table 7.3. Several poor-related measures (e.g. LPAPOOR2) were added to the core in regressions for 1970–74 and 1974–77 changes, and 1977 levels of general expenditures, which were consistently insignificant (appendix 5). The federal government is sometimes said to use more standard criteria for funding than cities, and to be more responsive to the disadvantaged. But intergovernmental grants to cities were virtually unrelated to poverty in the 1960s and early 1970s (chapter 9, note 9).

10. Question: "In your opinion, how important is each of the following in achieving real progress for blacks in America?" (Percent)

Robinson and Dye (1978:134) criticize the Joint Center for Political Studies data, and completed their own survey in 1976, but do not indicate disparities with the Joint Center figures. The Karnig and Welch results came from telephone surveys.

16. "Minority Objection," *New York Affairs* (Spring 1976), 3(3):69.

17. Between 1970 and 1976 (while Maynard Jackson was in office) black citizens in Atlanta increasingly reported that city government officials were honest and service delivery was good in their neighborhood. But whites reported declines (Abney and Hutcheson 1981). Cole (1976) found in New Jersey that 87 percent of blacks could identify the mayor by name if he was black, compared to 72 percent of blacks in municipalities with white mayors. But the proportions were similar for whites, 86 percent of whom could identify black mayors of their communities and only 75 percent of whom could identify white mayors. Only 15 percent of blacks did not support the statement that "it is important in your city that blacks hold elective office" compared to 24 percent of whites (for same statement). In a Los Angeles study (Sears 1970) black citizens expressed greater trust in black than white officials.

18. This result is strong:

Black political activity is related to the size of the black sector

Political Activity Measures	*Size of the Black Sector (Percent black = LPCBLK70)*
Index of severity of racial disorders (LRIOTSCR)	.66[a]
Importance of blacks supporting mayor in 1967 (LBLAKSMY)	.64
Power of racial and religious groups supporting mayor in 1967 (LIMETHMY)	.47

[a] Correlations exceeding ± .23 are significant at the .10 level.

Similarly, in Northern California cities, Browning, Marshall, and Tabb (1979) found that the percent of blacks strongly ($r = .77$) increased black electoral mobilization (measured by the degree of organized control over efforts to elect minority candidates to city councils).

19. How much a prospending mayor can implement his preferences depends on his power. Weighting the mayor's spending preferences by his power somewhat changes the impact of black political activity, as shown below. Severe riots seem to have increased liberal campaign statements, but active organized groups had a larger overall effect.

The association between black political activity and mayor's spending preferences changes when preferences are weighed by mayor's power

Political Activity Measures	*Mayor's Spending Preferences (MAYRTALK)*	*Mayor's Spending Preferences × Mayor's Power (LRPNTALK)*
Index of severity of racial disorders	.30	.17
Importance of blacks supporting mayor in 1967	.22	.28
Power of racial and religious groups supporting mayor in 1967	.29	.40

20. See also Piven and Cloward (1971). Threshold effects may also be present. That is, when blacks are less than about 15 percent of a city's population, it is hard to organize along racial lines, but as the number approaches a "minimal winning coalition" of 50 percent plus one vote, potential leaders are more likely to organize. Karnig and Welch's (1980) results support such threshold effects.

Blacks also supported losing candidates. We thus constructed a measure of campaign statements of the losing candidate from the 1967 PCS survey (OPPOTALK). It was added to the core for 1970–74 changes and 1977 levels of the four fiscal policy outputs, but was insignificant.

21.

	Index of Functional Performance (LFPDEC4)
Percent black (LPCBLK70)	.27
Importance of black support for mayor (LBLAKSMY)	.30
Mayor's spending preferences × mayor's power (LRPNTALK)	.43

22. Their cities with black mayors increased spending from 1969 to 1975 on education; a social welfare measure combining education, housing, and health; and inflows of intergovernmental revenue. Black mayors were negatively associated with spending on amenities (libraries, parks); protective services (police, fire); and physical facilities (except hospitals). But the percentage of black council members had no consistent effect on expenditures or revenues (Karnig and Welch 1980:ch. 7). Betz (1974) and Skura (1975) also suggest that cities with more riots increased welfare and social service spending.

23. In the core regression model (see chapter 4) both middle class and percent black were significantly negative. We were concerned that the black effect was just due to outliers—especially Amarillo and Gary—and to multicollinearity between the black and middle class measures (r = .55). Regressions thus were reestimated first excluding the middle class variable and then ex-

and other variables, initially:

CITYLAB3 = NGPOL72Z + PCEMPO72Z

(The Z suffix indicates z-score used.)

The Census also reported work stoppages (STEMyr) in terms of workdays lost after 1974; these were analyzed individually and combined with other measures, such as:

CITLAB5A = NGPOL72Z + PCEMPO72Z + STEM746Z

City officials stress that personnel relations are complicated by combined effects of unions plus civil service (see U.S. Conference of Mayors 1978). Civil service data are sadly sparse, but the Public Administration Service (Greisinger, Slovak, and Molkup 1979) interviewed several personnel officials in 42 of our PCS cities. They inquired if the local civil service commission played none, any, or all the following roles:

.17	Acts as an adviser to the city administration on personnel matters
.18	Administers routine personnel functions
.34	Acts as a regulatory body over local personnel decisions
.15	Adjudicates employees' appeals to personnel decisions
.26	Formulates personnel policies

The proportion of positive responses appears before each function. Six cities with no commission were scored 0. These five measures were analyzed individually and as a composite index.

In 36 cities, documents were obtained defining the civil service system, coded for extensiveness of coverage:

N of cities	
13	All groups of employees covered
18	Some groups of employees covered
2	No employees covered
3	Not clear (deleted)

This measure was computed separately for civilian and sworn personnel.

Individual civil service measures (designated SLOVno for Slovak) were correlated with other basic variables. Composite measures were also created, including:

CITLAB4 = NGPOL72Z + PCEMPO72Z + SLOV52 + SLOV72

CITLAB5 = CITLAB4 + STEM746Z

Some 15 multiplicative and additive versions of these indexes were created and analyzed. Virtually all civil service measures—individually, combined with each other and with Census employee measures—were insignificantly related to levels and changes in number and compensation of employees, and did not improve results over those of employee organization alone. The limited number of cities in the civil service survey may have weakened results. Yet the weak effect of the legal structure of civil service is consistent with chapter 9.

Change in percentage employees organized from 1972 to 1976 was uncorrelated with most variables in the chapter, especially numbers and compensation of employees.

7. The percentage organized in 1972 was the first year available from the Census. It was more appropriate than subsequent years for explaining (below) changes in compensation or numbers of municipal employees in 1960–1974. Organizational membership data for earlier years were available only from non-Census sources, involved missing cases, and proved less reliable in preliminary analyses.

The 1972 organization measure was also used to explain 1977 compensation and numbers because the 1977 levels reflect the whole prior history, and because the chapter 4 results suggested that organized groups had larger impacts in the earlier than the later 1970s.

8. Chapter 1 emphasizes sector impacts more on fiscal policy outputs than on this organized group measure, but the rest of this chapter fills in the linkages.

Other variables discussed in the text were added to table 6.3 and subsequent equations, usually one at a time, and the equation reestimated with no variables forced. No particular variable was thus favored by the estimation procedure. Strikes (or "work stoppages") for the late 1960s, from the late 1960s to 1975, and 1974 to 1976 were similarly analyzed. They were significantly related to employee organization, although the data came from different sources prior to 1974 when the Census began reporting work stoppages. More comparable data might generate clearer patterns. See also note 6 on strikes and civil service.

Effects of state laws on local labor-management relations have stirred debate (e.g., Stieber 1973; Burton and Krider 1975). We examined several measures of state laws (from our 1975 and 1976 PCS surveys and coded from ACIR [1976b] sources) and found most unrelated to local organization levels. (See chapter 9, note 20.) The causal direction is unclear even for positive relations, as state laws are so recent that they often reflect more than cause the balance of influence among municipal employees and other state-level interest groups. If an individual city differs from the rest in the state, it may thus be moved toward the state mean. More important than the laws is how they are enforced, especially in matters like arbitration settlements (see chapter 9.) Results for New York state in Kochan et al. (1979) are consistent with this interpretation.

9. Questions 1 and 2, Part II of the Survey. See appendix 1.F.

10. This was Q3, Part IV of the 1976 PCS Survey. See appendix 1.F.

11. Does a positive spending preference reflect responsiveness to municipal employees? While plausible, this is contradicted below by the effects of leaders' preferences (LRPNTALK) on compensation and numbers of employees.

Separate responsiveness scores for the mayor and council members generated results virtually identical to those in section C of table 6.4.

12. Note how this deals with fringes, including pensions. Our fiscal measure is the Census item labeled "personal services," for all municipal employees. This is gross compensation to all employees including wages and overtime, before deductions for fringes, pension contributions, and other purposes. It thus excludes employers' contributions to fringes or pensions that do not appear in the employees' paychecks; the Census does not report other employers' contributions. This is a definite reporting weakness that we hope the Census can correct in the future. Insofar as younger employees receive benefits that only come due in future years, in cities with underfunded or pay-as-you-go pension systems their benefits may be underestimated by current retirement payments. Favorable settlements for employees may be made by leaders who do not point out their costs to future taxpayers, but in the last decade this has grown harder as awareness of the issue has increased. Since what was done can be undone (through renegotiation or even bankruptcy), one could argue that until the city pays it, it is not compensation.

We did some analysis of employee numbers, compensation, and organization by separate functions. The most distinctive function in compensation is public education: teachers are paid more than other employees. And not all cities have teachers. We were concerned that this compositional effect of the labor force might distort compensation comparisons across cities. For cities providing public education, we therefore computed average compensation levels including and excluding public education. Although average levels were lower on the measure excluding education employees, when correlations with our basic variables for the two measures were compared, results were virtually identical. Hence the measure including all municipal employees was used. To disaggregate total compensation into components for overtime, fringes, and longevity of the employee demands extensive original data, as in Dickson, Hovey and Peterson's (1979) analysis for 12 cities.

We omit results for separate functions because of our concern for general urban policies. Similarly, Ehrenberg and Goldstein's (1975) careful compensation analysis suggests considerable spillover effects across functions.

13. See especially Bahl, Gustely, and Wasylenko (1978), Ehrenberg and Goldstein (1975), Gustely (1974), Ashenfelter (1971), and Johnson (1976). After completing the chapter we learned of Lewin et al. (1977), Mitchell (1979), Ichniowski (1980), and Methé and Perry (1980).

14. The specification started from the core model of seven variables in table 6.4. Additional variables were then added that others had used. While table 6.6 includes 11 variables, individual coefficients are consistent with those in simpler specifications and zero order relationships. See also note 8 on estimation procedures.

"Opportunity wages" in theory are those available in other jobs which municipal employees might accept, and with which the city government as employer must compete. Empirically, studies have used wages in manufacturing and services (e.g., Bahl, Gustely, and Wasylenko 1978). We computed both, but found manufacturing wages to vary considerably across cities, often reflecting differences in type of industry and distorting results for less diversified cities like Gary. Service activities and wages vary less across cities. Manufacturing wages were insignificantly related to municipal employee compensation, while service wages were strongly related. We thus operationalized opportunity wages with service wages.

15. Such minor fluctuations of opportunity wages and the City Wealth Index are accentuated by a .55 correlation between the two. We hesitated to include leaders' responsiveness for this period as it was measured in 1976, but decided to as it varies so much across cities that the ordering is unlikely to shift rapidly. This caveat applies here and in table 6.7.

Since compensation per employee in 1977 has the same denominator as the percentage organized (albeit for 1977 and 1972 respectively), one might wonder if their association is thereby increased. This is unlikely as number and compensation of employees correlate negligibly: $r_{LLGM77CA \cdot LPSEMP77} = -.098$.

16. While results for organization and opportunity wages are consistent with most cross-sectional studies, it is instructive to compare the 1977 results with those for identical independent variables, but 1960 compensation as the dependent variable. Employee organization in 1972 was equally related to 1960 and 1977 compensation; the respective *r*'s are .380 and .388, and betas from our table 6.6 model are .300 and .253. Many compensation differences across cities thus *predated* organizing activities of the 1960s. Hence wage elasticities estimated cross-sectionally will generate upwardly biased results. For example, results using our expanded core model to explain 1977 compensation levels suggest that the average effect of increasing organization of municipal employees from 0 to 100 percent is to increase compensation by 25.3 percent. This is slightly higher than the 17.5 percent of Bahl, Gustely, and Wasylenko (1978) for police, the 2 to 16 percent for employees in various common functions in Ehrenberg and Goldstein (1975), and 6 to 16 percent for firemen in Ashenfelter (1971). Our estimate may be higher due to better organization and compensation measures.

But estimates of effects of organization on compensation changes from 1960 to 1974 fall by half, to 13.7 percent. This suggests that earlier estimates were biased upward because of their cross-sectional design and omission of political process variables.

17. CETA workers were included only if they were city employees. (Many were employed by private agencies outside city governments.)

18. Pearson r = .29. Eisinger (1981) also found that in 49 U.S. cities, those more unionized hired fewer blacks from 1973 to 1978.

19. In New York City, compensation per employee for policemen rose 51 percent from 1971 to 1975, more than in either of the two previous four year periods. But the number of police officers simultaneously decreased 2.1 percent and hours worked dropped 3.7 percent. Further, "because no fundamental changes in the methods of delivering police services occurred during the pe-

riod, such as one-man patrol cars in low-crime areas, productivity declined very sharply." Temporary Commission on City Finances (1978:87–89). (See also Auletta 1979:290ff. on the politics.) Some compensation increases in cities like New York resulted from changes in average age or seniority of the work force. If employees with low seniority are terminated, or simply fewer hired, the net result is to increase compensation since a larger proportion of employees will hold higher-status positions. How much compensation changes are due to such compositional shifts cannot be determined from comparative data currently available for U.S. cities. A study of Los Angeles in the 1970s (Pascal et al. 1979: ch.3) found increases in total personal services expenditures due largely to increased compensation, due in turn largely to increases in the proportion of the work force in higher positions.

20. The negative relationship between numbers and compensation has been thoughtfully analyzed in Ehrenberg (1972), and Bahl, Gustely, and Wasylenko (1978), stressing market-related forces likely to maintain the negative relationship. Ehrenberg (1973) and Ehrenberg and Goldstein (1975) also document a positive relationship between compensation levels and reform government, suggesting that the reform government style may encourage use of fewer, more highly skilled workers. We looked for similar patterns in several ways. Cities were divided into halves on the median of our reform government index (LREFRMGV) and their means compared on numbers and compensation. More reformed cities had fewer employees per capita, but compensation differences were insignificant. Second, we added reform government to the models in tables 6.6 and 6.7, but found insignificant effects in most regressions. Next, we looked for possible interactions between reform government and the core political process variables, in two ways. First, by dividing the sample into halves on the reform index and reestimating the model; few results differed in the two halves, and most that did were not in the direction hypothesized. Second, we created interaction terms, multiplying the reform index by the core variables most likely to change with reform government (employee organization, leaders' spending preferences, and Irish), and reestimating the regressions. Again results differed little and usually not as expected.

These findings suggest that the compensation number trade off is indeed important, and associated with employee organization and perhaps reform government. But urban decision-making variables capture effects better. Ehrenberg and others without original data concerning political processes seem to have partially captured them using reform structure. Several intercorrelations among these variables (asterisked r's, $p \geq .10$) are significant:

	Reform government index LREFRMGV	LPAME	LLME76
Political Activities of MEs, LPAME	−.01		
Leaders' Responsiveness to MEs, LLME76	−.26*	.12	

	Reform government index LREFRMGV	LPAME	LLME76
Leaders' Spending Preferences × Power, LRPNTALK	−.45*	.23*	.43*

Future researchers might thus try to use direct measures of both leaders' and employees' power and policy preferences, although reform government relates to some of these.

In San Francisco, Katz (1979a, 1979b) showed that the trade off between compensation and numbers led high salaried departments like police and fire to have their positions frozen, while lower-paid office workers in these but especially other departments expanded. Katz also stresses that political activities of some unions increased compensation, while less politically active departments received fewer increases.

21. These are nine functions common to most cities: police, fire, sewerage, sanitation, highways, parks and recreation, financial administration, general control, and general building. Full-time equivalents were used.

22. Mayor Gibson made this point in several interviews in the late 1970s reported in the *New York Times* and in a symposium in *New York Affairs*.

23. Obviously variations of the Index could be computed by including only cities in a certain state or region, by adding or deleting certain demand variables, computing it for individual functions (police, fire, etc.), examining changes over time, or making other adjustments. Some cities have pursued such alternatives.

24. Of 72 fiscal policy outputs and fiscal strain indicators analyzed using our core regression model, only 6 were affected by the level of organization of municipal employees, 3 negatively.

7. The Middle Class: New Fiscal Populists, Republicans, and the Taxpayers' Revolt

1. This is from a National Opinion Research Center–General Social Survey item which includes "Independent, Close to Democrat," and "Independent, close to Republican." Surveys that ask only Republican, Democrat, and Independent elicit fewer Independent responses.

2. Most surveys of New Left views have focused on party identification, support for specific candidates, and social liberalism. (See Nie, Verba, and Petrocik 1976; Miller and Levitin 1976; Ladd 1978a.) Considering support for the New Class, Ladd dismisses fiscal conservatism and stresses social liberalism (Ladd 1978b:19–20). He uses NORC-GSS items to document the New Class, but creates extreme subgroups, like persons high and low in education, which show the more educated as more liberal on social and some fiscal issues. If instead of using subgroups the whole sample is analyzed for national trends, the opposite results emerge: persons higher in education and occupation prefer

for this family rose from 9.9 percent in 1970 to 12.0 percent in 1982. See Conference Board (1982).

11. For example, Mueller's (1963) review of three national surveys from 1960 and 1961 found that the more affluent preferred less spending on welfare, health, and unemployment. Similar results are in Bloom (1976), Wilson (1978), for welfare in Hochman and Rodgers (1974), and for Proposition 13 Turk (1979) and Citrin (1979). Ladd and Wilson (1981) report independent effects of support for more services and lower taxes on citizen support for Proposition 2 1/2. An ACIR (1980 S-9, 1982) survey from 1975 to 1982 found Americans favoring lower taxes over higher services about 7 to 1. The ACIR item: "Considering all government services on the one hand and taxes on the other, which of the following statements comes closest to your view?"

	Percent of U.S. Total Public					
	May 1982	May 1980	May 1979	May 1977	March 1976	May 1975
Keep taxes and services about where they are	42%	45%	46%	52%	51%	45%
Decrease services and taxes	36	38	39	31	30	38
Increase services and raise taxes	8	6	6	4	5	5
No opinion	14	11	9	13	14	12

Breakdowns by income were as follows:

Decreasing Services & Taxes		*Percent of U.S. Total Public*
Household Income:	Under $7,000	33
	7–9,999	36
	10–14,999	37
	15–24,999	38
	25,000 +	43

12. Differences between the two top income categories are significant at the .006 level. Empirical analysis is troubled by low cutting points for upper income groups. Altruism was also traditionally private, and may not extend to government. Altruism studies vary. Wilson and Banfield (1964, 1971) suggest that the affluent are more "public regarding" or "holistic," and support issues not to their benefit. Ewell and Meyers (1978) report similar results. Hochman and Rodgers (1974) found the affluent higher on a "net benevolence" measure which subtracted welfare spending preferences from beliefs that welfare decreases crime. But Hoffman and Clark (1979) found no support for more spending by the most affluent.

Another approach is to consider social contexts encouraging altruism. Appendix 2.E suggests that cities with high income citizens spend more. Colinearity with wealth makes inferences difficult, but if not spurious what might such results imply? They could follow from social and political pressures of other residents, especially the poor. If the affluent are seen as concerned with the "whole community," they can be more effective than if they simply press for low taxes. Such altruistic behavior should increase when the affluent are a minority in organizations with the less affluent. The most and least affluent may even join against the middle class, as John Lindsay attempted. The net result could be a curvilinear relationship between income and spending across cities, although income and spending preferences are linearly negative across individuals. This would reconcile some conflicting past results.

13. Hoffman and Clark (1979) analyzed the five spending areas in figure 7.2. Multiple regressions included 19 individual characteristics, six neighborhood measures (including service distribution, social, and housing characteristics), and a dummy variable for the city. This permitted decomposing the variance in spending items explained jointly and uniquely by each class of variable (individual, neighborhood, and city). Results also changed little when replicated within each of the 10 cities.

Schumaker similarly found consistent individual effects across cities. See chapter 4, note 2. Citizens also opposed taxes and spending more in high tax cities and states (Titus 1981).

14. "Do you think white students and Negro students should go to the same schools or to separate schools?" Answers by whites only.

Percent Answering "Same Schools"

1942	*1956*	*1963*	*1970*	*1972*	*1976*	*1980*
30	49	63	74	86	83	87

SOURCE: NORC Surveys; Sheatsley (1966); Taylor (1978).

"Now I want to ask you some questions about a man who admits he is a Communist.

A. Suppose this admitted Communist wanted to make a speech in your community. Should he be allowed to speak, or not?

B. Suppose he is teaching in a college. Should he be fired or not?

C. Suppose he wrote a book which is in your public library. Somebody in your community suggests that the book should be removed from the library. Would you favor removing it, or not?"

	Percent More Tolerant Responses		
	1954	*1972–73*	*1980*
Speech	28	57	56
Book	29	58	60
Teacher	6	38	43

SOURCE: Stouffer for 1954 and NORC-GSS surveys. See Davis (1975).

Percent of respondents who do not approve of abortion even if "the family has a very low income and cannot afford any more children":

1962	*1965*	*1969*	*1972*	*1974*	*1976*	*1978*	*1980*
82	80	74	51	45	47	53	48

SOURCE: AIPO for 1962–69, and NORC-GSS surveys.

Gallup wording differs slightly.

Other items in the text are in NORC-GSS surveys.

15. A survey of trends in 112 fiscal and social liberalism items (often 1950s–1980s) found that about 3/4 moved in a liberal direction. Most of the 1/4 that moved in a conservative direction were fiscal items, the major exception concerning treatment of criminals (T. Smith 1979).

16. Here are intercorrelations between three fiscal and seven social liberalism items:

	Federal taxes are too high (High = disagree) (V448)	*Federal taxes should be cut by 1/3 (High = disagree) (V449)*	*Proposition 13 (High = support) (V446)*
Civil liberties/crime (V365)	.009	.078	−.094
Race-govt. should play an active role (V373)	.053	.058	−.106
School integration (V444)	.022	.005	−.071
Affirmative action (V451)	.056	−.026	−.074
Women's rights—govt. should play an active role (V389)	−.034	.023	−.040
Abortion (V450)	−.030	−.022	−.065
ERA (V452)	.010	−.021	.012

NOTE: Social liberalism responses are scored positively.

Data are for about 2,000 U.S.citizens, surveyed in the 1978 National Election Study, University of Michigan. Statistics are simple r's, with values exceeding about .05 significant at the .01 level. (Our computations.)

Similar items are more strongly related: the three fiscal liberalism items, three race items, and three on women show within-cluster correlations of .12 to .38. Wording and marginals for the tax items: V448 "Despite all the complaints, federal taxes really are not too high considering the services the government provides for people." Agree 36%, Disagree 64%. V449 "Federal income taxes should be cut by at least one-third even if it means reducing military spending and cutting down on government services such as health and education." Agree 30%, Disagree 70%. V446 "If you had the chance, would you vote for or against a measure similar to Proposition 13 in your state?" Yes 71%, No 29%.

Knoke (1979) similarly reports minimal intercorrelation among fiscal and social liberalism in NORC-GSS and Michigan NES surveys. He shows distinct causes for each: income is the major determinant of fiscal liberalism, education that of social liberalism. Davis (1975) finds younger and more educated persons more socially liberal, but that period effects are a third cause; more recent interviews show more socially liberal respondents.

We have not found data for correlations over time between social and fiscal liberalism. While items have been used in hundreds of surveys, most sum them in a single liberalism scale and report inter-item correlations for the whole scale. One study that did distinguish "ethnocentrism" from "political-economic conservatism" found them weakly related (Adorno et al. 1950), but these two scales have been much criticized. See Robinson, Rusk, and Head (1968); T. Smith (1979).

17. Usage varies. The movement of William Jennings Bryan defined one meaning. Another contrasts two models of democracy: the populist, emphasizing citizen preferences as the legitimate basis for decisions, and the elitist, stressing leaders and organized groups. This populist-elitist distinction comes from Edward A. Shils and Robert Dahl (1956). Our NFP is more in the Shils-Dahl than the Bryan tradition.

18. The one study we have found concerning this hypothesis provides clear support. Schneider and Schell (1978) showed that post-1974 U.S. Congressmen were distinctly more conservative than their elders on fiscal issues, but more liberal on social issues (in roll call votes). A survey of challengers and incumbents in 1978 Illinois elections found that challengers stressed taxes and their reform far more than any other issue (*Illinois Issues*, 1978). See also Day (1978).

19. The fiscal conservatism of Democrats grew through the late 1970s. In the November 1978 elections, five months after Proposition 13, many past liberals either dramatically reversed themselves (Jerry Brown, Abner Mikva in Illinois) and stayed in office, or were defeated by conservative opponents (e.g., Michael Dukakis by Edward King as governor of Massachusetts). The next month at the Democratic National Convention in Memphis, Carter administration staff sought to mobilize support for fiscal conservatism—with slogans like "back the President on inflation." Delegates defeated three to two an effort by Teddy Kennedy and the United Auto Workers to prohibit reductions in social programs. (See *Washington Post*, December 11, 1978.) The Kennedy wing was again defeated soundly by Carter in the 1980 Presidential nomination, and when Reagan won, dozens of liberal Democrats lost.

Some ask if the Democratic party is "being used" by NFPs. Only if New Deal platforms are considered "genuine" and NFPs ungenuine. But Democrats have varied substantially across periods and regions. See Lipset (1978: parts I and II; 1963: esp. ch. 9).

20.

Preferred Spending Level Reported by Type of Leader	*Preferred by Leader Himself*	*Preferred by Active Local Groups*	*Preferred by Local Voters*
All leaders (n = 209)	23.3	23.7	20.6
Democrats (n = 135)	24.2	23.9	21.0
Republicans (n = 54)	21.5	23.4	19.3

Differences between all three types of leaders and voters were strongly significant (beyond the .001 level using t-tests). Democratic leaders were insignificantly different from organized groups; Republicans were. The 11 policy

thus computed 1975 population as a percentage of 1970 population, subtracting a constant of 100 so that the measure equaled zero if there were no change from 1970 to 1975.

$$\text{PRATIO75} = [(\text{POPC2575}/\text{POPC2570}) \times 100] - 100$$

where

PRATIO75 = 1975 population as a percent of the population in 1970, minus 100
POPC2575 = population on July 1, 1975 (as reported by the *Current Population Reports*, Series P-25, #709, September 1977)
POPC2570 = population on April 1, 1970 (same source as POPC2575)

The crude birth rate in 1970 was also computed:

$$\text{LBRTHR70} = \log_e[(\text{GROWTH70}/\text{POPC2570}) \times 1000]$$

where

GROWTH70 = number of births in 1970 (as reported in the *Vital Statistics of the United States, 1970, Vol. I, Natality*, Table 2-1, "births by place of residence")
POPC2570 = population in 1970 (as above)

Including the crude birth rate as an independent variable in the equation predicting PRATIO75 generates a population change measure free of birth rate effects. This assumes that crude birth rates were constant over the 1970 to 75 period. Death rates are sufficiently constant across the United States that they were omitted.

3. Local public policies include services and taxes. Ideally we thus might analyze service quality per tax dollar. Ingenious service quality measures have been devised (of road roughness, dimensions of police service, etc.) but have seldom been used in more than a few cities since data collection is so expensive (see Parks and Ostrom 1981; Lineberry 1977). Our policy measures are thus strictly fiscal. Service quality and expenditures may be correlated, but the relationship is often weak (Clark et al. 1981).

4. The 1972 data were used as they were early in the period studied. Measures for 1977 (the next Census of Governments) showed increases for most cities, but overall rankings changed little. Correlations for the two years were thus high, r = .82. Here are 1977 tax burdens for selected cities:

New York City	$1,549 per capita
San Francisco	$1,405
Boston	$1,284
Chicago	$ 915
San Diego	$1,006
Houston	$ 953
Tyler	$ 706
Waco	$ 698
Manchester	$ 773

Migration may slow with increased housing costs and condominium conversions, but a slowdown is not yet visible. Note that because we use counties,

New York City appears as five separate boroughs (all with the same tax burden, since the city government serves all five). Other counties are labeled with the city name to facilitate identification. Washington, D.C. fell into our 63-city sample, but we excluded it from city expenditure analyses in other chapters due to complex relations between the District of Columbia and federal government. Although the District receives substantial federal assistance, its local tax burden still exceeds that of any other PCS county area.

5. E.g., Pack (1973) and Cebula (1974). Katzman (1978) reviewed studies mainly of migration across neighborhoods and cities within metropolitan areas, concluding that higher taxes reduce net migration of middle- and upper-income citizens. Frey (1979), Jackson (1975), and Orr (1975) report similar results for metropolitan areas. While this volume was in draft, we learned of Mieszkowski and Straszheim (1979) and Wheaton (1979), which address related issues.

6. Maximum and minimum estimates come from the largest and smallest coefficients in the regression tables for the tax burden and welfare benefits. Estimates are based on changes at the mean level of the independent and dependent variables. The differences across periods are due largely to using data for nonwhites in 1960–70 and the total population in 1970–75. Results for total net migration (white plus nonwhite) are very close for 1960–70 and 1970–75: −1.78 and −1.16, respectively (regressions not shown).

7. In 1977, New Hampshire had the lowest per capita state taxes in the United States: $235. State legislators are paid $100/year, plus mileage. It was the eleventh fastest growing state in population 1960 to 1975 and east of the Rockies surpassed only by Florida. Many small firms started in New Hampshire in the 1970s, generating faster increases in jobs and lower unemployment rates than all other New England states (Shiff and Dorion 1978).

8. Welfare payments per recipient are an incomplete measure of benefits for poor residents, who may receive subsidized housing, hospitals, special education, etc. (see Anderson 1978). We began to assemble total benefit packages, but data were too poorly reported to proceed. If other benefits are associated with welfare payments across cities, they are reflected in the coefficients estimated; if uncorrelated with welfare payments, they should bias downward the coefficients for welfare payments. Variations in welfare payments alone are still substantial, from $1,496 per recipient in Duluth to $0 in Phoenix and Salt Lake City (county areas) in 1962.

9. One study of migration by race, age, and sex (Hinze 1977) found net migration by black men age 25–39 higher for more affluent SMSAs, and less affected by welfare benefits, while black women, especially older women, were more responsive to welfare benefits.

10. Correlations between the same variables for the city and county samples were usually .8 or above. We use Census variable titles to facilitate identification in the sources, the 1967 and 1972 *County and City Data Books*. *Tax burden* measures were FS27067 and FS27072, discussed here and in appendix 1.G. The *welfare* measure for 1962 divided column 54 by column 31, table 2,

1967 *CCDB*. The analogous 1972 measure was from column 76, table 2, 1972 *CCDB*. Total *nonagricultural employment* changes from 1970–75 were unavailable by county and taken from the "Detailed State and Area Characteristics" table for SMSAs in Bureau of Labor Statistics (1977). Missing data in this source for Butler County, Ohio, and Smith County, Texas, were obtained from local employment security offices. Corrections for border changes in four SMSAs 1970–75 were made using state trends. The five New York City boroughs were analyzed separately for variables reported for each.

11. These coefficients were troubled more than others by multicollinearity. Bonczar's Ph.D. in progress uses simultaneous equation procedures to provide more precise estimates.

9. Strategies That Often Failed: Intergovernmental Grants and Legal Reforms

1. Just one example is Bancroft's summary of the views of 1,031 local officials: "several city legislators commented that if present trends continue with state and federal bureaucrats making more important decisions concerning their cities, then local government will become little more than a 'clerical function' or a 'debating society'" (1974:22).

2. Comparing state and local expenditures across states, Giertz (1981) finds higher per capita spending in states where functional responsibilities are more centralized (performed by the state), controlling several other variables.

3. The b path indicates a statistical interaction effect; that is, intergovernmental revenues may reinforce or constrain local policy preferences, but not directly determine fiscal policy. By superimposing we could combine Models I and II in one diagram and analyze the importance of paths a, b, b*, and c. But we retain Models I and II to simplify exposition.

Numerous surveys show that American citizens feel their local governments are closer to them, doing a better job, officials are more trustworthy, and waste less. For example: "Which level of government do you think wastes the biggest part of its budget—the federal government, the state government, or local governments?"

Federal	62
State	12
Local	5
None/All equal	13
No opinion	8
	100%

The poll was conducted in June 1978. ACIR (1978b:4–5). This pattern weakened in the late 1970s, especially among older and lower-income persons. "Special-interest groups" representing these sectors may have been more successful in Washington than locally.

This section builds on earlier efforts (esp. Clark 1974c; Stonecash 1978; Przeworski and Teune 1970).

4. Nevertheless, much work on stimulation versus substitution effects of intergovernmental revenue is entirely compatible with this section. Stimulation-substitution research generally uses a variant of consumer preference theory. When "consumer" (read local government) demand is high for a service X, a reduction in its price or an increase in the "consumer's" income, should increase consumption of X. Intergovernmental revenue can reduce the price of goods and services for the local government, or increases its income. If the local government wants more of service X, intergovernmental revenue should stimulate spending on it. But if it does not want more, it will seek to substitute intergovernmental revenue for its own revenues normally spent on X. Local preferences, registered in price and income elasticities of demand, are the crucial variables determining the degree of stimulation or substitution. See Gramlich (1977). Like this research, in this section we often refer simply to "local preferences."

5. This procedure does not estimate separate paths of Models I and II. Without data for each program's goals and their fit with local policies, we cannot estimate b*. But if b* were important, it should lower a, b, and c, suppressing the core coefficients. Yet we find the opposite. The methodology and significance criteria are in appendix 5.

6. An ACIR (1977c) survey suggests that about 40 percent of federal grants to states are passed on to local governments, ranging from 14 percent for highways to 66 percent for criminal justice. See also Stephens (1974) and Anton (1979).

7. The distribution of federal grants to state and local governments follows (in millions):

	Actual		Estimated
	1972	*1978*	*1982*
General-purpose grants			
General revenue sharing	—	$ 6,823	$ 4,559
Other general purpose fiscal assistance and TVA	516	2,780	2,295
Subtotal, general-purpose grants	516	9,603	6,854
Broad-based grants			
Community development block grants	—	2,464	3,998
Comprehensive health grants	90	88	16
Employment and training	—	1,992	2,011
Social services	1,930	2,809	3,075
Criminal justice assistance	233	417	167
School aid in federally affected areas	602	706	346
Local public works	—	3,057	60
Subtotal, broad-based grants	2,855	11,533	9,673
Other grants	31,001	56,753	83,302
Total	$34,372	$77,889	$99,829

	Actual		Estimated
	1972	*1978*	*1982*
Addendum: Percent of total			
General-purpose grants	1.5	12.3	6.9
Broad-based grants	8.3	14.8	9.7
Other grants	90.2	72.9	83.4
Total	100.0%	100.0%	100.0%

SOURCE: Office of Management and Budget (1982:255).

Note the slight decline in "other grants," primarily categoricals, from 1972 to 1978. The drop in "broad-based grants" from 1978 to 1980 is due largely to termination of the counter-cyclical local public works program. Unfortunately, grants to cities are not reported separately; these data are for all state and local governments.

State grants to cities are harder to classify, but an ACIR (1977c:57) survey indicates that about 40 percent are for "general support" and 16 percent project categoricals (excluding federal "pass-through" grants). Less stimulation by GRS, CDBG, and CETA funds, compared to other federal grants, emerges from a regression analysis using the 62 PCS cities by Robert Y. Shapiro.

8. Examples: all Revenue Sharing funds to Chicago were impounded for 20 months by a federal judge over an affirmative action case. Regular buses in many cities have had to be cut back, and fares raised, to cover costs of special facilities for the handicapped.

9. This result has consistently emerged for federal public housing, urban renewal, and OEO expenditures (Aiken and Alford 1974); OEO and Model Cities (Magill 1976; Zimmermann 1979); various categoricals (Lovell and Korey 1975); total federal outlays in 1968 and 1973, separate totals for HEW, HUD, and OEO in 1968 and 1973, and state grants in 1967 and 1971 (Dye and Hurley 1978). All studies used national samples (or populations) of cities except Lovell and Korey who studied 97 Southern California cities. Magill and Zimmermann used the NORC-PCS. Dye included all central cities of SMSAs. Of course, these findings do not imply that funds are not allocated to the poor within individual cities.

10. Why these three functions? All functions have redistributive potentials—parks may cater to the poor, etc. To analyze these demands more disaggregated data than presently available. See Aaron (1975). Public housing is less ambiguous and one we would have preferred to include, but cities and Census data combine housing with other programs. These three are widely considered redistributive.

11. Financial data for this analysis come mainly from the 1974 Annual Survey of Governments tape and *City Government Finances* in 1974. Unfortu-

nately, this was the most recent year for which we could obtain data on intergovernmental transfers by function.

12. Local welfare offices exercised more control via discretionary payments or special grants in the 1960s (see Jackson and Johnson 1974). And of course many cities lobby actively to set state policies.

13. But there is enormous local resistance under almost every regime. See Fried (1974) on fiscal continuity of German cities under the Nazis, and Jambrek (1975) on local autonomy in Communist Yugoslavia.

14. More generally, participants seek to move decisions to arenas where they can be more successful (see Schattschneider 1960). Reformers who lost in cities often appealed them to the state level where they sometimes won. In this manner reforms were imposed on New York and Massachusetts cities near the turn of the century as American-born political leaders lost local control to new immigrants. See Litt (1965).

15. We coded the percentage of debt limitation used from city bond prospectuses. These were requested from finance directors of all 63 PCS cities, and a second letter sent to nonrespondents. Prospectuses of seven cities did not report debt limitations. Those which supplied adequate information appear here.

City	*(Amount of Non-Exempt Debt Issued/ Amount of Debt Limit) × 100*
Akron	55.9%
Boston	71.8
Buffalo	60.6
Chicago	52.7
Cleveland	66.2
Dallas	37.7
Detroit	72.7
Malden	79.9
Milwaukee	31.9
Phoenix	79.2
Pittsburgh	74.9
Salt Lake City	51.0
San Antonio	62.2
Schenectady	19.6
Waterbury	88.4
Average	60.3%

Cho (1972) found similar results.

16. MacManus (1978b) found more use of revenue bonds in states with more stringent g.o. limits.

17. More complex devices are used, but these illustrate our general point. See Davidson et al. (1977) and (W. E.) Mitchell (1967).

7. The standard error was for the leadership spending measure (SPEND11, explained in appendix 1.E). The subset of 15 "well measured" cities had response rates over 50 percent and standard errors below the median of .33; the rest were "poorly measured."

8. Robert Gordon and Lutz Erbring helped clarify these problems.

9. Formal tests for statistical interaction were also performed. See Wright (1976).

10. Homoscedasticity refers to similarity of dispersion as measured by variance. See Draper and Smith (1966).

11. Industrial leaders, retail merchants, bankers and executives of financial institutions, and other businessmen. Means for the 15 and factors loadings appear in Clark (1972c).

12. A note on acronyms. L indicates natural logarithm taken. FS indicates fiscal strain indicator. The last two digits are normally for the year. CA is per capita. Most expenditure, revenue, and debt measures were calculated per capita. Percentage change measures are percentage differences in the per capita amounts. For example, GEXP6070 = 100 × [(GEXP70/POP70) − (GEXP60/POP60)]/GEXP60/POP60).

Appendix 2

1. Margaret A. Troha supervised the analysis reported in this section.

2. Additional variations were estimated in exploratory manner with generally consistent results, many of which appear in notes.

3. The percentage of families for the entire United States in each income category follows:

Income Category		*Percentage of Families*
$15,000 and over		19.2
$10,000 to $14,999		26.7
$ 5,000 to $ 9,999		34.0
$ 3,000 to $ 4,999		10.7
Below $2,999		9.3
	Total	99.9

Median family income was $9,433.

SOURCE: U.S. Bureau of the Census. 1971. *Statistical Abstract: 1971*, p. 316.

4. Margaret A. Troha is coauthor of this section.

5. E.g., Ehrenberg (1972), Gustely (1974), Bahl et al. (1980), Inman (1979). A simpler version of the Index is in Clark et al. (1976).

Appendix 4

1. FP effects were insignificant in explaining common function expenditures even though common functions like general administration and general control might be larger in cities which support a broader range of activities.

2.

Per Capita Expenditures on Education

State	*Range*[a]	*n*	*State Mean*
Connecticut	\$179–433	16	\$275
Massachusetts	\$155–385	23	\$241
New Jersey	\$131–391	8	\$258
New York	\$ 85–334	6	\$245
Virginia	\$189–270	10	\$222
Wisconsin	\$225–287	7	\$251
FP (national) weight for expenditures on local schools =			\$253[b]

[a] Three cities were excluded (two in Wisconsin, one in New Jersey) because the per capita expenditures amounted to less than \$5.00.

[b] From table A.4.1.

Appendix 5

1. They number 72 including shorter time periods and certain variables only referred to occasionally in the text, e.g., compensation per municipal employee. See appendix 2.

2. We do not apply a formal significance test as in Goldberger (1964:108ff.) for several reasons. Models for the fiscal policy outputs (FPOs) and fiscal strain (FS) indicators are not identical; results may differ for a particular FPO or FS indicator or subset of them. Because some of the 72 FPOs and FS indicators are intercorrelated, the 72 regressions are not fully independent tests; effects on core coefficients could vary with magnitudes of direct effects of the other variable.

The core model specified here for FPOs omitted the City Wealth Index, which may lead to slight upward bias in coefficients of other variables associated with the Index. Both the City Wealth Index and "appropriate" private sector resource measure were included in the core for FS indicators. Some FS indicators were percentage changes in expenditures divided by percentage changes in resources, rather than ratios of ratios—unimportant since percentage and ratio indicators correlated over .85 (note 8, chapter 2). These slight inconsistencies with the rest of the volume did not warrant recomputing the six feet of printout summarized in table A.5.1.

3. The specific measure was the percent *over* 18.

Appendix 6

1. We particularly thank Sherman Landau, Chief, Governments Division, Bureau of the Census, and his staff. This section builds on their personal and written explanations of many complex details, as well as internal Census documents such as *Classification Manual, Government Finances*; *Compilation*

Ashenfelter, Orley. 1971. "The Effect of Unions on Wages in the Public Sector." *Industrial and Labor Relations Review* (January), 24:191–202.

Auletta, Ken. 1979. *The Streets Were Paved with Gold*. New York: Random House.

—— 1981. *Hard Feelings*. New York: Random House. (Includes *New Yorker* series on Edward Koch).

Bachrach, Peter and Morton S. Baratz. 1970. *Power and Poverty*. New York: Oxford University Press.

Bacon, Abigail R. 1980. "A Note on Selecting the Appropriate Pension Funding Method for Localities." *Public Administration Review* (May/June), 40:265–269.

Bahl, Roy. 1976. "Estimating the Equity and Budgetary Effects of Financial Assumption." *National Tax Journal* (March), 29:54–72.

—— 1980. "Prepared Statement" and "Special Study on Economic Change." *State and Local Government Finances and the Changing National Economy*. Hearing before the Special Study on Economic Change of the Joint Economic Committee, Congress of the United States. Ninety-Sixth Congress, Second Session, Washington, D.C., July 28.

Bahl, Roy, Richard D. Gustely, and Michael J. Wasylenko. 1978. "The Determinants of Local Government Police Expenditures: A Public Employment Approach." *National Tax Journal* (March), 31:67–80.

Bahl, Roy, Marvin Johnson and Michael J. Wasylenko. 1980. "State and Local Government Expenditure Determinants." In Roy Bahl, Jesse Burkhead, and Bernard Jump, eds., *Public Employment and State and Local Government Finance*, pp. 65–120. Cambridge, Mass.: Ballinger.

Bahl, Roy, Bernard Jump, Jr., and Larry Schroeder. 1978. "The Outlook for City Fiscal Performance in Declining Regions." In Roy Bahl, ed., *The Fiscal Outlook for Cities*, pp. 1–48. Syracuse: Syracuse University Press.

Bahl, Roy and Larry Schroeder. 1981. "Fiscal Adjustments in Declining Cities." In Robert W. Burchell and David Listokin, eds., *Cities Under Stress*, pp. 301–332. New Brunswick, N.J.: The Center for Urban Policy Research, Rutgers University.

Bahl, Roy and Walter Vogt. 1975. *Fiscal Centralization and Tax Burdens*. Cambridge, Mass.: Ballinger.

Baldasarre, Mark and William Protash. 1982. "Growth Controls, Population Growth, and Community Satisfaction." *American Sociological Review* (June), 47:339–346.

Baltzell, E. Digby. 1979. *Puritan Boston and Quaker Philadelphia*. New York: Free Press.

Bancroft, Raymond L. 1974. "Tomorrow's Municipal Government." *Nation's Cities* (April), 12:22–24.

Banfield, Edward C. 1961. *Political Influence*. New York: Free Press.

Barnett, Vic and Toby Lewis. 1978. *Outliers in Statistical Data*. New York: John Wiley.

Beame, Abraham D. 1972. *The Case for Upgrading New York City's Credit Rating*. New York: Office of the Comptroller, City of New York.

Beck, Paul Allen and M. Kent Jennings. 1979. "Political Periods and Political Participation." *American Political Science Review* (September), 73:737–750.

Becker, Gary S. 1982. "A Positive Theory of the Redistribution of Income and Political Behavior." Paper presented to Industrial Organization Workshop, University of Chicago.

Bell, Daniel. 1976. *The Cultural Contradictions of Capitalism*. New York: Basic Books.

Berry, Brian J. L. and D. C. Dahlmann. 1977. *Population Redistribution in the United States in the 1970s*. Washington, D.C.: Assembly of Behavioral and Social Sciences, National Research Council.

Betz, Michael. 1974. "Riots and Welfare." *Social Problems*, 21(3):345–355.

Birch, David L. 1979. *The Job Generation Process*. Cambridge, Mass.: MIT Program on Neighborhood and Regional Change.

Blanco, Cicely. 1963. "The Determinants of Interstate Population Movements." *Journal of Regional Science* (Summer), 5:77–84.

Blau, Peter M. 1977. *Inequality and Heterogeneity*. New York: Free Press.

Bloom, Harold Saul. 1976. "The Determination and Expression of Demand for Public Services." Ph.D. dissertation. Harvard University.

Bloom, Howard S., H. James Brown, and John E. Jackson. 1975. "Residential Location and Local Public Services." In John E. Jackson, ed., *Public Needs and Private Behavior in Metropolitan Areas*, pp. 73–98. Cambridge, Mass.: Ballinger.

Bohrnstedt, George. 1969. "Observations on the Measurement of

Change." In Edgar G. Borgatta, ed., *Sociological Methodology*, pp. 113–133. San Francisco: Jossey-Bass.

Bollen, Kenneth A. and Sally Ward. 1979. "Ratio Variables in Data Analysis." *Sociological Methods and Research* (May), 7:431–450.

Borcherding, Thomas, ed. 1977. *Budgets and Bureaucrats: The Sources of Government Growth*. Durham, N.C.: Duke University Press.

Borjas, George J. 1980. "The Politics of Racial Discrimination in the Federal Government." Presented to Industrial Organization Workshop, University of Chicago, October 23.

Bowles, Gladys K., Clavin L. Beale, and Everett S. Lee. 1975. *Population-Migration Report 1960–70*. Parts 1–6. Washington, D.C.: U.S. Department of Agriculture.

Boynton, Robert P. 1976. "City Councils." In *The Municipal Yearbook 1976*, pp. 67–77. Washington, D.C.: International Management Association.

Bradburn, Norman M. and Seymour Sudman. 1979. *Improving Interview Methods and Questionnaire Design*. San Francisco: Jossey-Bass.

Bradley, Robert, Paula England, and Richard Hula. 1980. "New Federalism and the Texas Urban Poor." *Texas Business Review* (March–April), 54:110–116.

Bradley, Tom. 1979. "Three Views of Financial Management." *Touche Ross Tempo*, 25(1):7–8.

Briggs, Vernon M. Jr. 1975. "Illegal Aliens." *Social Science Quarterly* (December), 56(3):477–484.

Browning, Rufus, Dale Rogers Marshall, and David Tabb. 1979. "Minority Mobilization and Urban Political Change, 1960–1979." Paper presented at Annual Meeting of the American Political Science Association, Washington, D.C.

—— 1982. "The Struggle for Political Equality." Draft manuscript. Berkeley, Calif.: Institute of Governmental Studies.

Bruce-Briggs, B., ed. *The New Class?* New Brunswick, N.J.: Transaction Books.

Buchanan, James M. 1971. "Principles of Urban Fiscal Strategy." *Public Choice* (Fall), 11:1–25.

Bunce, Harold L. 1979. "The Community Development Block Grant Formula." *Urban Affairs Quarterly* (June), 14:443–464.

Burchell, Robert W., David Listokin, George Sternlieb, James W. Hughes, and Stephen C. Casey. 1981. "Measuring Urban Distress." In Robert W. Burchell and David Listokin, eds., *Cities Under Stress*, pp. 159–230. New Brunswick, N.J.: The Center for Urban Policy Research, Rutgers University.

Burnett, Steve and Ches Gwinn. 1977. *Municipal Fiscal Crisis Research*. Atlanta: Touche Ross.

Burns, Kathy. 1981. "Mayoral Leadership and Fiscal Management in Waukegan, Illinois." Comparative Study of Community Decision-Making, Research Report 102. Chicago: University of Chicago.

Burt, Ronald S. 1981. "Comparative Power Structures in American Communities." *Social Science Research* (June), 10:115–176.

Burton, John F., Jr. 1979. "The Extent of Bargaining in the Public Sector." In Benjamin Aaron, James L. Stern, and Joseph R. Grodin, eds., *Public Sector Bargaining*, pp. 1–43. Washington, D.C.: Bureau of National Affairs.

Burton, John F., Jr. and Charles E. Krider. 1975. "The Incidence of Strikes in Public Employment." In Daniel S. Hamermesh, ed., *Labor in Public and Nonprofit Sectors*, pp. 135–177. Princeton: Princeton University Press.

Campbell, Alan K. and Judith A. Dollenmayer. 1975. "Governance in a Metropolitan Society." In Amos H. Hawley and Vicent P. Rock, eds., *Metropolitan America*, pp. 355–396. New York: Sage-Halsted-Wiley.

Campbell, Bruce. 1975. "Pittsburgh Boosts Services While Cutting Work Force." *Labor-Management Relations Service Newsletter* (December), 6(12):2–3.

Caputo, David A. and Richard L. Cole. 1977. "City Officials and Mailed Questionnaires." *Political Methodology*, 4:271–287.

Carmichael, Stokely and Charles Hamilton. 1967. *Black Power*. New York: Random House.

Caro, Robert A. 1974. *The Power Broker: Robert Moses and the Fall of New York*. New York: Knopf.

Castells, Manuel. 1972. *La question urbaine*. Paris: Maspero.

Cebula, Richard J. 1974. "Local Government Policies and Migration." *Public Choice*, 19:85–93.

Chickering, A. Lawrence, ed. 1976. *Public Employee Unions*. San Francisco: Institute for Contemporary Studies.

Cho, Yong Hyo. 1972. "Tax Structure and Municipal Debt in Large Ohio Cities." In John J. Gargan and James J. Coke, eds., *Political Behavior and Public Issues in Ohio*, pp. 56–94. Kent, Ohio: Kent State University Press.

Chomsky, Noam. 1968. *Language and Mind*. New York: Harcourt, Brace and World.

Citrin, Jack. 1979. "Do People Want Something for Nothing?" *National Tax Journal* (Supplement, June), 32:113–130.

Clark, Terry Nichols. 1968a. "Community Structure, Decision-Making, Budget Expenditures, and Urban Renewal in 51 American Communities." *American Sociological Review*, 33:576–593.

—— ed. 1968b. *Community Structure and Decision-Making: Comparative Analyses*. New York: Thomas Y. Crowell.

—— 1971. Expanded and revised version of Clark 1968a. In Charles M. Bonjean, Terry N. Clark, and Robert L. Lineberry, eds., *Community Politics*, pp. 293–313. New York: Free Press.

—— 1972a. "Urban Typologies and Political Outputs: Causal Models Using Discrete Variables and Orthogonal Factors, or Precise Distortion Versus Model Muddling." In Brian J. L. Berry, ed., *City Classification Handbook*, pp. 152–178. New York: Wiley.

—— 1972b. "Structural-Functionalism, Exchange Theory, and the New Political Economy: Institutionalization as a Theoretical Linkage." *Sociological Inquiry* (Spring), 42(3–4):275–311.

—— 1972c. "The Structure of Community Influence." In Harlan Hahn, ed., *Urban Affairs Annual Reviews, vol. 6, People and Politics in Urban Society*, pp. 283–314. Beverly Hills: Sage.

—— 1973a. *Community Power and Policy Outputs*. Beverly Hills and London: Sage.

—— 1973b. "Leadership in American Cities: Resources, Interchanges and the Press." Comparative Study of Community Decision-Making, Research Report 43. Chicago: University of Chicago.

—— 1973c. "Centralization Encourages Public Goods, But Decentralization Generates Separable Goods." Comparative Study of Community Decision-Making, Research Report 39. Chicago: University of Chicago.

—— 1974a. "Can You Cut a Budget Pie?" *Policy and Politics* (December), 3:3–32.

—— 1974b. "Theories of Policy Outputs." *Social Science Quarterly*, 55:787–791.

—— 1974c. "Community Autonomy in the National System." In Terry Nichols Clark, ed., *Comparative Community Politics*, pp. 21–51. New York: Wiley.

—— 1974d. "Quelques réflexions sur 'le pouvoir local'." *Revue française de sociologie*, 15:247–256.

—— 1975a. *Cities Differ—But How and Why? Inputs to National Urban Policy from Research on Decision-Making in 51 American Municipalities*. Washington, D.C.: U.S. Department of Housing and Urban Development.

—— 1975b. "Community Power." In Alex Inkeles, James Coleman, and Neil Smelser, eds., *Annual Review of Sociology*, 1:271–296. Palo Alto, Calif.: Annual Reviews, Inc.

—— 1975c. "The Irish Ethic and the Spirit of Patronage." *Ethnicity*, 2:305–359.

—— 1976. "How Many More New Yorks?" *New York Affairs* (Summer/Fall), 3(4):18.

—— 1977a. "Fiscal Management of American Cities: Funds Flow Indicators." *Journal of Accounting Research* (Supplement), 15:54–106.

—— 1977b. "Research in Progress Using the Permanent Community Sample." *Comparative Urban Research*, 5(1):60–71.

—— 1978. "Financial Management in Pittsburgh: Collective Bargaining, Managing for Productivity and Economic Development." In U.S. Conference of Mayors, 1978, pp. 62–80.

Clark, Terry Nichols, Ronald S. Burt, Lorna Crowley Ferguson, John D. Kasarda, David Knoke, Robert L. Lineberry, and Elinor Ostrom. 1981. "Urban Policy Analysis: Elements for an Agenda." In Terry Nichols Clark, ed., *Urban Policy Analysis*, pp. 23–78.

Clark, Terry Nichols and Lorna Crowley Ferguson. 1978. "Financial Management in San Diego: Revenue Forecasting, Productivity, and Pension Fund Management." In U.S. Conference of Mayors, 1978, pp. 43–61.

—— 1981. "Fiscal Strain and Fiscal Health in American Cities: Six Basic Processes." In Kenneth Newton, ed., *Urban Political Economy*, pp. 137–155. London: Frances Pinter.

Clark, Terry Nichols, Lorna Crowley Ferguson, and Robert Y. Shapiro. 1982 "Functional Performance Analysis: A New Approach to the Study of Municipal Expenditures." *Political Methodology* (Fall), 8:187–223.

Clark, Terry Nichols and Ester Fuchs. 1977a. "Financial Plight of Bay State Cities." *Boston Globe* (Supplement). January 11, 1977.

—— 1977b. "New York City in Comparative Perspective." In Temporary Commission on City Finances, 1977, pp. 295–311.

Clark, Terry Nichols and Ann Lennarson Greer. 1967. "Community Values, Decision-Making, and Outputs: Configurations of Inacment of Public and Nonprofit Enterprise, Graduate School of Business, University of Chicago.

Davis, James A. 1975. "Communism, Conformity, Cohorts, and Categories." *American Journal of Sociology* (November), 81:491–513.

Davis, James A., Tom W. Smith, and C. Bruce Stephenson. 1981. *General Social Survey Cumulative File, 1972–1980*. Ann Arbor, Mich.: Inter-University Consortium for Political and Social Research.

Day, Richard. 1978. "Controlling State Costs Is No. 1 Issue." *Illinois Issues* (November), 4:7–10.

Dearborn, Philip M. 1977. *Elements of Municipal Financial Analysis*. New York: First Boston Corporation.

—— 1978. "Urban Fiscal Studies." In John E. Petersen, Catherine Lavigne Spain, and Martharose F. Laffey, eds., *State and Local Government Finances and Financial Management*, pp. 156–164. Washington, D.C.: Government Finance Research Center, Municipal Finance Officers Association.

DeJong, Gordon F. and William L. Donnelly. 1973. "Public Welfare and Migration." *Social Science Quarterly* (September), 54:329–344.

DeLeeuw, Frank, Ann B. Schnare, and Raymond J. Struyk. 1976. "Housing." In William Gorham and Nathan Glazer, eds., *The Urban Predicament*, pp. 119–178. Washington, D.C.: The Urban Institute.

De Swaan, Abram. 1973. *Coalition Theories and Cabinet Formations*. San Francisco: Jossey-Bass.

Dickson, Elizabeth. 1978. "Fiscal Trends." In George E. Peterson, ed., *Urban Economic and Fiscal Indicators*, ch. 5. Washington, D.C.: The Urban Institute.

Dickson, Elizabeth, Harold Hovey, and George Peterson. 1979. *Urban Compensation Comparisons* (and Appendices). Washington, D.C.: The Urban Institute.

Domhoff, G. William. 1978. *Who Really Rules?* New Brunswick, N.J.: Transaction Books.

Dorfman, Robert. 1969. "General Equilibrium with Public Goods." In Julius Margolis and H. Guitton, eds., *Public Economics*, pp. 247–275. New York: St. Martin's Press.

Downes, Bryan T., ed. 1971. *Cities and Suburbs*. Belmont, Calif.: Wadsworth.

Downs, Anthony. 1957. *An Economic Theory of Democracy*. New York and Evanston, Ill.: Harper and Row.
Draper, Norman R. and Harry Smith. 1966. *Applied Regression Analysis*. New York: Wiley.
Duncan, Otis Dudley. 1966. "Path Analysis: Sociological Examples." *American Journal of Sociology* (July), 72:1–16.
Dye, Thomas R. and Brett W. Hawkins, eds. 1967. *Politics in the Metropolis*. Columbus, Ohio: Charles E. Merrill.
Dye, Thomas R. and Thomas L. Hurley. 1978. "The Responsiveness of Federal and State Governments to Urban Problems." *Journal of Politics* (February), 40:196–207.
Easton, David. 1957. "An Approach to the Analysis of Political Systems." *World Politics* (April), 9:383–400.
Eckel, Mark. 1980. "Political Instability and Policy Responsiveness in Fifty-One American Cites." Masters thesis, University of Chicago.
Edwards, Linda N. and Franklin R. Edwards. 1980. "Wellington-Winter Revisited: Public and Private Unionization in Municipal Sanitation Collection." Graduate School of Business, Research Working Paper 386. New York: Columbia University.
Ehrenberg, Ronald G. 1972. *The Demand for State and Local Government Employees*. Lexington, Mass.: D.C. Heath-Lexington.
—— 1973. "Municipal Government Structure, Unionization, and the Wages of Fire Fighters." *Industrial and Labor Relations Review* (October), 27:36–48.
Ehrenberg, Ronald G. and Gerald S. Goldstein. 1975. "A Model of Public Sector Wage Determination." *Journal of Urban Economics*, 2:223–245.
Eisenger, Peter K. 1974. "Racial Differences in Protest Participation." *American Political Science Review*, 68:250–268.
—— 1981. "The Economic Conditions of Black Employment in Municipal Bureaucracies." Institute for Research on Poverty, Discussion Paper 661-81. Madison: University of Wisconsin.
Elazar, Daniel J. and Joseph Zikmund II, eds. 1975. *The Ecology of American Political Culture*. New York: Thomas Y. Crowell.
Ellett, Charles A. 1976. "A Study of Data Requirements of Population-Based Formula Grants." *Statistical Reporter* (November), pp. 48–57.
Ensminger, Margaret E. 1978. "Welfare." Ph.D. dissertation, Department of Sociology, University of Chicago.

Galaskiewicz, Joseph. 1979. *Exchange Networks and Community Politics*. Beverly Hills and London: Sage.
Gans, Herbert J. 1967. *The Levittowners*. New York: Random House.
—— 1982. *The Urban Villagers*. Updated ed. New York: Free Press.
General Accounting Office. 1977a (July 20). *Anti-Recession Assistance Is Helping But Distribution Formula Needs Reassessment*. Washington, D.C.: GPO.
—— 1977b (November 29). *Anti-Recession Assistance: An Evaluation*. Washington, D.C.: GPO.
—— 1978. (February 22). *Impact of Anti-Recession Assistance on 21 City Governments*. Washington, D.C.: GPO.
Genevie, Louis E., ed. 1978. *Collective Behavior and Social Movements*. Itasca, Ill.: F. E. Peacock.
Giertz, J. Fred. 1981. "Centralization and Government Budget Size." *Publius* (Winter), 11:119–128.
Gifford, Bernard R. 1978. "New York City: The Political Economy of Cosmopolitan Liberalism." *Annual Report*. New York: Russell Sage Foundation.
Gilbert, Claire W. 1968. "Community Power and Decision-Making." In Terry Nichols Clark, ed., *Community Structure and Decision Making*, pp. 139–158. New York: Thomas Y. Crowell.
Goldberger, Arthur S. 1964. *Econometric Theory*. New York: Wiley.
Gordon, Wendell. 1975. "The Case for a Less Restrictive Border Policy." *Social Science Quarterly* (December), 56(3):485–491.
Grad, Frank P. 1970. "The State's Capacity to Respond to Urban Problems." In Alan K. Campbell, ed., *The States and the Urban Crisis*, pp. 27–58. Englewood Cliffs, N.J.: Prentice-Hall.
Gramlich, Edward M. 1977. "Intergovernmental Grants: A Review of the Empirical Literature." In Wallace E. Oates, ed., *The Political Economy of Fiscal Federalism*, pp. 219–240. Lexington, Mass.: Lexington Books.
—— 1978. "State and Local Budgets the Day after It Rained: Why Is the Surplus So High?" *Brookings Papers on Economic Activity*, 1:191–216.
Grasberger, Friedrich J. 1978. *Developing Tools to Improve Federal Grants-in-Aid Formulas*. Rochester, N.Y.: Center for Governmental Research, Inc.
Greeley, Andrew M. 1974. *Ethnicity in the United States*. New York: John Wiley.
—— 1981. *The Irish Americans*. New York: Harper & Row.

Greenberg, Stanley B. 1974. *Politics and Poverty*. New York: Wiley.

Greene, Kenneth and Thomas J. Parliament. 1980. "Political Externalities, Efficiency, and the Welfare Losses from Consolidation." *National Tax Journal* (June), 33:209–218.

Greenstone, J. David and Paul E. Peterson. 1973. *Race and Authority in Urban Politics*. New York: Russell Sage.

Greenwood, Michael J. 1975a. "Research on Internal Migration in the United States." *Journal of Economic Literature* (June), 13:397–433.

—— 1975b. "A Simultaneous-Equations Model of Urban Growth and Migration." *Journal of the American Statistical Association* (December), 70:797–810.

Greenwood, Michael J. and Douglas Sweetland. 1972. "The Determinants of Migration between Standard Metropolitan Statistical Areas." *Demography* (November), 9:665–681.

Greer, Ann Lennarson. 1974. *The Mayor's Agenda*. Cambridge, Mass.: Schenkman.

Greisinger, George W., Jeffrey S. Slovak, and Joseph J. Molkup. 1979. *Civil Service Systems*. U.S. Department of Justice, LEAA and NILECJ. Washington, D.C.: GPO.

Greytak, David and Bernard Jump, Jr. 1975. *The Impact of Inflation on the Expenditures and Revenues of Six Local Governments, 1971–1979*. Maxwell School of Citizenship and Public Affairs, Metropolitan Studies Program. Syracuse, N.Y.: Syracuse University.

Grimes, Michael, Charles M. Bonjean, Larry Lyon, and Robert Lineberry. 1976. "Community Structure and Leadership Arrangements." *American Sociological Review* (August), 4:706–725.

Gustely, Richard D. 1974. *Municipal Public Employment and Public Expenditure*. Lexington, Mass.: D.C. Heath-Lexington.

Hadden, Jeffrey K., Louis H. Masotti, and Victor Thiessen. 1969. "The Making of the Negro Mayors 1967." *Transaction* (January/February), 5:21–30.

Haider, Donald H. 1976. "Fiscal Scarcity: A New Urban Perspective." In Louis H. Masotti and Robert L. Lineberry, eds., *The New Urban Politics*, pp. 171–218. Cambridge, Mass.: Ballinger.

Hamilton, Edward K. and Francine F. Rabinovitz. 1977. *Whose Ox Would Be Healed? Financial Effects of Federalization of Welfare*. Durham, N.C.: Institute of Policy Sciences and Public Affairs and the Ford Foundation.

Hannan, Michael T. and Alice A. Young. 1977. "Estimation in Panel

Jacob, Nora B. 1979. "Butcher and Forde, Wizards of the Computer Letter." *California Journal* (May), 10:162–164.

Jacob, Philip E., ed. 1971. *Values and the Active Community*. New York: Free Press.

Jacobs, Bruce. 1981. *The Political Economy of Organizational Change*. New York: Academic Press.

Jambrek, Peter. 1975. *Development and Social Change in Yugoslavia*. Lexington, Mass.: Lexington Books.

Janowitz, Morris. 1978. *The Last Half-Century*. Chicago: University of Chicago Press.

Johnson, Marv. 1976. *The Effect of Unions on Public Sector Wages*. Metropolitan Studies Program, Maxwell School of Citizenship and Public Affairs. Syracuse, N.Y.: Syracuse University.

Johnston, Michael. 1979. "Patrons and Clients, Jobs and Machines." *American Political Science Review* (June), 79:385–398.

Johnstone, John W. C. and Ramon J. Rivera. 1965. *Volunteers for Learning*. Chicago: Aldine.

Joint Center for Political Studies. 1978. *National Roster of Black Elected Officials*. Washington, D.C.: Joint Center for Political Studies.

Joreskog, Karl G. 1969. "A General Approach to Confirmatory Maximum Likelihood Factor Analysis." *Psychometrika*, 34(2):183–202.

Jump, Bernard, Jr. 1976. "Compensating City Government Employees." *National Tax Journal* (September), 24:240–256.

—— 1980. "State and Local Government Employee Compensation." In Roy Bahl, Jesse Burkhead, and Bernard Jump, Jr., eds., *Public Employment and State and Local Government Finance*, pp. 155–194. Cambridge, Mass.: Ballinger.

Kain, John F. and John M. Quigley. 1975. *Housing Markets and Racial Discrimination*. New York: National Bureau of Economic Research.

Karnig, Albert K. and Susan Welch. 1980. *Black Representation and Urban Policy*. Chicago: University of Chicago Press.

Karp, Herbert and Dennis K. Kelly. 1971. *Ecological Analysis of Intrametropolitan Migration*. Chicago: Markham.

Kasarda, John D. 1976. "The Changing Occupational Structure of the American Metropolis." *Social Science Quarterly* (December), 61:369–400.

—— 1980. "The Implications of Contemporary Distribution Trends For National Urban Policy." *Social Science Quarterly* (December), 61:369–400.

Katz, Harry C. 1979a. "Municipal Pay Determination: The Case of San Francisco." *Industrial Relations* (Winter), 18:44–58.

—— 1979b. "The Municipal Budgetary Response to Changing Labor Costs: The Case of San Francisco." *Industrial and Labor Relations Review* (July), 32:506–519.

Katzman, Martin T. 1978. *The Quality of Municipal Services, Central City Decline, and Middle-Class Flight*. Research Report R78 1. Cambridge, Mass.: Department of City and Regional Planning, Harvard University.

Katzman, Martin T. and Harold Childs. 1979. "Black Flight." Southwest Center for Economic and Community Development, Discussion Paper 17. Dallas: University of Texas.

Kellar, Elizabeth K., ed. 1979. *Managing with Less*. Washington, D.C.: International City Management Association.

Keller, Edmond. 1978. "The Impact of Black Mayors on Urban Policy." *The Annals of the American Academy of Political and Social Science*. Special volume on Urban Black Politics (September), 439:40–52.

Kern, David A. 1978. "Municipal Revenue Estimation with a Focus on Sales Tax Revenue in Waukegan, Illinois." Comparative Study of Community Decision-Making Research Report 92. Chicago: University of Chicago.

Key, V. O. 1958. *Politics, Parties, and Pressure Groups*. New York: Crowell-Collier.

Kilson, Martin. 1975. "Blacks and Neo-Ethnicity in American Political Life." In Nathan Glazer and Daniel P. Moynihan, eds., *Ethnicity*, pp. 236–266. Cambridge, Mass.: Harvard University Press.

Kirby, David J., T. Robert Harris, Robert L. Crain, and Christine H. Rossell. 1973. *Political Strategies in Northern School Desegregation*. Lexington, Mass.: D.C. Heath.

Knoke, David. 1981. "Urban Political Cultures." In Terry Nichols Clark, ed., *Urban Policy Analysis*, pp. 203–225. Beverly Hills: Sage.

Koch, Edward I. 1980. "The Mandate Millstone." *The Public Interest* (Fall), 61:42–57.

Kochan, Thomas A., Mordehai Mironi, Ronald G. Ehrenberg, Jean

R. Grodin, and James L. Stern, eds., *Public Sector Bargaining*, pp. 118–149. Washington, D.C.: Bureau of National Affairs.

Mitchell, William E. 1967. "The Effect of Debt Limits on State and Local Government Borrowing." *The Bulletin* (New York University Institute of Finance) (October), Vol. 45.

Moak, Lennox L. and Albert M. Hillhouse. 1975. *Local Government Finance*. Chicago: Municipal Finance Officers Association.

Moak, Lennox and Kathryn W. Killian. 1963. *A Manual of Techniques for the Preparation, Consideration, Adoption, and Administration of Operating Budgets*. Chicago: Municipal Finance Officers Association.

Mollenkopf, John H. 1976. "The Crisis of the Public Sector in America's Cities." In Roger E. Alcaly and David Mermelstein, eds., *The Fiscal Crisis of American Cities*, pp. 113–132. New York: Random House-Vintage Books.

Monaghan, Henry. 1980. "Reflections on the Theme: Is There a Law of Federal Grants and Where Is It Leading Us?" In *Awakening the Slumbering Giant: Intergovernmental Relations and Federal Grant Law*, pp. 91–95. Report M-122. Washington, D.C.: GPO.

Morgan, David R. and Robert E. England. 1981. "Analyzing Fiscal Stress Among Large U.S. Cities." Revised from presentation to Southwestern Political Science Association, Dallas, Texas, March 26–28.

Morgan, William R. and Terry N. Clark. 1973. "The Causes of Racial Disorders: A Grievance-Level Explanation." *American Sociological Review* (October), 38:611–624.

Morlock, Laura L. 1973. "Black Power and Black Influence in 91 Northern Cities." Ph.D. dissertation, Johns Hopkins University.

—— 1974. "Business Interests, Countervailing Groups and the Balance of Influence in 91 Cities." In Willis D. Hawley and Frederick M. Wirt, eds., *The Search for Community Power*, pp. 309–328. Englewood Cliffs, N.J.: Prentice-Hall.

Mueller, Eva. 1963. "Public Attitudes Toward Fiscal Programs." *Quarterly Journal of Economics* (February), 77:210–235.

Mulford, Charles L., Gerald E. Klonglan, Richard D. Warren, and David A. Hay. 1978. "What Return Rate Is Necessary When Using Mailed Questionnaires?" *Political Methodology*, 5(1):87–108.

Muller, Thomas, 1975. *Growing and Declining Urban Areas*. Washington, D.C.: The Urban Institute.

—— 1979. "Prepared Statement." *Is the Urban Crisis Over?* pp. 88–95. Hearing before the Subcommittee on Fiscal and Intergovernmental Policy of Joint Economic Committee, Congress of the United States. Ninety-Sixth Congress, Washington, D.C., March 20.

Municipal Finance Officers Association. 1982. *Indicators of Urban Condition*. Washington, D.C.: Municipal Finance Officers Association.

Mushkin, Selma J., ed. 1972. *Public Prices for Public Products*. Washington, D.C.: The Urban Institute.

—— 1979. *Proposition 13 and Its Consequences for Public Management*. Cambridge, Mass.: Abt Books.

Muth, Richard F. 1971. "Migration: Chicken or Egg?" *Southern Economic Journal* (January), 37:295–306.

Nathan, Richard P. 1978. "The Outlook for Federal Grants to Cities." In Roy Bahl, ed., *The Fiscal Outlook for Cities*, pp. 75–92. Syracuse, N.Y.: Syracuse University Press.

Nathan, Richard P. and Paul R. Dommel. 1977. "The Cities." In Joseph A. Pechman, ed., *Setting National Priorities: The 1978 Budget*, pp. 283–316. Washington, D.C.: Brookings Institution.

—— 1981. "Issues and Techniques for Federal Grant-in-Aid Allocations to Distressed Cities." *Urban Affairs Papers* (Spring), 3:21–34.

Nathan, Richard P., Paul R. Dommel, Sarah Liebschutz, and Milton D. Morris. 1977. *Block Grants for Community Development*. Washington, D.C.: U.S. Department of Housing and Urban Development.

Nathan, Richard P., Allen D. Manvel, and Susannah E. Calkins. 1975. *Monitoring Revenue Sharing*. Washington, D.C.: Brookings Institution.

National Council on Governmental Accounting. 1981. *Objectives of State-Local Government Accounting and Financial Reporting: A Research Study*. Chicago: National Council on Governmental Accounting.

National Opinion Research Center. 1977. *National Data Programs for the Social Sciences: Cumulative Codebook for the 1972–1977 General Social Surveys*. Chicago: National Opinion Research Center.

Neenan, William B. 1972. *Political Economy of Urban Areas*. Chicago: Markham.

Nelson, Barbara J. 1980. "Purchase of Services." In George J.

Black Representation on City Councils." *Social Science Quarterly* (June), 59:133–141.
Rogers, David. 1971. *The Management of Big Cities*. Beverly Hills: Sage.
—— 1978. *Can Business Management Save the Cities?* New York: Free Press.
Rose, Richard and Guy Peters. 1978. *Can Governments Go Bankrupt?* New York: Basic Books.
Ross, John P. and James Greenfield. 1980. "Measuring the Health of Cities." In Charles H. Levine and Irene Rubin, eds., *Fiscal Stress and Public Policy*, pp. 89–112. Beverly Hills: Sage.
Rossi, Peter H., Richard A. Berk, and Bettye K. Eidson. 1974. *The Roots of Urban Discontent*. New York: Wiley.
Rossi, Peter H. and Robert L. Crain. 1968. "The NORC Permanent Community Sample." *Public Opinion Quarterly* (Summer), 32:261–272.
Rothenberg, Jerome. 1961. *The Measurement of Social Welfare*. Englewood Cliffs, N.J.: Prentice-Hall.
Rubin, Irene. 1979. *Running in the Red*. Albany, N.Y.: State University of New York Press.
Ruchelman, Leonard I., ed. 1969. *Big City Mayors*. Bloomington: Indiana University Press.
Salancik, Gerald R. and Jeffrey Pfeffer. 1977. "Constraints on Administrator Discretion." *Urban Affairs Quarterly* (June), 12:475–499.
Salisbury, Robert H. 1964. "The New Convergence of Power." *Journal of Politics* (November), 26:775–797.
Samuelson, Paul A. 1969. "Pure Theory of Public Expenditure and Taxation." In Julius Margolis and H. Guitton, eds., *Public Economics*, pp. 98–123. New York: St. Martin's Press.
San Diego Urban Observatory. 1976. *Report on Citizen Preferences*. San Diego: San Diego Urban Observatory.
Savas, E. S., ed. 1977. *Alternatives for Delivering Public Services*. Boulder, Colo.: Westview.
Schattschneider, E. E. 1960. *The Semi-Sovereign People*. New York: Holt, Rinehart and Winston.
Schick, Richard P. and Jean J. Couturier. 1977. *The Public Interest in Government Labor Relations*. Cambridge, Mass.: Ballinger.
Schlitz, Michael E. 1970. *Public Attitudes toward Social Security: 1935–1965*. Washington, D.C.: GPO.

Schneider, William and Gregory Schell. 1978. "The New Democrats." *Public Opinion* (November/December), 1:7–13.

Schoch, Eric. 1978. "General Revenue Sharing in Chicago." Masters thesis, University of Chicago.

Schuessler, Karl F. 1974. "Analysis of Ratio Variables." *American Journal of Sociology*, 80:379–396.

Schumaker, Paul D. and David M. Billeaux. 1978. "Group Representation in Local Bureaucracies." *Administration and Society* (November), 10:285–316.

Schumaker, Paul D., Russel W. Getter, and Terry Nichols Clark. 1979. *Policy Responsiveness and Fiscal Strain in 51 American Communities: A Manual for Studying City Politics Using the NORC Permanent Community Sample*. Washington, D.C.: American Political Science Association, SETUPS Series.

Schumaker, Paul D. and Burdett Loomis. 1979. "Responsiveness to Citizen Preferences and Societal Problems." In Samuel M. Hines and George W. Hopkins, eds., *South Atlantic Urban Studies*, 3:38–66. Columbia: University of South Carolina Press.

Schuman, Howard and Barry Gruenberg. 1970. "The Impact of City on Racial Attitudes." *American Journal of Sociology* (September), 76:213–261.

Schwartz, Mildred A. 1967. *Trends in White Attitudes Toward Negroes*. Report 119. Chicago: National Opinion Research Center.

Scott, Claudia DeVita. 1972. *Forecasting Local Government Spending*. Washington, D.C.: Urban Institute and Municipal Finance Officers Association.

Sears, David O. 1970. "Political Attitudes of Los Angeles Negroes." In Nathan Cohen, ed., *The Los Angeles Riots*, pp. 676–705. New York: Praeger.

Sen, Amartya K. 1970. *Collective Choice and Social Welfare*. San Francisco: Holden-Day.

Shapiro, Perry, David Puryear, and John Ross. 1979. "Tax and Expenditure Limitation in Retrospect and Prospect." *National Tax Journal* (Supplement, June), 32:1–10.

Sharkansky, Ira. 1968. *Spending in the American States*. Chicago: Rand-McNally.

Shaw, R. Paul. 1975. *Migration Theory and Fact*. Philadelphia: Regional Science Research Institute.

Sheatsley, Paul B. 1966. "White Attitudes Toward the Negro." In

Prospects and Policies for New York—The Final Report of the Temporary Commission on City Finances. New York, N.Y.: Arno Press, 1978.

Thompson, Frank J. 1975. *Personnel Policy in the City*. Berkeley: University of California Press.

Tideman, T. Nicolaus. 1976. "The Capabilities of Voting Rules in the Absence of Coalitions." In Terry Nichols Clark, ed., *Citizen Preferences and Urban Public Policy*, pp. 23–44. Special issue of *Policy and Politics* (June), vol. 4.

Tiebout, Charles M. 1956. "A Pure Theory of Local Expenditures." *Journal of Political Economy*, 64:416–424.

Tilove, Robert. 1976. *Public Employee Pension Funds*. New York: Columbia University Press.

Titus, A. Constandina. 1981. "Local Governmental Expenditures and Political Attitudes." *Urban Affairs Quarterly* (June), 16:437–452.

Tolley, George S., Philip E. Graves, and John L. Gardiner. 1979. *Urban Growth Policy in Market Economy*. New York: Academic Press.

Touche, Ross and First National Bank of Boston. 1979. *Urban Fiscal Stress*. New York: Touche Ross.

Truman, David. 1951. *The Governmental Process*. New York: Knopf.

Turk, Herman. 1977. *Organizations in Modern Life*. San Francisco: Jossey-Bass.

—— 1979. "Imageries of Social Control." *Urban Life* (October), 8:335–358.

Uhlman, Wes. 1976. "Seattle." In A. Lawrence Chickering, ed., *Public Employee Unions*, pp. 77–84. San Francisco: Institute for Contemporary Studies.

U.S. Bureau of Labor Statistics. 1973. *Work Stoppages in Government*. (Also, for 1974, 1975, 1976). Washington, D.C.: GPO.

U.S. Bureau of Labor Statistics. 1977. *Employment and Earnings, 1939–1975* (Bulletin 1370–12). Washington, D.C.: GPO.

U.S. Bureau of the Census. 1964. *Census of Population: 1960, Vol. 1, Characteristics of the Population*, Part 1, United States Summary. Washington, D.C.: GPO.

—— 1967. *County and City Data Book, 1967*. Washington, D.C.: GPO. (Also for 1972 and 1977.)

—— 1968. *Census of Governments: 1967*. Washington, D.C.: GPO. (Also for 1972.)

—— 1972. *Census of Population: 1970*. Subject Reports, Negro Populations. Final Report PC(2)-1B. Washington, D.C.: GPO.

—— 1973. *Census of Population: 1970, Vol. 1, Characteristics of the Population*, Part 1, United States Summary—Section 2. Washington, D.C.: GPO.

—— 1975. *Mobility of the Population of the United States: March 1970 to March 1975*. Current Population Reports. Series P-20, No. 285. Washington, D.C.: GPO.

—— 1977. "Population Estimates and Projections." *Current Population Reports*. Series P-25, No. 709. Washington, D.C.: GPO.

—— 1977b. *Census of Governments*. Vol. 4, *Governmental Finance*, no. 5, Compendium of Governmental Finances. Washington, D.C.: GPO.

—— 1981. *Statistical Abstract of the United States: 1981*. Washington, D.C.: GPO.

U.S. Conference of Mayors. 1978. *Issues in Financial Mangement of Local Governments*. Washington, D.C.: U.S. Conference of Mayors and HUD.

U.S. Conference of Mayors. 1982. *A Mayor's Financial Management Handbook*. 2d ed. Washington, D.C.: U.S. Conference of Mayors.

U.S. Congress, Joint Economic Committee. 1969. *The Analysis and Evaluation of Public Expenditures*. Ninetieth Congress. Washington, D.C.: GPO.

U.S. Congress, Subcommittee on Economic Progress, Joint Economic Committee. 1968. *Financing Municipal Facilities*. Ninetieth Congress, First Session. Washington, D.C.: GPO.

U.S. Department of Health, Education, and Welfare, Public Health Service, National Center for Health Statistics. 1975. *Vital Statistics for the United States, 1970, Vol. 1, Natality*. Washington, D.C.: GPO.

U.S. Department of the Treasury, Office of State and Local Finance. 1978. *Report on the Fiscal Impact of the Economic Stimulus Package on Urban Governments*. Washington, D.C.: GPO.

Urban and Regional Policy Group. 1978. *A New Partnership to Conserve America's Communities: A National Urban Policy*. HUD-S-297. Washington, D.C.: U.S. Department of Housing and Urban Development.

Vanecko, James J., Susan Orden, and Sidney Hollander. 1970a. *Community Organization Efforts, Political and Institutional Change, and the Diffusion of Change Produced by Community Action Programs*. NORC Report 122. Chicago: National Opinion Research Center, University of Chicago.

—— 1970b. *Community Organization in the War on Poverty*. Chicago: National Opinion Research Center, University of Chicago.

Van Meter, Donald S. 1974. "Alternative Methods of Measuring Change." *Political Methodology* (Fall), 1:125–140.

Vaughan, Roger J. 1976. *Public Works as a Countercyclical Device*. Report R-1990-EDA. Santa Monica, Calif.: Rand.

—— 1977. *The Urban Impacts of Federal Policies: Vol. 2, Economic Development*. Report R-2028-KF/RC. Santa Monica, Calif.: Rand.

Verba, Sidney and Norman H. Nie. 1972. *Participation in America*. New York: Harper & Row.

Verba, Sidney, Norman H. Nie, and Jae-On Kim. 1978. *Participation and Political Equality: A Seven-Nation Comparison*. New York: Cambridge University Press.

Vernez, Georges, Roger J. Vaughan, Burke Burright, and Sinclair Coleman. 1977. *Regional Cycles and Employment Effects of Public Works Investments*. Report R-2052-EDA. Santa Monica, Calif.: Rand.

Vernez, Georges, Roger J. Vaughan, and Robert K. Yin. 1979. *Federal Activities in Urban Economic Development*. Report R-2372-EDA. Santa Monica, Calif.: Rand.

Walsh, Annmarie Hauck. 1978. *The Public's Business*. Cambridge: MIT Press.

Walton, John. 1970. "A Systematic Survey of Community Power Research." In Michael Aiken and Paul E. Mott, eds., *The Structure of Community Power*, pp. 443–463. New York: Random House.

Walzer, Norman. 1978. *Fiscal Note and Reimbursement Programs for State Mandates*. Macomb, Ill.: Public Policy Research Institute, Western Illinois University.

Ward, Sally K. 1977. "The Impact of Community Characteristics on Local Social Programs and Policies." Ph.D. dissertation, Brown University.

Washnis, George J., ed. 1980. *Productivity Improvement Handbook for State and Local Government*. New York: Wiley.

Weicher, John C. 1970. "Determinants of Central City Expenditures." *National Tax Journal* (December), 23:379–396.

—— 1971. "The Allocation of Police Protection by Income Class." *Urban Studies* (October), 8:207–220.

—— 1972. "The Effect of Metropolitan Political Fragmentation on Central City Budgets." In David C. Sweet, ed., *Models of Urban*

Structure, pp. 177–204. Lexington, Mass.: D.C. Heath-Lexington Books.

Weicher, John C. and R. J. Emerine II. 1973. "Econometric Analysis of State and Local Aggregate Expenditure Functions." *Public Finance*, 28(1):69–83.

Welch, Susan and Albert K. Karnig. 1978. "Representation of Blacks on Big City School Boards." *Social Science Quarterly*, 59:162–172.

Wellington, Harry H. and Ralph K. Winter. 1971. *The Unions and the Cities*. Washington, D.C.: The Brookings Institute.

Wheaton, William C., ed. 1979. *Interregional Movements and Regional Growth*. Washington, D.C.: The Urban Institute.

White, Sheila. 1969. "Work Stoppages of Government Employees." *Monthly Labor Review* (December), 92:29–34.

Whyte, William Foote and Donald McCall. 1980. "Self-Help Economics." *Society* (May/June), 17:22–29.

Wiener, Norbert. 1948. *Cybernetics*. New York: Wiley.

Wildavsky, Aaron. 1964. *The Politics of the Budgetary Process*. Boston: Little, Brown.

Wilensky, Harold. 1975. *The Welfare State and Equality*. Berkeley: University of California Press.

Williams, Anne S. 1980. "Relationships Between the Structure of Local Influence and Policy Outcomes." *Rural Sociology*, 4(45):621–643.

Williams, John A. and Erwin Zimmermann. 1981. "American Business Organizations and Redistributive Preferences." *Urban Affairs Quarterly* (June), 16:453–464.

Wilson, James Q. 1960. *Negro Politics*. New York: Free Press.

Wilson, James Q. and Edward C. Banfield. 1964. "Public Regardingness as a Value Premise in Voting Behavior." *American Political Science Review* (December), 58:876–887.

—— 1971. "Political Ethos Revisited." *American Political Science Review* (December), 65:1048–1062.

Wilson, William J. 1978. *The Declining Significance of Race*. Chicago: University of Chicago Press.

Woody, Bette. 1975. "Impact of Racial Transition on the Management of City Government." Ph.D. dissertation, MIT.

—— 1981. "Managing the New Urban Crisis." Draft paper. Harvard University.

Wright, Gerald C. 1976. "Linear Models for Evaluating Conditional

Relationships." *American Journal of Political Science* (May), 20:349–373.

Yates, Douglas. 1977. *The Ungovernable City*. Cambridge, Mass.: MIT Press.

Ziegler, Martin. 1977. "Efforts to Improve Estimates of State and Local Unemployment." *Monthly Labor Review* (November), pp. 12–18.

Zimmerman, Jerold L. 1977. "The Municipal Accounting Maze." *Journal of Accounting Research* (Supplement), 15:107–155.

Zimmerman, Joseph F. 1975. "The Patchwork Approach." In Amos H. Hawley and Vincent P. Rock, eds., *Metropolitan America*, pp. 431–474. New York: Sage-Halsted-Wiley.

Zimmermann, Erwin. 1979. *Interest and Control in Community Decision-Making*. Ph.D. dissertation, University of Chicago. Bern, Frankfurt, Las Vegas: Peter Lang, 1981.

Author Index

Subject Index

Bei Fragen zur Produktsicherheit wenden Sie sich bitte an:
If you have any questions regarding product safety,
please contact:

Walter de Gruyter GmbH
Genthiner Straße 13
10785 Berlin
productsafety@degruyterbrill.com